WITCH HUNTS
in Europe and America

An Encyclopedia

WILLIAM E. BURNS

GREENWOOD PRESS
Westport, Connecticut • London

Library of Congress Cataloging-in-Publication Data

Burns, William E., 1959–
    Witch hunts in Europe and America : an encyclopedia / by William E. Burns.
       p. cm.
    Includes bibliographical references and index.
    ISBN 0–313–32142–6 (alk. paper)
    1. Witchcraft—Europe—History—Encyclopedias. 2. Witchcraft—United States—History—
Encyclopedias. 3. Persecution—Europe—History—Encyclopedias. 4. Persecution—United States—
History—Encyclopedias. 5. Trials (Witchcraft)—Europe—History—Encyclopedias. 6. Trials
(Witchcraft)—United States—History—Encyclopedias. I. Title.
BF1584.E9B87   2003
133.4′3′09—dc21   2003044074

British Library Cataloguing in Publication Data is available.

Library of Congress Catalog Card Number: 2003044074
ISBN: 0–313–32142–6

First published in 2003

Greenwood Press, 88 Post Road West, Westport, CT 06881
An imprint of Greenwood Publishing Group, Inc.
www.greenwood.com

Printed in the United States of America

The paper used in this book complies with the
Permanent Paper Standard issued by the National
Information Standards Organization (Z39.48–1984).

10 9 8 7 6 5 4 3 2 1

Dedicated to Miriam and Tonya, wise women

CONTENTS

LIST OF ENTRIES

INTRODUCTION

Few subjects in European history exert as much continuing fascination as the persecution of witches in the early modern era. Witchcraft and witch-hunting are topics that touch on nearly every aspect of European life in the period, from great events such as the Reformation or the scientific revolution, to society, politics, law, medicine, culture and colonialism. Over the last three decades, there has been an explosion of exciting scholarship on witches, witchcraft and witch-hunting. Old myths, such as the prevalence of midwives as victims, have been debunked, and many new sources have been opened and explored. The subject of early modern witchcraft has been attacked with a range of tools as diverse as literary criticism, climatologic history and epidemiology.

Witches and witch-hunters also play a significant role in modern culture and society outside historical scholarship. The "Halloween witch," with her pointed hat, broom and black cat, is a familiar stereotype, and the "wicked witch," usually shorn of her diabolical affinities, appears frequently in fairy tales and children's stories. Neopagans and feminists often look back on witches positively, seeing them as aboriginal nature priestesses or assertive women victimized by a patriarchal society. Witch-hunters and witch-hunts function as metaphors across a huge range of political and cultural positions. The Salem witch-hunt has been called the best-known event in American history between the Pilgrims landing at Plymouth Rock and the American Revolution, and the Puritans of New England—perhaps unfairly—remain better known for hunting witches than for any of their numerous other activities. Witch-hunting is often used as a symbol of the "barbaric" and "superstitious" practices of medieval and early modern people, now happily forgotten in our own enlightened era, an interpretation that actually emerged in the later stages of the witch-hunt.

Despite the variety of activities described pejoratively as witch-hunting, the actual witch-hunt remained limited in space and time. Although many societies have believed and still believe that some people could have magical powers—and have punished people alleged to have used these powers in a destructive or illicit way—the full-fledged stereotype of the witch is unique to the culture of western and central European Christianity. The witch combined the power and desire to do ill with a close alliance with Satan, the principle of evil. It was the Devil, and not the witch's own power and knowledge, that she, or less commonly he, drew on to wreak damage upon individuals or the community at large. The fully developed mythology of European witchcraft included explicit pacts with Satan, gatherings and revels called sabbats, grisly deeds including infanticide and cannibalism, as well as a huge variety of harmful acts.

The similarity of ideas about witches across Europe and European colonies does not obscure many fascinating differences across both space and time. Why did the Inquisitions of Rome, Spain and Portugal virtually ignore witches through vast swathes of the territories under their jurisdiction? How different was England from the Continent, and even from Scotland? What made those few areas where men comprised the majority of witch-hunt victims so different from the mainstream? Why was Germany the center of the witch-hunt? How and where did the witch-hunt start, and from what ingredients and in what time was the witch stereotype born? One of the most puzzling questions of all is why the witch-hunt ended.

Witch-hunting is not a phenomenon with precise boundaries. Not all magic-using criminals fit the definition of a witch. Some were merely charged with having used magic, without it being claimed that the magic was malevolent or of demonic origin. (This pattern was particularly common in the Mediterranean world.) Distinguishing these "sorcery" trials from witch trials can be difficult. Witches also had much in common with heretics, particularly in the late Middle Ages. As giving worship to devils that rightly belonged to God, witchcraft was even defined as a heresy, and thus the witch-hunt was sometimes seen as part of a larger struggle against heresy—a topic much on European minds during the struggles of the Reformation and Wars of Religion. Many people in both Europe and the European colonies in America also saw the struggle to extirpate Native American religion as intimately tied to the witch-hunt, as both Native Americans and witches were charged with worshipping the Devil. The witch-hunt also interacted in complex ways with the drive on the part of European elites to purify the culture of the common people. In the beginning of mass witch-hunting during the sixteenth century, champions of the Protestant and Catholic Reformations often viewed the culture of ordinary Europeans as permeated with magic and witchcraft, and treated ordinary people's ready recourse to magical "fixes" as an even bigger problem than witchcraft. By the end of the witch-hunt during the Enlightenment, Europe's intellectual leaders were more likely to identify witch-hunting than witchcraft with popular superstition.

This book covers witch-hunting in Europe, from Portugal to Russia (two areas with little witch-hunting) and those colonies in the Americas where Europeans exercised political domination. It covers the span of time between the cluster of political sorcery trials in the beginning of the fourteenth century, mostly associated with the French and Papal courts, to the last witch executions by formal legal process at the end of the eighteenth century. The topics covered include the witch-hunt in various countries, major individual witch-hunts and trials, aspects of the witch-hunting process, demonological writers who were both supporters and opponents of witch-hunting, and subsequent interpretations of the witch-hunt by historians and others. (Words which refer to other articles are boldfaced on their first appearance in an article.)

I thank the Folger Library, the Library of Congress and the libraries of the University of Maryland at College Park, Howard University and Mary Washington College for the use of their resources.

CHRONOLOGY

1307–1308	The French government employs charges of devil worship in its attack on the Templars.
1308–1314	Bishop Guichard of Troyes is imprisoned while charged by French officials with magical and other crimes.
1310–1311	French king Philip IV brings proceedings against the late pope, Boniface VIII, charging him with ritual magic and dealings with demons.
1312	The final suppression of the Templars by the pope takes place at the behest of Philip IV.
1317	Pope John XXII has the French bishop Hughes Geraud arrested, tortured and burned at the stake for trying to kill the pope by poison and sorcery.
1320	Galleazzo Visconti is tried at Milan for attempting to kill Pope John XXII by image magic.
1324	The trial of Alice Kyteler and her associates in Ireland for witchcraft takes place.
1325	Ragnhildr Tregagas of Bergen in Norway is sentenced to penance for witchcraft, diabolism and heresy.
1326 or 1327	Pope John XXII issues a bull against ritual magic, *Super illius Specula*.
1327	The Inquisition in Florence executes by burning the university professor and astrologer Cecco d'Ascoli on charges of practicing magic.
1360	The first recorded witch trial takes place in Croatia.

1376	Nicholas Eymeric's *Directorium Inquisitorum* is first circulated. It includes an extensive discussion of the heretical nature of ritual magic.
1384–1390	Two women in Milan are placed on trial and then executed as followers of Diana.
1392–1406	Bernese magistrate Peter von Greyerz carries out major antiwitch campaign as governor of the Simme Valley.
1398	The theology faculty of the University of Paris issues an opinion denouncing magic and magicians as idolaters.
1406	Charges are made of a magical plot to kill the pope of Avignon, Benedict XIII.
1409	The Council of Pisa charges Benedict XIII with sorcery and the invocation of demons.
1410	The Great Council of Venice decrees that secular courts have jurisdiction over most magical offenses.
1411	During a plague, 12 women are burned as witches in the Russian town of Pskov.
1413	The burning of a woman for poisoning and witchcraft takes place in Maastricht, the first recorded execution of a witch in the Netherlands.
1419	Use of the German word *Hexerei* is first documented, describing a witch in the Swiss city of Lucerne.
1419–1422	The dowager queen of England, Joan of Navarre, is imprisoned on charges of plotting the death of King Henry V by sorcery.
1426	Magistrates of the Italian town of Todi adopt a new antiwitch law with the death penalty at the behest of preacher Bernardino of Siena; Bernardino is also involved in witch-hunt in Rome.
1427	Bernardino's sermons in Siena are unsuccessful in starting a witch-hunt there.
1428	A major witch-hunt in the Valais region of Switzerland takes place, possibly with more than one hundred victims. The trial and execution of Matteuccia di Francesco takes place at Todi.
1428–1447	A witch-hunting campaign in the Dauphiné region of France leads to 167 executions.

1430–1436	Approximate date of the composition of Bernardino's Latin treatise on witchcraft, *On the Cult of Idols*.
1431	The trial of Jehanne Darc involves some witch-related charges, which are withdrawn before the final verdict.
1435–1438	Probable date of the composition of Johannes Nider's *Formicarius*, incorporating material derived from von Greyerz.
1436–1437	Composition of Claude Tholosan's *The Errors of Magicians and Witches*.
1437	Approximate date of the composition of the anonymous *Errores Gazariorum*.
1441	English noblewoman Eleanor Cobham and her associates are condemned for witchcraft and sorcery.
1442	Probable date of composition of Martin Le Franc's *The Defender of Ladies*.
1453	Guillame Adeline is condemned and faces trial for flying to the sabbat on a broomstick.
1458	French Dominican inquisitor Nicholas Jacquier writes *A Scourge for Heretical Witches*, expounding many aspects of the developing witch stereotype.
1459–1460	Vauderie of Arras, the first mass witch-hunt based on the concept of the sabbat, takes place; at least 12 witches are executed by burning.
1460	Approximate date of the composition of Girolamo Visconti's two treatises on witchcraft.
1466	The Basque Province of Guipuzcoa in Spain petitions the king of Castile to grant local magistrates the power to try and execute witches. The petition is granted.
1467	Ivan the Great of Muscovy charges witches with causing the death of his wife, Maria of Tver.
1470	Johann Sprenger is appointed inquisitor for the Rhineland. Approximate date of the composition of Giordano da Bergamo's *Inquiry of Witches*.
1471	First recorded Swedish witch trial, in Arboga.
1474	Heinrich Kramer is appointed inquisitor for southern Germany.
1476	First printed edition of Nider's *Formicarius*.

1477–1486	A series of witch-hunts in Switzerland is precipitated by agrarian crisis.
1479	Several witches are executed in Scotland for attempted murder of the king.
1483	Protector of England, Richard, duke of Gloucester, accuses the late King Edward IV's wife, Elizabeth Woodville, and mistress, Jane Shore, of having attacked his body through sorcery. Jean Vineti's *Treatise Against the Invokers of Demons* is published.
1484	Kramer's persecution in Ravensburg results in two executions. Pope Innocent VIII issues *Summus Desiderantes Affectibus*, endorsing Kramer and Sprenger's German witch-hunt.
1485	Forty-one witches are burned by the Inquisition at Bormio. Kramer leads an unsuccessful witch-hunt at Innsbruck. *The Defender of Ladies* is published.
1486	Kramer's *Malleus Maleficarum* is published. The text includes *Summis Desiderantes Affectibus*.
1489	Ulrich Molitor's *Of Witches and Fortunetelling Women* is published.
1490	Girolamo Visconti's treatises on witchcraft are published.
1491	A thirty-year investigation by the Parlement of Paris results in clearing the names of those executed in the Vauderie of Arras.
1497	The first important piece of witch art is created, Albert Dürer's *The Four Witches*.
1498	The first known witch trial by the Spanish Inquisition takes place.
1501	Papal bull *Cum Acceperimus* commissions the Inquisition against witches and poisoners in Lombardy.
1503	The first printed edition of Eymeric's *Directorium Inquisitorum* appears.
1505	The execution of a witch at Tübingen prompts Martin Plantsch to give a course of sermons emphasizing God's providence and the impotence of the Devil, demons and witches.
1507	Plantsch's sermons are published in an expanded version as *Opusculum de Sagis Maleficis*. A witch-hunt in the

Basque country of Spain results in about 30 executions. The first surviving mention of the German magician Georg Faust.

1508   Twenty-six of Johann Geiler von Kaysersberg's Lenten sermons at Strasbourg discuss witches.

1510   First surviving English reference to the idea of a familiar drinking blood from a witch's body.

1512–1516   Hans Baldung Grien, while in the city of Freiburg, creates a classic series of witch images.

1516   Johann Geiler von Kaysersberg's Lenten sermons are published as *The Ant-Hill.*

1519   Heinrich Cornelius Agrippa defends an accused witch in Metz.

1520   Gianfrancesco Ponzinibio's *Treatise on Witches* is published.

1521   Pope Leo X orders Venetian bishops to proceed against witches, ignoring complaints from the secular courts. Silvestro Mazzolini's *On the Marvels of Witch-sorceresses and Demons* is published.

1522–1523   A witch-hunt in the territory of Mirandola and the adjacent territory of Concordia in Italy, actively supported by territorial lord Gianfrancesco Pico della Mirandola, results in the execution of 10 witches.

1523   An antiwitch decree from Pope Adrian VI is addressed to Modesto of Vincenza. Gianfrancesco Pico della Mirandola's *Strix* is published. Bartolommeo Spina's *Inquiry on Witches* is published.

1525   About 30 witches are burned by the Royal Council of Navarre in Spain.

1526   The Spanish Inquisition draws up witch-hunting policy, emphasizing procuring repentance over execution.

1527   The first recorded witch burning in Estonia takes place.

1529   The Spanish demonologies, Martin de Castañega's *Treatise on Superstition and Witchcraft* and Pedro Ciruelo's *A Reproof of Superstitions and Witchery*, are published, incorporating information from recent witch-hunts in the Basque country. Castañega's is the first treatise on witchcraft originally written in a vernacular language.

1532	Janet Douglas, Lady Glamis, is burned for attempting to assassinate the king of Scotland, James V, by witchcraft and poisoning. The *Carolina* criminal code is proclaimed for the Holy Roman Empire by Emperor Charles V. It includes Article 109 on witchcraft, emphasizing *maleficia* rather than demonism.
1540	Approximate date of the death of Georg Faust.
1542	Passage of the first English Parliamentary statute to address witchcraft. A Papal decree establishes the Roman Inquisition.
1543	Polish law reserves jurisdiction over witch cases to the church courts. The law will be widely ignored.
1544	Date of Hans Baldung Grien's *The Bewitched Groom*.
1545	A witch-hunt takes place in the territory of Geneva, with one execution.
1547	A witch-hunt takes place in the Groninger Ommelands in the northern Netherlands, with 20 executions. The English statute of 1542 is repealed. Danish Copenhagen articles provide procedural safeguards against witchcraft accusations. The first recorded appearance in Wales of the English word "wits" for witch.
1554	Joost de Damhouder's *Criminal Practice* is published, calling for the extermination of witches.
1559	Five witches are executed by a public burning in Lisbon, Portugal. Along with another case occurring shortly thereafter, this is the only known witch execution in sixteenth-century Portugal. Jacob Vallick's *Bewitching, what kind of work it is* is published.
1562	The first witch execution takes place in the Channel Islands.
1562–1563	A witch-hunt in the southern German territory of Wiesensteig leaves about 63 dead.
1563	Passage of a new English law against witches provides for the death penalty for *maleficium*. Passage of the Witchcraft Act by the Scottish Parliament. Johann Weyer's *Of the Tricks of Demons* is published.
1564	Elizabeth Lowys of Great Waltham is the first person tried and convicted under the English Act of 1563.

1564–1565	Public exorcisms of Nicole Obry take place at Laon, France.
1565	The first unauthorized German translation of Weyer's *Of the Tricks of Demons* appears.
1566	The first surviving pamphlet accounts of English witchcraft, *The Examination and Confession of certaine Wytches* and *The Examination of John Walsh*, are published. Weyer's own German translation of *Of the Tricks of Demons*is published. The forged account of a fourteenth-century devil-worshipping witch by Giovanni Battista Piotto is published.
1567	Sir William Stewart is burned for attempting to assassinate the regent of Scotland by witchcraft. The first unauthorized French translation of Weyer's *Of the Tricks of Demons* is published.
1568	A large witch-hunt, with about 40 accused, is carried out in Angus and the Mearns, Scotland, by the Protestant clergyman John Erskine of Dun.
1570	The duke of Alva, Spanish commander in the Netherlands, issues the Decree on Criminal Justice, promising harsher treatment of witches and cunning folk.
1571	A plague in Geneva inspires largest witch-hunt in the city's history, with at least 29 executions. The Spanish Inquisition and the separate Inquisition for Indians are established as the principal judicial bodies dealing with witchcraft and sorcery in the Spanish New World Empire.
1571–72	Jesuit Juan Maldonado gives a popular series of lectures on demonology in Paris. Among his audience are Martin del Rio and Pierre de Lancre.
1572	The Criminal Constitutions of Electoral Saxony define satanic pact or dealings with the Devil, whether or not any harm was caused by magic, as punishable by death by burning.
1573	The Scottish Privy Council declares witchcraft a *crimen exceptum*. The Assembly of the Scottish Kirk declares that all found to consult witches or cunning folk will be made to repent in church wearing sackcloth. The Parlement of Dôle permits Franche-Comte villagers to carry weapons when hunting a werewolf.

1574	The Parlement of Dôle executes Gilles Garnier for were-wolfism, infanticide and cannibalism Lambert Daneau's *On Witches*, the first major Protestant demonology supporting witch-hunting, is published.
1575	The first trial of Anne Pedersdottir Absalon at Bergen in Norway takes place. The first recorded case of a *benandante* comes before the Inquisition. Niels Hemmingsen's *Admonition on Superstitious Magic to be Avoided* is published. Daneau's *On Witches* appears in English translation.
1576	The Danish Kalundborg articles provide for automatic appeal to county courts of all death sentences for witchcraft imposed by juries in local courts, becoming the first secular legal system to follow this procedure. Nicolas Remy is appointed duumvir of Nancy in Lorraine, the beginning of his career as a witch-hunter.
1577	Weyer's *Book of Witches* is published, featuring a reply to Erastus.
1578	English authorities, claiming to be acting under "natural law," execute three witches in Ireland. Eymeric's *Directorium Inquisitorum* appears in an expanded edition sponsored by the Roman Inquisition with a commentary by the Spanish canon lawyer Francisco Pena that discusses many issues of magic and witchcraft.
1579	The hanging of Elizabeth Stiles and three other witches at Abingdon in England is described in two pamphlets. Three witches are hanged at Chelmsford Assizes. The first case of the Spanish Inquisition dealing with the "ladies from outside" in Sicily.
1579–1580	The Morosini case of a conspiracy to use magic to find hidden treasure is tried before the Inquisition of Venice.
1580	Jakob Bithner is appointed *Landprofos* in Styria. He carries on a vigorous witch-hunt for the next 20 years. Fra Felice de Montefeltro, Iinquisitor, revives the case of the *benandanti*, firmly identifying them as witches. Andrea Cesalpino's *Aristotelian Investigation of Demons*, defending the compatibility of Aristotelian philosophy and belief in witches and demons, is published. Jean Bodin's *On the Demonmania of Sorcerers* is published.

1581	German Carmelite friar Johannes Minzenberg publishes a collection of texts on witchcraft and magic, including the first appearance in print of Jacquier's *A Scourge for Heretical Witches*.
1582	The trial of the Saint Osyth witches takes place at Chelmsford Assizes. Eighteen witches burned in Avignon by the inquisitor Sebastien Michaelis.
1583	About 25 witches are killed in Wiesensteig. The last edition of Weyer's *Of the Tricks of Demons* features a reply to Bodin.
1584	Reginald Scot's *Discoverie of Witchcraft* is published. At the behest of the bishop, the death penalty is introduced for magical acts in the Norwegian diocese of Stavanger. Jesuit Georg Scherer carries out well-publicized exorcism at Vienna, identifying the victim's grandmother as a witch.
1585	The bull of Pope Sixtus V, *Coeli et Terrae*, reaffirms the Church's opposition to divination and ritual magic.
1586	John Darrell's first recorded exorcism case takes place, that of Katherine Wright of Mansfield. The English witchcraft statute of 1563 is enacted into Irish law.
1586–1588	A witch-hunt in the German territory of Obermarchthal claims at least 53 victims. The 1587 burning of Conrad Stoeckhlin touches off a major witch-hunt in southern Germany. Execution of more than one hundred witches takes place in the territory of Pfalzel under Johann Zandt von Marll. George Gifford's *A Discourse of the Subtill Practises of Devilles by Witches and Sorcerers* is published. The German Faustbook first appears in print.
1587–1588	A witch-hunt in the Champagne region of France is halted by the Parlement of Paris and the cardinal of Guise, leader of the Catholic League.
1587–1593	A major witch-hunt in the archbishopric of Trier, with nearly four hundred witches killed, takes place.
1588	Scottish witch Alison Pearson is executed.
1589	In a single day, 133 witches are burned in the lands of the Convent of Quedlinburg in Germany. The trial and execution of Dietrich Flade takes place in Trier. The Cologne werewolf Peter Stubbe is executed. Three witches are convicted and hanged at Chelmsford Assizes.

1590	The torturer and executioner Hans Vollmair carries out great persecution in Ellingen, resulting in 72 executions. The second trial of Anne Pedersdottir Absalon ends in execution. The first execution for witchcraft takes place in the Prince-Bishopric of Würzburg. Henry Holland's *A Treatise Against Witchcraft* is published.
1590–1592	The North Berwick trials take place in Scotland.
1590–1593	Several dozen witches are burned in the prince-bishopric of Eichstätt
1591	Peter Binsfeld's *Treatise on the Confessions of Evildoers and Witches* is published.
1592	A royal decree against witchcraft is pronounced in the Spanish Netherlands. Publications of the Dutch and English translations of the German Faustbook are recorded. Cornelius Loos's attack on witch-hunting, *Of True and False Magic* is published.
1593	The Stavanger antimagic law is extended throughout the Norwegian kingdom. Cornelius Loos is forced to repent publicly in the presence of Peter Binsfeld and other Catholic authorities for his attack on witch-hunting. George Gifford's *A Dialogue Concerning Witches and Witchcraftes* is published.
1594	The faculty of the University of Leiden rules against flotation tests. Bodin's *On the Demonmania of Sorcerers* is placed on the Catholic Index of Forbidden Books.
1595	Nineteen witches are executed at Peelande in the northern Netherlands. Gwen ferch Ellis, the first case of maleficent witchcraft in Wales, ends in conviction. Nicholas Remy's *Demonolatry* is published. Robert Holland's *Tudor and Gronow*, the only demonological work in Welsh, is published at approximately this time.
1596	Witch-hunting magistrate and demonologist Henri Boguet is appointed grand judge of the territories of the Abbey of Saint Claude in Franche-Comte. John Darrell's exorcises Thomas Burton. Remy's *Demonolatry* is published in German translation.
1597	King James VI of Scotland's *Daemonologie* is published. To bring witch-hunting under control, James reserves all cases to the central government. John Darrell exorcises members of the household of Nicholas Starkie in Lancashire and begins the exorcisms of William Sommers of

	Nottingham. The trial of the monk-witch Jean de Vaulx arouses Martin del Rio's interest in magic and witchcraft.
1598	The French translation of the German Faustbook is published. Anton Praetorius's *On Sorcery and Sorcerors* is published.
1598–1599	Marthe Brossier's career in Paris as a victim of demonic possession lasts until she is revealed as a fraud and exiled by the Parlement of Paris.
1599	John Darrell is sentenced to imprisonment by the authority of the archbishop of Canterbury. Samuel Harsnett's *A Discovery of the Fraudulent Practices of John Darrell* is published.
1599–1600	The first edition of del Rio's *Disquisitions on Magic* is published.
1600	The Pappenheimer case in Munich ends with 12 executions.
1601	The witch-pricker Jean Minard is arrested and sentenced to the galleys by the Parlement of Paris after causing the deaths of more than two hundred persons in Northern France and the Spanish Netherlands. The Parlement of Paris forbids flotation tests in its jurisdiction.
1602	The Mary Glover case occurs in London. Henri Boguet's *Discourse on Sorcerers* is published. Johannes David's *Sentinel for Guarding Against False Cunning Men and Witches* is published.
1603	Trial of the werewolf Jean Grenier takes place at Bordeaux. James VI ascends to the English throne as James I. Edward Jorden's *A Briefe Discourse of a Disease Called the Suffocation of the Mother*, ascribing Glover's symptoms to hysteria, is published.
1604	Passage of a new English witchcraft act criminalizes dealings with spirits and the use of body parts in magic, as well as *maleficia*. A decree from Brussels gives seignorial courts in Franche-Comte the right to administer the death penalty for witchcraft.
1605	Publication of Juan Maldonado's lectures in French as *Treatise on Angels and Devils*.
1606	An anti-witchcraft decree is proclaimed by the court of the archduke in the southern Netherlands. William Shakespeare writes *Macbeth*; it receives its first performance either very late in 1606 or very early in 1607.

1607	Frans Francken the Younger paints *Witches Sabbath*, with detailed depictions of a number of witch activities.
1608	The last burning of a witch takes place in the Dutch Republic. Pierre de Lancre is appointed by royal decree to investigate witch activity in Pays de Labourd area of the Basque region of France. Swedish national code provides for the death penalty only for witches convicted of murder. Francis Maria Guazzo's *Compendium Maleficarum* is published. William Perkins's *A Discourse on the Damned Art of Witchcraft* is published. The last edition of del Rio's *Disquisitions on Magic* to appear in his lifetime, with his final revisions, is published.
1609	Pierre de Lancre's tour of the Basque country results in the execution of about 80 witches and the trial and imprisonment of many more. The witch-hunt at Bregenz in Austria ends with 16 executions. The Croatian Assembly empowers any citizen to take a suspected witch before the district magistrate.
1610	Auto-de-fé of the Zugurramurdi witches takes place, resulting in six executions. Johann Gottfried von Aschausen, Bamberg prince-bishop, issues a decree against sorcerers and diviners. Pierre de Lancre interviews Jean Grenier shortly before his death.
1610–1612	Antonio de Salazar Frias journies through the Basque country of Spain with the Edict of Grace.
1610–1619	Charges are brought against 163 people in a witch-hunt in the district of Bouchain in the Spanish Netherlands.
1611	Father Louis Gaufridi is convicted of witchcraft before the Parlement of Aix on the evidence of the possessed girl, Madeline de Demandolx de la Palud, and executed.
1611–1618	A witch-hunt in Ellwangen claims more than four hundred lives.
1612	Annexation and re-Catholicization of the Protestant town of Freudenberg by the prince-bishop of Würzburg, Julius Echter von Mespellbrun, is accompanied by a witch-hunt with more than 50 victims. Ten witches are executed in the English county of Lancashire. A Bavarian mandate against magic, superstition and witchcraft provides for the death penalty for dealing with demons or *maleficium*. Johann Christoph von Westerstetten, prince-provost of Ellwangen, becomes prince-bishop of Eich-

stätt. Pierre de Lancre's *Description of the Inconstancy of Bad Angels and Demons*, based on his witch-hunting experience and incorporating materials from his investigations, is published.

1613   A witch-hunt in Roermond in Spanish Limburg in the northern Netherlands results in 40 death sentences. The case of three possessed nuns in Lille in the Spanish Netherlands results in the execution of two nuns as witches. The corrupt Bavarian witch judge Gottfried Sattler is executed. Trial of the Sutton witches includes the first documented use of a flotation test in England. Publication of Sebastien Michaelis's account of the Gaufridi case, *The Admirable History of the Possession and Conversion of a Penitent*.

1614   Supreme Council of the Spanish Inquisition vindicates Salazar's skeptical position on witches. The Inquisition's involvement in large-scale witch-hunting ends.

1615   Jean De Nynauld, *On Lycanthropy*, is published.

1615–1620   Legal troubles of the accused witch Katharina Kepler end in her exoneration.

1616   Salazar's intervention results in the transfer of 289 witch cases from the civil courts at Vizcaya to the jurisdiction of the Inquisition, where accusations are suspended. John Cotta's *The Triall of Witch-Craft*, is published.

1616–1617   A witch-hunt in Würzburg claims more than three hundred victims.

1616–1618   A witch-hunt in Bamberg claims about three hundred victims.

1617   New Danish witchcraft law sets off the most intense period of Danish witch-hunting, lasting into the mid-1620s. Johann Christoph von Westerstetten begins large-scale witch-hunting in Eichstätt. Witches will be burned in Eichstätt every year until 1630.

1621   Elizabeth Sawyer is executed in London for committing murder by witchcraft. Henry Goodcole's pamphlet describing the case, *The Wonderfull Discoverie of Elizabeth Sawyer, a Witch*, is published; a play based on the case by John Ford, Thomas Dekker and William Rowley, *The Witch of Edmonton*, premiers.

1622	Pierre de Lancre's *Incredulity and Misbelief in Sorcery Plainly confuted*, is published.
1623	Jean Le Normant's *True and Memorable History of the Exorcism of Three Possessed Girls in Flanders* is published on the Lille case.
1624	The Parlement of Paris orders that all witchcraft cases in its jurisdiction be automatically appealed to it.
1625	Catherine Bouillion is executed; she is the last witch executed by regular procedure in an area under the jurisdiction of the Parlement of Paris until 1691. Jon Rognvaldsson is the first witch executed in Iceland. Gabriel Naudé's attack on de Lancre, *Apology for all the Great People who have been Falsely Suspected of Magic*, is published.
1626	The Holy Office in Rome, ruling body of the Roman Inquisition, intervenes to quell a witch panic in Florence. A witch is executed by the Inquisition in Portugal–the only known execution of a witch by the Portuguese Inquisition. Hermann Samson's *Nine Selected and Well-Grounded Witch Sermons*, is published. Friedrich Förner's *A Display of the Weaponry of God against all Superstition, Divination, Enchantments and Devil-Worship* is published.
1626–1630	Massive witch-hunts in the Franconian bishoprics take place. As many as six hundred die in Bamberg under Bishop Fuchs von Dornheim.
1627	Richard Bernard's *A Guide to Grand Jury Men with respect to Witches* is published. De Lancre's reply to Naudé, *On Sorcery* is published.
1627–1630	At least 62 witches are killed in witch-hunts in the free imperial city of Offenburg.
1627–1631	As many as nine hundred witches are executed in the territory of the prince-bishopric of Würzburg, under Prince-Bishop Philipp Adolf von Ehrenberg. About two hundred witches are executed in the territory of Baden-Baden in a witch-hunt led by Dr. Martin Eschbach.
1628	English astrologer and witch Dr. John Lambe is murdered by a London mob.
1628–1631	A witch-hunt in German territory of Mergentheim results in 122 executions.

1630	The Diet of Regensburg in the Holy Roman Empire brings an end to large-scale witch-hunting in Franconia. The Danish witchcraft decree of 1617 is read before the Icelandic Allthing and recognized as Icelandic law.
1631	Friedrich von Spee's *Warning to Prosecutors* is published anonymously.
1632	First cases of possession among the nuns of Loudun are recorded. The first German translation of *Warning to Prosecutors* is published.
1633	Boy witch-finder Edmund Robinson is active in Lancashire.
1634	The trial and execution of Urbain Grandier takes place at Loudun. Johannes Kepler's *Somnium* is published; its hero, modeled on Kepler, has a sorceress mother, possibly modeled on Katharina Kepler. Thomas Heywood and Richard Brome's play *The Late Lancashire Witches* appears.
1636	Hermann Löher flees his home of Rheinbach in the electorate of Cologne in fear of witch judge Franz Buirmann.
1638	Jane Hawkins of Boston is indicted, bringing about the first witchcraft case in New England.
1641	Massachusetts Bay Colony passes a statute providing for the death penalty for witchcraft, defined as having dealings with familiar spirits.
1642	Friend of von Spee and a witch-hunting opponent, Johann Phillip von Schonborn becomes bishop of Würzburg. Connecticut Colony passes a witchcraft law similar to that of the Massachusetts Bay Colony.
1643	Battle of Newbury in the English Civil War are preceded by the shooting of a witch.
1643–1644	Severe witch-hunts take place in many parts of France.
1644	The first recorded weighing of a witch suspect takes place at Oudewater in the northern Netherlands.
1645–1646	Matthew Hopkins's East Anglian witch-hunt is the largest in English history, with about two hundred executions.
1647	Johann Philipp von Schonborn becomes elector and archbishop of Mainz and issues a decree against witch-hunts in the electoral territories. Alice Young of Windsor, Connecticut, is executed; it is the first execution of a witch recorded in the English colonies in America.

1651	The last time the Spanish Inquisition in Sicily hears a case involving the "ladies from outside."
1651–1655	Five witches are hanged in the English colony of Bermuda, under governor Josias Fforster.
1652	Michée Chauderon is the last witch executed in the territory of Geneva.
1653	Sir Robert Filmer's *An Advertisement to the Jury-Men of England, touching Witches. Together with a difference between a Hebrew and an English Witch* is published. Francois Perraud's *Demonology, or a Treatise on Demons and Sorcerers* is published. John Lambe's servant Anne Bodenham is convicted of witchcraft and executed. Madeline de Demandolx de la Palud is convicted of witchcraft and causing a girl's possession.
1656	Thomas Ady's *A Candle in the Dark* is published.
1657	A Dutch translation of von Spee's *Warning to Prosecutors* is published by Nicholas Borremans.
1657–1659	Severe witch-hunt takes place in Franche-Comte, led by the inquisitor Father Symard.
1659	Abraham Palinghe's *Witchcraft Unmasked* is published.
1661	George Ludwig Geisz's Lindheim witch-hunt leads to 30 executions.
1661–1662	A major Scottish witch-hunt results in more than three hundred executions.
1662	Two English women are executed as witches at Lowestoft in a case presided over by the future lord chief justice, Matthew Hale.
1662–1666	A witch-hunt led by Daniel Hauff in the German city of Esslingen results in at least 37 executions.
1665	A Swedish law associates witchcraft and diabolism.
1666	Joseph Glanvill's *A Philosophical Endeavour towards the Defense of the Being of Witches and Apparitions* is published.
1668	Meric Casaubon's *Of Credulity and Incredulity in things Natural, Civil and Divine* is published.
1668–1676	The Mora witch-hunt in Sweden results in about two hundred executions.

1669–1672	The Bohuslan witch-hunt in Sweden results in 29 executions.
1669	John Wagstaffe's *The Question of Witchcraft Debated* is published.
1672	A royal decree in Poland ineffectively reiterates the reservation of witch cases to the church courts.
1676	Hermann Löher's *The most Pressing Humble Complaint of Pious Innocents* is published.
1677	The investigation that will lead to the discovery of the Affair of the Poisons in France begins. John Webster's *The Displaying of Supposed Witchcraft* is published.
1677–1678	The exorcisms of Johann Christoph Haizmann take place at Mariazell in Austria.
1677–1681	Zaubererjackl trials take place in Salzburg, with at least 140 executions.
1679	The Chambre Ardente in Paris is established to investigate the Affair of the Poisons.
1680	A Native American Pueblo revolt in northern New Spain is blamed on witches.
1681	The fourth and final edition of Glanvill's witchcraft book, *Sadducismus Triumphatus*, is published.
1682	Three Bideford witches are executed. Louis XIV's proclamation identifies witchcraft in France as poisoning and sacrilege. Thomas Shadwell's play *The Lancashire Witches* is performed.
1684	Richard Bovet's *Pandaemonium, or the Devil's Cloyster. Being a further Blow to modern Sadducism, proving the Existence of Witches and Spirits*, is published.
1685	Alice Molland is executed in the last known execution of a witch in England. Halldor Finnbogason is executed in the last execution of a witch in Iceland. Rebecca Fowler is executed, the only known witch execution in Maryland history. A bad harvest in Croatia is followed by the lynching of several witches. The Imperial Chamber Court of the Holy Roman Empire condemns the use of ordeals, including flotation tests. George Sinclair's *Satan's Invisible World Discovered* is published.

1686	Denmark imposes automatic appeal of all death sentences from county courts to the supreme court, leading to the end of witch-hunting.
1688	The Goodwin case in Massachusetts leads to the execution of the poor Irishwoman Goody Glover and the first direct involvement of Cotton Mather in a witch case.
1689	Cotton Mather's *Memorable Providences, Relating to Witchcrafts and Possessions* is published; it is his first demonological work and recounts the Goodwin case and others. Balthasar Bekker publishes a Dutch translation of an English broadside on a recent witch case, *Great News from the West of England*, with a commentary ridiculing witch-hunting.
1690	Andrei Beobrazov and his associates are executed for having attempted to bewitch the tsar of Russia.
1691	The first two volumes of Balthasar Bekker's *The Enchanted World* are published. Richard Baxter's *The Certainty of the World of Spirits* is published. Two shepherds are executed as "so-called witches" by the Parlement of Paris in the last witch-related execution by the Parlement.
1691–1692	Multiple cases of demonic possession occur in the Mexican city of Querétaro.
1692	The Salem Witch Trials result in 20 executions. Because of his beliefs, Balthasar Bekker loses his job as a minister in the Dutch Reformed Church. The last edition of Nider's *Formicarius* is published.
1693	A shepherd and his wife are executed by the Parlement of Rouen, in the last witch-related execution by the Parlement. The last execution of a witch in Denmark takes place. Increase Mather's *Cases of Conscience Concerning Witchcraft* is published. Cotton Mather's *Wonders of the Invisible World* is published. Publication of the second two volumes of Balthasar Bekker's *The Enchanted World* are published.
1695	The first volume of Balthasar Bekker's *The Enchanted World* is published in English as *The World Bewitch'd*.
1696	Benedict Carpzov's *Practica Rerum Criminalium* becomes law in Hungary, after the recent conquest of the Turks by the Habsburgs; legal change encourages witch-hunting. Sarah Spencer is the last person charged with witchcraft in Bermuda.

1697	The last mass execution of witches in western Europe takes place with the deaths of the seven Paisley witches in Scotland. The last witchcraft indictments are made in New England.
1698	The last witchcraft indictment is made in Wales.
1699	The burning of Tattra Santi Michel is the last witch execution in Estonia.
1700	Robert Calef's *More Wonders of the Invisible World* is published.
1701	Christian Thomasius's Latin *On the Crime of Magic* is published. A German translation of Glanvill's *Sadducismus Triumphatus* is published.
1702	The Reverend John Hale's *A Modest Enquiry into the Nature of Witchcraft* is published.
1703	Johann Reiche's German translation of Thomasius's *On the Crime of Magic* is published.
1705	John Bell's *The Tryal of Witchcraft* is published.
1706	Ann Putnam, leader of the accusers at Salem, admits to having been deluded by Satan and begs the forgiveness of the families of those executed.
1711	Seven Island Magee witches are sentenced to a year in jail in last witchcraft case in Ireland. The General Court of Massachusetts reverses the attainders of 22 Salem witches and their families. The governor of Massachusetts allocates funds for their compensation.
1712	Jane Wenham becomes the last person in England convicted of witchcraft. Her case sets off major debate.
1713	A royal decree in Poland ineffectively reiterates the reservation of witch cases to the church courts.
1715	Richard Boulton's *A Compleat History of Magick, Sorcery and Witchcraft* is published.
1717	The trial of the witches of Great Wigston in Leicester ends in dismissal of the case. It is the last witch trial in England.
1718	Francis Hutchinson's *A Historical Essay concerning Witchcraft. With Observations of Matters of Fact, tending to Clear the Texts of the Sacred Scriptures, and Confute the Vulgar Errors about that Point* is published in response to Boulton.

1723	Nearly 20 children are imprisoned as witches in the imperial city of Augsburg. The last is released in 1729.
1725	The last recorded witch trial takes place in Estonia.
1727	Janet Horne is excuted in the last witch execution in Scotland.
1728–1729	The Szeged witch-trial in Hungary results in 14 executions.
1729–1731	The case of the possession of Marie Catherine Cadière in Toulon, France, takes place.
1734	A Swedish code provides for the death penalty for all cases of *maleficia*. but it is not enforced.
1736	The English Statute of 1604 and Scottish witchcraft statutes are repealed by the Parliament of Great Britain.
1746	The first recorded performance of the German Faust puppet-play takes place.
1749	Girolamo Tartarotti's *Nocturnal Meetings of Witches* is published.
1751	Ruth Osborne is lynched. Publication of Benedetto Bonelli's response to Tartarotti, *Critical Animadversions on the Nocturnal Meetings of Witches*.
1752	The last recorded witch trial takes place in Zagreb, capital of Croatia.
1754	The last edition of del Rio's *Disquisitions on Magic* is published.
1756	The execution of Veronica Zerritsch is the last witch execution in Bavaria. Empress Maria Theresa reserves all Hungarian witch cases to courts of appeal.
1762	William Hogarth's print *Credulity, Superstition and Fanaticism* features an early appearance of the "Halloween witch," with broomstick, pointed hat and black cat.
1766	Father Ferdinand Sterzinger attacks witch-hunting before the Bavarian Academy of Sciences, setting off Bavarian "witchcraft war."
1768	The imperial Habsburg government bans witch-hunting in Hungary.

1775	Anna Maria Schwägel is executed in the territories of the prince-abbacy of Kempten, Schwägel was the last witch executed in Germany.
1777	The last witch execution in Hungary takes place.
1779	Swedish King Gustavus III abolishes the death penalty for witchcraft, although it had not been inflicted for decades.
1782	Anne Goldin is executed at Glarus in Switzerland. It is the last witch execution in western Europe.
1791	The offense of witchcraft is eliminated from French law with the issuing of a new penal code by the Constituent Assembly.
1793	The legally dubious execution of two women accused of witchery takes place in the city of Posen in Prussian Poland. It is the last execution for witchcraft in Europe, although murder and lynching continue into the twentieth century.

A

ABSALON, ANNE PEDERSDOTTIR

Anne Pedersdottir Absalon, executed in 1590, was the most famous victim of the Norwegian witch-hunt. Her husband was a Lutheran minister, Absalon Pedersen Beyer. At that time, Norwegian Lutherans, supported by **Norway's** Danish rulers, were attempting to purify Norwegian churches of Catholic remnants, particularly artistic objects conducive to idolatry. The initial **accusation** of Absalon, in 1575, seems to have been an attempt to strike at her husband and the reforming party through her. She was acquitted then, but, now widowed, was accused of a wide variety of offenses in 1590. Some were standard *maleficia,* including causing sickness or death to people who had offended her. Her own servant claimed that Absalon had changed her into a horse and rode her to a **sabbat** on the Lyderhorn, where a gathering of witches had planned to wreak devastation on the town of Bergen in various ways. There had been a severe storm at the time of the alleged sabbat. The sabbat itself was fairly tame, lacking more bizarre features such as cannibalism. Absalon was convicted, in a civil court, on the evidence of others, including that of two women previously executed for witchcraft. She did not confess, nor was she **tortured** to induce confession or accusations of other witches. She was executed by burning. The Absalon case is the basis of the Danish director Carl Dreyer's (1889–1968) classic, although historically inaccurate, film, *Day of Wrath* (1943).

REFERENCE: Brian Levack, *The Witch-Hunt in Early Modern Europe.* London and New York: Longman, 1987.

ACCUSATIONS

The process by which a man or woman was legally brought before a court to answer charges of witchcraft was often complex. Accusations took many forms and came from many sources. One of the most common patterns by which accusations were made was as the culmination of a long process of suspicion and hostility between the suspected witch and others in her community. Usually it was people who thought themselves or their households victims of *maleficia* who made these allegations, but legal accusation was seldom the first response of an early modern villager who suspected his or her neighbor of witchery. There were many reasons not to go to court. Accusers risked entanglement in the legal process, which was often nearly as harsh in its treatment of plaintiffs as of defendants. The accuser's specifically legal risks diminished in the early modern period with the abandonment of the *lex talionis*, under which an accuser was liable to the same penalties a convicted defendant would suffer if the defendant was acquitted, but countersuits by accused witches against accusers for defamation did continue. Suspected witches could also gain revenge on accusers by accusing them of witchcraft, or use the threat to accuse others as a way of deterring potential accusers. Another risk of accusation, run outside the legal system, was the prospect of personal revenge from the accused witch. Although it was often claimed that being arrested or held for legal proceedings deprived witches of their power, in all but the most savage witch-hunts there was a distinct possibility that the accused would be acquitted. Acquitted witches would then be able to take either demonic or more mundane vengeance. The witch's family might also strike against the accuser.

In patriarchal early modern households, the husband was more likely to represent the family before the legal process. Although women accused each other of witchcraft in informal settings, adult men were more likely to make formal accusations of witchcraft in court. This was not true in the case of another kind of accusation that grew increasingly common in the late sixteenth and seventeenth centuries: an accusation made by a person possessed or otherwise afflicted by a demon. Possessed people were usually women or children, who while in the throes of torment could ascribe responsibility for the demonic presence to a witch. Unlike cases of more common *maleficium* such as the destruction of livestock, the accused need not be one who had established a long-standing reputation for witchcraft. Such accusations could be made for the sake of revenge, or for a member of one of these often powerless groups in early modern society to assume a powerful role. The most famous example of such accusers and accusations are the possessed girls who inaugurated the **Salem** witch-hunts. In other cases, the accuser acted as a mouthpiece for a person in authority who wanted to act covertly, as Anne **Gunter** did for her father Brian or as possessed persons in Catholic countries sometimes did for exorcists.

Once witch proceedings actually began, another kind of accusation played a central role. This was the accusation by an accused witch herself, sometimes voluntarily and sometimes under harsh interrogation or **torture.** Once a witch confessed, getting her to make more accusations was the principal goal of many torturers and interrogators. These accusations were sometimes of cooperation in *maleficium*, but also of presence at the **sabbat.** The process of eliciting accusations of sabbat attendance could lead to spiraling accusations, as in the great German witch-hunts. Unscrupulous interrogators could also force the accused to implicate others who the interrogator already viewed as witches, or simply as enemies. Many of the standard treatments of witchcraft urged caution in evaluating such accusations, and an expanding cycle of accusations was one of the central features distinguishing the small-scale witch trial or groups of trials from the large-scale witch-hunt. There was some controversy about the legal standing of accusations made by an accused witch, particularly whether the accusations, without supporting evidence, justified torturing the accused.

REFERENCES: Robin Briggs. *Witches and Neighbors: The Social and Cultural Context of European Witchcraft*. New York: Penguin, 1996; Joseph Klaits. *Servants of Satan: The Age of the Witch Hunts*. Bloomington: Indiana University Press, 1985; Keith Thomas. *Religion and the Decline of Magic*. New York: Charles Scribner's Sons, 1971.

ADELINE, GUILLAME (D. 1457)

The French university professor Guillame Adeline was among the first to be charged with the fully developed crime of witchcraft after its long period of development in the Middle Ages. In 1453, the church court of Evreux in Normandy charged Adeline with having made a compact with **Satan** to preach against the reality of the **sabbat,** thus hindering the persecution of witches in the area and advancing the cause of the Devil. Under **torture,** Adeline confessed to **flying** to the sabbat on a broomstick and there **kissing** the anus of a demon named Monseigneur (My lord) who transformed himself into a goat. Adeline also claimed that attendants at the sabbat were required to renounce the Christian faith. His social position kept Adeline from the pyre, and his confession did not lead to a large-scale witch-hunt, but he was sentenced to perpetual imprisonment on bread and water. He died four years later.

REFERENCE: Norman Cohn. *Europe's Inner Demons: The Demonization of Christians in Medieval Christendom*. Rev. ed. Chicago: University of Chicago Press, 2000.

ADY, THOMAS

The English **physician** Thomas Ady was the author of a strong denunciation of witchcraft belief, *A Candle in the Dark* (1656). Ady was inspired by revulsion at recent witch-hunts in **England,** notably that of Matthew **Hopkins,** and Ady was probably an inhabitant of Essex, where Hopkins had been active. Drawing on previous English witchcraft writers including George **Gifford** and Reginald **Scot,** he described the tensions of early modern villages that caused witchcraft **accusations.** Poor physicians and unscrupulous **cunning** men, he claimed, also denounced those ills they were unable to cure as the handiwork of witches. His basic strategy, however, was to denounce the hunting of witches as antibiblical and as Roman Catholic. He denounced the techniques of contemporary witch-hunters, such as **torture, flotation tests** and "waking the witch"—torture by prolonged sleep deprivation. Ady attacked these practices as having no biblical warrant. The witch's or **Devil's mark** or the **satanic pact** were also unscriptural. More fundamentally, Ady denied the biblical basis for the belief that **Satan,** or witches, actually possessed supernatural powers. Instead, the Devil was a spiritual tempter only. The word "witch," Ady pointed out, occurs only twice in the **Bible** (Exodus and Deuteronomy) and there refers to an idolater rather than someone with supernatural powers. He also claimed that biblical witches, unlike those most likely to be accused in England, were usually men. All admitted witches, as well as cunning folk, were frauds, and the only real *maleficium* was poisoning. The idea of witchcraft had been invented by Roman Catholics to stigmatize those beliefs and practices that opposed their church. Although Ady's chief venom was reserved for Catholics, he also denounced Protestant writers who supported witchcraft belief, including William **Perkins** and the Danish theologian Niels Hemmingsen (1513–1600).

REFERENCES: Stuart Clark. *Thinking with Demons: The Idea of Witchcraft in Early Modern Europe.* Oxford: Clarendon Press, 1997; Frederick Valetta. *Witchcraft, Magic and Superstition in England, 1640–1670.* Aldershot, England: Ashgate, 2000.

AFFAIR OF THE POISONS

The last great political sorcery case in western Europe was Affair of the Poisons in **France.** Its exposure began with an investigation by the lieutenant of police of Paris, Nicholas-Gabriel de la Reynie, into a group of alchemists, counterfeiters and poisoners in late 1677. This led to discovery of a group of poisoners and makers of love potions with connections to the high court nobility. Early in 1679, the police arrested three fortunetelling women, Marie Bosse, La Vigoreaux and Catherine Deshayes, known as "La Voisin." La Voisin, a **midwife,** abortionist and witch, became particularly celebrated. On April 7, 1679, papers were issued by the government for the formation of a special tribunal called a "Chambre Ardente" to try those charged. The Chambre Ardente met in a special room, draped in black and illuminated by torches. The judges were chosen for their piety as well as their legal knowledge and were assisted by **physician**s and apothecaries with expertise in poisons. The Chambre Ardente aroused opposition from the Parlement of Paris, always jealous of its supreme judicial power in the city, but went forth anyway. Unlike the Parlement, the Chambre Ardente made great use of **torture** in interrogation. It quickly convicted Bosse and her associates, including a son and daughter. They, along with other members of the group, were burned on May 8, 1679. (La Vigoreaux had died under torture.) Such were the rumors and excitement surrounding the affair, that Reynie encouraged two authors, Thomas Corneille (1625–1709) and Donneau de Visé (1638–1710), to write a play ridiculing pretenders to **magic** power, *The Fortuneteller, or the False Enchantments,* which ran for several months at the end of 1679 and the beginning of the next year. Reynie also studied the classic demonology of Jean **Bodin,** however.

The confessions of the poisoners implicated high court nobility, including persons associated with Louis XIV's (r. 1643–1715) mistress, Madame de Montespan (1641–1707). Several were arrested at the beginning of 1680. La Voisin refused to confess to poisoning, even under extreme torture, and was burned at the stake in February 1680. Her daughter and assistant, Margaret, confessed to poisoning, however, and charged that Montespan had been among her mother's clients. The ingredients of the poisons ranged from actual poisons, such as arsenic, to magical substances such as human remains.

The charges spread from poisoning to witchcraft, when it was revealed that individuals associated with the group had carried on various magical rituals, including the first appearance of the Black Mass, involving ritual **infanticide** and celebrated on the naked body of a woman, widely thought to be Montespan. It was found that Montespan had participated in rituals and used **image magic** to keep the king's love and make the queen sterile. Even worse, it was believed that Montespan had at one time even worked magic for the king's death and that several nobles, including some of the highest ranking, had made **satanic pacts.** Such was the sensitivity of the matter that the king ordered much of the evidence, particularly that involving Montespan, kept secret and separate so that it could be easily disposed. Much of it he burned many years later, after Reynie's death. The investigation continued until 1682, although the Chambre Ardente was suspended in 1680. It was also widely believed that poison or malicious magic caused the death of Montespan's rival for the king's affections, Mademoiselle de Fontanges (1661–1681).

The toll of the affair was dramatic—367 persons were arrested, 36 sentenced to death, five sent to the galleys and 23 banished. Others were merely held in prison until they died, like the priest-sorcerer Etienne Guiborg who had assisted La Voisin. Although many persons from the nobility and upper classes had been charged with poisoning and witchcraft, the only persons officially punished or tortured were from the lower **social classes.** Montespan lost the king's trust and affection and was essentially held under house arrest for the rest of her life. The affair stood in the background of the king's decree against witchcraft in 1682, by which he attempted to reassert his control over the supernatural.

REFERENCES: Ian Bostridge. *Witchcraft and Its Transformations, c. 1650–c. 1750.* Oxford: Clarendon Press, 1997; Frances Mossiker. *The Affair of the Poisons: Louis XIV, Madame de Montespan, and One of History's Greatest Unsolved Mysteries.* New York: Alfred A. Knopf, 1969; Joanna Richardson. "Madame de Montespan and the Affair of the Poisons." *History Today* 23 (1973): 588–592.

AGRIPPA VON NETTESHEIM, HEINRICH CORNELIUS (1486–1535)

The German humanist and occultist Heinrich Cornelius Agrippa stood beside his much more shadowy fellow countryman Georg **Faust** as the archetypal demonic magician. Ironically, Agrippa was greatly concerned to distinguish between his own **magic** and demonic magic. His *On Occult Philosophy* (1533) was one of the most influential of all early modern magical texts. It was published in three books, but a fourth book claiming to be by Agrippa and containing formulas for the invocation of demons also appeared. It was this book that ruined Agrippa's reputation. He became known as a satanic magician, and one particularly widespread legend claimed that he was always accompanied by a demonic **familiar** in the shape of a black dog. Jean **Bodin** and Martin **del Rio,** among other demonologists, attacked Agrippa as a magician. Agrippa's pupil, the witch-hunting opponent Johann **Weyer,** defended his old master's good name in his *On the Tricks of Demons* by claiming, correctly, that Agrippa had not in fact authored the fourth book.

Weyer's opposition to witch-hunting could have originated from Agrippa's teaching, for the magician claimed that most accused witches were merely deluded old women. Agrippa put his beliefs into effect in 1519, when he was serving the imperial city of Metz as its town orator. Agrippa intervened to defend an old woman from the village of Woippy who was being persecuted as a witch by a Dominican inquisitor, Nicolas Savini. Agrippa won the woman's freedom not by denying the reality of witchcraft, but by attacking Savini's use of irregular and even illegal procedures, such as kidnapping, and playing on the rivalry between Savini as an inquisitor and the bishop's court, which had jurisdiction over the area. He also claimed that the argument based on hereditary taint that the woman's enemies made, charging that she was a witch because her mother was a witch, was heretical in denying the efficacy of baptism.

REFERENCE: Charles G. Nauert, Jr. *Agrippa and the Crisis of Renaissance Thought.* Urbana: University of Illinois Press, 1965.

ANDERSON, SIR EDMUND (1530–1605)

Sir Edmund Anderson, Lord Chief Justice of the Common Pleas from 1582, was a rarity among senior English magistrates—a dedicated witch-hunter. In his most famous witch-related trial, that of Elizabeth Jackson for bewitching Mary **Glover** in 1602, Anderson declared the following in his charge to the jury: "The land is full of witches, they abound in all places, I have hanged five or six and twenty of them. There is no man here, can speak more of them than myself; few of them would confess it, some of them did; against whom the proofs were nothing so manifest, as against those that denied it." Anderson went on to endorse the theory of the **witch's mark** and to argue for relaxed standards of proof in witch cases, claiming that, given the power and subtlety of **Satan,** it was necessary to go on presumptions and circumstances rather than direct proofs. He argued that if **physicians** could not give a natural cause or cure for Glover's bewitchment, it must be concluded to be witchcraft. Other witch cases in which Anderson was involved include those of Alice Gooderidge in 1596, convicted for bewitching Thomas Darling, and the London witch Anne Kerke, convicted for bewitching several children, one to death, around 1599. Kerke was hanged, although Gooderidge was not, because under the statute of 1563 it would have been necessary for her to have been charged with murder by witchcraft. On at least one occasion Anderson's notorious dislike for accused witches was overcome by his equally notorious dislike for Puritans, when he dismissed a case against a witch who had been accused by an allegedly possessed person exorcised by the Puritan John **Darrell.** Anderson also served on a committee of lawyers that advised Parliament on drawing up the new and harsher witchcraft statute of 1604.

REFERENCES: C. L'Estrange Ewen, *Witchcraft and Demonianism: A Concise Account Derived from Sworn Depositions and Confessions Obtained in the Courts of England and Wales.* London: Heath Cranton, 1933; James Sharpe. *Instruments of Darkness: Witchcraft in Early Modern England.* Philadelphia: University of Pennsylvania Press, 1996.

ANIMALS

Several species of animals were strongly associated with witches and witchcraft by early modern Europeans. Prominent among these were toads, cats, goats and hares. All of these animals had generally negative cultural associations. Toads were considered ugly and poisonous, goats were lustful and, in Christian culture, were negatively contrasted with sheep. Cats were considered demonic and were charged with drinking blood or killing children. Hares were believed to be hermaphrodites or to change gender and were often linked with sodomy.

Toads had great **magical** power, and many magical practices used by witches, **cunning folk,** and ordinary people made use of toads, dried toads, powdered dried toads, toad bile, toad feces and toad blood. The toxic liquids exuded by toads' skin associated them with poisoning and sickness, but also with healing and health—toads were an ingredient in many magical cures for both humans and livestock. Toads played their most prominent role in **Basque** witchcraft, where "dressed toads" monopolized the role of **familiars** and witches described entire herds of toads at **sabbats.** In **England,** the other area where familiars were common, toads frequently, although not exclusively, appeared in that role. Sometimes the mere discovery of a toad in a person's house was treated as evidence of witchcraft. Toads were associated with devils and demons—John Milton's (1608–1674) epic *Paradise Lost* (1667) pictured **Satan** taking the form of a toad to pour poison into the ear of Eve, and devils and demons were frequently depicted in **art** as toadlike.

Although it was claimed that the Devil sometimes took the form of a toad at sabbats, a far more common depiction was as a goat. The goat's associations with lust go back to the goat-human combinations of classical mythology, fauns and satyrs, which influenced the Christian depiction of Satan. The biblical reference to the sheep on the right hand and the goats on the left at the last judgment also contributed to goats' satanic associations. It was frequently claimed that the Devil took the form of a goat at the sabbat in order to have **sex** with witches or to be **kissed** by them. Witches were also sometimes believed to be carried on **flying** goats to the sabbat.

Witches' Sabbath by Francisco de Goya y Lucientes. © Scala/Art Resource, New York.

Cats fulfilled many of the same functions as goats, carrying witches to the sabbat and having their form taken by Satan or demons. The idea that witches worship Satan in the form of cat at the sabbat goes back to descriptions of medieval heretical meetings. (Satan was also recorded to appear as a wolf, a bear, a dog, a bull, a sheep, a monkey, a hare, a horse, a cow, a bird, or a fox.) Cats also played a major role outside the sabbat, however, in less glamorous day-to-day witchcraft. Witches were often believed to transform themselves into the likeness of cats, and in that form to kill babies and children by biting or scratching them. This idea can be found both in common folklore and the writings of demonologists, as can stories of how wounds made on cats later showed up on the witch who had taken the cat's shape. The cat attained its greatest connection with witchcraft in England, where its main role was as a familiar. (Other forms taken by familiars included dogs, rats, chickens and insects.)

Stories of witches taking the form of a cat have many similarities with stories of witches in hare form, but the most common purpose of hare form was somewhat less malevolent. Witch-hares are associated with the stealing of milk from cows. There was also a Scandinavian belief in a harelike creature, the "milk-hare" that a witch could create for that specific purpose. There were also stories of witches taking the form of hares that could not be caught or killed for the purpose of frustrating hunters.

The Toad of Death. From a pen drawing in the nineteenth-century French manuscript, *La Magie Noir.* © Dover Pictorial Archive.

REFERENCES: Robert M. De Graaf. *The Book of the Toad: A Natural and Magical History of Toad-Human Relations.* Rochester, Vermont: Park Street Press,

1991; Gustav Henningsen. *The Witches' Advocate: Basque Witchcraft and the Spanish Inquisition (1609–1614)*. Reno: University of Nevada Press, 1980; William Monter. "Toads and Eucharists: The Male Witches of Normandy, 1564–1660," *French Historical Studies* 20 (1997): 563–595; Eilis Ni Dhuibhne. " 'The Old Woman as Hare': Structure and Meaning in Irish Legend." *Folklore* 104 (1993): 77–85; Boldil Nildin-Wall and Jan Wall. "The Witch as Hare or the Witch's Hare: Popular Legends and Beliefs in Nordic Tradition." *Folklore* 104 (1993): 67–76; Jeffrey Burton Russell. *Witchcraft in the Middle Ages*. Ithaca: Cornell University Press, 1972; Walter Stephens. *Demon Lovers: Witchcraft, Sex, and the Crisis of Belief*. Chicago and London: University of Chicago Press, 2002.

A witch rides through the starlit sky on her goat carrying a child she has stolen from its mother. Illustration from Collin de Plancy, *Dictionaire Infernal*, 1863. © Mary Evans Picture Library.

ARRAS WITCH-HUNT

The first large-scale witch-hunt, as opposed to the persecution of single witches or small groups, in an urban community was in the French city of Arras in 1459. A single witch who had been sentenced to be burned named other people he had seen at the **sabbat.** More **torture** led to more names, in the classic witch-hunt pattern. Five were burned alive on May 9, 1460. This did not end the hunt, which was carried out in the absence of the Bishop of Arras by two local clerics, the bishop of Beirut who was administering the diocese in the absence of the diocesan, and the head of the local Dominicans, Jacques du Boys. Both seem to have been obsessed with witches, who they claimed had representatives in the highest circles of the church.

The hunt the two carried on was based on Devil worship and the sabbat rather than *maleficia*, which played little role in the charges against the accused. As the arrests, trials and tortures continued, the citizens of Arras were gripped by a terror many communities would know in the following centuries. Even those who were not accused of witchcraft suffered economically, as Arras businessmen found that their peers in other towns were unwilling to extend credit to them while the witch-hunt lasted, given the difficulty of collecting from a convicted witch's estate.

The Four Witches by Albrecht Dürer, 1497. © Dover Pictorial Archive.

About twelve accused witches were burned in the Arras witch-hunt. Many more could have suffered, but the bishop of Beirut and Du Boys were hindered by the resistance of the local Inquisition, whose leaders were skeptical of the sabbat stories accused witches told under torture. What brought the killings to an end was the intervention of the sovereign of Arras, the duke of Burgundy, concerned about the economic and social damage the hunt was causing. The duke actually called an assembly of scholars from the university of Louvain to debate the sabbat's reality. They did not reach a unanimous conclusion, but the duke sent a representative to attend further trials. This action halted the killings, and Du Boys went mad and died shortly thereafter. One wealthy citizen of Arras who had been arrested appealed to the Parlement of Paris, the supreme court of appeal for the area. The Parlement launched an investigation, removing prisoners from Arras to Paris, and after thirty years, in 1491, cleared the name of everyone condemned and fined the surviving prosecutors to pay for masses for the souls of the condemned and the erection of a cross at the site of the burnings. The affair is sometimes referred to as the Vauderie of Arras after the **Waldensian** heretics whose name had become synonymous with "witch," although the accused do not appear to have been Waldensians.

REFERENCES: Norman Cohn. *Europe's Inner Demons: The Demonization of Christians in Medieval Christendom*. Chicago: University of Chicago Press, 2000; Joseph Klaits. *Servants of Satan: The Age of the Witch Hunts*. Bloomington: Indiana University Press, 1985.

ART

Although witchcraft never became a major theme of early modern European art, several artists did create witch images. The first body of "witch art" was associated with a group of South German and Swiss printmakers around Albert Dürer (1471–1528) in the late fifteenth and early sixteenth centuries. Their reasons for interest in witches include the heightened presence of demonological literature, notably the works of Ulrich **Molitor** and Heinrich **Kramer;** humanist interest in ancient literature featuring witches such as Circe; and the desire to explore the female nude, which could only be depicted in a narrow range of contexts, of which witchcraft was one. The first important artistic image of witches, Dürer's etching *Four Witches* (1497), was in fact mostly a study of four female nudes, with little witch paraphernalia. Dürer's second witch image, *The Witch*, produced between 1500 and 1507, was much more recognizable, showing an old woman riding a goat backward. It drew on the ideas of being made to ride backward as a mark of shame and of Lust as a personified figure riding a goat. Associates of Dürer who produced witch art include Hans **Baldung Grien**, the most prolific, as well as Albrecht Altdorfer (1480–1538), Hans Schauffelein the Elder (c. 1482–1539/40) and Urs Graf (1485–1527/8).

Flanders was another area where witches often appeared in art. The art of Hieronymous Bosch (c. 1450–1516), particularly the triptych *The Temptation of Saint Anthony,* often contained witch-related imagery. Bosch's admirer Pieter Bruegel the Elder (c. 1527–1569) included **sabbats** in two prints on the legend of the defeat of the wizard

Saul and the Witches of Endor by Salvator Rosa (1615–1673). © Scala/Art Resource, New York.

Hermogenes by Saint James. One of the most skillful and elaborate Flemish paintings on the subject of witchcraft was the *Witches' Sabbath* by Frans Francken the Younger (1581–1642). This painting showed a range of witch activity, including demon worship and *maleficia*. It appeared the year after a decree against witchcraft from the rulers of the **Southern Netherlands** and may have been connected to a witch-hunting campaign. Other Dutch artists who painted witches include the prolific David Teniers the Younger (1610–1690) and Jacques de Gheyn II (1565–1629). Most witch art was produced in northern Europe, where painters had a greater interest in everyday contemporary life than in **Italy** and Spain. One exception to this pattern was the Neapolitan Salvator Rosa (1615–1673), responsible for several witch paintings, the most celebrated being *The Witch of Endor* and *Witches and Their Incantations*. Rosa had a particular interest in witches and also wrote a poem on the subject.

By the eighteenth century, witches were often treated as comic, or as symbols not of supernatural evil but of irrationality and superstition, a tendency that would reach its apogee in the work of Francisco de Goya (1746–1828). One particularly influential image appeared in William Hogarth's (1697–1764) print, *Credulity, Superstition and Fanaticism* (1762). This attack on all forms of irrational belief features the first appearance of the "Halloween witch," with pointed hat (associated only with witches in **England** and there only from the late seventeenth century), broomstick and black cat.

REFERENCES: Jane P. Davidson. *The Witch in Northern European Art, 1470–1750*. Freren: Luca Verlag, 1987; Lene Dresen-Conders. "Witches as Devil's Concubines: On the Origin of Fear of Witches and Protection against Witchcraft." In *Saints and She-Devils: Images of Women in the 15th and 16th Centuries*, ed. Lene Dresen-Conders, 59–82. London: Rubicon Press, 1987; Charles Zika. "Durer's Witch, Riding Women and Moral Order." In *Durer and His Culture*, ed. Dagmar Eichberger and Charles Zika, 118–140. Cambridge: Cambridge University Press, 1998.

AUSTRIA AND BOHEMIA, WITCH-HUNTING IN

The hereditary lands of the Habsburg dynasty in central Europe came to witch-hunting late and only had their most intense witch-hunts in the late seventeenth century. There was one large case in the late fifteenth century, Heinrich **Kramer's** witch-hunt at **Innsbruck,** but no one was executed; there was little further witch-hunting in Austria until the late sixteenth century. Witch-hunting rose alongside the Catholic Reformation. The great Jesuit preacher Georg Scherer (1540–1605) exorcised a girl in Vienna of 12,652 demons in 1584, incidentally identifying the girl's grandmother as the witch responsible for her **possession.** The witch-hunting activities of the Lutheran magistrate Jakob **Bithner** in Styria also began around this time, as did the use of the concept of the **satanic pact** in Austrian witch trials. By the early seventeenth century, Austria was suffering from large witch-hunts, such as one in

Capture of Jan Hus, Czech religious reformer (later burnt at the stake for heresy), from the fifteenth-century *Chronicle of Ulrico de Richental*. © The Art Archive/University Library Prague/Dagli Orti.

Bregenz in 1609 that led to sixteen **executions.** Bohemia also developed witch-hunting relatively late, in the final stages of the Thirty Years' War. In the 1640s, a witch-hunt in the province of Silesia saw as many as 250 deaths.

Austrian witch-hunts were usually carried out by regional secular courts, including the courts of priestly landowners. There were few appeals to the ruler's central courts. Unlike **Germany,** in the Habsburg lands magistrates seldom appealed to university law faculties for their opinions on witch cases. An unusually high percentage of Austrian witches were men—as many as one-third in some areas. Roma, or Gypsies—an especially persecuted population—as well as vagrants were often associated with witchcraft as well. In addition to *maleficia*, Austrian and Bohemian witches also were frequently charged with desecrating the sacred Host.

The high point of witch-hunting in the late seventeenth century is associated with iterant judicial officials called *Bannrichter*. These officials used **torture** to promote truly large witch-hunts. The most notorious, Frantisek Boblig, was active in Moravia and the Sudetenland and carried on large witch-hunts in Sumperk and Velke Losiny (Ullersdorf). The central government began to exert more control over local witch-hunts in the early eighteenth century, but large witch-hunts continued sporadically until the 1730s, and individual cases continued until the 1750s. R. J. W. Evans gives an estimate of approximately 1,500 executions in Austria and approximately a thousand in Bohemia, of whom a majority came from the German population.

REFERENCES: R. J. W. Evans. *The Making of the Habsburg Monarchy: An Interpretation.* Oxford: Clarendon Press, 1979; Edmund Kern. "Confessional Identity and Magic in the Late Sixteenth Century: Jakob Bithner and Witchcraft in Styria." *The Sixteenth Century Journal* 25 (1994): 323–340.

B

BADEN-BADEN WITCH-HUNT

Like many other German territories, Baden-Baden had a severe witch-hunt in the period 1627 to 1632. The territory, a dominion of the margrave of Baden, had recently been forcibly changed from Protestant to Catholic, and thus religious tensions were high. The witch-hunt was restricted to three places, the town of Baden and two other cities, Buhl and Steinbach. It was led by one man, a councillor to Margrave William, Dr. Martin Eschbach, who was a resident in the town of Baden from September 16, 1627, to October 3, 1628. He spent the time from October 1628 to April 10, 1631, as a consultant to Buhl and Steinbach in their witch-hunting campaigns. Eschbach's hunt, like many other German witch-hunts, reached beyond the old women who were stereotypical witches to include men, who comprised about one-third of the accused, and government officials. Prominent men accused included the margrave's official in Steinhalter (accused after his wife and sisters had already been executed) and the church superintendent and director of the city hospital in Baden. Characteristics of the Baden-Baden witch-hunt include fierce and repeated **torture,** the violation by Catholic priests of the sanctity of the confessional to provide information to witch-hunters, and a heavy emphasis on getting tortured witches to implicate others whom they had allegedly seen at the **sabbat.** The average number of other witches named by suspects was about 15, and Eschbach and his associates accumulated lists of hundreds of names. One woman named 150 other witches. Eschbach also made extensive use of children's **accusations** to implicate parents (and vice versa), foreshadowing the **Mora** and **Salem** witch-hunts.

Although not all accused were brought to trial, 97 percent of those tried were convicted—among the highest conviction rates of the entire European witch-hunt. About two hundred witches were executed. Accumulated doubts among the magistrates who assisted Eschbach, rather than external factors, seem to have caused the witch-hunt's end.

REFERENCE: H. C. Erik Midelfort. *Witch Hunting in Southwestern Germany, 1562–1684.* Stanford: Stanford University Press, 1972.

BALDUNG GRIEN, HANS (1485–1545)

The German Hans Baldung Grien, a disciple of Albrecht Dürer (1471–1528), was the first and one of the few European artists to treat witches as a major subject of his **art,** although he worked at a time when witch-hunting was not vigorous or culturally prominent. Witches were a particularly congenial subject for Baldung because of his combination of misogyny and an extreme fascination with the female body. The extensive set of drawings Baldung produced while in the city of Freiburg to paint the high altar between 1512 and 1516 is a repository of fifteenth- and early-sixteenth-century ideas about witches, many deriving from the humanist revival of the classical tradition. Baldung's witches in these drawings were always women, fleshy and engaged in **magical** activities such as preparation for flight. They were often shown in a distorted or gruesome fashion, characteristic of Baldung's art in general. Baldung linked witchcraft both to the female capacity to be deluded by **Satan** and to unbridled sexuality, often associated with the demonic. Some images, such as the 1515 *Witch and Dragon*, were explicitly pornographic and meant for private circulation among Baldung's friends. *Witch and Dragon* features a dragon directing a stream of fire from its mouth between a witch's legs.

Baldung's later works, including the painting *The Weather Witches* (1523) and the popular woodcut of 1544, *The Bewitched Groom*, shift from predominantly ridiculing witches to presenting them as objects of fear and allies of the Devil. *The Bewitched Groom* shows a stable groom with a resemblance to Baldung himself stretched out unconscious or dead while a malevolent or maddened-appearing horse looks on. A witch looking through a stable window at the groom is much more realistically portrayed than the exotic and sensual nudes of the Freiburg drawings. She is an old, lower-class woman, typical of the people most commonly charged as witches. The presence of horses, symbols of sexuality for Baldung, associates the witch's power over the groom with her power over the sexual realm. This is a complex image with no obvious antecedents in the literature of witchcraft or folk tradition and has been subject to a variety of interpretations.

REFERENCES: Dale Hoak. "Art, Culture and Mentality in Renaissance Society: The Meaning of Hans Baldung Grien's *Bewitched Groom* (1544)." *Renaissance Quarterly* 38 (1985): 489–510; Linda C. Hults. "Baldung's *Bewitched Groom* Revisited: Artistic Temperament, Fantasy and the 'Dream of Reason.'" *The Sixteenth Century Journal* 15 (1984): 259–279; Linda C. Hults. "Baldung and the Witches of Freiburg: The Evidence of Images." *Journal of Interdisciplinary History* 18 (1987): 249–276; Margaret A. Sullivan. "The Witches of Durer and Hans Baldung Grien." *Renaissance Quarterly* 53 (2000): 332–401.

BAMBERG WITCH-HUNT

Some of the worst witch-hunts of the entire early modern period took place in Bamberg, one of the small independent Catholic bishoprics of **Germany's** Franconia region, in the early seventeenth century. The first large Bamberg witch-hunt took place under the reforming Catholic prelate, Prince-Bishop Johann Gottfried von Aschausen, who held office from 1609 to 1622. Von Aschausen's crusade against witchcraft began with a decree against sorcerers and diviners in 1610. In 1612 and 1613, this decree led to a small witch-hunt, with about six victims. The first mass panic was between 1616 and 1618, when about three hundred witches were executed. The real moving spirit behind this and subsequent persecutions in Bamberg and Franconia appears to have been not the prince-bishop, but the suffragan, or assistant bishop, Friedrich Förner, a leader of the Catholic Reformation in Germany. Förner was an avid witch-hunter and demonologist, frequent preacher against witchcraft and author of the sermon collection A *Display of the Weaponry of God against all Superstition, Divination, Enchantments and Devil-Worship* (1626). (The book was dedicated to the notorious persecutor of **Eichstätt** and **Ellwangen,** Johann Christoph von Westerstetten [1565–1636].)

The next major wave of Bamberg persecution took place from 1626 to 1630, during the reign of the *Hexenbischof*, or "witch-bishop," Johann Georg Fuchs von Dornheim (bishop, 1623–1633). Such was the sheer volume of witchcraft persecution that Bamberg even had to build a special "witch-prison" to hold the suspects and set up a special state bureau, the Witch Commission, exclusively devoted to witchcraft cases. Experienced persecutors from other territories, such as Dr. Schwarzkonz from Eichstätt, were recruited to carry on the persecution, and Bamberg subjects were forbidden to criticize witch-hunting officials, on pain of public flogging and banishment. **Torture** was extreme, and the restrictions on it laid down in the *Carolina* were ignored. The sometimes elaborate confessions of Bamberg witches feature the standard witch stereotype, with *maleficia*, witch flight, the **sabbat** (usually referred to as the "witches' dance"), **sex** with the Devil or lesser demons, **satanic pact,** (often in the form of baptism by the Devil) and the desecration of sacred objects. **Execution** of convicted witches was frequently by burning alive, without the mercy of preliminary strangulation. Like all the major Franconian persecutions, this witch-hunt did not respect the traditional class boundaries that limited witch persecution to the poor and politically powerless. It extended to councillors, leading families of the urban patriciate, including that of the burgomaster Johannes **Junius** and even the bishop's chancellor, along with his wife and children. Unlike the contemporary **Würzburg** witch-hunt, however, Bamberg witch-hunters took relatively little interest in child witches. Although the Bamberg prince-bishops were also fierce opponents of Bamberg's Protestants, there was no correlation, positive or negative, between the areas of substantial Protestant presence and the areas of intense witch-hunting.

What eventually ended the persecution was Fuchs von Dornheim's radicalism in going after leading families, who could invoke the support of outside rulers far more powerful than the prince-bishop. The case that brought about Fuchs von Dornheim's fall and exile was that of the accused witch Dorothea Flockhlin, whose husband, a Bamberg official, had managed to flee to the free imperial city of Nuremberg, a center for many refugees from the Franconian persecutions. From there he and members of Dorothea's Nuremberg family appealed to the pope and the Holy Roman Emperor. In early April of 1630, the imperial court issued a mandate calling Fuchs von Dornheim to account for the charges against him. Personal interventions from leading imperial officials followed, but the prince-bishop paid little heed, renewing the proceedings against Flockhlin in a harsher form on April 28. A stronger imperial mandate, forbidding all further proceedings against Flockhlin, was issued on May 11, and the pope also prepared an intervention. Before the official messages from the emperor and pope could arrive, Fuchs von Dornheim had Flockhlin executed on May 17, enraging imperial officials.

In a Diet of the Empire at Regensburg, the increasingly scandalous Franconian situation was on the agenda. Fuchs von Dornheim sent representatives, including Förner, to the Diet to plead with imperial officials, but in vain. The imperial court had definitively turned against Fuchs von Dornheim and the other Franconian witch-bishops, but he continued his delaying tactics. Another imperial mandate was issued on September 20, and the persecutions ended shortly after, although accused witches were not yet released. A fourth mandate issued in June 1631 appointed a Bamberg official known to be opposed to the hunts, Anton Winter, as head of the Bamberg Witch Commission and set up stronger standards of evidence and procedure for witch trials. Finally Fuchs von Dornheim fled Bamberg (allowing the Bamberg authorities to free the imprisoned accused witches), dying in exile in 1633.

REFERENCES: Wolfgang Behringer. *Witchcraft Persecutions in Bavaria: Popular Magic, Religious Zealotry, and Reason of State in Early Modern Europe.* Trans. J. C. Grayson and David Lederer. Cambridge: Cambridge University Press, 1997; Hans Sebald. *Witch-Children: From Salem Witch-Hunts to Modern Courtrooms.* Amherst, Mass.: Prometheus Books, 1995; Robert S. Walinski-Kiehl. "The Devil's Children: Child Witch-Trials in Early Modern Germany." *Continuity and Change* 11 (1996): 171–189; Robert S. Walinski-Kiehl. " 'Godly States,' Confessional Conflict and Witch-Hunting in Early Modern Germany." *Mentalities* 5 (1988): 13–25.

BASQUES

The witchcraft beliefs of the Basque people of the Pyrenees region between Spain and **France** are some of the best-documented in early modern Europe, thanks to the exhaustive investigations carried out by the **Spanish Inquisition** in connection with the **Zugurramurdi** witches and the writings of the French demonologist and witch-hunter Pierre de **Lancre.** Through de Lancre's widely distributed work, they also influenced the ideas of witch-hunters throughout Europe.

The association of the Basques with witchcraft begins early in the history of the witch-hunt. By the early fifteenth century, French and Spanish magistrates were carrying out trials. In 1466, the province of Guipuzcoa petitioned Enrique IV of Castile (r. 1454–1474) for vigorous action against witches who were causing damage in the area. The petitioners complained that local legal codes lacked anti-witchcraft provisions and asked that the king grant local mayors the power to try and execute witches, without the right of appeal. The petition was granted. Witch persecutions, some severe, are recorded in the Spanish Basque provinces in 1507 (when about 30 witches were burned), 1517 and 1527. The early sixteenth century Spanish persecutions were discussed in Spanish language demonologies such as Martin de **Castañega's** *Treatise on Superstitions and Witchcraft* (1529) and Pedro Ciruelo's *A Reproof of Superstitions and Witchery* (1529). Persecution on the Spanish side of the Pyrenees dwindled for most of the sixteenth century, particularly after the Inquisition changed its procedures for investigating witchcraft cases. The most eager witch-hunters in the Spanish Basque country were secular magistrates, but the Inquisition managed to maintain control over the entire process. Few persecutions ended in **execution.**

La Murqui, the noted witch-finder of the French Basque country, indicates the tell-tale marks that prove the victim is in league with Satan. © Mary Evans Picture Library.

Aggressive witch-hunting in the Basque country in the seventeenth century began on the French side of the border, with a petition from local officials in the Pays de Labourd to the king of France complaining of witches and asking for royal help. In 1609, Henri IV (1589–1610) responded by appointing a lawyer, Pierre de Lancre, and the president of the Parlement of Bordeaux, the scholar Jean d'Espagnet, to constitute a traveling court for witch cases. De Lancre, much the dominant personality of the two, and d'Espagnet did not begin their tour of the region until the summer of 1609, but local authorities did not wait. They were already trying and imprisoning witches in large numbers. The exact number of witches executed in de Lancre's persecution is unknown but was probably around 80, including several priests. De Lancre thought this was barely the tip of the iceberg and concluded that Basque society generally was permeated with witchcraft.

The French witch-hunt spilled over into Spain, eventually leading to the execution of six witches from Zugurramurdi at the auto-da-fé at Logroño in 1610. The confessions taken from the many witches investigated by the Spanish inquisitors, with intense psychological pressure but without **torture,** constitute the most detailed source for Basque witchcraft beliefs and rank high among sources for popular witchcraft beliefs anywhere in Europe. The Zugurramurdi Basque witches described a secret society of devil worshippers. The Devil was sometimes seen in the form of a monstrous man with a deformed body and horrible eyes, and sometimes in the form of a he-goat. The word Basques used to describe the **sabbat,** *akellarre* (Castilianized as *aquelarre*) literally means "he-goat meadow." The *akellarres* took place frequently—every Monday, Wednesday and Friday in addition to the evenings before the great festivals of the Church. They began late in the evening and continued until dawn. Before the witches left their homes for the sabbat, they rubbed themselves with a foul-smelling ointment while repeating vows of loyalty to the Devil. They either flew or walked to the sabbat, where they prostrated themselves before the Devil, **kissing** him on his hands, chest, penis and anus (some witches claimed that he farted in their faces). The main business of the sabbat was dancing, cavorting and promiscuous **sex,** witches with each other and male and female witches with the Devil. Witches also feasted on the flesh of corpses. The highly colored descriptions of the Basque sabbat were influential throughout Europe, after being publicized, with their drama heightened even further, in de Lancre's *Description of the Inconstancy of Bad Angels and Demons* (1612). On the festival eves, the witches and the Devil would hold a special ceremony parodying and blaspheming the mass.

Basque witchcraft was presented more as a matter of tradition, often handed down through families, than of the Devil recruiting individual witches. The Basque witches claimed to have been initiated as children, when adult witches, often parents, persuaded them to deny God and the saints and presented them to the Devil. The Devil gave them a mark by scratching them with his claw. The witches themselves were organized in a hierarchy, with greater power and responsibility accruing to senior witches. Particularly distinguished senior witches would participate as queen, or king, of the *akellarre*. As witches, the Basques had toads as **familiars** (the Basque country is the only place in Continental Europe where the belief in familiars played a large role in the witch-hunt), who were treated with great honor. The toads were frequently referred to as "dressed" toads, signifying the robes they wore. At the *akellarre* a child witch would keep herd over the toads (shepherding was a common profession among the Basques). Regular toads were used as one of the ingredients in the poisons and ointments the witches concocted, as were the remains of human bodies they had eaten and many other substances, most of them disgusting. Like witches everywhere, Basque witches were supposed to harm other humans, and the Devil punished them when they could work harm and did not do so.

Which parts of the witches' confessions reflect actual Basque beliefs, and which the demonological expectations of Spanish inquisitors and French magistrates, is a difficult question, complicated by the cultural and linguistic barriers between the Basques and the French and Spanish. Few magistrates or inquisitors could understand Basque or be understood by Basques without an interpreter. The investigators sometimes saw distinctive Basque cultural practices as contributing to witchcraft—de Lancre was particularly repulsed by the high status of Basque women, some of whom participated in the celebration of the Mass. The question of the truth of the confessions was thoroughly disposed of by the inquisitor Alonzo de **Salazar Frias.** Salazar's painstaking investigations in the years 1610–1612 involved searching witches' houses for ointments and dressed toads, feeding ointments and poisons (the searchers never found a dressed toad) to **animals** and observing the effect, which was usually none, and taking blindfolded witches to the areas where they had claimed the *akellarre* had been held and asking them to describe it and then comparing the descriptions to those of others who claimed to have attended. Physical examination of women claiming to have had sex with the Devil revealed that some were virgins. Acceptance of Salazar's findings by the Supreme Council of the Spanish Inquisition led to a diminution of witch-hunting in the Spanish Basque region, then carried on principally by secular authorities and hindered by the Inquisition. Witch-hunting in the French Basque region also moderated after de Lancre's witch-hunt. Belief in witchcraft, on the other hand, persists in the Basque country to the present day.

REFERENCES: Julio Caro Baroja. *The World of the Witches*. Trans. O. N. V. Glendinning. Chicago: University of Chicago Press, 1965; Gustav Henningsen. *The Witches' Advocate: Basque Witchcraft and the Spanish Inquisition (1609–1614)*. Reno: University of Nevada Press, 1980.

BAVARIA, WITCH-HUNTING IN

The Duchy of Bavaria was the largest and most powerful state in southeastern **Germany** and the leader of the Catholic Reformation in the Holy Roman Empire. It was also an active witch-hunting state, but its level of activity varied greatly over time, and it was never as active as some smaller German states. Witchcraft and the appropriate policies for dealing with it produced complex political and theoretical struggle and debate in Bavaria.

Large-scale witch persecution began in Bavaria in 1589 as part of the great wave of South German witch-hunting around 1590. This was a time of widespread crop failure, and the major Bavarian witch-hunts were all associated with dearth. The first wave of persecution ended around the fall of 1590. This was the most severe persecution in Bavarian history, but the spotty survival of records makes the number of victims irrecoverable. The persecution introduced witch-hunting theory and practice to the duchy, and a party of hard-line persecutors was formed in subsequent years. Politically, their leader was Johann Sigismund Wagnereckh, court chancellor from 1606 until his death in 1617 and a zealous champion of the Catholic Reformation. From a middle-class background—his father was a customs official—Wagnereckh had great influence with the duke of Bavaria, Maximilian I (r. 1597–1651), but never enough to shut out opposing views. The severely Catholic Maximilian was usually sympathetic to witch-hunting but sometimes treated it as an open question. His indecisiveness permitted the continued existence of factions both supporting and opposing persecutions.

Although no member of Bavaria's elite denied witches' existence or the necessity of punishing them, some pressed for milder treatment of the accused, narrower definitions of "witchcraft" and the application of regular rather than extraordinary procedures in criminal trials. Although the pro-persecution party was initially made up of the powerful Bavarian Jesuits, officials who had risen from relative obscurity like Wagnereckh, foreigners in the duke's service and even converts from Protestantism, the anti-persecution party was dominated by Bavaria's traditional elites, both the rural nobility and the urban patriciate. Their see-saw struggle continued for decades. The next agrarian crisis, from 1597–1601, saw the **Pappenheimer** case, in which Wagnereckh promoted a trial of a family of vagrants. They were convicted, violently tortured, and burned, as were several other witches, but the resistance of the anti-persecution party prevented these events from developing into a major witch-hunt. Wagnereckh charged his opponents with being bad Catholics, and they responded by attacking alleged irregularities in the trials, including the subjecting of accused witches to **torture** merely on the basis of denunciation. An appeal for a ruling was made to the University of Ingolstadt, the leading academic institution in Bavaria. The Ingolstadt theologians supported active persecution, whereas the lawyers had their doubts. In the hope of a clearer mandate, Wagnereckh and the persecutors broadened their enquiries to other universities in south Germany and the Catholic world. These, too, were contradictory and inconclusive. The next step was to get the opinions of the greatest Catholic authorities on witchcraft, the Jesuit Martin **del Rio** and the **Lorraine** magistrate Nicholas **Remy.** Their opinions, not surprisingly endorsing a zealous hunt with unrestricted use of torture, still did not end the debate, which the anti-persecution party seemed to be winning simply by preventing persecution while it went on.

Wagnereckh's ascendancy to the court chancellorship in 1606 and another agrarian crisis from 1607 to 1608 changed the situation. Wagnereckh loosened restrictions on the use of torture and included various forms of popular **magic** as witchcraft. Even so, the opponents of persecution often managed to block his interventions in particular cases. Wagnereckh attempted to remedy this situation by drafting the Mandate against Superstition, Magic and Witchcraft in 1611. It was signed by Duke Maximilian in 1612 and renewed in 1665 and 1746. The mandate set forth the program of Wagnereckh's faction, prescribing death as the punishment for dealing with the Devil or *maleficium* and treating many forms of popular magic and soothsaying as evidence of witchcraft or an implicit **satanic pact.** Even this, however, did not open the doors to persecution on the level of the 1590s. The anti-persecution party scored a victory with the **execution** of the corrupt witch judge Gottfried **Sattler** in 1613, and the next agrarian crisis, in 1615, produced a wave of trials but few, if any, executions.

Even the Jesuits, who had been the intellectual mainstay of the persecution party, were developing divisions over the issue. Adam Tanner (1572–1632) in

1601 was the first German Jesuit to express doubts over witch persecution. He was a lecturer at Ingolstadt from 1603 to 1627 and published his doubts in his theological treatise, *Theologica Scholastica* (1626–1627). (The section on witch trials was published separately in Cologne in 1629.) Tanner did not deny the reality of witchcraft or witch flight (although he thought actual flights were rare), but attacked the procedures and free use of torture characteristic of witch persecutions. His controversial work greatly influenced subsequent and more radical German anti-persecution writers, notably two of his fellow Ingolstadt Jesuits, Paul Laymann (1574–1635) and Kaspar Hell (1588–1634), as well as Friedrich von **Spee** (1591–1635) and the Lutheran professor Johann Meyfahrt (1590–1642).

The period 1629 to 1630, coinciding with another agrarian crisis and severe suffering caused by the Thirty Years' War, saw an attempt by the government to persecute witches rigorously on the model of the great hunts in the Franconian prince-bishoprics. This was controversial, because the Franconian persecutions were actually widely condemned by Bavarian opinion. Perhaps for this reason, the new persecution policy was applied most rigorously to Wemding, a small, isolated fragment of Bavaria separated from the main body of the duchy. Thirty-nine witches were burned in the two years in Wemding under the supervision of the witch commissioner Dr. Wolfgang Kolb, an experienced persecutor from Franconia. Kolb died in 1630, but the pace of the persecution at Wemding was already slowing down because of opposition from the other parts of the duchy. The number of deaths was much smaller in other parts of Bavaria, not at all on the Franconian scale of hundreds of executions. This was the last major persecution in Bavaria.

Subsequent persecutions usually consisted of single trials of individuals and families rather than large-scale witch-hunting. In the late seventeenth century, Bavaria followed the pattern of most of south Germany after the Salzburg **Zaubererjackl trials** (1677–1681) of shifting witch persecution away from old women to young beggar boys. The last execution of a witch in Bavaria was of a 14-year-old girl named Veronica Zerritsch, convicted and burned for a satanic pact and the stealing of consecrated hosts in 1756. Ten years later, Ferdinand **Sterzinger's** speech before the Bavarian Academy of Sciences inaugurated the Bavarian witchcraft controversy, won by the opponents of persecution. The Mandate against Superstition became a dead letter until its abolition on the revision of the Bavarian criminal code in 1813.

REFERENCES: Wolfgang Behringer. *Witchcraft Persecutions in Bavaria: Popular Magic, Religious Zealotry, and Reason of State in Early Modern Europe.* Translated by J. C. Grayson and David Lederer. Cambridge: Cambridge University Press, 1997; Michael Kunze. *Highroad to the Stake: A Tale of Witchcraft.* Translated by William E. Yuill. Chicago and London: University of Chicago Press, 1987.

BEKKER, BALTHASAR (1634–1698)

Balthasar Bekker, a minister in the Dutch Reformed Church, was the author of one of the most thoroughgoing attacks on witch belief, the four-volume *The*

Enchanted World (1691–1693). *The Enchanted World,* however, covered a far larger range of topics than witch belief alone. From early in his career, Bekker opposed conservative Calvinist church authorities in the Dutch Church. *The Enchanted World* boldly attacked religious dogmatism and biblical literalism, as well as belief in the powers of spirits, whether good or evil.

Bekker arrived at his opposition to orthodox demonology slowly—a commentary on the Heidelberg Catechism he published in 1671 accepted the existence of witchcraft. *The Enchanted World* was immediately preceded in 1689 by Bekker's translation of a recent English broadside, *Great News from the West of England* (1689) on the case of an accused witch, Elizabeth Carrier, from the town of Beckenton. She was being held for the Assizes on charges of having caused a young man and woman to vomit strange objects, including pins. Bekker included a commentary deploring witch persecution and ridiculing the charges in the case. He satirically hoped that Carrier would die in prison rather than be subjected to the humiliation of a trial and **execution.** (Carrier was eventually released.)

The first two volumes of *The Enchanted World* appeared in 1691, when Bekker was a minister in Amsterdam. The first volume was a historical account of superstitious belief in **magic** and demons, which Bekker identified as of pagan, rather than Christian, origin. The second, more controversial volume, combined Cartesian mechanism with biblical exegesis to attack the idea that spirits affected the material world in any way. As a Cartesian, Bekker claimed that spirit and matter were two entirely different categories of things and could not affect each other. (The obvious exception, human beings, were so because God had worked an ongoing miracle.) God was not a spirit. As a biblical exegete, Bekker claimed that references to angels in the **Bible** were really references to God's power (although he acknowledged that purely spiritual angels existed) and references to **possession** in the New Testament were really references to illness. He used examples from his own pastoral work to show how illness caused people to believe themselves possessed. **Satan,** Bekker claimed, was bound up in Hell, unable to harm or make pacts with humans.

Bekker's work was extremely popular and extremely controversial. Several responses to it were printed the same year, and eventually there were 175 publications in the controversy, of which 131 were hostile. Church authorities tried and failed to get the Dutch government to suppress the book. Bekker's opponents feared that denying the power of spirits promoted atheism—a far more important issue at that time and place than witchcraft or witch-hunting. Bekker was deposed as a pastor the following year. In 1693, he published two more volumes of *The Enchanted World*. Volume 3 focused specifically on sorcery and magic, dismissing it as trickery and sleight of hand. Volume 4 analyzes contemporary cases and closes with a denunciation of witch trials. Although there had not been a conviction or execution of a witch in the Dutch Republic for many decades, Bekker was familiar with recent cases in **England** and **Sweden.** Much of his argument was derived from previous literary opponents of the witch-hunt, particularly Johann **Weyer** and Reginald **Scot.** Bekker's work, originally in Dutch, received many translations, including a 1695 English translation of the first volume, *The World Bewitch'd*.

REFERENCES: Andrew Fix. *Fallen Angels: Balthasar Bekker, Spirit Belief, and Confessionalism in the Seventeenth Century Dutch Republic*. Dordrecht: Kluwer, 1999; Anna E. C Simoni. "Balthasar Bekker and the Beckington Witch." *Quaerendo* 9 (1979): 135–142; J. G. Stronks. "The Significance of Balthasar Bekker's *The Enchanted World*." In *Witchcraft in the Netherlands from the Fourteenth to the Twentieth Century*, ed. Marijke Gijswit-Hofstra and Willem Frijhoff, 149–156. Rotterdam: Universitaire Pers Rotterdam, 1991.

BELGIUM

See Southern Netherlands.

BELL, JOHN (1676–1707)

John Bell, a Scottish Presbyterian minister, is the probable author of the anonymous *The Tryal of Witches* (1705), one of the last statements of classical demonology. The text is divided into three parts, the first of which discusses how one knows oneself to be bewitched. Bell's principal opponent in this discussion is not witchcraft skepticism, the existence of which he does not acknowledge, but those eager to ascribe disease to witchcraft. (He scorned the credulity of those who believed the **Paisley** witches guilty on flimsy evidence.) He emphasizes that only those conditions for which there are no natural causes can be considered the result of witch activity. The second section discusses how to remedy witch-caused conditions. Bell attacks **countermagic,** recommending fasting and prayer. The third section is on proofs and presumptions of witchcraft. Bell endorsed many aspects of the traditional witch stereotype, including *maleficia,* **satanic pact,** the **Devil's mark** and **familiars.** In addition to the **Bible,** Bell's sources include late-sixteenth and early-seventeenth-century English demonology, notably Richard **Bernard's** Guide to Grand Jury Men (1627). Bell is also sometimes credited with writing another tract supporting witch belief, Witch-Craft Proven (1697), but Cristina Larner has conclusively established that the two tracts have different authors.

REFERENCE: Cristina Larner. "Two Late Scottish Witchcraft Tracts: *Witch-Craft Proven* and *The Tryal of Witchcraft*." In *The Damned Art: Essays in the Literature of Witchcraft*, ed. Sydney Anglo, 227–245. Boston: Routledge and Kegan Paul, 1977.

BENANDANTI

The *benandanti*, or "good walkers," of Friuli provide the most striking example of the folk beliefs of European peasants coming into confrontation with the learned stereotype of the demonic witch in the early modern period. Friuli was a small territory subject to the Venetian Republic with a particularly rich popular culture composed of German, Slavic and Italian components. Friulians were often associated with **magic**—those who emigrated to Venice frequently practiced as **cunning folk** and magical healers. The *benandanti* were a group of men and women born with cauls, traditionally a sign of supernatural power, who battled against witches. Details of their activities differ somewhat among the different *benandanti* who described them, but the common elements are that *benandanti* armed with fennel stalks fought male and female witches armed with sorghum stalks and that the *benandanti* fought in defense of the harvest four times a year on Thursdays during the Ember Days (the weeks of Saint Lucia in December, Ash Wednesday, Whitsunday and Holy Cross Sunday in September). Those whose destinies were to become *benandanti* commenced their activity around the age of twenty and could retire around the age of forty. Both the *benandanti* and the witches were organized in military units with banners and captains, and both were usually described as going to the battle in spirit while their bodies were asleep. Also in spirit, the *benandanti* were sometimes claimed, by themselves or others, to have witnessed processions of the dead and to know the final fate of departed souls. Some *benandanti* informed people of the fate of their departed relatives for a fee or practiced as cunning folk or **witch-finders,** and many peasants and workers who were not *benandanti* themselves credited them with the supernatural power to heal victims of witchcraft and to recognize witches. Indeed, some witches spoke of fearing the power of the *benandanti*.

The *benandanti* first came to the attention of the Inquisition of Aquileia, the part of the **Roman Inquisition** with jurisdiction over Friuli, in 1575. The village priest of Brazzano, Dom Bartolomeo Sgabarizza, had heard of a man named Paolo Gasparutto who had supposedly used magic to heal a small boy afflicted by witchcraft. Sgabarizza summoned Gasparutto before him, and heard that Gasparutto was a *benandante* and that he and other men fought female witches on the Ember Days. The priest referred the matter to the Inquisition, and Gasparutto and the father of the bewitched boy told the story of the *benandanti* and the witches, now including both sexes. At this point the matter ended, partly because the Inquisition was more concerned with Protestant heresy than with popular superstition and witchcraft.

The case was revived five years later by a new inquisitor, Fra Felice de Montefalco. He summoned Gasparutto before him, who began by denying being a *benandante* and having anything to do with the healing of the boy. Fra Felice's persistent questioning failed to shake him. Gasparutto was imprisoned, but another *benandante,* the town crier Battista Moduco, gave the inquisitor a full description of *benandanti* activities, and after a day of imprisonment had loosened his tongue, Gasparutto concurred. He also made a terrible mistake by claiming that an angel had summoned him to be a *benandante*. Inquisitors knew that devils frequently disguised themselves as angels, and Fra Felice's questioning grew more hostile as he tried to force both Gasparutto and Moduco to admit that the gatherings of the *benandanti* were in reality witch's **sabbats.** Both eventually gave in to the persistent inquisitor and admitted themselves witches. Both received a sentence of six months imprisonment and a series of penances, although in the end they got off with a public admission of their errors. During the whole course of the Inquisition's involvement with the *benandanti,* none was executed or even sentenced to death.

The subsequent history of the *benandanti* was that of a struggle between the *benandanti,* wishing to define themselves as good orthodox Catholics and opponents of evil witches, and inquisitors, along with the foot soldiers of Catholicism, the confessors, preachers and parish priests, to define them as witches. The first indication that the inquisitors were winning the battle occurred in 1618, when a thief and accused witch named Maria Panzona, identifying herself as a *benandante,* admitted spontaneously, without leading questions from the inquisitors, that she was a witch and derived her powers from the Devil. Panzona later retracted this confession and affirmed herself a traditional *benandante,* a good Catholic and opponent of witches and was eventually sentenced to three years imprisonment. Subsequent accused *benandanti* were to give descriptions of the sabbat that more or less coincided with the picture held by the inquisitors, although they sometimes emphasized their own separateness from the witches who also attended. By midcentury the inquisitors's theory of witch-*benandanti* had vanquished the traditional picture, but the Roman Inquisition's loss of interest in witch persecution meant that the remaining *benandanti* suffered relatively little.

REFERENCE: Carlo Ginzburg. *The Night Battles: Witchcraft & Agrarian Cults in the Sixteenth & Seventeenth Centuries.* Trans. John Tedeschi and Anne Tedeschi. Baltimore: Johns Hopkins University Press, 1983.

BENEDICT XIII, POPE (AVIGNON SUCCESSION) 1394–1417

In 1409, a Church Council at Pisa was attempting to solve the schism between the Roman line of popes and the popes resident at Avignon, of whom the current representative was the Spaniard Pedro de Luna, who had taken the style of Benedict XIII. The council's intent was to formally depose both popes. For this purpose, charges were declared against them for failing to end the schism, and when this seemed inadequate, there were additional charges against them, including sorcery. The Roman pope, Gregory XII (pope from 1406–1415), was charged only with the comparatively minor offense of having consulted a Jewish doctor, but Benedict was charged with having sought the aid of necromancers and diviners, of having summoned demons, and having tried to obtain a sorcerous book from the Islamic lands. Certainly some of the Pope's inner circle had bad reputations as sorcerers, including the Spanish monk Francisco Aranda and the Franciscan Francesco Eximenis. Witnesses before the council named other associates of the pope and the papal inner circle as magicians. Several connected the pope with books of **magic,** such as one which claimed that all the miracles of Christ had actually been performed by magic, and a book called *Yeezael,* by the ninth-century Jewish astrologer Zahel Benbriz. Witnesses charged that Benedict foresaw future events or beheld those happening at a distance by the power of his magic and controlled the weather with a demon servant. These charges suited the council's purpose of being grave enough to justify the deposition of a pope, although they were not mentioned in the formal sentence of deposition.

Because there were no defense witnesses at the council, and several witnesses did not refer to their own experiences but "common fame," or rumor, it is difficult to know what the pope's involvement in magic really was. He seems to have believed in astrology, as did virtually all his contemporaries, and astrological prediction could be viewed as demonic. Benedict certainly took magic very seriously, as when a plot to kill him by magic was exposed in 1406. Whatever the merit of the charges against him, Benedict ignored them and continued to claim the papacy until his death.

REFERENCE: Margaret Harvey. "Papal Witchcraft: The Charges against Benedict XIII." In *Sanctity and Secularity; the Church and the World. Papers read at the eleventh summer meeting and the twelfth winter meeting of the Ecclesiastical History Society*, ed. Derek Baker, 109–116. Oxford: Blackwell, 1973.

BERMUDA, WITCH-HUNTING IN

Four women and one man were hanged as witches in the English colony of Bermuda from 1651 to 1655 under the governor Josias Fforster, a supporter of the new Puritan regime in **England.** The first was Jeane Gardiner, accused of having caused the temporary blinding and deafening of a mulatto woman named Tomasin. Gardiner was searched for witch marks, and a **flotation test** revealed that she floated. **Maleficia** and **witch's marks,** rather than the **sabbat** or the **satanic pact,** were central to Bermuda witchcraft investigations. The last of the five was Jane Hopkins, a recent arrival, hanged on January 5, 1655. A drizzle of witchcraft cases continued in Bermuda, with the last that of the widow Sarah Spencer in 1696, accused of having caused the death of Sarah Harmon by witchcraft. Records of the final disposition of Spencer's case do not survive, but it is unlikely that she was executed. The case of Sally Basset, an old slave woman burned in 1730 for having planned the death of her master and his family by poisoning, is sometimes identified as a witch case, but witchcraft did not actually figure in the charges against her.

REFERENCE: J. H. Lefroy. *Memorials of the Discovery and Early Settlement of the Bermudas or Somers Islands 1511–1687.* Bermuda: Bermuda Government Library, 1932.

BERNARD, RICHARD (1568–1641)

Richard Bernard was a prominent English Puritan minister and religious controversialist who had assisted John **Darrell** at his well-publicized exorcisms. Bernard's principal contribution to demonology was A *Guide to Grand Jury Men with respect to Witches*, inspired by a case at Taunton in 1626 and first published in 1627 and then republished in 1629. Bernard was not an original demonologist, but he synthesized much of the previous English literature, from the works of George **Gifford** and Reginald **Scot** to the many published English accounts of trials such as Thomas Potts's *The Wonderful Discoverie of Witches in the Countie of Lancaster* (1612). The only Continental demonologists of whom he made great use of were Martin **del Rio** and Jean **Bodin.** Bernard firmly believed in witches, using Scot mainly to refute him, but he also advised caution in witch persecution, pointing out that many ordinary maladies were falsely ascribed to the work of witches. Like many clerics, he strongly opposed **countermagic** and **cunning folk,** some of whom he had interviewed. Distrusting most magistrates' ability to handle the complex issues involved in witch cases, he recommended that they work with a godly minister.

Despite its lack of originality, Bernard's work, the last major English demonology before the civil war of the 1640s, was influential, although it did not immediately lead to a revival of witch-hunting. Surprisingly, as Bernard was not a lawyer, he was the primary source for the discussion of witchcraft in the later editions of Michael Dalton's *The Country Justice* (1618), a frequently reprinted and much-used handbook for justices of the peace, the unpaid magistrates who were the source of day-to-day justice in most of **England.** Bernard also greatly influenced Matthew **Hopkins** and John Stearne, the leaders in the great East Anglian persecution of 1645–1647, as well as **Increase Mather** and **Cotton Mather** in **New England.**

REFERENCES: James Sharpe. *Instruments of Darkness: Witchcraft in Early Modern England.* Philadelphia: University of Pennsylvania Press, 1996; Keith Thomas. *Religion and the Decline of Magic.* New York: Charles Scribner's Sons, 1971.

BERNARDINO OF SIENA (1380–1444)

The great Franciscan preacher Bernardino of Siena passionately denounced witchcraft in early fifteenth-century **Italy.** Bernardino preached in front of audiences of thousands from all ranks of society throughout northern Italy during his career. He claimed that his preaching had led to a campaign against witches, culminating in **executions** by burning, that took place in Rome, probably in the year 1426. (These executions are known from other sources as well.) Bernardino described this campaign in a sermon cycle he gave in his hometown of Siena in 1427, unsuccessfully urging the Sienese to launch a similar assault on witches, to "send up some of the same incense to God." The sermons give an elaborate description of the Roman witches and of witches in general. Although Bernardino acknowledged that both men and women can be witches, he concentrated on women, particularly those he described as "dog-faced old women." (The principal witch in the Roman witch-hunt was described in some but not all sources as an old woman. Her name also varied but was something like "Finicella.") He charged witches with drinking children's blood, making agreements with **Satan** (although not with the full **satanic pact**) and making **magic** powders from the corpses of murdered children. The *Canon Episcopi* was one of Bernardino's chief authorities on witchcraft, and like the *Canon,* he described witch **transformation** (he agreed with other accounts of the events in claiming that the Roman witches had smeared ointment on themselves to be transformed to cats) and **flying** as demonic delusions. He also viewed the **sabbat,** which he referred to by the Italian term *tregenda,* as a demonic illusion, although sometimes he seemed to take it as real. A popular preacher rather than a theoretician, Bernardino was not always consistent.

Bernardino had had more success in encouraging witch-hunting at the small town of Todi than at Siena. On March 10, 1426, Todi adopted a new set of ordinances at the behest of Bernardino, there on a preaching mission, mandating death by burning for all who conjured devils or perpetrated acts of witchcraft and legitimating **torture** in investigations of such cases. In addition to adopting new laws, a common response to Bernardino's preaching, his emphasis on witchcraft's diabolical nature may have led the inhabitants of Todi to take a new, more hostile attitude to magic users in their midst, such as Matteuccia Di **Francesco,** who was burned in 1428.

Witchcraft preoccupied Bernardino throughout his long career. He described it on several occasions as among the worst of all sins and claimed that Italy was particularly rife with it. He also denounced secret and horrible gatherings of heretics as similar to those of witches. In the period 1430–1436, Bernardino composed a Latin treatise on witchcraft for the benefit of his fellow preachers, *Of the Cult of Idols*.

REFERENCE: Franco Mormando. *The Preacher's Demons: Bernardino of Siena and the Social Underworld of Early Renaissance Italy.* Chicago and London: University of Chicago Press, 1999.

THE BIBLE

The Bible permeated early modern culture, and many passages directly affected witch-hunting and demonology. Women's greater vulnerability to **Satan's** wiles was related to Eve's falling prey to the serpent's temptation in the garden, and Eve was sometimes treated as the archetypal witch. The Bible teems with villainous **magic** users, although most were men. They included Pharaoh's magicians, who were vanquished by Moses; Simon Magus, the archetypal evil magician in the Christian tradition; and the Jewish magician Elymas, vanquished by Saint Paul. All made frequent appearances in demonological literature.

One change affecting witch-hunting was the increasing importance of the Ten Commandments among both Protestants and Catholics. In the Middle Ages, sins had been categorized more often in terms of the Seven Deadly Sins than in terms of the Decalogue, but the Decalogue became dominant in early modern times. Witchcraft and other magical crimes were categorized as violations of the first, and most important commandment, "Thou shalt have no other Gods before me." (Witchcraft skeptics, by contrast, favored the Ninth Commandment, against bearing false witness.) Prohibitions on magic thus figured prominently in the endless stream of commentaries on the Command-

The fall of Simon Magus, first century practitioner of magic, from *Speculum historae* (Mirror of History), encyclopedia compiled by the French scholar, Vincent de Beauvais (1190–1264). © The Art Archive/Cava dei Tirreni Abbey Salerno/Dagli Orti.

ments, catechisms, confessor's manuals and handbooks of pastoral care that proliferated in Europe. The Mosaic Law, particularly fascinating to Protestants, also forbid all types of divination and magic. This was used to support broad, harsh penalties (never actually carried out in practice). John Calvin (1509–1564), for example, used the Mosaic law to argue for the death penalty for "witches," but the context in which he called of this practice makes it clear that he was thinking of **cunning folk** and popular magicians rather than maleficient witches. The Bible was interpreted more literally during the early modern period than during the Middle Ages. (The group least likely to interpret the Bible literally, religious radicals such as the Anabaptists, were also the least interested in persecuting witches.) The most famous Mosaic passage attacking witches, Exodus 22.18 "Thou shalt not suffer a witch to live," had been viewed in the twelfth century as referring to exclusion from the community of the faithful rather than literal death. Its literal sense was frequently invoked during the witch-hunt, particularly by demonologists and others hoping to prod derelict magistrates into doing their duty. It was also used as an argument against the idea that only the evil-doing witch deserved death.

Another passage frequently invoked in this context was Romans 13, the most important chapter of the Bible for early modern political theory. The idea of the godly magistrate whose power came from above implied an obligation to zealously root out witches. King Josiah, who banished all workers of magic and possessors of **familiar** spirits from the land, was contrasted favorably with King Saul, who had consulted the "witch" of Endor and been punished by God for it.

Although the gospels had no direct statements about witches, they were frequently referred to in the contexts of exorcism and the activities of demons. The idea that witches could fly was defended by pointing out that Satan had carried Jesus to the mountaintop, and therefore demons could carry witches through the air. The gospel stories of Jesus freeing people from the demons that possessed them were considered the archetypal exorcisms. The words of the Bible were viewed as having power against witches and demons—it was commonly believed into the eighteenth century that witches could not recite the Lord's Prayer.

One problem for witch-hunters was that so much of the early modern stereotype of the witch—the **sabbat,** the **satanic pact,** the **Devil's mark** and other commonplaces—had no biblical basis. This problem could be finessed by pointing out that things had changed, and Satan had refined his methods since biblical times. Some Protestant biblicists such as William **Perkins** tried to build a completely biblical demonology, shunning many aspects of traditional demonology. But if the Bible presented problems for supporters of witch-hunting, it was the single greatest intellectual obstacle for witch- hunting opponents, particularly before the late seventeenth century. The most important sixteenth-century opponents of witch-hunting, Johann **Weyer,** followed by Reginald **Scot,** had to explain away Exodus 22.18 by claiming a mistranslation, that the Hebrew word in the passage referred to poisoners rather than evil users of magic. Scot had a torturous explanation of the Witch of Endor as a charlatan and ventriloquist rather than an actual witch. Such arguments were easily refuted. It was only with the rise of critical and historical understanding of the Bible and the decline of literalism in the early Enlightenment that it ceased to be the intellectual bulwark of witch-hunting.

REFERENCES: Stuart Clark. *Thinking with Demons: The Idea of Witchcraft in Early Modern Europe.* Oxford: Clarendon Press, 1997; Edward Peters. *The Magician, the Witch and the Law.* Philadelphia: University of Pennsylvania Press, 1978.

BIDEFORD WITCHES

The last **execution** of a group of witches in **England** took place at Exeter in 1682, when three women from the Devonshire town of Bideford were hanged at the summer assizes. Bideford was an expanding port town with a large surplus of men over women. Elderly women without wealth or family connections were marginal. Two widows, Temperance Lloyd and Susanna Edwards, and one single woman, Mary Trembles, were accused of a range of *maleficia*, including fatal bewitchment, and diabolical activities including the **satanic pact, sex** with the Devil (referred to in testimony as "the black man") and possessing **familiars** and **witch's marks.** Lloyd, the most prominent of the three, had a long reputation as a witch, which had led to previous brushes with the law. In 1671, Lloyd had been accused of causing the death of William Herbert but had been acquitted. In 1679, Lloyd was accused of causing the death of Anne Fellows, but the charges were dropped. She was arrested in 1682 for bewitching a woman named Grace Thomas. Zealous investigation by local magistrates led to Edwards and Trembles, both of whom confessed to satanic pacts. A jury of women examined the suspects for witch's marks, which were found on Lloyd's genitals. She confessed that the Devil had sucked on them repeatedly and claimed to have had sex with him nine nights running. The witches were clearly differentiated in a hierarchy, with Lloyd the chief and Edwards the superior of Trembles.

A surviving letter from one of the assize judges, Francis North, indicates some skepticism about the women's guilt. Given the fact that all had confessed, however, and the heavy local hostility against the three, North and the other judges convicted and sent the women to the gallows. The case attracted more interest than any other English case until the conviction of Jane **Wenham** in 1712. Three pamphlets and a ballad were published in its immediate aftermath.

REFERENCES: James Sharpe. *Instruments of Darkness: Witchcraft in Early Modern England.* Philadelphia: University of Pennsylvania Press, 1996; Janet A. Thompson. *Wives, Widows, Witches and Bitches: Women in Seventeenth-Century Devon.* New York: Peter Lang, 1993.

BINSFELD, PETER (1540–1598)

The suffragan, or assistant bishop, of Trier, Peter Binsfeld, was one of **Germany's** leading witch-hunters and demonologists. He served under archbishop Johann von Schonenburg during the fierce Trier witch-hunt from 1587 to 1593. Binsfeld's demonology, *Treatise on the Confessions of Evildoers and Witches* (1591), reflected the conditions of the Trier witch-hunt, including the prosecution of Dietrich **Flade,** and focused on practical legal problems witch-hunting presented. Binsfeld realized that ordinary procedures did not produce the confessions needed to get convictions and **executions.** He argued that witchcraft, due to its secrecy, was *crimen exceptum*, requiring different rules.

Binsfeld accepted most aspects of the witch figure as it had developed in early modern Europe, including **satanic pact,** the **sabbat,** witch flight, *maleficia*, **infanticide** and human-demon **sex.** He had his doubts about the **Devil's mark,** which he believed too unreliable for practical use, and like most demonologists denied the possibility of witches or demons working actual **transformations.** His short treatment of **gender** claimed that women were more likely to become witches because of their propensity for more intense despair and desire for revenge. He attacked those who relied on the **Canon Episcopi** to argue against the reality of the sabbat and even cast doubt on the *Canon's* authenticity. Binsfeld believed that every human being had a personal demon, corresponding with the guardian angel, and the personal demon sought to lead people into witchcraft. Binsfeld's view on *maleficia* fitted into the context of the Trier witch-hunt, which was driven by people's frustration and rage after several years of bad harvests. Binsfeld suggested that witches conspired to send bad weather and drive up the price of grain for the benefit of the speculators with whom they worked.

Binsfeld argued that as a *crimen exceptum*, witchcraft needed to be investigated with far looser controls on **torture.** He believed that torture could be inflicted on the basis of one credible charge of witchcraft, and that persons under age 14 could be tortured in witch cases. He asserted that the Devil could not take the form of an innocent person at the sabbat (this had been Flade's defense), and therefore a claim that someone had been seen there justified torture. Binsfeld argued that whereas ordinarily parents and children should not testify against each other, in witchcraft trials they should be encouraged to do so, because they would possibly save the souls of the persons on whom they informed. He railed against lazy magistrates who did not zealously pursue witches and ignorant parish priests who did not combat witchcraft in their own neighborhoods. His *Enchiridion of Pastoral Theology* (1595), aimed at the parish clergy, also contained much on witches and devils.

Binsfeld was a learned man, familiar with demonological and other literature. Among previous demonologists, he drew on Heinrich **Kramer,** Paulus **Grillandus,** Bartolommeo de **Spina,** and Jean **Bodin.** He also referred to the witch-hunting opponent Johann **Weyer,** whom he denounced. Another witch-hunting opponent he attacked was the Dutchman Cornelius Loos (1546–1595), who had published a radical attack on witch-hunting, *On True and False Magic* (1592). On March 15, 1593, Loos was forced to recant his opinions publicly in the presence of Binsfeld and other Catholic authorities.

REFERENCES: Stuart Clark. *Thinking with Demons: The Idea of Witchcraft in Early Modern Europe.* Oxford: Clarendon Press, 1997; Henry Charles Lea. *Materials toward a History of Witchcraft.* New York and London: Thomas Yoseloff, 1957; P. G. Maxwell-Stuart. *Witchcraft in Europe and the New World, 1400–1800.* Houndsmills, England and New York: Palgrave, 2001.

BITHNER, JAKOB

As *Landprofos*, or local official in charge of maintaining social order, Jakob Bithner was involved in 23 of the 39 witch cases in the Habsburg territory of Styria (now divided between Slovenia and **Austria**) from 1578 to 1600. This is all but three of Styria's sixteenth-century cases. Appointed *Landprofos* in 1580 by the Styrian Estates, the nobility-dominated provincial representative body, Bithner launched a drive against witches in which he employed a number of demonological concepts, such as the **sabbat, satanic pact** and intercourse with the Devil. These concepts had previously seen little use in Styria. For example, Bithner reported to the Estates that after intercourse with **Satan,** a woman gave birth to a demon in the form of a raven, which had actually flown out of her side, leaving a gaping wound. Bithner viewed all forms of **magic,** including such peripheral activities as astrology, as demonic.

Bithner, a Lutheran, was eventually caught in the conflict between the Catholic Habsburg court and the Lutheran-dominated Styrian Estates. For years, the two powers had agreed on the necessity and value of witch-hunting, but by the late 1590s, witch cases had become sites for struggle between them. One Protestant village, assigned a Catholic priest by the government, accused the priest of weather magic after his threat that God would punish the village for its heresy was followed by bad weather and poor harvests. The Catholic Court not only cleared the priests reputation, but held the villagers responsible for defaming him, a judgment Bithner was unwillingly forced to carry out. Catholic exorcists were also carrying out public exorcisms, in which the alliance between demons and Protestants was emphasized. Bithner was eventually forced to resign and exiled in 1600, but the witch-hunting he had promoted in Styria long survived his departure.

REFERENCE: Edmund Kern. "Confessional Identity and Magic in the Late Sixteenth Century: Jakob Bithner and Witchcraft in Styria." *The Sixteenth Century Journal* 25 (1994): 323–340.

BODIN, JEAN (1529?–1596)

The French political thinker and provincial magistrate Jean Bodin was the author of *On the Demonmania of Sorcerers* (1580), one of the most impressive and popular works of demonology. *Demonmania* followed by four years Bodin's classic book of political theory, *Six Books on the Republic* (1576) and expanded on it, by demonstrating how holders of political and judicial authority should treat witchcraft. It also refuted Johann **Weyer's** *On the Tricks of Demons* (1563) and had a separate appendix specifically devoted to attacks on Weyer, who Bodin claimed was a witch.

Bodin viewed witchcraft—which he defined as the use of demonic **magic** in general, whether practiced by the village witch or the learned male magician— as the worst of all crimes, as direct treason against God. His work was highly unusual in defining witchcraft in a way transcending **confessional** differences. Bodin supported religious toleration and civil peace at a time when **France** was torn by wars between Calvinists and Catholics, whereas the dominant tradition of French demonology was strongly Catholic, identifying witchcraft with heresy. Most late-sixteenth-century French demonologists called for increased persecution of both witches and Protestants. Bodin took confessional debate out of witch-hunting by universalizing the witch, claiming that all religions that acknowledged a God, or gods, could produce rebels against that obedience. Even classical pagans, he pointed out, knew of witches, so clearly they did not require Christianity in order to exist. Bodin accepted the idea of the witch as it had developed in the last two centuries, including the **sabbat, flying** witches, *maleficia*, **infanticide,** the **satanic pact,** cannibalism, the dedication of children to the Devil and human-demon **sex.** Bodin was actually more radical than mainstream demonologists in that he was prepared to consider **transformations** worked by witches and demons to be real rather than mere illusions, suggesting that human knowledge was not sufficient to set limits to demonic power. Bodin's eclectic demonological sources included the work of

Weyer, Paulus **Grillandus** and Lambert **Daneau,** as well as Heinrich **Kramer's** *Malleus Maleficarum* (1486).

Bodin accepted that women were more vulnerable to the Devil's wiles because of their weakness, suggesting that their viscera were larger and their heads smaller than those of men. He reserved his discussion of women for the separate appendix refuting Weyer, however, and misogyny did not play a major role in *Demonmania*.

Bodin's mission was to arouse the magistrates of **France** to more zealous action against witches, at which he thought they had been shamefully lax. The crushing of witchcraft was a prime duty of government, and Bodin emphasized the opposition of magistrates and witches, enthusiastically endorsing the doctrine of **magisterial immunity.** Bodin refers to one case in which he had been involved as a magistrate, that of Jeanne Hervillier, a witch and the daughter of a witch, and many others of which he had been informed by fellow judicial officials. He attacked the government of the previous monarch, Charles IX (r. 1560–1574), as lax on witchcraft and urged the new government of Henri III (r. 1574–1589) to do better. Part of the reason he attacked Weyer was that he feared that Weyer's ideas would encourage judges to fail in their god-given duty to crush witchcraft. A judge who did not act zealously against witchcraft was little better than a witch and deserved death.

The part of *Demonmania* of most direct interest to magistrates was Bodin's discussion of **trial procedure,** evidence and the proper conditions for **torture.** Bodin supported a loose, but not totally subjective, application of the standards of proof derived from Roman law, where eyewitnesses or confessions (whether or not extracted through torture) were the major proofs. He argued that witchcraft was *crimen exceptum*, however, seldom committed before witnesses. Therefore, it was necessary for the magistrate to be alert to "presumptions," which by themselves could justify torture to produce confession. (Bodin endorsed the use of hot irons.) Things giving rise to presumption of witchcraft included widespread rumor, the inability to weep or having witch parents. Those persons "presumed" but not proven by confession or eyewitness were not to be executed as witches but were subject to other penalties, including fines, prison, mutilation or branding. Few if any persons accused of witchcraft should get off with no penalty at all. Witchcraft's exceptional nature also meant that persons whose testimony would not be given much weight in a trial of another crime, such as women and persons already convicted, could testify in a witch case. Children could also testify against their parents. In addition to torture, Bodin endorsed deceiving witch suspects in the magistrate's quest for conviction.

Bodin scorned countermagic, whether secular or ecclesiastical. Although he was officially a Catholic and later in his life supported the French Catholic League, his predilection seems to have been for a strict monotheism, based on Judaism and denying divine status to Jesus Christ. He even denied the efficacy of exorcism, holding that possessed persons should be treated with music and prayer rather than ceremonies designed to expel demons. He somewhat grudgingly accepted countermagic using incense, fish liver and salt, as sanctioned in the Old Testament.

The influence of Bodin's work is not clear. It was certainly popular, having been published in 23 editions and translated into Latin, Italian and German. The German translation by Johann Fischart, who added much material of his own, was in particularly wide circulation. Many subsequent demonologists drew on Bodin's work and used the authority of his learning to support witch-hunting. Others, however, rejected Bodin's arguments or treated them as negligible. *Demonmania* inspired two major refutations, one by Weyer in the 1583 edition of *On the Tricks of Demons* and one by Reginald **Scot,** *The Discoverie of Witchcraft* (1584). In France, Bodin's eccentricity limited the acceptability of his arguments. Mainstream Catholic demonologists, such as Martin **del Rio** and Pierre de **Lancre,** sometimes quarried *Demonmania* for examples, but were too suspicious of Bodin's religious reliability to trustingly accept it. It was actually placed on the Catholic Church's Index of Forbidden Books in 1594. French secular magistrates, too, did not fully accept Bodin's work. Although Bodin dedicated *Demonmania* to the first president of the Parlement of Paris, Christophe de Thou, the work of a provincial magistrate such as Bodin was beneath the official notice of France's judicial elite. The Parlement continued to follow a much more lenient policy against witches than Bodin recommended. Another factor limiting Bodin's influence was his acceptance of the reality of transformations worked by witches and demons, which attracted much ridicule extending through the seventeenth century. Bodin's credulity was held up to scorn in works such as Jean de Nynauld's *On Lycanthropy* (1615).

REFERENCES: Christopher Baxter. "Jean Bodin's *De La Demonomanie des Sorciers: The Logic of Persecution.*" In *The Damned Art: Essays in the Literature of Witchcraft,* ed. Sydney Anglo, 76–105. Boston: Routledge and Kegan Paul, 1977; Stuart Clark. *Thinking with Demons: The Idea of Witchcraft in Early Modern Europe.* Oxford: Clarendon Press, 1997; Jonathan L. Pearl. *The Crime of Crimes: Demonology and Politics in France, 1560–1620.* Waterloo, Ontario: Wilfred Laurier University Press, 1999; Gerhild Scholz Williams. *Defining Dominion: The Discourses of Witchcraft and Magic in Early Modern France and Germany.* Ann Arbor: University of Michigan Press, 1995.

BOGUET, HENRI (D. 1619)

Henri Boguet was a witch-hunting magistrate and demonologist in **Franche-Comte.** He became grand judge of the territories of the abbey of Saint Claude in 1596, an appointment that coincided with an upswing in witch-hunting in Franche-Comte and a switch from Inquisitorial to secular jurisdiction over witch cases. As a magistrate, Boguet tried 35 people, condemning 28 to death (many without the mercy of being strangled before being burned) in addition to four others who died in prison. This is a high conviction and **execution** rate by European standards.

Boguet's *Discourse on Sorcerors*, first published in 1602, was republished every year from 1605 to 1608 and then again in 1610 and 1611. It drew on Boguet's work as a judge, which was mainly with demonic **possession** cases in rural areas and on Catholic legal demonologies, such as Heinrich **Kramer's** *Malleus Maleficarum* (1486) and the works of Jean **Bodin,** Nicholas **Remy** and Paulus **Grillandus.** The **physician** Paracelsus (1493–1541) was also a major source. Boguet was naturalistic in his explanations of demonic action—demons and **Satan** used their superior knowledge of nature, rather than occult or supernatural means, to work evil deeds. Boguet also emphasized the apocalyptic relevance of witchcraft, declaring that the increased prevalence of witches was surely a sign of the nearness of the Antichrist. His expertise on witches was recognized outside his immediate jurisdiction. In 1604, the free imperial city of Besancon appealed for his advice in dealing with witches.

After 1611, the supreme legal authority of Franche-Comte, the Parlement of Dôle, greatly moderated the persecution of witches, and Boguet may have prevented his work from going into further editions to avoid clashing with the new direction of the Parlement. Boguet wanted to be admitted to the Parlement and eventually was a few months before his death in 1619.

REFERENCES: Stuart Clark. *Thinking with Demons: The Idea of Witchcraft in Early Modern Europe* Oxford: Clarendon Press, 1997; William Monter. *Witchcraft in France and Switzerland: The Borderlands during the Reformation.* Ithaca and London: Cornell University Press, 1976.

BOHEMIA

See Austria and Bohemia, Witch-hunting in.

BOVET, RICHARD (B. CA. 1641)

Richard Bovet, author of *Pandaemonium, or the Devil's Cloyster. Being a further Blow to modern Sadducism, proving the Existence of Witches and Spirits* (1684) was an English demonologist in the tradition of Joseph **Glanvill** and Henry More (1614–1687), to whom *Pandaemonium* was dedicated. What he added to the alliance of witch-hunting and the new philosophy was a passionate anti-Catholicism. Bovet came from a family of radical Protestants at odds with the Church of **England** and the dominant culture of the English Restoration. The Catholic menace was much on the minds of English Protestants in the early 1680s, because Charles II had no legitimate children to inherit his throne. This meant it would go to his brother, the openly Catholic James, duke of York. *Pandaemonium* was intended as a blow in the struggle against Popery, and Bovet consistently assimilated the practices of witches with those of Roman Catholics. Catholic reverence for relics and statues of the saints was idolatry, leading by natural progression to the explicit devil worship that witches practiced. Glanvill's work was the inspiration for Bovet, and like its predecessor

Pandaemonium contained several full and well-attested stories of supernatural actions of witches and demons.

REFERENCE: Ian Bostridge. *Witchcraft and Its Transformations, c. 1650–c. 1750.* Oxford: Clarendon Press, 1997.

BROOMSTICKS

See Flying.

BROSSIER, MARTHE (B. CA. 1573)

Marthe Brossier was among the most celebrated of the demonically possessed French girls of the late sixteenth century. This was not because her fits were convincing—in fact, she was a transparent fraud—but because she came along at a time when conservative Catholic forces in Paris needed a demoniac. Brossier was born around 1573 in Romorantin, one of four daughters of the draper Jacques Brossier. The Brossier family had come down in the world, and Marthe Brossier's prospects for marriage were slim. She expressed her discontent by running away from home disguised as a man but was quickly captured and returned to her family. Early in 1598, she claimed to have been bewitched by a neighbor, Anne Chevreau. Chevreau's sister had married a prominent local landlord who had been a possible match for Brossier's eldest sister, before the family's economic decline, so there was bad blood between the Brossier and Chevreau families. As an unmarried, middle-aged woman, Chevreau was the type of person vulnerable to witchcraft **accusations.** A local priest with a grudge against the Chevreaus encouraged Brossier in her accusations. Chevreau was imprisoned for about a year, during which time a fellow prisoner accused her of bewitching her, but she was eventually released after Brossier's **possession** was discredited. A statement by Chevreau blamed Brossier's accusation on her mental state, rather than deliberate or malicious fraud.

Chevreau and the original circumstances of Brossier's possession, however, played only a minor role as Brossier toured the Loire Valley as a demonically possessed woman, being publicly exorcised in front of huge crowds. Church authorities treated her with skepticism—one official found that she would react to ordinary water as if it were holy water if she were simply told that it was and vice versa. Brossier arrived in Paris shortly after the promulgation of the Edict of Nantes in 1598, which guaranteed tolerance to French Protestants. This appalled many Catholics, particularly members of religious orders, and a Paris monastery of Capuchin Friars promoted exorcisms of Brossier in which the demon who possessed her, Beezlebub, would denounce the Huguenots, or French Protestants, as slaves of the Devil. These exorcisms were popular events among the Catholic population of Paris. Brossier and her handlers closely modeled her career on that of Nicole **Obry,** an account of whom Brossier possessed. Beezlebub was the same demon that had possessed Obry. Brossier's possession by male demons may have been related to her original fleeing of her home in male disguise—both allowed her to abandon womanhood temporarily.

Brossier attracted the attention of the government of Henri IV (r. 1589–1610), a convert from Protestantism strongly identified with the toleration policy. The king's **physician** Michael Marescot examined Brossier and found her possession to be fraudulent. The Parlement of Paris, at the king's behest, imprisoned her and eventually sent her home. From there she was abducted by Alexander de la Rochefoucauld, a high-ranking ecclesiastic who took her to Rome, where she repeated her exorcisms for the Jubilee year of 1600. Eventually, French government pressure forced her out of Rome, and she last appears in the historical record in Milan, still claiming to be possessed. Brossier became the archetypal fraudulent demoniac. Marescot's 1599 tract denouncing her was translated into English the same year as part of the campaign against the Puritan exorcist John **Darrell,** and she appeared in skeptical literature into the eighteenth century.

REFERENCES: Anita M. Walker and Edmund H. Dickermann. " 'A Woman under the Influence': A Case of Alleged Possession in Sixteenth-Century France." *The Sixteenth Century Journal* 22 (1991): 534–544; D. P. Walker, *Unclean Spirits: Possession and Exorcism in France and England in the late Sixteenth and early Seventeenth Centuries.* London: The Warburg Institute, University of London, 1981.

BURT, RICHARD

Richard Burt, a victim of a witch called Mother Atkyns, was the subject of a witchcraft pamphlet dated 1592 and titled *A Most Wicked Work of a Wretched Witch*. The pamphlet, by an unidentified "G. B., maister of arts," tells the story of an affliction that Atkyns laid on Burt, a servant to a gentleman in the parish of Pynner in Middlesex, after he called her a witch. A spirit, presumably sent by Atkyns, interrupted him at his threshing and took him on a brief visit to hell, which G. B. treats humorously, with an uncredited reference to Robert Greene's (1558–1592) play *Friar Bacon and Friar Bungay*, performed early in 1592. The humorous treatment extends to the characterization of Burt himself, who is depicted as a comic, clownish rustic. The spirit demanded that Burt speak to no one of what he had seen, and when Burt refused to comply, the spirit took away his ability to speak. Burt went into hiding after his return to Pynner. His voice was restored when the local parish minister reached into his mouth and unfolded his tongue. Burt then demanded to be taken before Mother Atkyns and employed the common **countermagical** technique of scratching her until he drew blood. Unlike some witchcraft writers who disapproved of countermagic, G. B. described it as successful and not a "Capital error." The pamphlet concludes with two stories of *maleficia* worked by Mother Atkyns on others. In one instance she caused cream to swell and burst a churn; in the other she caused two lambs to die. *A Most Wicked Work of a*

Wretched Witch is one of the earliest surviving English witchcraft pamphlets that was not based on a trial record—indeed, it makes no mention of any legal process whatsoever. This, along with the use of Greene's play, may indicate that the whole narrative is fictional.

REFERENCE: Marion Gibson, ed. *Early Modern Witches: Witchcraft Cases in Contemporary Writing*. London and New York: Routledge, 2000.

C

CADIÈRE, MARIE CATHERINE (B. CA. 1710)

The case of Marie Catherine Cadière of Toulon was the last great French **possession** case, but its outcome was strikingly different from those of Louis **Gaufridy** or the possessed nuns of **Loudon.** Cadière was a pious Catholic girl whose devout family was grooming her for sainthood. In 1728, when Cadière was eighteen, a 48-year-old Jesuit priest named Louis Girard came to Toulon to head the Royal Seminary for Naval Chaplains and soon became Cadière's confessor and spiritual director. Under Girard's direction, Cadière began to show signs of sainthood, including clairvoyance, levitation and the stigmata (wounds in the hands and feet in imitation of those of Christ on the cross). Girard and local church authorities avidly promoted Cadière's sainthood, and she became a widely known and admired figure in Provence. At some time in 1729, according to Cadière's later testimony, Girard began to abuse his spiritual authority to take sexual advantage of her. She charged that he breathed on her in a peculiar way that caused her to desire him, as well as forcing her to submit to him sexually as a sign of her humility to God. In November, she also began publicly exhibiting the signs not of a saint, but of a victim of demonic possession, including profanity, convulsions and blasphemy.

Cadière's possession suited the purposes of her brothers, the Dominican Etienne Cadeire and the secular priest Francois Cadière, who urged the bishop to transfer her to another spiritual director, the Carmelite Nicholas Girieux. All of them were opponents of the local Jesuits, of whom Girard was the leader. Girieux suggested exorcism as the cure for Cadière's symptoms, and in November 1730, a year after she had first displayed the symptoms of possession, she was publicly exorcised by her brothers and Girieux. At this point she named Girard as the person who had bewitched her. This touched off an enormous controversy, not only in Provence but throughout **France.** The faction in the French Catholic Church most opposed to the Jesuits, the Jansenists, used the case to attack their enemies. Anti-Girard writers deliberately placed him in the tradition of the sorcerer-priests of the great seventeenth-century French possession cases, Gaufridy (d. 1611), Urbain Grandier (d. 1634) (see **Loudon Witch-Hunt)** and Thomas Boulle of Louviers (d. 1647). The Cadière faction, building on Marie Catherine's previous reputation for saintliness, had by far the most popular support in the Toulon area, and it became dangerous for Jesuits to appear in the streets.

The faction of Girard and the Jesuits, however, had the support of the royal government. After inconclusive investigations by the secular and ecclesiastical authorities of Toulon, the case was reserved to the Parlement of Aix by royal decree. Cadière was held in Jesuit-controlled convents and not allowed to see her family or Girieux. Under intense pressure, she withdrew the charges, then withdrew her withdrawal. She was threatened with **torture** to get her to withdraw the charges again. The investigating magistrate found Girard completely innocent and Cadière guilty of making false charges as well as faking both saintliness and possession. He recommended that Cadière be tortured to divulge the name of her accomplices and then hanged in accordance with the royal decree on witchcraft of 1682. This was only an advisory judgment, however, and the case still had to be heard by the Parlement itself, which gave its verdict on October 11, 1731. The Parlement, in accordance with the 1682 decree, ignored the witchcraft aspects of the case, concentrating on the sexual charges. The Parlement itself proved divided, twelve members recommending that Cadière be hanged and twelve recommending that Girard be burnt. The president of the Parlement, who was also the *intendant*, or royal governor of Provence, compromised by acquitting both, remanding Cadière to her family and Girard to his ecclesiastical superiors. Despite the judgment's seeming impartiality, the Cadières were the losers. They were saddled with the costs of the trial, and government troops were called out to suppress pro-Cadière demonstrations. The Cadières were forced to leave the area, and Marie Cadière dropped entirely from sight. Girard, having avoided the fate of Gaufridy, Grandier and Boullé, died two years later, in what his fellow Jesuits claimed was the odor of sanctity. Although witchcraft did not formally appear among the charges against him, the Cadière case is often considered the end of the French witch-hunt.

REFERENCE: B. Robert Kreiser. "The Devils of Toulon: Demonic Possession and Religious Politics in Eighteenth Century Provence." In *Church, State, and Society under the Bourbon Kings of France*, ed. Richard M. Golden, 173–221. Lawrence, Kans.: Coronado Press, 1982.

CALEF, ROBERT

The Boston merchant and weaver Robert Calef was the most outspoken opponent of witchcraft belief in late seventeenth-century **New England,** partially motivated by his strong personal dislike of **Cotton Mather.** Calef had immigrated to Boston from **England** in the 1680s and, despite his orthodox Congregationalism, disliked New England Puritanism, its domineering ministers and its view of everyday life as a supernatural drama, with both God and **Satan** constantly intervening. He and Mather had been debating witchcraft throughout the 1690s, but Mather's writings on **Salem** eventually prompted Calef into print. Calef's 1700 *More Wonders of the Invisible World* mocked Mather's *Wonders of the Invisible World* in its title and was sufficiently controversial that it had to be printed in London rather than New England. In publishing it, Calef was a spokesman for a Boston-based group influenced by current English thought, opposed to the Mathers and disgusted with the Salem proceedings. Calef's arguments include standard ones against the applicability of **Bible** passages supporting witch persecution. He also attacked the idea that anyone, ministers included, could identify specific acts as caused by God or the Devil. Calef argued that Cotton and **Increase Mather** were reviving the ancient heresy of Manicheism, which ascribed independent power to the Devil rather than restricting all power to God. He ridiculed the idea of special providence by pointing out the disasters that had overtaken many of the persecutors of witches. He also somewhat unfairly mocked the Mathers as lechers obsessed with the bodies of hysterical young girls claiming to be possessed. Calef recounted the Salem case at length, emphasizing the culpability of the minister Samuel Parris, and may have had connections with the anti-Parris faction in Salem Village. His work remains one of the principal historical sources for the Salem cases. Despite the refusal of Boston booksellers to handle it, *More Wonders of the Invisible World* was widely circulated in New England. The Mathers replied the next year in a work written ostensibly by a group of their defenders, *Some Few Remarks upon a Scandalous Book*.

REFERENCE: Peter Lockwood Rumsey. *Acts of God and the People, 1620–1730.* Ann Arbor, Mich.: UMI Research Press, 1986.

CANON EPISCOPI

The "canon of the bishops" (so-called because it began with the word "bishops"), was a piece of Church legislation about witches originating in the ninth century and surviving in its first copy from the early tenth century. In addition to recommending that bishops and priests zealously combat sorcery and *maleficia*, the canon also identified the belief that some women traverse great distances in the night led by the pagan goddess **Diana** as diabolical illusion and superstition. It also condemned belief in the reality of the power of witches and demons to work **transformation.** The canon emerged at a time when much of Europe had only recently been converted officially to Christianity and the struggle against residual pagan beliefs was much on the minds of clerics. The clerical writers of the canon identified pagan deities with demons and thought women were particularly vulnerable to remaining pagan beliefs.

The canon was received as authoritative throughout the Middle Ages, particularly because it was mistakenly thought to have originated at the 314 Church Council of Ancyra and thus to have the authority of the early church behind it. It was included in the standard collections of Catholic church law in the Middle Ages, most importantly that of Gratian in the twelfth century, which remained valid in the early modern period. Early modern catholic witch-hunters were then presented with the problem of reconciling their own belief that witches did indeed fly through the air or in other ways traverse great distances at night, often on their way to the **sabbat,** with the canon's clear condemnation of such belief. Nicholas **Jacquier's** fifteenth-century *A Scourge for Heretical Witches* was written specifically to refute the canon's assertion of the impossibility of bodily flight. Jacquier and Heinrich **Kramer** argued that modern witches were different from those who the canon discussed. Another possibility was to argue that the belief in having flown through the air by diabolical means was as blameworthy as actually having done so, whether or not that was possible. Demonologists also asserted that some witches, like those the canon envisioned, merely thought they journeyed to the sabbat, whereas others actually did. As witch-hunting theory developed and gained intellectual legitimacy, other Catholic theorists, such as Francesco Maria **Guazzo,** were able simply to ignore the canon in their discussion of witches' flight. Catholic witchcraft skeptics, on the other hand, tended to endorse the canon's description of witch flying as illusion. Protestants, whose churches had rejected canon law, were, of course, always free to ignore the canon.

REFERENCE: Jeffrey Burton Russell. *Witchcraft in the Middle Ages.* Ithaca: Cornell University Press, Oxford: Clarendon Press, 1972.

CASAUBON, MERIC (1599–1671)

The scholar and churchman Meric Casaubon defended belief in witchcraft as part of the structure of traditional political and intellectual authority in late-seventeenth-century **England.** Because the English had already had a revolution, publicly executing King Charles I (r. 1625–1649) in 1649, the previously established order required defenders. Even the Restoration of Charles II (r. 1660–1685) in 1660 did not end the struggle in Casaubon's eyes, as the forces of "enthusiasm" could launch another revolution at any moment. His main work on demonology and witchcraft was *Of Credulity and Incredulity in things Natural, Civil and Divine*, first published in 1668 and then posthumously in 1672 as *A Treatise proving Spirits, Witches and Supernatural Operations*. Casaubon systematically wove the acceptance of God's political and monarchical wonders, such as the miraculous preservation of Charles II from his enemies or the miraculous cures performed by Charles I while being held prisoner by his enemies, with the possible wonders performed by witches and demons. To deny the latter was at least potentially to deny the former—and all legitimate political authority along with it. Unlike the other leading Restoration Church of England defender of witchcraft belief, Joseph **Glanvill,** Casaubon was an intellectual conservative distrustful of the new **science** and innovation in general. His association of a divinely sanctioned political order and the existence of witchcraft as its negation resembles that of King **James VI and I,** but his concern with atheism and skepticism as opposed to witchcraft per se marks him as a participant in the English Restoration witchcraft controversy. Along with Glanvill, Casaubon was attacked by anti-witch-hunting writers such as John **Wagstaffe** and John **Webster.**

REFERENCE: Ian Bostridge. *Witchcraft and Its Transformations, c. 1650–c. 1750.* 1997.

CASTAÑEGA, MARTIN DE

The Spanish Franciscan friar Martin de Castañega was the author of the first original treatise on witchcraft to appear in a European vernacular (previous vernacular works had been translations from the Latin) *Treatise on Superstition and Witchcraft* (1529). The work was published at Logroño, a center of the **Spanish Inquisition,** and built on recent trials and **executions** in the **Basque** region. Castañega's informally written treatise accepts the reality of diabolical witches, the **satanic pact** and **sex** with devils (which he describes as extremely pleasurable for the human participant, whether a male witch having intercourse with a devil in female shape or vice versa), although he does not discuss the **sabbat.** He presented the witch-cult as **Satan's** systematic inversion of the true Catholic Church. One reason he gave for the greater number of witches who are women was that as in the true church, power to dispense the sacraments was held by men, so in Satan's church the power to work magic was primarily exercised by women. Other reasons included women's weakness, talkativeness and curiosity. In linking witchcraft with idolatry, Castañega paralleled the **infanticide** practiced by European witches with the human sacrifice practiced by some recently encountered or conquered **Spanish American** peoples.

Castañega's sources included the **Bible,** the writings of the medieval theologians Augustine (354–430) and Thomas Aquinas (1224?–1274), the *Canon Episcopi* and some conversations he had had with confessed witches. He accepted the authority of the canon but suggested that witch-flight was sometimes illusion, as described in the canon, and sometimes real flight made possible by the power of Satan. Castañega allowed a broad range of possibility for the exercise of unknown, natural, nondemonic causes and criticized making **accusations of witchcraft too hastily.** Even the **evil eye,** he suggests, can operate through natural causes. Castañega's target was popular credulity as much as witchcraft—he attacks the performance of weather magic and the common Spanish custom of responding to plagues of locusts by excommunicating the locusts.

REFERENCE: David H. Darst. "Witchcraft in Spain: The Testimony of Martin de Castañega's *Treatise on Superstition and Witchcraft* (1529)." *Proceedings of the American Philosophical Society* 123 (1979): 298–322.

CAT

See Animals.

CATHOLICISM

See Canon Episcopi; Confessionalism; Roman Inquisition; Spanish Inquisition; *Summis Desiderantes Affectibus.*

CHANNEL ISLANDS, WITCH-HUNTING IN

The most ferocious witch-hunting in any territory under the early modern British crown took place in the small islands of Jersey and Guernsey, which were legally and culturally French but politically English. With a population of about 15,000, the islands saw 167 trials for which records survive and 90 witches executed between 1562 and 1661 (15 men and 75 women). Many of the witches were linked by family. The **sabbat** appeared frequently in the trials, and **torture** was employed, sometimes even after conviction, to elicit information on it. Unlike **England,** the Channel Islands executed witches by burning. The Channel Islands' high conviction rate appears to have been due to their judicial autonomy. Their unique position meant, as in small ecclesiastical territories in the Holy Roman Empire such as **Ellwangen,** that local courts operated without any supervision by higher courts. Witch persecution continued later in the Channel Islands than on the British mainland as well. As late as 1736, an accused witch, Marie Godfroy, was brought before an ecclesiastical court in Jersey and made to promise to stop doing witchcraft and report anyone who came to consult her.

REFERENCES: G. R. Balleine. "Witch Trials in Jersey." *Societe Jersaise* 13 (1939): 379–398; William Monter. "Toads and Eucharists: The Male Witches of Normandy, 1564–1660." *French Historical Studies* 20 (1997): 563–595.

CHELMSFORD WITCH TRIALS

Chelmsford Assizes in Essex, the most active witch-hunting county in **England,** was the scene of a number of trials of groups of witches. (In the English legal system, assizes were occasions when traveling judges would try the major cases that emerged in the provinces.) A Chelmsford trial in 1566 was the first English witch trial to be the subject of a surviving pamphlet. *The Examination and Confession of certaine Witches* (1566) describes the trial of three witches, Agnes and Joan Waterhouse (a mother and daughter) and Elizabeth Frauncis. The other principal was Frauncis's **familiar,** a cat named Sathan. Frauncis's confession, as recounted in the pamphlet, describes how she received the cat from her grandmother, Eve, and how the cat did favors for her when fed with a drop of her blood. The favors were of varying usefulness—Sathan procured sheep for Frauncis, but they all disappeared. When Frauncis wanted to marry a well-off villager, Andrew Byles, Sathan told her she had to sleep with him first. After she did so, Byles refused to marry her, so Frauncis claimed that she requested and received from Sathan first the wasting of Byles's goods and then his death. After fifteen or sixteen years she traded Sathan to Agnes Waterhouse for a cake. Waterhouse used her new familiar for *maleficia*, to kill the livestock and spoil the beer and butter of villagers she disliked, to kill one neighbor, and finally to kill her husband. Waterhouse also changed Sathan from a cat to a toad for easier keeping. Joan Waterhouse was accused of calling Sathan in the form of a black dog to bewitch a child named Agnes Browne who had refused to give her a piece of bread and some cheese. The published confessions, however, were not that for which the witches were under trial. Agnes Waterhouse pleaded guilty to the murder by witchcraft of William Fynee and was hanged under the Statute of 1563. The pamphleteer places particular emphasis on Waterhouse praying in Latin and her familiar's approval of that practice, suggesting that like many early English witchcraft pamphlets this one had an anti-Catholic agenda. Joan was acquitted, and Frauncis, who pleaded guilty to bewitching a child, John Auger, was sentenced to a year in prison and four appearances in the pillory.

Depiction taken from a sixteenth-century English pamphlet of the public hanging of three Chelmsford witches, Joan Prentice, Joan Cony, and Joan Upney. © The Art Archive/The Art Archive.

The next major Chelmsford trial, in 1579, also involved Frauncis. In the intermediate time she had been convicted of another offense in 1573, serving another year in prison. In four unrelated trials, Frauncis and two other women were hanged for murder by witchcraft. Along with another woman, Margery Staunton, who was acquitted because of a flaw in the indictment, the three witches were the subject of another pamphlet, *A Detection of Damnable Driftes* (1579). Frauncis was convicted of the murder of a woman named Alice Poole, who denied her some yeast for brewing. The spirit she claimed to have used this time was not Sathan but a familiar in the shape of a little white, shaggy dog. Ellen Smith of Maldon, whose mother had been executed for witchcraft years before, was convicted and hanged for the murder of a four-year-old girl, Susan Webbe, who had quarreled with Smith's daughter. Alice Nokes of Lamborne was convicted and hanged for the murder of Elizabeth Barfott. All the witches were also charged with having familiar spirits.

The year 1582 saw witches from the small Essex town of Saint Osyth tried. The moving spirit in this case was a local justice of the peace, Brian Darcy, who was also connected with the printing of a pamphlet narrating the case in detail, "W.W.," *A True and Just Recorde, of the Information, Examination, and Confession of All the Witches, taken at St. Oses in the Countie of Essex* (1582). This was the longest and most elaborate English witchcraft pamphlet to date, and the first to refer to Continental learned demonology—the preface includes a passage translated from Jean **Bodin's** *Of the Demonmania of Sorcerors*. The pamphlet preserves an account of Darcy's high-pressure interrogations, showing what a zealous magistrate could achieve in the way of getting confessions without **torture.** The first **accusation,** of a local **cunning** woman named Ursula Kempe, came from one of Darcy's servants, a woman named Grace Thorlowe. Prolonged interrogations produced accusations and confessions of *maleficia* and keeping familiars from over a dozen local women, although trial at the assizes produced only two **executions,** Kempe and another woman named Elizabeth Bennett, both convicted of multiple murder. The case received wide publicity, and Darcy's abuses played a part in inspiring Reginald **Scot's** anti-persecution *Discoverie of Witchcraft* (1584).

The next notable set of trials at Chelmsford Assizes occurred in 1589, when three witches, Joan Cony of Systed, Joan Upney of Dagenham and Joan Prentice, were all convicted and hanged. The cases are described in *The Apprehension and Conviction of Three Notorious Witches* (1589). The pamphlet claims that Cony had actually worshipped **Satan,** that she had received two familiar spirits in the shape of black frogs and that she had trained her two daughters to be witches. Cony was convicted of the murder of Elizabeth Finch, who had refused her charity, and of bewitching three other people. Her daughters' illegitimate sons were among those who testified against her. Upney was convicted of using her familiars, in the shape of toads, to murder Joan Harwood and Alice Foster, whose husbands had called Upney a witch. Joan Prentice of Sible Hedingham is described as having conversed with the Devil in the shape of a ferret. This is an early example of how the idea of the familiar was starting to merge with the ideas of Satan and the **satanic pact.** Joan Prentice made a pact with the ferret-Satan to give him her soul, but the pact was sealed in the traditional way of English witches and their familiars, by the ferret sucking blood from her finger. Prentice was convicted for killing a young girl named Sara Glascock, whose family had denied her charity, although she claimed she had told the ferret only to harm the child but not kill it.

Chelmsford was also the site of many witch trials and executions during the Matthew **Hopkins** witch-hunt in the 1640s. The mass trial of 36 witches, with possibly 19 executions, on July 17, 1645, at Chelmsford is the largest trial and execution of witches in English history.

REFERENCES: James Sharpe. *Instruments of Darkness: Witchcraft in Early Modern England.* Philadelphia: University of Pennsylvania, 1996; Marion Gibson, ed. *Early Modern Witches: Witchcraft Cases in Contemporary Writing.* London and New York: Routledge, 2000.

COBHAM, ELEANOR (D. 1454)

Eleanor Cobham, second wife of Duke Humphrey of Gloucester (1390–1447) and aunt by marriage of the king of **England,** Henry VI (1421–

1471), was condemned as a witch in 1441 in one of the most prominent late medieval political witchcraft trials. She was already widely believed to have used **magic** to win Humphrey's love before their marriage, when she had been his mistress and a lady-in-waiting to his first wife, and to procure the annulment of his first marriage, freeing Humphrey to marry her.

Political enemies of Cobham and her husband, the legitimate heir of the childless Henry VI, exploited her connection with magical practitioners to ruin her. The enquiry began with Roger Bolingbroke, a learned clerk and astrologer charged with plotting the death of the king by sorcery. Under strict interrogation, Bolingbroke confessed that Cobham had asked him to divine her future, with the implication that she had asked whether the king would die and she would become queen. Cobham fled for sanctuary to Westminster the same day, confirming ideas of her guilt. After being removed, because sanctuary did not cover the offenses with which she was charged, Cobham was tried by a church court, although her enemies tried to move the case to a secular court, which would presumably have been more harsh. Probably due to her aristocratic standing, Cobham was treated relatively mercifully on conviction—she was sentenced to carry a lighted taper through the streets of London for three days as a mark of repentance (a punishment ordinarily associated with prostitutes and other women convicted of sexual offenses) and then imprisoned for life in relative comfort. Her associates were not all so lucky—a woman named Margery Jourdemayne, who had previously been charged with witchcraft, was burned, and Bolingbroke was hung, drawn and quartered for high treason. Humphrey, who had been almost entirely passive during the entire affair, was not charged, but his political career was destroyed and his marriage to Cobham annulled. Cobham's story is recounted, without much historical accuracy, in William Shakespeare's (1564–1616) *The Second Part of King Henry VI*.

REFERENCES: James Sharpe. *Instruments of Darkness: Witchcraft in Early Modern England*. Philadelphia: University of Pennsylvania Press, 1996; K. H. Vickers. *Humphrey Duke of Gloucester: A Biography*. London: A. Constable, 1907.

COLE, EUNICE (D. CA. 1680)

Although she was never actually convicted of witchcraft, Eunice Cole of Hampton (now in the state of New Hampshire) established fame as a witch that lasted through the twentieth century. Cole was a marginal figure in colonial **New England**—a poor, childless, old woman. Her reputation as a witch had been growing for years before she was first brought before the courts in 1656. Depositions sent to the General Court in Boston accused her of a variety of *maleficia* and of possessing **familiars.** Although the verdict on this case is not recorded, it is unlikely that Cole was convicted, because she was not executed. Cole spent most of the 1660s back and forth between Hampton and the jail in Boston, for crimes unrelated to witchcraft. Her reputation as a witch, though, continued to flourish, becoming known to many people outside of Hampton. The next indictment occurred in 1672, by which time Cole, now a widow, had become wholly a public charge. More depositions charged *maleficia* and the making of a **satanic pact** in 1662. In April 1673, the Essex County grand jury cleared Cole of the legal guilt of witchcraft—and thus the legal penalty—but declared that there was "just ground of vehement suspicion of her having had familiarity with the Devil." Cole was arrested for witchcraft once again, in a general witch scare in Hampton in 1680. Her death is not recorded, but there is a tradition in Hampton that she was found dead in her house, after which the townspeople hurriedly buried her with a stake through her body and a horseshoe attached to prevent her from rising again.

Cole's legend persisted after her death, and she was a protagonist of folktales and ghost stories in that corner of New England for centuries. John Greenleaf Whittier (1807–1892) wrote a poem, "The Wreck of Rivermouth" in which Cole punishes a girl for mocking her by causing the girl's boat to sink with all hands. In 1938, on the 300th anniversary of Hampton's founding, the town legally declared its disbelief in her guilt and affirmed her position as a citizen of Hampton.

REFERENCE: John Putnam Demos. *Entertaining Satan: Witchcraft and the Culture of Early New England*. New York: Oxford University Press, 1982.

COMMUNITY-BASED HISTORIOGRAPHY

The interpretation of early modern witchcraft in terms of the social functions that witchcraft and witchcraft **accusations** played in local communities began outside the history of the witch-hunt itself, in work done by anthropologists studying contemporary witchcraft in African communities. Particularly influential in this regard was the work of the British anthropologist E. E. Evans-Pritchard, *Witchcraft, Oracles and Magic among the Azande* (1937). The insights of anthropologists were brought to bear on the early modern witch-hunt in the 1970s by two English historians, Keith Thomas and Alan Macfarlane. Although Thomas and Macfarlane made the most explicit use of anthropological theory, their work was part of a broader trend in the 1970s toward close study of community interactions in understanding witch-hunts. Other historians putting forth similar interpretations were William Monter on **Switzerland**, H. C. Erik Midelfort on **Germany**, and Paul Boyer and Stephen Nissenbaum on **Salem.**

Unlike the previously dominant school, the **liberal** historians, anthropology-influenced work has been much less interested in trials and the witchcraft theory of learned demonologists and magistrates than in the circumstances out of which accusations arose. Whereas the liberal historians, had emphasized the uniquely diabolical nature of European witchcraft, the functionalists, while not denying that European witchcraft had its peculiarities, viewed it as broadly similar to witchcraft traditions existing in other societies and times. Anthropology influenced witchcraft historians to analyze witchcraft cases by considering the role of the witch and the accuser in the community. For community-based interpretations, witchcraft beliefs existed to serve a social function. For example, Thomas and Macfarlane identified many (not all) witchcraft accusations in rural **England** in the sixteenth and seventeenth centuries as responses to capitalist development A classic pattern in the cases Thomas and Macfarlane investigated was the "denial of charity." This type of witchcraft accusation followed a poor beggar or other poor person being denied charity by a well-off member of the community. When disaster later struck the well-off person, he or she would accuse the poor person of revenge-motivated *maleficia*. Thomas and Macfarlane identified this pattern as a result of the decline of individual charitable obligation and its replacement by individual charity, at a time when poverty was increasing in England and Europe as a whole. Deniers dealt with their failure to live up to traditional expectations of charitable behavior by projecting their guilt onto witches. Boyer and Nissenbaum put forth a similar interpretation of the Salem witch-hunt as a response to capitalist modernity but inverted it by identifying witch-hunters and accusers as the side that was losing in the great transition and accused witches as representatives of the forces of capitalist modernity.

A different kind of community-based interpretation located the drive to hunt witches stresses on communities rather than within them. One of its most distinguished exponents is the German historian Wolfgang Behringer, much of whose work focuses on the close connection between large-scale German witch-hunts, bad weather, poor harvests and widespread hunger and famine.

Attacks on anthropological and community-based interpretations came from several sources. Some anthropologists warned of too facile cross-cultural applications of theory, or even questioned whether the concept of "witch" was valid cross-culturally. Liberal historians of witchcraft claimed that studies of community dynamics may have explained individual cases but could not explain big witch-hunts, which seemed dysfunctional. Given that tensions within small communities and accusations of witchcraft have had a history in European society stretching back to the classical world and extending to the present day, community-based interpreters had difficulty explaining why hostility to witches took the form of a witch-hunt in early modern and not at other times. The peculiar mythology of the European witch-hunt, including the **sabbat** and **satanic pact,** was difficult to explain solely as a product of interactions in local communities. **Feminist** historians argued that anthropological interpretations such as Thomas's gave exaggerated weight to differences between **social classes** and status groups and insufficient weight to **gender.** Some of these objections have been taken into account in the latest attempt at a general analysis of European witchcraft using a community-based approach, Robin Briggs's *Witches and Neighbors*.

REFERENCES: Wolfgang Behringer, *Witchcraft Persecutions in Bavaria: Popular Magic, Religious Zealotry, and Reason of State in Early Modern Europe.* Trans. by J. C. Grayson and David Lederer. Cambridge: Cambridge University Press, 1997; Paul Boyer and Stephen Nissenbaum. *Salem Possessed: The Social Origins of Witchcraft.* Cambridge and London: Harvard University Press, 1974; Robin Briggs, *Witches and Neighbors: The Social and Cultural Context of European Witchcraft.* New York: Penguin, 1996; E. E. Evans-Pritchard. *Witchcraft, Oracles and Magic among the Azande.* Oxford: Clarendon

Press, 1937; Alan Macfarlane. *Witchcraft in Tudor and Stuart Essex: A Regional and Comparative Study.* London: Routledge and Kegan Paul, 1970; H. C. Erik Midelfort. *Witch Hunting in Southwestern Germany, 1562–1684.* Stanford: Stanford University Press, 1972; William Monter. *Witchcraft in France and Switzerland: The Borderlands during the Reformation.* Ithaca and London: Cornell University Press, 1976; Andrew Sanders. *A Deed without a Name: The Witch in Society and History.* Oxford and Washington, D.C.: Berg, 1995; Keith Thomas. *Religion and the Decline of Magic.* New York: Charles Scribner's Sons, 1971.

CONFESSIONALISM AND WITCH-HUNTING

The age of the great witch-hunt was also the age of the Protestant and Catholic religious Reformations, and the relation of the religious struggle to witch persecution has been a topic of great controversy. A great deal of ink was spilled in the nineteenth and early twentieth centuries over whether Protestants or Catholics were more severe in their persecution of witches. The modern consensus is that this is not a useful question to ask. There were many similarities between Protestant and Catholic demonology and witch-persecution, and in practice a broad spectrum of approaches to witches can be found in both Catholic and Protestant Europe. The Catholic world ranged from the lack of interest in witch persecution found in large areas of **Italy** and the Iberian peninsula to the severe witch-hunts found in the German prince-bishoprics. The Protestant world ranged from the Dutch Republic, which stopped persecution entirely by the early seventeenth century, to **Scotland** and some of the German Calvinist states on the other extreme. A variety of other factors, political and social, seem to have more influence over a region's actions against witches than confessional affiliation.

This does not mean that there are no important differences between Protestant and Catholic witch-hunts, however. In addition to a common heritage including the **Bible,** the early Church Fathers and medieval Christianity, Protestants and Catholics also drew on different intellectual and spiritual sources to understand a witch's crimes. Broadly speaking, Catholics leaned toward assimilating witchcraft to heresy, and Protestants linked it to idolatry, a crime with which they often charged Catholics. Protestants had less interest in the **sabbat,** which Catholics saw as a diabolical inversion of the sacrament of the Mass. Catholics were much more horrified by the idea of the witch desecrating the Host or turning it to diabolical use, because for them the consecrated Host was the actual flesh of God. Host desecration had a much lower profile in the Protestant world. Both sides used witchcraft as a polemical weapon in religious controversy, but they used it in different ways. For example, Protestants found prayer to saints as practiced by Catholics identical to prayer to demons practiced by witches, whereas Catholics such as Martin **del Rio** claimed that lands that turned from Catholicism to Protestantism saw a vast increase in witches, witchcraft and heresy being indissolubly linked. Protestants also accused popes of practicing sorcery. Ironically, Protestant writers against witchcraft belief, like Reginald **Scot,** also attacked Catholicism as fostering superstitious belief in **magic** as against rationality. Protestants and Catholics also recommended different religious remedies for witch victims. Both condemned **countermagic** as blasphemous or even demonic, but devout Protestants were limited to prayer, fasting and repentance, whereas Catholics were also urged to use the sacraments of the church, as well as "sacramentals" such as holy water. Protestant powerlessness against witchcraft was a favorite charge of Catholic demonologists.

During the periods of highest conflict between Protestants and Catholics, there was usually little governmental energy to spare for witch-hunts. The period of the Reformation itself, from about 1520 to about 1550, saw little witch-hunting. The great Protestant religious reformers Martin Luther (1483–1546) and John Calvin (1509–1564), although they endorsed the death penalty for witches, had little interest

Martin Luther. Engraving by Theodor Knesing, from the picture by Lucas Cranach. © Library of Congress.

in the subject of witchcraft itself. Even in times of intense religious conflict, it was uncommon for one religious group to employ the machinery of witch-persecution against another. Protestants may have charged Catholics with being witches, for example, but neither Protestants nor Catholics routinely persecuted their religious opponents for the crime. They were more likely to link witches with the religious opposition than the other way around; in Scotland during the late sixteenth century, for example, many accused witches were accused of being Catholics, but their primary identity was that of witches. The situation was further complicated by the similarity between some claimants to religious power and witches—the Puritan William Hacket, an illiterate maltmaker from Northamptonshire, was proclaimed in London as the second coming of Christ in 1591, with the special mission of overthrowing the English bishops and establishing Presbyterianism. Despite his alleged divine mission, many of the powers Hackett claimed, such as control of the weather, were witchlike, and he was portrayed in government propaganda before and after his **execution** as having made a witchlike **satanic pact.**

One link between witch-hunting and the religious changes of confessionalization was through the process of reformation itself, one which displayed many similarities between Protestants and Catholics. Generally speaking, those areas in which there was a concerted effort with the backing of the state to reform the morals and beliefs of ordinary people along either Catholic or Protestant lines saw more witch-hunting than those in which the church and state were relatively indifferent to popular morals and beliefs. Several of the German witch-hunting prelates had reputations as devoted workers for the improvement of the church and the promotion of piety in their territories. Another pattern was for areas where confessions directly confronted each other—large states with established religious minorities such as **France** or areas of many small jurisdictions such as **Switzerland** and the Holy Roman Empire where Protestant and Catholic states lived in close proximity—to see more witch persecution than areas, such as Catholic Spain or Lutheran Scandinavia, where the dominant creed was relatively unchallenged. (The Dutch Republic, highly mixed religiously but with little persecution either of religious minorities or witches, was the great exception to this pattern.) In some areas, authorities turned to witch persecution as an alternative when forbidden to persecute their religious opponents. In France, political settlements between the Catholics and Protestants in the late-sixteenth-century Wars of Religion were often followed by witch-hunts. Confessionalism did not always promote witch-hunting. The use of possessed individuals to advance particular religious agendas, as in the cases of John **Darrell** and Marthe **Brossier,** actually tended to discredit witchcraft and demonology when they were revealed as fraudulent.

One group of sects and religious traditions in early modern Europe tended to oppose witch-persecution. These were those that sprung from the Radical Reformation, the Anabaptists and Spiritualist groups that did not emphasize reforming society in a godly way but withdrawing from society into small, self-contained colonies or pursuing individual spiritual perfection. Witchcraft was simply irrelevant to these goals. Many of the most important anti-persecution writers of early modern Europe—Johann **Weyer,** Reginald **Scot,** John **Webster** and Balthazar **Bekker,** among others—had social or intellectual connections to religious radicals, although they belonged to more conventional groups.

REFERENCES: Robin Briggs. *Witches and Neighbors: The Social and Cultural Context of European Witchcraft.* New York: Penguin, 1996; Stuart Clark. *Thinking with Demons: The Idea of Witchcraft in Early Modern Europe.* Oxford: Clarendon Press, 1997; Brian P. Levack. *The Witch-Hunt in Early Modern Europe.* London and New York: Longman, 1987; Alexandra Walsham. " 'Frantick Hacket': Prophecy, Sorcery, Insanity and the Elizabethan Puritan Movement." *Historical Journal* 40 (1998): 27–66; Robert S. Walinski-Kiehl. " 'Godly States,' Confessional Conflict and Witch-Hunting in Early Modern Germany." *Mentalities* 5 (1988): 13–25.

COUNTERMAGIC

The first recourse of many early modern people who thought themselves victims of witchcraft was not to seek the aid of the magistrate or the local clergyman, but to fight fire with fire by employing countermagic. Countermagic had a number of purposes, and an immense variety of techniques were employed across Europe. Countermagic could be employed by the bewitched person and his or her family or friends, by **cunning folk** or even by priests.

Probably the most widely practiced form of countermagic was strictly defensive—the use of herbs, amulets or charms to prevent the attacks of witches. In **England** and **Ireland,** hanging a horseshoe above the threshold was thought to keep witches from attacking a house. Once such defensive measures had failed and a particular situation had been identified as having been caused by a witch, one use of countermagic was to make the witch reveal herself. A common technique was the application of fire to something associated with the witch, causing pain. Bewitchment created **magical** links that could be exploited by victims and their families, in German villages burning the excrement of a bewitched person was thought to burn the witch herself, revealing her identity. Excrement was frequently associated with countermagic. A common practice in some parts of England was burying or burning "witch-bottles"—flasks containing some of the victim's urine along with hair or fingernail clippings and sometimes thorns, pins and nails. It was thought that this would cause the witch intense pain when she urinated. Alternatively, things associated with the witch herself rather than her victim could be attacked, for example burning thatch from a witch's house. Brooms, often associated with witches, were sometimes credited

The Counter-Spell by the Image by Gaston Vuillier (1847–1915). © Giraudon/Art Resource, New York.

with antiwitch powers. Sweeping salt with a broom was an effective counter to witch-sent disease in **Lorraine,** and in England laying a broom across the threshold was thought to prevent a witch from leaving the victim's house.

Identification of a witch could be followed by negotiation to cause her to lift her bewitchment by more countermagic. The most direct form of countermagic was simply to attack the witch physically. In many areas, drawing blood from a witch was thought to neutralize her power. Demonologists differed on whether it was licit to beat a witch to force her to remove a spell. Nicholas **Remy** and others argued that because this did not involve any kind of pact or agreement, it was licit, while Martin **del Rio** and others argued that any dealing with magic or devilry to remove magic was sinful. Using physical force in countermagic could easily become an expression of the rage and frustration of the witch victim, and there are numerous cases of witches being beaten to death by their victims. Other measures against a witch were less severe. Some peasants believed that simply eating food from a witch's house would cure her harms. Not all countermagic attacked the witch directly. Sometimes part of that which the witch was attacking would be sacrificed to save the whole—one technique for dealing with witch-caused sickness of livestock was to kill and bury one or more of the afflicted beasts, sometimes accompanied by magical objects. This may have actually functioned to break chains of infection. Particularly in Catholic areas, countermagic could employ sacred objects such as holy water or consecrated wafers, or the recitation of particular prayers. Some priests were experts in countermagic, but the practice was open to criticism from Protestants, who identified many Catholic practices with witchcraft, and from church authorities. There is some evidence that the gap created by Protestantism's attack on church magic was filled by **cunning folk,** but "unofficial" countermagic also flourished in Catholic countries, and some Protestant pastors distributed charms and amulets to protect from witches.

Whether or not it employed specifically religious items or practices, countermagic was always religiously questionable. Many authorities, particularly Protestants, claimed the proper response to bewitchment was prayer and lamentation of one's sins. These would demonstrate to God one's repentance, thus causing him perhaps to lift the penalty of the bewitchment for which he was ultimately responsible, the witch and the Devil acting only by God's permission. This kind of argument was of little comfort to witch victims and was never widely accepted outside the clergy. A wider range of religious responses, including pilgrimages to the shrines of the saints, was available to afflicted Catholics. Some cunning folk claimed expertise in magical procedures to determine which were the appropriate saints to visit.

Besides prayer and repentance, the only other fully legitimate countermeasure in the minds of most representatives of the church and state was the **accusation** of the witch before an authorized court. The idea that legal proceedings took away a witch's powers was common among ordinary people as well as demonologists. As opposed to these legitimate procedures, clerical authorities saw countermagic as a blasphemous attempt to frustrate the will of God, although many witch victims were perfectly willing to combine countermagic, prayer and legal proceedings. Countermagic could also be seen as implicitly satanic, the use of the Devil's devices to counter the witch, saving the body at the expense of the soul's damnation. The form of countermagic with which clerical authors were often most comfortable was simple physical attack, which did not involve an implicit pact with the Devil.

Whatever clerics' reservations, countermagic performed an important function in early modern society in giving people a feeling that they were not powerless against witches. It also functioned as a way to resolve conflicts in village society, albeit sometimes violently.

REFERENCES: Robin Briggs. *Witches and Neighbors: The Social and Cultural Context of European Witchcraft.* New York: Penguin, 1996; Keith Thomas. *Religion and the Decline of Magic.* New York: Charles Scribner's Sons, 1971.

CROATIA, WITCH-HUNTING IN

Most of the Balkan Slavic peoples, among whom belief in witchcraft was common, were spared a witch-hunt in the early modern period because they were ruled by the Ottoman Turks, who did not persecute witches. The Croats, outside the Turkish Empire, were an exception. Witch trials in Croatia date to the late fourteenth century—the earliest surviving record dates from a trial of two women, Alicia and Margareta, in 1360. They were required to produce witnesses to swear that they were not witches, and this seems to have been the most common procedure in late medieval Croatia.

Persecution intensified in the early modern period. In 1609, the Croatian Assembly empowered all citizens to seize suspected witches and hand them over to the nobleman responsible for the area. If the nobleman found the witches guilty and did not punish them, his sword, the emblem of his status, was to be confiscated. Between 1640 and 1752, there were 28 witch trials in Zagreb, the capital of Croatia, of which records survive. All the suspects were women. The **accusations** were typical, including the **satanic pact** and attendance as **sabbats** featuring **infanticide** and cannibalism. By the mid–eighteenth century, Croatian sabbats were sometimes referred to as "Copernicus guilds," after the heretical astronomer. Croatian witches were also accused of *maleficia* including **weather witching,** causing the illness or death of humans or livestock and milk theft. Witches were described as stealing milk by gathering dew at a crossroads with their left hands during the week of the new moon and giving it to other people's cows to drink. **Torture** was commonly used in Croatian witch trials, and **execution** was by burning. There were also extrajudicial killings. Following a poor harvest in 1685, peasants carried out a series of witch murders. The murderers were made to repent publicly.

REFERENCE: T. P. Vukanovic. "Witchcraft in the Central Balkans I: Characteristics of Witches." *Folklore* 100 (1989): 1–24.

CUNNING FOLK

The most common **magical** practitioners in early modern Europe were not witches but those people usually referred to by the English term as "cunning" men and women. Many ordinary Europeans turned to cunning folk to deal with the vicissitudes of their lives—stubborn illness, the theft of property and assaults by witches could all be eased by their ministrations. The need for such services was great in a society without police forces and in which few people, particularly the rural poor, had access to learned medical practitioners. The cunning folk may have benefited from the Reformation in Protestant areas, because Protestant ministers were less willing to endorse the efficacy of religious artifacts such as holy water or pictures of the saints than Catholic priests had been. But cunning folk were also numerous and successful in Catholic Europe.

Cunning folk presented a problem for clerical writers on witchcraft, both Protestant and Catholic. Many denounced cunning magic as simply another form of witchcraft, infinitely worse than that of the witch because the witch damaged only life or property, whereas use of the cunning folk—"white witches"—led directly to the loss of the soul. The magical powers of the cunning folk could only come ultimately from the Devil, who used the seeming benevolence of cunning magic into luring people to deal with him. Nevertheless, the clerical animus against cunning folk, which may have had its roots in professional rivalry because clerics and cunning folk dealt with many of the same kinds of problems, had little to no effect on law enforcement throughout most of Europe. Most magistrates and nearly all the common people had no difficulty making a distinction between the witch, who performed harmful acts of *maleficia*, and the cunning person, who employed magic to help. Cunning folk, particularly women and itinerants, were sometimes accused of being witches, but given their large numbers only a small proportion ran afoul of the law in this way. Even in many of these cases, fraud, as the promising of magical detection of buried treasure in return for a payment, was the issue rather than magic per se. Cunning folk and their magic were more likely to be criminalized in Mediterranean areas, particularly **Italy,** which lacked a strong tradition of persecution of diabolic witches.

Although a few writers on witchcraft, notably Reginald **Scot,** believed the cunning folk to be conscious frauds, most cunning people seem to have believed in their own power and the efficacy of their spells or magical acts. Most other people seem to have agreed with them. Being a cunning man or woman was generally not a full-time occupation, but practiced as a lucrative sideline. Cunning folk often claimed their activities were community service, charging their clients only modest amounts.

Resort to a cunning person was often the first recourse of people who suspected themselves to be bewitched, including some quite far up the social scale. Certain cunning folk specialized in detecting and countering witchcraft. One **Lorraine** cunning man, for example, poured the urine of a person suspected of being bewitched on a hot iron. If it boiled away, the illness or other affliction was natural, if it remained the illness was caused by witchcraft. John **Walsh** of Netherbury claimed that he spoke with white, green and black fairies on the tops of hills, who identified the bewitched for him. If the bewitched person knew him or herself to be a victim of witchcraft but was uncertain as to the witch's identity, the cunning folk had techniques to identify the malefactor. Some cunning folk claimed the ability to provide a countercharm, or even to turn the affliction back on the witch—a practice that could lead to witchcraft **accusations** against themselves. The cunning folk, and **countermagic** generally, were an alternative to judicial proceedings against an alleged witch; cunning folk seem to have discouraged a resort to law.

As the early modern period wore on, educated and upper-class persons were less and less likely to consult cunning folk or believe in their magic. The clientele of the later cunning folk was more exclusively drawn from the poor and working class, with a concomitant drop in the wealth and prestige of the cunning folk themselves. Despite their decline, however, the cunning folk far outlasted both witches and witch-hunters and were still active in Europe in the nineteenth century, and in some areas well into the twentieth.

REFERENCES: Robin Briggs. *Witches and Neighbors: The Social and Cultural Context of European Witchcraft.* New York: Penguin, 1996; Keith Thomas. *Religion and the Decline of Magic.* New York: Charles Scribner's Sons, 1971.

D

DANEAU, LAMBERT (1530–1595)

The minister and theology professor Lambert Daneau, a leading Calvinist thinker, was the first important Protestant demonologist. His *On Sorcerers* (1574) drew on information from recent trials in Savoy and **Geneva,** as well as vast classical and patristic learning. Written in the form of a dialogue, *On Sorcerers* endorsed the witch stereotype, including *maleficia*, the **sabbat, flying** witches and the **satanic pact.** Daneau placed great emphasis on the **Devil's mark,** and his work is one reason for its importance for subsequent Protestant demonologists and witch-hunters. He believed that witchcraft was strong—and increasing as the world grew more evil and approached its final end. He called for vigorous persecution of witches and **cunning folk,** attacking overly lenient magistrates. Daneau believed that simple condemnation of witchcraft based on the **Bible** was more effective than elaborate Scholastic inquiries, which he argued led to unhealthy curiosity. He condemned the Paris lectures of Juan **Maldonado** for this reason.

Daneau's work was influential in **England** (although, surprisingly, far less so in Calvinist **Scotland**) as well as the Francophone Protestant world. It was translated into English in 1575 as *A Dialogue of Witches in Foretime named Lottellers and now commonly called Sorcerers* and was one of the first unimpeachably Protestant works of demonology available in English.

REFERENCE: Julio Caro Baroja. *The World of the Witches.* Trans. O. N. V. Glendinning. Chicago: University of Chicago Press, 1965.

DARC, JEHANNE (JOAN OF ARC) (1412–1431)

Jehanne Darc (also known as Jeanne D'Arc or Joan of Arc) tried in 1431, was neither convicted nor executed as a witch. Some of the charges against her in the bishop's court at Rouen involved **magical** or demonic activity, such as invoking demons, making a **satanic pact** and dancing in a ring with fairies.

These charges were withdrawn in the course of the proceedings, however, probably for lack of evidence and to keep the focus on the main charges. When she was finally burned alive, it was as a relapsed heretic, not as a witch. Nevertheless, Jeanne's enemies continued to circulate stories of her magical and diabolical actions. This tradition culminates in William Shakespeare's (1564–1616) *Henry VI, Part One*. Shakespeare, an Englishman writing from the point of view of Jeanne's English enemies, treated her as a witch whose successes against the English came with the aid of demons.

REFERENCE: Jeffrey Burton Russell. *Witchcraft in the Middle Ages*. Ithaca: Cornell University Press, 1972.

DARRELL, JOHN

The Puritan minister John Darrell was the most celebrated exorcist of Elizabethan **England.** He first came to public notice with the attempted exorcism of a seventeen-year old woman named Katherine Wright in Mansfield in 1586. A local woman named Margaret Roper was charged with bewitching Wright, although the charges were eventually dropped. Ten years later, Darrell was involved in a well-publicized dispossession of a thirteen-year-old boy named Thomas Darling of Burton-on-Trent. Darling, a pious Puritan lad, was afflicted with convulsions, vomiting, visions and loss of use of his legs, all of which he attributed to a local old woman named Alice Gooderidge, whom he had offended by farting in her presence. Gooderidge was held in prison, where she died. Darling's story was told in a pamphlet by Jesse Bee, *The Most Wonderful and True Storie of a Witch named Alice Gooderidge* (1597). Darrell's exorcisms did not rely on the formulas and holy artifacts that Catholic exorcists used, but on intense prayer and fasting, which Darrell employed in all the exorcism cases after Wright's.

Shortly after exorcising Darling, Darrell intervened in a case of **possession** in the household of a Lancashire gentleman named Nicholas Starkie, whose children, John (age 12) and Ann (age 10), first showed signs of bewitchment. When a Catholic priest had failed to exorcise the children, a local **cunning** man, Edmund Hartley, managed to calm them with an application of herbs and Catholic charms. Shortly after Hartley's arrival, however, five other members of Starkie's household, all female, began to show signs of possession. Starkie sought the advice of a learned magician, Dr. John Dee (1527–1608), who warned him against Hartley and suggested that he seek the aid of godly Protestant ministers. Hartley was identified as a witch and executed for conjuring in March 1597; Darrell and another minister, George More, were successful in exorcising the possessed members of Starkie's household. Darrell's last case began at the end of the year in Nottingham, with the spectacular possession of a young musician named William Sommers. In addition to the usual symptoms of bewitchment, Sommers had a large lump the size of an egg and engaged in public **sex** acts, including bestiality with a dog. Darrell waged a see-saw struggle with the demons possessing Sommers, expelling them only to have them return. The drama attracted a great deal of interest in Nottingham, and Darrell received a regular position—his first—at a local church. His preaching was devoted nearly exclusively to demons and witches, and he claimed that Sommers when bewitched had the power to identify witches brought before him. (Others who had tried Sommers's ability doubted it.) Darrell claimed that by using Sommers, every witch in the land could be identified and routed out. 13 witches were arrested, although 11 were released shortly after. One of the two remaining, an old woman named Alice Freeman, was acquitted—interestingly, by the witch-hunting judge Sir Edmund **Anderson,** on this occasion letting his dislike for Puritans overcome his dislike for supposed witches.

Freeman's family was influential in the area and counterattacked with an arrest of Sommers in January 1598 on charges of having bewitched to death a person named Sterland. The principal point was to get Sommers to confess to fraud in identifying witches, however, which he did, although he withdrew the confession shortly thereafter. By this time, word of what was going on in Nottingham had reached the central authorities of the Church of England, concerned to rein in freelancers like Darrell, particularly Puritan ones. The archbishop of Canterbury, John Whitgift (1530?–1604), summoned Darrell to his palace at Lambeth, where he was tried by an ecclesiastical commission. Wright, Darling and Sommers all confessed to having faked their seizures and other possession-related behavior. Darling withdrew his confession, but Wright and Sommers went on to make the far more damaging charge that Darrell had coached them. In May 1599 Darrell was condemned and imprisoned, although he was eventually released.

The Darrell affair attracted a great deal of interest. No less than thirteen publications on it appeared between late 1598 and 1601, the most important being Samuel Harsnett's (1561–1631) A Discovery of the Fraudulent Practices of John Darrell (1599), which denied that possession was caused by witchcraft at all. Darrell himself was aware of the importance of publicity, and all four of his exorcism cases were recorded in print. He himself published several pamphlets, including A Detection of that Sinnful, Shamful, Lying and Ridiculous Discours of Samuel Harshnet, published at an underground Puritan press in 1600. The result of the Darrell affair was to increase suspicion of exorcisms and witch cases among the leadership of the early-seventeenth-century Church of England. Sympathizers with Puritanism, on the other hand, referred to Darrell's exorcisms as genuine throughout the seventeenth century.

REFERENCES: Freeman, Thomas. "Demons, Deviance and Defiance: John Darrell and the Politics of Exorcism in late Elizabethan England." In Orthodoxy and Conformity in the English Church, c. 1560–1660, ed. Peter Lake and Michael Questier, 34–63. Woodbridge, England: Boydell Press, 2000; James Sharpe. Instruments of Darkness: Witchcraft in Early Modern England. Philadelphia: University of Pennsylvania Press, 1996; D. P. Walker. Unclean Spirits: Possession and Exorcism in France and England in the Late Sixteenth and Early Seventeenth Centuries. London: Warburg Institute, University of London 1981.

DENMARK, WITCH-HUNTING IN

Denmark was the most active witch-hunting society in Scandinavia, but large-scale witch-hunts did not develop there. The most important reason for the country's freedom from large-scale witch-hunting was the legal restrictions embedded in Danish criminal codes. The Copenhagen Articles of 1547 decreed that **accusations** from dishonest persons, including witches and sorcerers, could not be the basis of another's conviction and forbade the use of **torture** before the final sentence. The Kalundborg Statutes of 1576 subjected all capital sentences handed down by juries to automatic appeal to county courts. This would become a common strategy for dealing with witchcraft convictions, but Denmark was the first secular court system to adopt it.

Patchy survival of records makes it difficult to estimate the extent of witch-hunting in Denmark. Very approximate figures are 2,000 trials and 1,000 **executions** for the sixteenth and seventeenth centuries. Approximately 85 percent of the trials took place in rural areas, roughly mirroring the distribution of the Danish population. About 90 percent of the victims were women, mostly old and from the poorest class. Execution was by burning. Danish trials focused on **maleficia**, its most common forms being the infliction of illness or death on people or livestock or, in coastal areas, interference with fishing. **Satanic pact, infanticide, magically** caused impotence and demonic **possession** played little role in Danish witchcraft cases. One unusually prominent evil deed ascribed to witches was the storms that delayed King **James** of **Scotland** and his Danish bride Anne on their return to their native land in 1590. These were blamed on witches in both Scotland and Denmark, and it has been argued that James's experiences in Denmark were one way in which the idea of the satanic pact was introduced to Scotland through his contact with Denmark's leading demonologist, the Lutheran theologian Niels Hemmingsen (1513–1600), author of *Admonition on Superstitious Magic to be Avoided* (1575). There is, however, no direct evidence to support this claim.

In Denmark, the fully developed idea of the **sabbat** was quite rare, although individual witches and sometimes small groups did meet with the Devil. One unique feature of Danish witchcraft accusations was the prominent role played by churches as settings for these meetings. Churches were a surprisingly commonplace for witches to meet the Devil, perhaps because of the wall paintings of the Devil or demons that were common in them. Danish witches were also frequently accused of having denied Christ and renounced Christianity by blowing through a keyhole in a church door. The Devil, or demons, usually appeared in the testimony of accused witches not as the lordly master of the sabbat, but as a large black dog to whom witches swore loyalty—although they sometimes claimed to have beaten the dog to get it to perform evil acts.

The reforming Lutheran bishop Peder Palladius (1503–1560) called for a witch-hunt as part of an anti-Catholic campaign as early as the 1540s, but the peak of Danish witch-hunting was in the second and third decades of the seventeenth century. In 1612 and 1613, 11 women were killed in a witch-hunt in the town of Koge. This drew more attention to witchcraft, and a new witch-craft law was promulgated in 1617 as part of an overall effort led by King Christian IV (r. 1596–1648) and some of his councillors, in alliance with some of the Lutheran Church leadership, to reform the morals of the Danish people. The new law restricted the death penalty to cases of satanic pact. In conjunction with government policy, it greatly increased witch trials, although most continued to be for *maleficia*. In Jutland, the Danish peninsula, over half of the known trials are concentrated in the decade after 1617. As the persecution progressed in the early 1620s, there was increased interest in the **Devil's mark** as evidence of witchcraft. (The Danes also employed **flotation tests.**) By the end of the decade, the panic had largely ended, possibly due to exhaustion of the supply of suspected witches.

In 1686, it was decreed that all death sentences in the county courts would be automatically appealed to the supreme court, and judicial witch-hunting ended shortly thereafter. The Danish Lutheran clergy also steadily lost interest in witch-hunting, while continuing vigorous preaching against **countermagic** and recourse to **cunning** men, which had been a common topic of sermons in Denmark since the Reformation. The last judicial execution of a witch was the burning of a woman in Falster in 1693. Belief in witchcraft continued long after the end of the witch-hunt. Commentators on Danish law continued to treat the witchcraft statute as current throughout the eighteenth century, and it was only finally abolished in 1866. Popular hostility toward witches also continued. The murder of an alleged witch named Dorte Jensdatter in 1722 was followed by wide publicity and the execution of the ringleaders. The last known witch murder in Denmark occurred in 1800.

REFERENCES: Gustav Henningsen. "Witchcraft in Denmark." *Folklore* 93 (1982): 131–137; Gustave Henningsen. "Witchcraft Prosecutions after the End of the Era of the Witch Trials: A Contribution to Danish Ethnology." ARV: *Scandinavian Yearbook of Folklore* 43 (1987): 147–165; Jens Christian v. Johansen. "Denmark: The Sociology of Accusations." In *Early Modern European Witchcraft: Centres and Peripheries,* ed. Bengt Ankarloo and Gustav Henningsen, 339–365. Oxford: Clarendon Press, 1990; Jens Christian v. Johansen. "Witchcraft in Elsinore 1625–1626." *Mentalities* 3 (1985): 1–8; Jens Christian v. Johansen. "Witchcraft, Sin and Repentance: The Decline of Danish Witchcraft Trials." *Acta Ethnographica Hungarica* 37 (1991/1992): 413–423; Brian P. Levack. *The Witch-Hunt in Early Modern Europe.* London and New York: Longman, 1987.

THE DEVIL

See Satan.

DEVIL'S MARK

An increasingly prominent belief in the witch-hunt was that in a small, insensitive area of the witch's skin—a mark, usually on a concealed part of the

Satan applying his clawmark on an apprentice sorcerer. From Guazzo, *Compendium Maleficarum*, 1626. © Dover Pictorial Archive.

body, left by the Devil when the witch first made the **satanic pact,** the Devil's mark. (Multiple marks on one witch were uncommon, but not unheard of.) This belief was a relative latecomer to the European definition of witchcraft—it was not known in the Middle Ages or at the beginning of the witch-hunt in the fifteenth century. Heinrich **Kramer's** *Malleus Maleficarum* (1486) does not mention it. The Devil's mark began to emerge in witch-hunting in the early sixteenth century. Beginning with the revival of large-scale witch-hunting around 1560, the Devil's mark played an important role in the judicial process in many parts of Europe, particularly in Protestant areas. The first important Protestant demonologist, Lambert **Daneau,** placed great emphasis on it. The Catholic Inquisition, by contrast, never used it. Catholic demonologists and supporters of the witch-hunt such as Peter **Binsfeld** and Martin **del Rio** were skeptical, although Nicolas **Remy** was a strong believer. In **England,** belief in the Devil's mark contributed to the somewhat different idea of the **witch's mark.**

Evidence of the Devil's mark was useful to witch-hunters because it demonstrated the pact the witch had made with the Devil. The stripping of the suspected witch, particularly female witches, to search for the concealed Devil's mark was a ritual of humiliation justified because it was believed that the Devil often marked women, but not men, on the breasts, anus or genitals. Belief in the Devil's mark was exploited by "witch-prickers," who marketed their expertise in identifying Devil's marks and demonstrating their insensibility and that they did not bleed when pierced. Witch-pricking was practiced by many **witch-finders** and torturers, like Hans **Vollmair,** but was also the principal profession of some. The executioner of Rocroi, Jean Minard, pricked hundreds of suspects, boasting of having been responsible for the death of more than two hundred, before the Parlement of Paris put a stop to his activities by sentencing him to the galleys for life in 1601. **Scotland** was particularly active in witch-pricking. Scottish witch-prickers, including the notorious James Kinkaid, active in the mid–seventeenth century, practically constituted a profession, even taking their special expertise to the north of England for witch-hunts. Witch-prickers in this region were often paid per witch identified, which encouraged fraud. Fraudulent witch-prickers could usually find warts or other insensitive spots on the human body, and the whole concept of the Devil's mark was sometimes attacked by claiming that everyone bore similar blemishes. Another technique of fraudulent witch-prickers was the use of a special knife with a retractable blade. (One witch-pricker active in Scotland and the north of England was reputed to fraudulently identify women as witches by using an "enchanted pin," **magically** enabled to pierce the human body without drawing blood or causing pain.) The end of the great Scottish witch-hunt of 1661–1662 was accompanied by a series of scandals whereby witch-prickers, including Kinkaid, were revealed as frauds. The decline of witch-hunting in western Europe in the late seventeenth and early eighteenth centuries saw a related decline in judges' willingness to accept Devil's marks as evidence.

REFERENCES: Joseph Klaits. *Servants of Satan: The Age of the Witch Hunts.* Bloomington: Indiana University Press, 1985; Brian P. Levack. *The Witch-Hunt in Early Modern Europe.* London and New York: Longman, 1987; W. N. Neill. "The Professional Pricker and His Test for Witchcraft. *Scottish Historical Review* 19 (1922): 205–213.

DIANA

In the Middle Ages, there were widespread beliefs, particularly among the peasantry, in a powerful female supernatural being, often associated with fertility. This belief seems to have been a vestige of pre-Christian paganism that the Church never entirely succeeded in erasing. Learned writers, such as those who penned the **Canon Episcopi,** identified this powerful being with the ancient Roman Goddess Diana, who was herself sometimes identified with the Greek

Goddess Diana and nymphs while Actaeon is torn to pieces by his hounds in the background, by Giovan Battista Pittoni. © The Art Archive/Museo Civico Vicenza/Dagli Orti (A).

Hecate, goddess of **magic.** This supernatural being was also identified with Herodias, the wife of Herod who had demanded the **execution** of John the Baptist. Other names were Holda in Germanic areas and Lady Habundia, or abundance, in **France.** The queen of the fairies in **Scotland** had similar qualities. Whatever her name, the goddess was believed to travel at night, particularly on Thursdays, accompanied by swarms of followers, including the living and the souls of the dead. Honoring or welcoming the goddess and her followers could cause them to reward one with prosperity or gifts. From the *Canon Episcopi* to the thirteenth century, the Church identified this belief as a demonic illusion, again and again forbidding Christians from honoring Diana or believing that they or others traveled with the goddess and her followers. These beliefs were fairly minor sins, atoned for with a light penance.

This official attitude slowly changed in the later Middle Ages, when authorities began to believe that the goddess and her followers were not illusions, but real demons. Now honoring Diana and her followers was not superstition but demon worship, a much graver crime. In the late 1380s, two women, Sibillia and Pierina, were tried and condemned to death before the Inquisition in Milan for being followers of Diana, whom they called "Signora Oriente." The followers of Diana were also conceived in a much more hostile way, as evil beings who devoured children, essentially as demons. Diana crossed the **gender** barrier to be identified with the Devil only rarely—usually she was conceived of as a powerful demon. Diana played a much smaller role in the period of the early modern witch-hunt, where she and her troop were often replaced by **Satan** and his **sabbat.** Nevertheless, belief in this being continued in some places, as in the Sicilian **"Ladies from Outside,"** and was found by folklorists in Europe into the twentieth century.

REFERENCES: Norman Cohn. *Europe's Inner Demons: The Demonization of Christians in Medieval Christendom*, Rev. ed. Chicago: University of Chicago Press, 2000; Carlo Ginzburg. *Ecstacies: Deciphering the Witches's Sabbath*. Trans. Raymond Rosenthal. New York: Pantheon Books, 1991; Jeffrey Burton Russell. *Witchcraft in the Middle Ages*. Ithaca: Cornell University Press, 1972.

DOMINICAN ORDER

See Eymeric, Nicholas; Giordano da Bergamo; Jacquier, Nicholas; Kramer, Heinrich; Mazzolini, Silvestro; Nider, Johannes; Roman Inquisition; Spina, Bartolommeo; Vineti, Jean; Visconti, Girolamo.

DRUGS

See Medical Interpretations.

DUTCH REPUBLIC

See Northern Netherlands.

E

EICHSTÄTT WITCH-HUNTS

The small German prince-bishopric of Eichstätt became one of the most notorious centers of witch-hunting in the sixteenth and early seventeenth centuries. Witch trials occurred in 1494, 1532, 1535 and 1562, generally a time when German witch-hunting was a lull. The account of the 1532 trial was particularly widely distributed. There was a severe persecution, of which little record survives, during the first peak of German witch-hunting in the late sixteenth century. Several dozen people were burned from 1590 to 1593, while the principality was ruled by the zealous Catholic Reformation bishops Martin von Schaumburg, bishop from 1560 to 1590, and Caspar von Seckendorf, bishop from 1590 to 1595. Eichstätt was viewed as a model witch-hunting state in the legal opinion issued by the law faculty of the University of Ingolstadt in 1590, recommending harsher witch persecution in **Bavaria.**

The next peak in Eichstätt witch-hunting occurred under one of the most notorious of the Franconian "witch-bishops," Johann Christoph von Westerstetten (1565–1636). Fresh from initiating the great **Ellwangen** persecution as prince-provost, Westerstetten was appointed prince-bishop of Eichstätt in 1612. Witch-burnings began in 1617, a time of active persecution, but although many states abandoned witch-hunting in the early 1620s, Eichstätt continued, eventually executing witches every year from 1617 to 1630. Incomplete preservation of the records make it impossible to know the precise number of witches executed, although the witch-commissioner, Dr. Maximilian Kolb, active in Eichstätt from 1624 to 1628, claimed to have personally examined 274 witches that had subsequently been executed. The identities of 150 executed witches are documented. Like many German Catholic ecclesiastical states, Eichstätt had a special government body devoted to witch-hunting, the Witch Commission. The hunt was characterized by unrestrained **torture** and an obsession with getting tortured witches to name other witches. Two women from a village near the city of Eichstätt, one a fishwife and one a peasant, named 223 and 261 accomplices, respectively. Like all the great German witch-hunts, the Eichstätt hunt reached high into the social scale, often attacking the women associated with Eichstätt's male elite. Victims included three former burgomasters, eight burgomasters' wives, several innkeepers and brewers, the wife of the Town clerk, the daughter of the bishop's provincial administrator and other leading figures. The most distinguished victim was Maria Richel, wife of Chancellor Bartholomaus Richel. Maria was burned at the stake in 1621, after which Bartholomaus left Eichstätt and entered the service of the duke of Bavaria. One accused witch, the priest Johann Reichard (1573–1644), himself the son of a woman from the Bavarian town of Wemding who was burned as a witch in 1609, was tortured several times with great brutality, despite his priesthood. Reichard stubbornly refused to confess, passing the rest of his life in house arrest. Another priest residing in Eichstätt, the Jesuit and former Ingolstadt professor Kaspar Hell (1588–1634), bravely criticized the witch-hunt but had no ability to stop it. The hunt actually ended in 1630 during the general move against large-scale witch-hunting associated with the meeting of the Diet of the Holy Roman Empire held at Regensburg that year. Westerstetten was driven from Eichstätt by the Swedish army and died in exile.

REFERENCE: Wolfgang Behringer. *Witchcraft Persecutions in Bavaria: Popular Magic, Religious Zealotry, and Reason of State in Early Modern Europe*. Trans. J. C. Grayson and David Lederer. Cambridge: Cambridge University Press, 1997.

ELLWANGEN WITCH-HUNT

The principality of Ellwangen, in southwestern **Germany,** was about 155 square miles and governed by the head of the cathedral chapter of the town of Ellwangen, the prince-provost. There is documented evidence of witch-hunting in Ellwangen in 1528 and 1588–1589, but the territory is best known in witch-hunting history for an exceptionally bloody persecution from 1611 to 1618. Ellwangen, a Catholic territory, was remarkably free from both secular and higher Church authority. The prince-provost was exempt from the jurisdiction of the local bishop and subject only to the pope, and Ellwangen successfully forbade all appeals from its criminal courts. The witch-hunt was preceded by several years of bad weather, plague, the sickness and death of livestock and severe inflation. The first witch to be tried, in the spring of 1611, was a 70-year-old woman named Barbara Rüfin, who had a long-standing reputation as a witch; even her husband had called her one. She was initially accused of having killed **animals** by witchcraft and attempting to poison her son. After a series of interrogations under **torture** increasing in duration and intensity, Rüfin confessed to these crimes as well as to having made a pact with the Devil and having had **sex** with him. At this point, she lost mental control and continued alternately to confess to the charges against her and to deny them. Rüfin was executed on May 16, 1611.

This was only the beginning. The course of events is unclear because of the haphazard survival of documents, but by the end of the year more than one hundred witches had been executed over the course of 17 public **executions.** An annual letter from the Ellwangen Jesuits (the Jesuits had been established in Ellwangen in 1611) in 1612 mentioned 167 executed witches, and another Jesuit document from September 1613 mentioned a total of 303 victims of the witch-hunt. The hunt quickly expanded to reach accused witches differing from the old woman stereotype that Rüfin had presented. The wife of a judge was executed in the autumn of 1611, followed by the judge himself. In 1615, three priests and an organist were executed, after a long and painful ceremony degrading them from their priestly rank.

The witch-hunt was marked by increasingly perfunctory legal procedure and open corruption and abuse. Two guards confessed to revealing information about the prisoners' interrogations in exchange for bribes, as well as raping many of the imprisoned women. The usual form of confession in the hunt was of a woman confessing to intercourse with the Devil, usually claiming that she had not initially known him to be so. The Devil usually appeared in human as opposed to animal or monstrous form. Witches also confessed to various forms of *maleficium*. The **sabbat** played a central role in the witch-hunt, with witches constantly pressed to name those they had seen there. Some denunciations from the witch-hunt in 1588 were also revived.

Ellwangen's independence meant that no outside force could stop the hunt, although the nearby Protestant community of Oettingen protested Ellwangen's campaign. After a final flurry of 10 executions in 1618, the hunt ended, possibly due to exhaustion of the supply of suspects and fear that the reputation Ellwangen had acquired as a center of both witchcraft and witch persecution would hurt the town's economy. More than four hundred accused witches had met their deaths in Ellwangen during the hunt, but its effects extended far beyond the borders of the small community. **Accusations** from Ellwangen witches touched off another major hunt in nearby Schwabisch-Gmund, claiming more than 70 lives. The prince-provost of Ellwangen at the start of the hunt, Johann Christoph von Westerstetten (1565–1636), became prince-bishop of **Eichstätt** in 1612 and led a savage persecution there as well.

REFERENCE: H. C. Erik Midelfort. *Witch Hunting in Southwestern Germany, 1562–1684.* Stanford: Stanford University Press, 1972.

ENGLAND, WITCH-HUNTING IN

The witch-hunt in England, although not isolated from developments elsewhere, possessed a number of special characteristics, both at the level of the legal system and its treatment of witches and at the level of popular beliefs about witches and their powers.

The main difference between how England dealt with witches and Continental and Scottish witch-hunts was that England possessed a unique legal system, the common law developed in the Middle Ages, that differed from the systems used elsewhere in Europe, which were derived from Roman law. **Torture** as practiced on the Continent had no place in the English legal system, although

The Witch of Berkeley, said by William of Malmesbury to have been exhumed by her friend, the Devil, who took her away on his horse. Illustration appearing in Schedel's *Nurnberg Chronicle*, 852. © Mary Evans Picture Library.

milder and less effective forms of torture, such as repeated duckings, were sometimes employed. Without sanctioned torture to extract a confession, witchcraft was a difficult crime to prove, and English conviction rates were usually low, about one-fifth of the accused. In other jurisdictions in the early modern period, witches were burned, an adaptation of punishments for heresy. In England, the vast majority of witches were hanged for felony like common criminals. (A few were burned if their witchcraft was aggravated by another crime that merited burning. Women convicted of murdering their husbands, whether or not through witchcraft, were guilty of "petty treason" and burned.) The total number of witches executed in the English witch-hunt is estimated between five hundred and a thousand, although many more accused witches died in the notoriously filthy English jails or as victims of mob violence. The percentage of accused and executed witches who were women was even higher than the European average, about 90 percent. English witches were poor and often accused by richer neighbors. One of the most common charges against a witch in the English literature, particularly before 1590, was that she performed **maleficia** against a richer member of the community as revenge after being denied charity.

There were scattered instances of witch persecution in England in the later Middle Ages and the early sixteenth century, mostly political cases such as those of Edward III's (r. 1327–1377) mistress Alice Perrers (d. 1400) and Henry VI's (r. 1422–1471) aunt Eleanor **Cobham.** The first parliamentary statute addressing witchcraft was not passed until 1542, however, and it was hardly followed by a burst of **accusations** or trials. In 1547, it was repealed. What began active witch persecution in England was the accession of Queen Elizabeth (r. 1558–1603) in 1558. Elizabeth reestablished Protestantism after succeeding her Catholic half-sister Mary (r. 1553–1558), and many of the returning Protestant exiles from Mary's reign had been exposed to Protestant witch persecution on the Continent and were fired with the idea of making England a truly godly society. A necessary part of this project was rooting out **Satan's** agents, the witches, and the returned exiles were the first English promoters of an active campaign of persecution. A new act providing for the punishment of witches was passed in 1563. This act reserved the death penalty solely for killing or destroying human beings through witchcraft. Other offenses, such as destroying goods or chattel by witchcraft, was punishable by a year's imprisonment, or, on a second offense, forfeiture of the witch's property to the crown and life imprisonment. The first person known to have been charged under the act was Elizabeth Lowys of Great Waltham in Essex, charged in 1564 with *maleficia* including the killing of a child. She was sentenced to death, although no record of her **execution** has survived.

The offense of witchcraft as defined by the act of 1563 was fundamentally one of *maleficium*, causing harm by **magic,** rather than more explicitly demonic activities such as attendance at **sabbats** or entering into a **satanic pact.** The judicial apparatus of the English state in dealing with witchcraft usually reacted to the **accusations** brought before it, mostly those emerging from the disagreements inevitable among people living in small communities. The courts engaged in little aggressive witch-hunting during the Elizabethan and early Stuart periods. Lack of interest in the sabbat meant that witches were usually treated as individual malefactors, rather than being interrogated to name other witches whom they had encountered at a sabbat or otherwise knew. The English professional judiciary, the assize judges, seem often to have been more concerned with containing witch cases, keeping them from generating more accusations, than with rooting out witches.

The legal situation changed shortly after the accession of King **James I** in 1603. In his previous career as king of **Scotland,** James had established a reputation as a demonologist and fierce foe of witches, and his accession to the English throne was followed by a new witchcraft statute much more influenced by theoretical Continental and Scottish demonology. The act of 1604 broadened the range of *maleficia* subject to the death penalty to inflicting physical harm short of death to a person and destroying his or her goods. The act provided for a death sentence on all convictions on a second witchcraft offense. It also defined witchcraft not solely as *maleficium* but expanded the range of behavior subject to capital punishment to having any dealings with wicked spirits or stealing bodies or body parts from graves for magical purposes. In practice, however, the difference between the 1563 and 1604 acts had little influence on how courts dealt with witchcraft. Their primary interest remained *maleficium*, and the number of trials and persecutions actually diminished under James (despite some spectacular cases such as the 10 witches executed in **Lancashire** in 1612) and dwindled to almost nothing under his son Charles I. Intervention by the king and Privy Council prevented the execution of several more Lancashire witches in 1633. The waning of persecution was accompanied by a waning of interest in witch cases in the general society, judging by the fact that no pamphlets on witches or accounts of trials were published between 1621 and 1643.

One reason for the diminishing interest in persecuting witches was the opposition of the central government to the Puritan faction in the Church of England. Witch-hunting in Elizabethan and Early Stuart England had strongly puritan associations. The county of Essex, where Puritanism was strong, had by far the highest incident of witch-hunting. Some anti-Puritan members of the

Church of England were suspicious of persecuting witches because of its Puritan associations. The affair of the Puritan exorcist John **Darrell** in the late sixteenth century turned many leaders of the Church against witch-hunting as well as exorcism.

In demonology, England had a strong tradition of denial of the reality of witchcraft, founded by the country gentleman Reginald **Scot** and his *Discoverie of Witchcraft* (1584), the first major English demonology. Subsequent English skeptical writers, most of them drawing on Scot, included Sir Robert **Filmer,** Thomas **Ady,** John **Webster** and John **Wagstaffe.** There were also, however, distinguished English supporters of witchcraft belief and persecution, the most notable being William **Perkins,** an internationally respected Calvinist theologian, at the beginning of the seventeenth century and the promoter of the new **science,** Joseph **Glanvill,** in the late seventeenth century. Other English demonologists supporting witch persecution included George **Gifford,** Richard **Bernard,** Richard **Bovet,** Richard Baxter (1615–1691) and Richard Boulton.

Like English law, English popular witch belief had its peculiarities. Ordinary English people's concern with witchcraft always focused on *maleficium,* and ideas about the sabbat do not seem to have existed in English culture. English witches were conceptualized as performing *maleficium* on a small scale, rather than raising floods and plagues as some Continental witches did. Following a northern European pattern, disasters that English witches caused were also much less likely to be sexual than those of witches farther south—there are few English cases in which witches were charged with causing impotence or stillbirth. **Sex** with the Devil also rarely figured in English witchcraft episodes. Another difference was that the English were much more likely to associate witches with **familiar** spirits and animal familiars than were Continental people. Because it was believed that the witches suckled the familiars through "witches' teats" the search of the body of an accused witch for **witch's marks,** often carried out by women, was common in England and its colonies. In some ways, the relationship with the familiar occupied the place in English witchcraft belief that on the Continent and in Scotland was occupied by the relationship of the witch and the Devil.

The popular culture of England in its relation to witchcraft was not static and changed during the early modern period. Contact with learned ideas about witchcraft through trials affected some people's thinking and new ideas about witchcraft were also disseminated through the active English press. More than one hundred reports about witches and cases of witchcraft were published between 1563 and the repeal of the 1604 statute in 1736. These works shifted from their origins, which were close to bare transcriptions of trial documents, to richly detailed and partly fictional narratives in the 1590s. English popular thinking about witches was marked by an increasing interest in the dealings of witches and spirits, even if not necessarily the Devil. More emphasis was placed on witches meeting together, even if not in sabbat-style devil-worshipping orgies.

After the relative quiet on the witch front that characterized Charles's reign, witch-hunting began again in the religiously polarized English Civil War between Charles's Royalists and the Puritan-Parliamentary army. Matthew **Hopkins,** the Puritan "witch-finder general," demonstrated that in the peculiar situation of the Civil War, English culture and institutions did have the potential for developing large-scale witch panic. Hundreds of accused witches were brought before courts in East Anglia, with perhaps more than a hundred executed. The Hopkins persecutions also resembled European persecutions in that there was much more frequent mention made of contact with the Devil by the accused witches. The seeming anomalies of the scale and Satanic nature of the Hopkins panic have provoked much speculation on Hopkins's alleged importation of Continental demonology. Evidence for Hopkins's direct awareness of Continental writers is slim, but some of the English demonologists he read, such as King James and Bernard, did employ Continental concepts that Hopkins could have received secondhand. Many of the ideas about the Devil and his relationship with witches that appear in the records of Hopkins's witch-hunt, however, could have arisen in the English cultural context as an extension of ideas about familiar spirits.

Witch-hunting continued with diminishing intensity through the Puritan regimes of the 1650s and after the Restoration of the monarchy in 1660. In 1662, the **Lowestoft** witches, Rose Cullender and Amy Denny (often referred to in later literature as Amy Duny), were condemned by the Lord Chief Justice Matthew Hale (1609–1676), a leading figure in the development of the common law. One exception to the chronological pattern of English witch-hunting was the county of Devon in the west country, where witch-hunting seems to have peaked after 1650 and which is only recorded as executing four witches in the entire witch-hunt, all in the 1680s—the three **Bideford** witches in 1682, the last execution of a group of witches in England, and Alice Molland, the last English person known to have been executed as a witch, in 1685.

Generally persecution was waning in the late seventeenth century, accompanied by a rise in judicial doubts, not so much about the existence of witchcraft but about the possibility of proving it in a court. Chief Justice John Holt (1642–1710) got a particularly notorious reputation as a foe of witchcraft persecutions, dismissing several of them and even bringing a boy named Richard Hathaway to trial for falsely accusing a woman named Sarah Morduck of bewitching him. The last person convicted of witchcraft was Jane **Wenham,** who was later pardoned in 1712. The last witch trial occurred in Leicester in 1717, when an old woman and her daughter and son were accused of being witches. They were subjected to **flotation tests,** searched for witches marks and attacked with countermagic including the drawing of blood. The assize judges put a stop to it by declaring no true bill.

The late seventeenth and early eighteenth centuries were marked by growing disdain on the part of the upper classes for the beliefs of ordinary people—their "vulgar superstition." Belief that common people were too credulous of the powers of witches and the Devil was one source of upper-class skepticism. Upper-class people who continued to promote witch belief and advocated witch-hunting were increasingly identified with reactionary "Tory" opinions, divine right monarchy and opposition to religious toleration. The "Whigs," opponents of the Tories, presented themselves as defenders of rationality, and in 1736 a Whig-dominated Parliament repealed the statute of 1604. Ordinary people did not necessarily share opposition to witchcraft persecution, nor did all educated people. The founder of Methodism, John Wesley (1703–1791), accepted the existence of witchcraft and believed that doubt of its existence led to doubt of the truth of the **Bible.** Wesley's theological opponents often used charges of superstition against him, and after his death, Methodist leaders condemned belief in witches. The persistence of witch belief among ordinary people in the eighteenth century (and later) sometimes endangered suspected witches, such as Ruth **Osborne,** killed by an organized mob in 1751.

REFERENCES: Ian Bostridge. *Witchcraft and Its Transformations, c. 1650–c. 1750.* Oxford: Clarendon Press, 1997; Owen Davies. "Methodism, the Clergy, and the Popular Belief in Witchcraft and Magic." *History* 82 (1997): 252–265; C. L'Estrange Ewen. *Witchcraft and Demonianism: A Concise Account Derived from Sworn Depositions and Confessions Obtained in the Courts of England and Wales.* London: Heath Cranton, 1933; Marion Gibson. *Reading Witchcraft: Stories of Early English Witches.* London and New York: Routledge, 1999; Louise Jackson. "Witches, Wives and Mothers: Witchcraft Persecution and Women's Confessions in Seventeenth-Century England." In *The Witchcraft Reader,* ed. Darren Oldridge, 353–366. London and New York: Routledge, 2002; Alan Macfarlane. *Witchcraft in Tudor and Stuart Essex: A Regional and Comparative Study.* London: Routledge and Kegan Paul, 1970; Wallace Notestein. *A History of Witchcraft in England from 1558 to 1718.* Washington, D.C.: American Historical Association, 1911; James Sharpe. *Instruments of Darkness: Witchcraft in Early Modern England.* Philadelphia: University of Pennsylvania Press, 1996; Keith Thomas. *Religion and the Decline of Magic.* New York: Charles Scribner's Sons, 1971; Janet A. Thompson. *Wives, Widows, Witches and Bitches: Women in Seventeenth-Century Devon.* New York: Peter Lang, 1993; Frederick Valetta. *Witchcraft, Magic and Superstition in England, 1640–1670.* Aldershot, England: Ashgate, 2000; Alan R. Young. "Elizabeth Lowys: Witch and Social Victim." *History Today* 22 (1972): 251–261.

ERGOT

See Medical Interpretations.

ERRORES GAZARIORUM

Errores Gazariorum is an anonymous manuscript tract, probably written by a Savoyard inquisitor in the late 1430s. The literal meaning of the title is "Errors of the Cathars," but the work had little to do with the historical Cathars, a heretical group of the Middle Ages. Along with the contemporary work of Johannes **Nider** and Claude **Tholosan,** *Errores Gazariorum* is one of the earliest discussions of the full witch stereotype that would be the basis of the witch-hunt. It includes an elaborate description of the **sabbat** (which the author calls a "synagogue") and one of the earliest descriptions of an explicit **satanic pact** concluded between a witch and the Devil, and written in blood. *Errores Gazariorum* also endorses the reality of witch flight. The author does not distinguish by **gender** in discussing witches and refers to witches as male. The sabbat includes the devouring of murdered children, the **kiss** bestowed on the Devil's anus, **sex** orgies including male-male and incestuous sex, and the desecration of the Host. The author emphasizes the preparation of **magical** potions and powders under **Satan's** direction, giving elaborate recipes.

REFERENCES: Michael Bailey. "The Medieval Concept of the Witches' Sabbath." *Exemplaria: A Journal of Theory in Medieval and Renaissance Studies* 8 (1996): 419–439; Alan Charles Kors and Edward Peters, eds. *Witchcraft in Europe 400–1700: A Documentary History.* 2d ed. Revised by Edward Peters. Philadelphia: University of Pennsylvania Press, 2001.

ESCHATOLOGY

By far the most common explanation for the increase in witchcraft cases to be put forth in the early modern period was that **Satan** was raging in the last period before the end of the world. This belief drew on the **Bible,** notably Revelations and Paul's Second Epistle to the Thessalonians. It was held by both Catholics and Protestants, by learned demonologists and ordinary people. During exorcisms, even devils were made to endorse this theory. Demonologists who supported this theory included Heinrich **Kramer,** Lambert **Daneau,** Anton **Praetorius, James VI and I,** Henri **Boguet,** Martin **del Rio,** William **Perkins** and **Cotton Mather,** as well as a host of others. Even Johann **Weyer,** who denied the guilt of accused witches, believed that the increase in false **accusations** was a sign of Satan's frenzied activity in the last days.

The early modern period was a great age of apocalyptic thinking, and it was generally believed that the perceived increase in sin, bloody conflicts, bizarre natural phenomena and witchcraft and **magic** were all linked as harbingers of the second coming of Christ. Witchcraft was also linked to the apocalypse through the growing obsession with Antichrist. This played out differently in Protestant and Catholic **confessional** thinking. For Catholics, for whom Antichrist was a person, his power to perform false miracles with the help of the Devil was perfectly analogous to the power of witches and magicians, and he was the greatest of witches. For Protestants, for whom Antichrist was an institution, usually the Catholic Church or the Papacy, the proclaimed "magical" powers of Catholic priests to perform such supernatural acts as changing wine into blood with words during the Mass or exorcise devils made them anti-Christian witches. The dubious reputation of many medieval popes as witches also enabled Protestants to link them with Antichrist's witchcraft. Both Protestants and Catholics used the identifications of witches with Antichrist to urge magistrates to more zealous persecution of witches in the last days.

REFERENCE: Stuart Clark. *Thinking with Demons: The Idea of Witchcraft in Early Modern Europe.* Oxford: Clarendon Press, 1997.

ESSLINGEN WITCH-HUNT

The Free Imperial city of Esslingen in southwest **Germany** saw a severe witch-hunt in the period 1662–1666. Esslingen was a Lutheran city, and the ground for the witch-hunt had been prepared by the Lutheran minister Johann Jakob Faber, who called for a rigorous witch-hunt based on the idea of the **satanic pact** (while also calling for moderation in the use of **torture**). The witch-hunt began when a 10-year-old boy from the village of Vaihingen (most of the witch-hunt victims would come from villages subject to Esslingen rather than from the city itself) confessed voluntarily to witchcraft, setting off a chain of confessions by other children. The importance placed on children as informers would be a characteristic Esslingen shared with other major late-seventeenth-century Protestant witch-hunts such as **Mora** and **Salem.** One denounced child, a 17-year-old boy, denounced 17 others. The boy, along with all those he denounced whose fates are known, was executed. In 1662, the first year of the witch-hunt, at least 56 people were suspected of witchcraft, and many were executed. That summer, the magistrates appealed for a legal opinion on **execution** to the law faculty of Tübingen, Lutheran Germany's leading university. When Tübingen's response proved unsatisfactory, suggesting that the confessions had been produced by demonic delusions and rebuking Esslingen for its enthusiastic use of torture, they turned to Strasbourg, which obligingly recommended execution. (On a subsequent occasion when Strasbourg's response to a request for authorization of torture proved unsatisfactory, Esslingen procured a favorable opinion from the obscure law faculty of the University of Altdorf.)

The leading spirit of the Esslingen persecution was the judge of the town, Daniel Hauff, who was unusually learned in demonology and projected his personal obsessions with the control of adolescent sexuality onto the trials. Male homosexuality and bestiality played unusually prominent roles in the Esslingen witch-hunt. The Esslingen persecution provides one of the few examples in the entire European witch-hunt of a male witch, in this case an adolescent boy, confessing to **sex** with the Devil. This may have been based on the boy's actual recollections of being seduced by another servant. Instances of bestiality also figured heavily in the confessions Hauff extorted.

After starting with great activity, the Esslingen persecution became more quiescent in 1663 and 1664, when only one execution is recorded. The pace picked up again in 1665, when eight executions are recorded, then wound down again in 1666, after Hauff's premature death. No executions are recorded that year, and the remaining suspects were given minor penalties or simply let go. In all, at least 214 persons were under suspicion of witchcraft in the Esslingen witch-hunt, at least 79 arrested, and at least 37 executed. Along with a similar but smaller persecution in the nearby city of Reutlingen, the Esslingen witch-hunt was the last witch-hunt involving large numbers of defendants in southwestern Germany.

REFERENCES: Robin Briggs. *Witches and Neighbors: The Social and Cultural Context of European Witchcraft.* New York: Penguin, 1996; H. C. Erik Midelfort. *Witch Hunting in Southwestern Germany, 1562–1684.* Stanford: Stanford University Press, 1972.

ESTONIA, WITCH-HUNTING IN

Estonia lay in the eastern Baltic, the last area of Europe to be Christianized. Both Protestant and Catholic church authorities (the territory passed from Polish to Swedish rule) were concerned to end remaining pagan practices, such as worship in sacred groves. This did not lead to large-scale witch-hunting, however. No large witch-hunt emerged in the territory, and the small trials that did occur, involving an individual or small group, emerged from peasant **accusations** of *maleficia*. Common types of *maleficia* in Estonia included cursing beer so that the drinker would be infected with frogs, toads, worms or serpents and wreaking damage as a **werewolf** or werebear. Notions of the **satanic pact** and night flight were introduced by magistrates or forced from accused witches under **torture,** which was commonly used. **Flotation tests** were also common, with the first recorded example in 1558.

The first recorded **execution** of a witch in Estonia occurred in 1527, in an area close to Tallinn. Witch-hunting reached a first peak in the 1620s and 1630s, with a total of 48 recorded trials out of the 140 which historian Maia Madar has recovered (patchy survival of records makes any definitive conclusions about the Estonian witch-hunt impossible). This peak is associated with the work of the Swedish ecclesiastical agent Hermann Samson (1579–1643), author of *Nine Selected and Well-Grounded Witch Sermons* (1626). The second peak of Estonian witch-hunting was in the 1690s, with 24 recorded trials. The campaign against paganism might have contributed to the fact that many of the accused were **cunning folk,** and they were disproportionately male. The overall total of the indicted is 116 men to 77 women, although men comprise a minority of the recorded executions, 26 men to 29 women (there are a total of 65 recorded executions, but some are of unknown **gender**). Execution was by burning, rarely commuted to beheading. The last execution was of Tattra Santi Michel in 1699, and the last recorded trial was in 1725, shortly after the territory had passed from Swedish to **Russian** rule.

REFERENCES: Juhan Kahk. "Estonia II: The Crusade Against Idolatry." In *Early Modern European Witchcraft: Centres and Peripheries*, ed. Bengt Ankarloo and Gustav Henningsen, 273–284. Oxford: Clarendon Press, 1990; Maia Madar. "Estonia I: Werewolves and Poisoners." In *Early Modern European Witchcraft: Centres and Peripheries*, ed. Bengt Ankarloo and Gustav Henningsen, 257–272. Oxford: Clarendon Press, 1990.

EVIL EYE

Belief in the evil eye or fascination, a persons' ability to cause harm by their glance, was and is widespread throughout Europe, Asia and Africa. Magicians and witches were not the only persons thought to possess it; the belief that a menstruating or an old woman can cause harm by her glance is an ancient phenomenon. The person casting the evil eye was not always thought to wish harm. Italians had a concept of a peculiar sort of involuntary witch called a *jettator*, whose glance caused harm and bad luck completely unbeknownst to him or her. Scholars might identify this kind of evil eye as a form of natural **magic.** The death of babies and small children, a common event in any early modern community, was frequently blamed on the evil eye, and medical manuals treated the evil eye along with other normal hazards of childhood should a young person be suspected of possessing it. **Countermagic** to the evil eye took many forms. In **Scotland,** livestock could be protected from the evil eye by braiding rowan in their tails, and a witch's evil eye could be neutralized by drawing blood from her forehead. Countermagic often included wearing protective amulets, but as with other kinds of countermagic, these were identified by religious authorities as illicit, possibly Satanic.

In witchcraft cases, the evil eye was a form of *maleficium*, arguably the purest form of *maleficium* because it operated solely by the witch's malice, rather than the properties of herbs, ointments, potions or charms. Witches were frequently accused of employing an evil eye to cast their spells both by ordinary people and by learned demonologists. Sometimes bewitched persons seem to feel particular torment when a witch cast her gaze at them. The evil eye provided an easy explanation for how a witch caused children or livestock to die, and any interest in a particular person shown by a suspected witch would be cause for thinking her preparing to cast the evil eye.

REFERENCE: Alan Dundes, ed. *The Evil Eye: A Folklore Casebook.* New York and London: Garland, 1981.

EXECUTIONS

The use of burning as the ultimate judicial punishment for a witch, standard in Continental Europe and **Scotland,** derived from the identification of witchcraft as heresy. Burning was the punishment given relapsed heretics, for whom it was appropriate given its similarity to the flames of hell they would soon be entering. The practice claimed biblical sanction, referring to the Gospel of John, 15:16, in which burning is described as the punishment for "withered branches." Burning was also associated with the purification of the community.

The importance of burning was mainly symbolic, and many jurisdictions, even ones of intense witch-hunting activity, provided the small mercy of actually killing the witch before burning, usually by strangulation. In **Sweden** and parts of **Germany,** witches were killed by the sword and then burned. On the other extreme were those rare occasions, notably the execution of the **Pappenheimer** witches in **Bavaria,** where **torture** and mutilation was added to the execution before the burning to make the whole event more horrific and presumably to deter any potential witches observing the incident. Executions for all crimes were nearly always public in early modern Europe, and part of their function was as a "theater of justice," where both the evil of the criminals (and, it was hoped, their repentance) and the justice of the authorities were represented.

The exception to the overall pattern was **England** and its offshoots in North America. There the crime of witchcraft was not related to heresy (heretics

Public burning of witches at the stake at Derneburg Harz, Germany. From a broadside newsletter dated October 1555. © The Art Archive / The Art Archive.

were burned in England in the sixteenth century) but to harm. Hanging was the appropriate punishment. There were a few occasions when witches were burned in an English jurisdiction, but that was when they were guilty of a crime meriting punishment by burning, in addition to their witchcraft.

REFERENCE: Brian P. Levack. *The Witch-hunt in Early Modern Europe*. London and New York: Longman, 1987.

EYMERIC, NICHOLAS (1320–1393)

The fourteenth-century Aragonese inquisitor Nicholas Eymeric was the most influential writer on inquisitorial procedures well into the early modern period. Eymeric twice came to grips with the problem of witchcraft and sorcery, once in a treatise of 1369, "Treatise against invokers of demons" and then as part of his massive summation of inquisitorial principles and practices, *Directorium Inquisitorum*, first circulated in 1376. Eymeric's *Directorium*, which incorporated much of the "Treatise," remained the basis of inquisitorial practice for centuries. No book in the field could rival its authority, and most other inquisitorial manuals relied heavily on it. With the advent of printing, the *Directorium* was printed in 1503, and in an expanded edition sponsored by the **Roman Inquisition** with a commentary by the sixteenth-century Spanish canon lawyer Francisco Pena in 1578. This version went through four more editions in the following decades.

Eymeric drew on wide reading, particularly in the works of his fellow Dominican, the theologian Thomas Aquinas (1224?–1274), and in the **magical** texts that he had encountered in his career. He also drew on decades of experience in the Inquisition. His approach to witchcraft was characteristic of the late medieval period in that his principal concern was not the satanic witch but the demon-invoking ritual magician. The key issue for Eymeric and subsequent inquisitors working in the tradition he defined was magic's heretical nature. This was the only factor making magic an Inquisition matter at all, and part of Eymeric's agenda was establishing that the Inquisition did possess jurisdiction over magicians. In determining the heresy of a magician or a magical act, attention should be paid to two issues. The first is whether the magician rendered to devils that worship and honor that should be reserved to God, *latria*, or the saints, *dulia*. Sacrifice to a demon, promising it obedience—these things were latria. Latria could also take more subtle forms—to ask a demon to do something beyond his powers is to ascribe to him powers belonging to God, and thus heretical latria. Pena applies this concept to the case of love magic, common in the sixteenth century. If the magician or witch expects the Devil to tempt the person bewitched to fall in love, this is in accordance with the nature of the Devil as a tempter, and not in itself heretical. If **Satan** or another devil is expected to force the person to fall in love, overriding free will, this is a power belonging to God, and thus to ascribe it to the Devil is heretical. Dulia could take the form of invoking God for assistance through a demon as if it were a saint. Eymeric thought most magical actions involved paying reverence to Devils on some level, whether or not the magician consciously thought so. Pena stated that those forms of magic that depended only on an object's natural properties, such as natural magic, astrology and alchemy, were not heretical.

The second question in determining the heretical nature of a magical act was whether the magician misused anything associated with the sacraments of the church, such as the ceremony of baptism or a consecrated wafer. The degree of heresy depended on what the magician thought he was doing, which made inquisitorial courts, unlike secular courts, which focused on a witch's actions, interested in suspected witches' beliefs about their actions. Eymeric's picture of heretical magic differed from that of early modern texts such as Heinrich **Kramer's** *Malleus Maleficarum* (1486), which pictured the offender not as a learned man, but as an old woman, and paid far less attention to the procedures used. Eymeric also paid far less attention to the goal of magic; divination was much more important to him than ***maleficia***. Eymeric's influence on the Roman Inquisition was one reason why the early modern witch stereotype played little role in Italian witch-hunting.

REFERENCES: Norman Cohn. *Europe's Inner Demons: The Demonization of Christians in Medieval Christendom*. Rev. ed. Chicago: University of Chicago Press, 2000; Ruth Martin. *Witchcraft and the Inquisition in Venice, 1550–1650*. Oxford: Blackwell, 1989.

F

FAMILIARS

The belief that witches had personal demons who assisted them in their wicked deeds, usually taking the form of small **animals,** was not universal during the witch-hunt. Although it is found in many places, the major areas where belief in familiar spirits was strong were **England** (and its cultural offshoot in America, **New England**) and the Basque country. For the **Basques,** familiars nearly always took the form of toads wearing clothes. The toads were fed with a special mixture prepared in the witch's house, and were powerful beings that had to be treated well and propitiated. Sometimes a child being taught to be a witch would have the responsibility of herding the toads (shepherding was a common occupation among Basques) while the adult witches were at the **sabbat.** If the child touched or harmed the toad, she would be punished. The **Spanish Inquisition** searched the witch's houses for dressed toads, among other things, but never found one.

The most developed mythology surrounding familiars was found in England, although even in England familiars did not appear in all witchcraft **accusations** or trials. English familiars were sometimes toads, but could take many other forms. The most common were cats and dogs, common domesticated animals, but they could also be ferrets, rats or insects. The familiars were not animals, but spirits taking on their shape. Familiars were often described in ways similar to fairies, particularly one type of fairy called a fairy hobman. The familiar, or sometimes several familiars, was given to the witch by the Devil or sometimes inherited from a witch-mother or other witch. It performed evil deeds itself and encouraged and assisted the witch in doing them as well. Usually, the familiar was actually fed from the witch's body in a diabolic parody of motherhood. Sometimes the familiar merely sucked blood from a witch's finger, or licked up blood after she pricked herself with a pin, but increasingly during the English witch-hunt, female witches were described as possessing a "**witch's mark**" or "witch's teat," a supernumerary nipple through which the familiar sucked her blood.

The magic circle of a witch with skull and her familiars from *De Spectris*, by Ludovicus Lavater, 1527–1586. © The Art Archive/Dagli Orti (A).

The familiar seems to have originally been associated with medieval learned magicians who were reputed to command devils. The idea of the familiar feeding from the witch's blood shows up early in the history of the English witch-hunt. The first surviving reference to it was in Yorkshire in 1510, when an investigation into **magical** treasure seeking by the archbishop produced an account of a schoolmaster, John Steward, who had three familiars in the shape of bees who fed on drops of blood from his fingers. The first use of the idea presented in a trial of the blood-drinking familiar was in 1566, when an Essex witch, Elizabeth Francis, claimed that she had been given a familiar in the form of a cat named **Satan** as a gift from her grandmother, who first compelled her to renounce God and the **Bible.** Satan was fed with a drop of her blood every time he performed a service for her, including procuring 18 sheep and killing a man who had refused to marry her after having had **sex** with her. The importance of familiar spirits was accentuated by the witchcraft act of 1604, which made dealings with evil spirits a crime in itself, something which previously had not been the case. Familiars served a number of purposes in witchcraft stories. Sometimes accused witches blamed the most potent acts of *maleficium* on their familiar spirits. Another Elizabethan witch, Joan Prentice, claimed in her trial at **Chelmsford** that she had ordered her familiar, a ferret, to nip a neighbor's child but not to hurt it, but the familiar had disobeyed her orders and boasted of nipping in such a way as to cause the child's death. The defense strategy was unsuccessful. Familiars could also be used as evidence against a witch, and sometimes a close relationship between a person and an animal, or the finding of an animal such as a toad in a search of a person's house, was considered evidence of witchcraft. Familiars also served to take the place of the Devil, given that many English witches did not deal with the Devil directly. This is fairly obvious in the case of Elizabeth Francis's "Satan," with whom her relationship resembled that of a witch with the Devil in **satanic pacts.** (Familiars did not always have names that referred directly to their status; many had names usually given to pets, such as Jack or Piggin.) Sometimes the familiar demanded the witch's soul in exchange for carrying out evil deeds. As the familiar mythology developed along with the English witch-hunt, familiars became more closely linked with the Devil.

REFERENCES: Gustav Henningsen. *The Witches' Advocate: Basque Witchcraft and the Spanish Inquisition (1609–1614)*. Reno: University of Nevada Press, 1980; James Sharpe. *Instruments of Darkness: Witchcraft in Early Modern England*. Philadelphia: University of Pennsylvania Press, 1996; Emma Wilby. "The Witch's Familiar and the Fairy in Early Modern England and Scotland." *Folklore* 111 (2000): 283–305.

FAUST LEGEND

Changing ideas about witchcraft, **magic** and the Devil in the early modern period are reflected in the changing forms of the legend of Faust, the German magician who sold his soul to the Devil for twenty-four years of knowledge and power. Faust was based on a real person, Georg or Johann Faust, the first surviving mention of whom comes in a letter by the Benedictine abbot and magician Johannes Trithemius (1462–1516), dated 1507. Georg Faust (the name "Faust," meaning "fortunate" in Latin, may have been an assumed one), a graduate of the University of Kraków, seems to have been a disreputable professor, one of the many magicians and occult charlatans who haunted the universities and courts of early-sixteenth-century **Germany.** Faust was a colorful character, who referred to the Devil as his brother-in-law. He was fairly well-known— Martin Luther (1483–1546), who despised the magic Faust practiced, mentioned him in table talk as one of the Devil's allies. Georg Faust was often charged with satanic magic, but the specific idea of the **satanic pact** was not yet associated with him. Faust ceases to be referred to as a living man around 1540.

Faust's literary afterlife begins with collections of *exempla*, anecdotes for Lutheran pastors to use in their sermons. Faust figures as a satanic magician, and his ultimate fate of damnation warns hearers against trafficking with the Devil. The witch-hunting opponent Johann **Weyer** also referred to Faust in his *Of the Tricks of Demons* (1586), pointing out that magicians like Faust, rather than poor and deluded old women, were appropriate targets for legal punishment. Collections of Faust stories also circulated in manuscript. A "biography" of Faust based on the legends and incorporating the idea of the satanic pact appeared in 1587 in a German book *Historie of Dr. Johann Faustus, the World-Famous Sorcerer and Black Magician, How he Contracted Himself to the Devil for a certain Time, What Strange Adventures he Saw and Pursued during this Time, Until in the End he Received his Just Reward, Compiled and Printed, Mostly from his own Writings, as a Dreadful Example, Ghastly Case Study, and Faithful Warning to all Ambitious, Curious, and Godless Men*, known as the Faustbook. Although the book is entertaining with a variety of amusing anecdotes of Faust's pranks, its primary purpose was didactic. Its publisher, Johann Spies, was a prominent conservative Lutheran, whose usual output consisted not of entertaining books for the common people, but works of Lutheran theology and church law.

HISTORIA

Von D. Johañ
Fausten/dem weitbeschreyten
Zauberer vnd Schwartzkünstler/
Wie er sich gegen dem Teuffel auff eine be-
nandte zeit verschrieben/ Was er hierzwischen für
seltzame Abentheawr gesehen/ selbs angerich-
tet vnd getrieben/ biß er endtlich seinen wol verdienten Lohn
empfangen.

Mehrertheils auß seinen eygenen
hinderlassenen Schrifften/ allen hochtragen-
den fürwitzigen vnd Gottlosen Menschen zum schecklí-
chen Beyspiel/abschewlichem Exempel/vnnd trew-
hertziger Warnung zusammen gezo-
gen/ vnd in Druck ver-
fertiget.

IACOBI IIIL
Seyt Gott vnderthänig widerstehet dem
Teuffel/so fleuhet er von euch.

CVM GRATIA ET PRIVILEGIO.

Gedruckt zu Franckfurt am Mayn/
durch Johann Spies.

M. D. LXXXVII.

Title page from the oldest extant book about Dr. Johannes Faust, printed by Johann Spies, Frankfurt, 1587. © Dover Pictorial Archive.

Spies's book, the actual author or compiler of which is unknown, had several didactic functions. The story of Faust's agreement with Mephostophiles (an invented name of a demon appearing for the first time) both links the hermetic and learned magic associated with Faust with demonism and witchcraft and furnishes an object lesson of the degradation to which pride and arrogant curiosity like Faust's can lead. Unlike previous medieval stories of satanic pact, Faust specifically promises to harm Christian people, a provision associated with the satanic pacts of early modern witches. Spies's Lutheranism can be seen in the fiercely anti-Catholic tone of the work, which features Faust's visit to a Rome pictured as overrun with prostitutes and clerical debauchery. The Faustbook's association of Faust with the University of Wittenberg, then controlled by liberal, or "crypto-Calvinist," Lutherans, also served Spies's conservative Lutheran purposes.

Whether or not the Faustbook's readers were deriving the proper moral lessons from it, the book was wildly popular, going through further printings and a pirated edition the same year, being brought out again by Spies in 1588, and eventually going through 18 German editions as well as expansions and adaptations before the end of the sixteenth century. A Dutch translation was published in 1592 and a French in 1598. The first surviving edition of the English translation by "P. F." dates from 1592, although there is some evidence of an earlier edition. The English Faustbook, which differs in many areas from the German original, is the basis of the most important artistic work to emerge from the Faust legend in the early modern period, Christopher Marlowe's (1564–1593) play *Doctor Faustus*, written between 1588 and 1593. Marlowe's play differs from the Faustbook in its more sympathetic portrayal of Faust, with which whose desire for power and learning Marlowe at times sympathizes, and its portrayal of Mephistopheles—the first devil figure in Western literature to show psychological complexity and hints of moral ambiguity. Such was the power of Marlowe's portrayal of Faust that some early modern audiences feared that the stage Faust's conjurations would actually raise the Devil. Faust plays, possibly based on Marlowe, played on several recorded occasions in central Europe in the seventeenth century.

Interest in Faust diminished in the early seventeenth century, but then revived again in 1674 with the publication of a new German Faustbook, adapted from an older version by the **physician** Nicolaus Pfitzer. In 1683, a German scholar published a work investigating the origins of the Faust story. Faust plays continued to be put on into the eighteenth century, and 1746 saw the first recorded performance of a Faust puppet play, a theatrical form in which Faust would continue to be presented to European audiences into the nineteenth century. Faust himself remained a theme for high as well as popular culture, being the subject of a never-completed play by the German Enlightenment thinker Gotthold Ephraim Lessing (1729–1781) and the famous *Faust* of Johann Wolfgang von Goethe (1749–1832), which broke dramatically with the legend by having Faust saved rather than damned at the end. The ideas of the Devil and the satanic pact could now be treated as principally of literary interest.

The Faustian witch, the learned man interested in knowledge and political power, played a considerably lesser role in the witch-hunt than the standard witch stereotype—the marginal old woman interested mainly in the power to perform **maleficia** and win a modest degree of economic security. Nonetheless, "Faustian" witches did suffer during the witch-hunt. The same year as the first publication of Spies's Faustbook saw the first **accusation** against another German, Dr. Dietrich **Flade,** among the most learned men ever to be tried, convicted and executed for witchcraft.

REFERENCES: Peter Boerner and Sidney Johnson, eds. *Faust through Four Centuries: Retrospect and Analysis*. Tübingen, Max Niemeyer Verlag, 1989; R. J. Fehrenbach. "A Pre-1592 English Faust Book and the Date of Marlowe's Doctor Faustus." *The Library*, Seventh Series 2 (2001): 327–335; Philip Mason Palmer and Robert Pattison More. *The Sources of the Faust Tradition: From Simon Magus to Lessing*. New York: Haskell House, [1911] 1965; Jeffrey Burton Russell. *Mephistopheles: The Devil in the Modern World*. Ithaca and London: Cornell University Press, 1986.

FEMINIST HISTORIOGRAPHY

Although witches had been associated with outcast and rebellious women in general since the Romantic Era of the early nineteenth century, dynamic interaction between the feminist movement and the historiography of European witchcraft began in the late 1960s, with the rise of feminism in and out of the academy. The first group to identify radical feminists with witches was the Women's International Terrorist Conspiracy from Hell, a radical feminist group founded in 1968 in New York City. Interaction between feminism and witchcraft studies took a number of different forms. One which has had a great deal of influence on American culture at large, although not much among historians or European feminists, was the construction of the myth of the "Burning Times." This viewed the witch-hunt as a male campaign against women, an extreme case of the male violence that many feminists saw as the underlying principle of patriarchy. This analysis of the witch-hunt coincided with the early 1970s shift in American feminism away from public sphere issues like equal pay for equal work to issues of rape and domestic violence. Its foremost champions were not early modern scholars, but feminist theoreticians and intellectuals such as Mary Daly, Barbara Ehrenreich and Deirdre English. These and other feminist painted early modern witches as wise natural healers and **midwives,** representatives of a millennia-old tradition of women deriving wisdom from their connection to the earth, and victims of male authority in state, church and organized medicine. This invocation of a continuous underground female wisdom tradition has affinities to neopagan and Wiccan interpretations of the witch-hunt and is supported by many modern feminist witches. It also can be combined with the **Murray thesis,** a less **gender-**specific version of the same argument. For these feminist writers, witches were martyrs to male violence, part of a continuum with victims of Chinese foot binding, clitoridectomy and rape. Writers in this tradition tended to estimate the **numbers of victims** in the millions, the figure of nine million being one of the most common. The witch-hunt, the "Holocaust of Women," has sometimes been paralleled explicitly to the Nazi attempted genocide of the Jews in World War II. Daly's coinage for the witch-hunt was "gynocide." Work in this tradition is not based on empirical study of the witch-hunt.

Feminism affected the professional scholarly study of the witch-hunt in a somewhat different way—by making the question of gender central to explanation and analysis. Although everyone knew that the vast majority of accused and executed witches had been women, this was not usually put at the center of the analysis. Feminist scholars analyzed the gender of witches as an expression of the Western tradition of misogyny. Witches, essentially, were punished because they were women, particularly because they were women who, through their economic, social or sexual independence, threatened patriarchal authority. (Feminist historians have tended to ignore male victims of the witch-hunt until recently.) The favorite demonological text of feminist scholars of witchcraft (and of feminist writers in general) was the *Malleus Maleficarum* (1486) of Heinrich **Kramer**, precisely because it was by far the most misogynist of the classical witch-hunting writings and provided a number of juicy quotes. Contemporary practitioners of this school of feminist analysis include Anna Llewellyn Barstow, Marianne Hester and Carol F. Karlsen.

Feminist historiography had a complex relation to the preceding dominant tradition, **liberal historiography.** Feminists and liberals agreed on treating the witch-hunt as important and relevant to modern society, rather than being merely of antiquarian interest. Both sympathized with the victims and denounced the theorists and practitioners of witch-hunting. Where they differed is that feminists placed their emphasis on gender and misogyny rather than intolerance and repressive church authority. Feminists were less inclined to distinguish between Protestant and Catholic witch-hunters and were also much more skeptical of the heroes of the liberal story, male opponents of witch-hunting such as Johann **Weyer** and Reginald **Scot.** They pointed out that the opponents of witch-hunting tended to portray women as mentally limited and emotionally unstable fools prone to a variety of delusions, which were mistaken for witchcraft. Rather than male opponents of witch-hunting, feminist historians tended to identify with witches themselves. This sometimes led them to underestimate the degree to which women were not only accused witches, but also accusers.

During the 1980s and 1990s, feminist scholarship on the witch-hunt, like feminist scholarship in general, has moved away from simplistic "men versus women" interpretations. It has also moved away from the emphasis on accused witches as pure victims and has attempted to reconstruct the rhetorical and other strategies accused women used. New analyses, such as those of Purkiss, Willis, Lyndal Roper and Sigrid Brauner, have focused on gender-specific aspects of witchcraft and witch-hunting such as the connection between witchcraft and motherhood or the construction of the witch as an antonym of the good woman. Feminist scholars have used **psychoanalytic** categories to understand both witches and witch-hunters. Scholars have also examined the ways differences between women could result in witch **accusations.** Feminist scholarship has also influenced witchcraft scholarship in general in that all serious historians of the subject, feminists or not, now recognize the necessity of dealing with gender issues and gender analysis.

REFERENCES: Anne Llewellyn Barstow. *Witchcraze: A New History of the European Witch Hunts.* San Francisco: Pandora, 1994; Sigrid Brauner. *Fearless Wives and Frightened Shrews: The Construction of the Witch in Early Modern Germany.* Amherst: University of Massachusetts Press, 1995; Mary Daly. *Gyn/Ecology: The Metaethics of Radical Feminism.* Boston: Beacon Press, 1978; Barbara Ehrenreich and Deidre English. *Witches, Midwives and Nurses: A History of Women Healers.* New York: Feminist Press, 1973; Marianne Hester. *Lewd Women and Wicked Witches: A Study in the Dynamics of Male Domination.* London and New York: Routledge, 1992; Carol F. Karlsen. *The Devil in the Shape of a Woman: Witchcraft in Colonial New England.* New York: Norton, 1987; Diane Purkiss. *The Witch in History: Early Modern and Twentieth-Century Representations.* London and New York: Routledge, 1996; Lyndal Roper. *Oedipus and the Devil: Witchcraft, Sexuality and Religion in Early Modern Europe.* New York: Routledge, 1994; Deborah Willis. *Malevolent Nuture: Witch-Hunting and Maternal Power in Early Modern England.* Ithaca: Cornell University Press, 1995.

FILMER, SIR ROBERT (C. 1590–1653)

Although better known as a conservative political theorist, the English baronet Sir Robert Filmer also anonymously published a short but ingenious work of witchcraft skepticism, *An Advertisement to the Jury-Men of England, touching Witches. Together with a difference between a Hebrew and an English Witch* (1653). Filmer was an experienced magistrate in the county of Kent and former believer in witches, who had been shocked by a recent witch-hunt in Maidstone in 1652. He used clever legal arguments to demonstrate the questionable status of witchcraft trials. For example, if, as all witchcraft theorists agreed, the true power came not from the witch but from the Devil, the witch was but an accessory to the crime and could not be convicted until the crime was proved on the true perpetrator, **Satan.** Because Satan could hardly be brought before an English court, the convictions of witches had no legal standing.

Filmer's principal target among demonologists was William **Perkins.** As a conservative Royalist in the aftermath of the English Civil War, Filmer detested

Perkins's Calvinist theology, which he blamed for rebellion and the **execution** of Charles I in 1649. He makes a slashing and somewhat unfair attack against Perkins's 18 types of evidence of the guilt of a witch. He also denies the central concept of Perkins's demonology, the **satanic pact.** This is one way in which Filmer's thought on witches is connected to his political theory. Just as Filmer detested theories that based political authority on contracts between subjects and sovereigns, theories which had in his mind led to civil war and regicide, he attacked theories of witchcraft resting on the Satanic pact—a contract between a witch and the Devil. Filmer claimed, with some justification, that although the witchcraft act of 1604 made dealings with spirits criminal in themselves, the usual practice of English judges was to convict only for actual evil deeds, *maleficium*. Filmer attacked the ambiguities inherent in the idea of the pact, pointing out that because the witch could evade the contract simply by repentance, it had no legal force, and "the devill without doubt notwithstanding all his craft hath far the worse part of the bargain." Theories of contract, Filmer claimed, had no scriptural warrant but had been taken over by Protestant writers like Perkins from Catholics like Martin **del Rio.**

REFERENCES: Ian Bostridge. *Witchcraft and Its Transformations, c. 1650–c. 1750,* Oxford: Clarendon Press, 1997; James Sharpe. *Instruments of Darkness: Witchcraft in Early Modern England.* Philadelphia: University of Pennsylvania Press, 1996.

FINLAND, WITCH-HUNTING IN

Finland, a possession of the Swedish crown in the early modern period, went through two distinct phases of witch-hunting. In the first, the principal targets were practitioners of traditional **magic,** whose primary offense was the commission of *maleficia* and who were usually men. In the second, which lasted for a few decades in the late seventeenth century, the importation of European notions of demonology lend to something much more resembling a traditional witch-hunt, with a concentration on women. This witch-hunt was restricted to the western provinces that were largely inhabited by Swedish immigrants and their descendants and were more prosperous than the Finnish-speaking interior. The key base for the importation of foreign demonology was the University of Turku, founded in 1640, Finland's first university. Its vice-chancellor and bishop of Turku from 1627 to 1652, the Swede Isaac Rothovius, encouraged a zealous campaign against sorcery and superstition. Ironically, the university had some trouble with sorcerers on its faculty. The full demonological concept of witchcraft was introduced into the Finnish judicial system by Nils Psilander (d. 1682), a judge in the Swedish-inhabited province of Ahvenanmaa. Psilander presided over a long hunt from 1666 and 1674, which despite taking so many years only resulted in six **executions.**

There are 710 known cases of witchcraft **accusation** in Finland covering the period from 1520–1699, with 115 known death sentences. Because many court records have not survived, there were undoubtedly more cases that are unrecorded, with probably over a thousand total. Slightly more than half of all cases were women, concentrated in the period 1650–1690. More than half of all death sentences were handed down in the 1660s and 1670s. One factor making for the increased volume of witch accusations in the 1670s was a spillover effect from the Swedish **Mora** trials. Some of the informants spoke of attending **sabbats** on the Blokulla, a mythical Swedish mountain. The Finnish witch-hunt, however, never fully followed the Swedish pattern with mass trials and the widespread use of child accusers. Other factors limiting the development of witch-hunting in Finland were the lack of **torture** and the omission of the search for the **Devil's mark.**

REFERENCES: Antero Heikkinen and Timo Kervinen. "Finland: The Male Domination." In *Early Modern European Witchcraft: Centres and Peripheries*, ed. Bengt Ankarloo and Gustav Henningsen, 319–338. Oxford: Clarendon Press, 1990; Brian P. Levack. *The Witch-Hunt in Early Modern Europe.* London and New York: Longman, 1987.

FLADE, DIETRICH (D. 1589)

Dietrich Flade was the most socially eminent victim of the German witch-hunt. He was dean of the Law Faculty of the University of Trier and had served as its rector. He was also judge of the city of Trier, in which capacity he presided over at least one witch case. Persecution of witches began in the region by 1572, reaching the city itself by 1582. Flade was the judge in the case of Braun Grethe in that year, which probably ended in Grethe's banishment.

Flade does not seem to have been an enthusiastic witch-hunter, in which quality he was increasingly isolated. The witch-hunt in Trier, largely a response to several bad harvests compounded by the disastrous effects of the war between the Spanish and the Dutch in the nearby Netherlands, had great popular support, with ordinary people in many cases taking the initiative in rooting out witchcraft from their communities. It was also supporter by many political and religious leaders, including the ruler of the area, the Elector of Trier Johann von Schonenburg, the suffragan bishop and demonologist Peter **Binsfeld,** and the governor of the city of Trier from 1584, Johann Zandt von Merl. Zandt was also the administrative head of a small territory outside the city called Pfalzel, where he had carried out a witch-hunt in 1587 with more than a hundred **executions.**

Accusations of Flade began to emerge in 1587, when a boy confessed to involvement in a **magical** plot to kill the elector, who suffered several days of illness, and implicated Flade. Several witches from villages outside Trier claimed to have seen him at **sabbats.** Flade heard about this, and petitioned the elector to be allowed to clear his name, but the accusations kept coming. In April 1588, an accused witch called Margarethe of Euren accused Flade of coming to the sabbat in a golden chariot and arguing for the destruction of all crops. Possibly indicating an element of **social class** resentment underlying accusations of Flade, Margarethe said the poor witches at the sabbat argued against this. She also accused Flade of taking part in crop destruction and cannibalism. A commission was appointed to investigate the charges. In October, Flade attempted unsuccessfully to flee the electorate.

Flade was not arrested until April 1589, and his trial took place in August. He defended himself by pointing out that what his accusers had seen at the sabbat was not him, but merely his appearance, and that this could be a trick of **Satan's.** Following multiple sessions of **torture,** Flade confessed. He was sentenced to execution by burning, with the mercy of preliminary strangulation. Flade's exalted social position meant that his case attracted an unusual amount of attention. Although the case was not discussed in Binsfeld's writings, he made a particular point of refuting Flade's central defensive claim, that the Devil could impersonate people at sabbats. Martin **del Rio** did discuss the case as an example of the harm witches could do in positions of power.

REFERENCES: Robin Briggs. *Witches and Neighbors: The Social and Cultural Context of European Witchcraft.* New York: Penguin, 1996. *George Lincoln Burr: His Life by Roland Bainton: Selections from his Writings edited by Lois Oliphant Gibbons.* Ithaca and New York: Cornell University Press, 1943.

FLOTATION TESTS

The idea that guilt or innocence could be determined by water's acceptance or rejection of a person's body—the ordeal by water—was old in European culture by the time of the witch-hunts. Judicial ordeals had been banned by a Church council in 1215, but they made their way back during the early modern period. The flotation test was justified for use in witch cases by the argument that water was the element of baptism and that the witch, by making her pact with **Satan,** had rejected baptism. Belief in it was widespread among ordinary people—some accused witches even volunteered for it in hopes of clearing their name. The judicial use of the flotation test seems to have originated in the German region of Westphalia in the mid–sixteenth century. From there it spread throughout northern and western **Germany** and into Scandinavia. The water test was used in some English cases, particularly during the Matthew **Hopkins** witch-hunt. It was used only a few times in the English North American colonies and very little in **Scotland.** It had little impact in **Italy,** the Iberian Peninsula, or southern **France.** It had been used in **Russia** and the Ukraine during the Middle Ages, but was abandoned in the fourteenth century. Ukraine, but not Russia, began to use it again in the beginning of the eighteenth century, continuing well into the nineteenth.

The flotation test is a good example of how witchcraft deviated from general tendencies in criminal justice, which was moving away from such supernatural means of investigation. The flotation test was justified by the difficulty of finding evidence of witchcraft, which legitimized unusual ways to acquire evidence, including flotation tests and pricking for the **Devil's mark.** Many jurists were unhappy with flotation—the Parlement of Paris banned it in territories under its jurisdiction in 1601, and the Imperial Chamber Court of the Holy

Roman Empire denounced it along with other ordeals in 1685. The assize judges of **England** opposed the flotation test, and it never enjoyed formal legal status in England. Some demonologists were also skeptical, but others, including **James VI and I,** endorsed it.

In a judicial flotation test, the suspect was stripped to a single garment, bound and immersed in the water by a rope. Persons who sank were quickly pulled out, rather than being allowed to drown. Persons who floated were deemed to be witches. The principal use of the flotation test most places it was used was to provide evidence—not for conviction but for the application of **torture.** (This also meant that those who passed the flotation test and managed to sink usually were not deemed innocent or set free.)

The real popularity of the flotation test in many areas occurred outside the legal process, particularly after the end of the judicial witch-hunt. Flotation tests provided an excuse and a template for mob action against witches, who could be simply tossed into the nearest body of water. This action led to the death of Ruth **Osborne** in 1751.

REFERENCES: Heikki Pihlajamak. "'Swimming the Witch, Pricking for the Devil's Mark': Ordeals in the Early Modern Witchcraft Trials." *Journal of Legal History* 21 (2000): 35–58; James Sharpe. *Instruments of Darkness: Witchcraft in Early Modern England.* Philadelphia: University of Philadelphia Press, 1996; Russell Zguta. "The Ordeal by Water (Swimming of Witches) in the East Slavic World." *Slavic Review* 36 (1977): 220–230.

FLOWER WITCHES

The case of Joan Flower and her daughters Margaret and Phillip provide a striking example of how even powerful aristocrats could feel themselves and their families threatened by witches of the humble **social class.** The evidence for the case is an anonymous pamphlet, *The Wonderful Discovery of the Witch-crafts of Margaret and Phillip Flower* (1619), which went through two subsequent editions after the first. (There was also a ballad produced by the same publishers, titled *Damnable Practices of three Lincoln-shire Witches, Joane Flower, and her two Daughters, Margaret and Phillip Flower, against Henry Lord Ross, with others the Children of the Right Honourable the Earle of Rutland, at Beaver Castle, who for the same were executed at Lincolne the 11 March last.*) The pamphlet was probably produced at the behest of the witch's victim, Francis Manners, sixth earl of Rutland (1578–1632). He is portrayed throughout as an altogether innocent victim and a man of noble, charitable and godly character. The author had some education and acquaintance with demonological literature, referring to the description of a witch in Virgil's *Aeneid* and lifting some general thoughts on witches from Reginald **Scot's** *Discoverie of Witchcraft.* He also quoted extensively from the works of George **Gifford,** and referred to the **Sutton witches** and the **Lancashire** witch-hunt. There are no surviving trial documents to check against the pamphlet, and the chronology of the events is not altogether clear.

The principal crime of which the witches were accused was the murder by witchcraft of Rutland's young son, Henry, Lord Roos, who died in 1613. The trouble actually began shortly after Manners inherited the earldom and the estate of Belvoir castle. Joan Flower was employed as a char-woman, and her daughter Margaret as a chicken-woman and laundress. Rutland and his countess, Cicily Manners, heard rumors that Joan was a great swearer of oaths and a witch, and that Margaret was stealing food from the castle and bringing it to her mother. Phillip was supposed to have bewitched a local man, Thomas Simpson, to love her. Margaret was dismissed from the Castle by the countess, albeit the pamphleteer emphasizes that she received forty shillings and other gifts as compensation. In a classical story of the witch's revenge, the Flowers, with the aid of **familiar** spirits acquired through a **satanic pact,** killed the earl's livestock, afflicted he and the countess with sickness, and eventually killed Henry. The couple's other son, Francis, and their daughter Lady Katherine Manners, were also afflicted with illness. (Francis eventually also died of it.) It took some time for suspicion to light on the Flower family, but they were arrested around Christmas, probably of the year 1618. Joan Flower died shortly after she and her daughters were jailed at Lincoln, but her daughters confessed that she had worked Henry's death by taking his glove, which Margaret had stolen from the castle, boiling it in a mixture of water and blood and rubbing it on a cat familiar named Rutterkin. They also confessed to causing the subsequent infertility of Lord and Lady Rutland, a matter of great importance because Henry and Francis were their only male children. The witches were hanged March 11, probably 1619.

The investigation, in which Manners played a quasi-magisterial role, spilled over into the neighboring county of Leicestershire. The pamphlet includes interrogations of three women, Anne Baker, Joane Willimot and Ellen Greene. Willimot confessed to witchcraft and having a familiar spirit and claimed that she had associated with Joan and Margaret Flower. She blamed Joan Flower for Henry's death. Greene also confessed to being a witch, receiving familiar spirits from Willimot and using them to kill. Baker, a **cunning** woman, admitted to having a familiar spirit, but not to being a witch or performing *maleficia*. The legal fate of the Leicestershire women is unknown.

REFERENCE: Marion Gibson, ed. *Early Modern Witches: Witchcraft Cases in Contemporary Writing.* London and New York: Routledge, 2000.

FLYING

One of the most commonly held beliefs about witches among both the educated and popular classes is that they could fly. Popular belief in flying witches can be traced far back in European history. Belief in women who travel long distances by night, often accompanying the pagan goddess **Diana,** was among the superstitions condemned in the ninth-century **Canon Episcopi**. A less pleasant form of belief was that in women who transform themselves into *strigae*, birds resembling owls who fly by night, searching for people whose blood they could suck or babies whose entrails they could devour. This belief can be traced to the ancient Romans and also seems to have been widespread among the German barbarians who came to rule large parts of Europe after the fall of Rome. Belief in the *strigae* was also condemned in the early Middle Ages. Whereas Roman law never dealt with the *strigae*, several early medieval law codes provide punishment for people who accuse others of being *strigae*, or who murder them for that reason. Despite their dubiousness about human flight, medieval authorities endorsed the idea of demonic flight, as demons were spirits. The Scholastic philosopher William of Auvergne (c. 1180–1249) argued that the ladies who ride with Diana do fly, but that this was because they were demons and not witches. **Satan**'s removal of Jesus to the high place to view all the kingdoms of the earth during the temptation in the wilderness provided an unimpeachable precedent for a demon carrying a human body in flight, but rather an awkward one to apply to witches.

Despite the condemnation of the learned, belief in witch flight continued in the Middle Ages. Medieval flying witches were seldom thought of as flying under their own power, but often pictured as fly-

A depiction by Hans Baldung Grien of witches concocting an ointment to be used for flying to the Sabbath, Strassburg, 1514. © Dover Pictorial Archive.

ing on the backs of enchanted **animals** or household objects, including broomsticks. The earliest illustration of a witch flying on a broomstick occurs in the cathedral at Sleswig, dating from the late thirteenth century. As domestic objects, broomsticks were particularly appropriate for female witches (distaffs were also popular), but this association was not inevitable—the French male witch Guillame **Adeline** confessed to flying to the **sabbat** on a broomstick in 1453.

What changed during the witch-hunt was that educated people, including demonologists and witch-hunting magistrates, became willing to accept the possibility of witch flight. Classic demonological texts, including Heinrich **Kramer**'s *Malleus Maleficarum* (1486), endorsed the idea, although conceding that some witches might be transported only in spirit. Although independent of it, belief in witch flight complemented belief in the sabbat, because it answered the question of how dozens or even hundreds of witches could get to a sabbat many miles away and back in a single night. The alternative belief, that witches went to the sabbat only in spirit while their bodies remained in their beds, was a minority opinion. Demonologists tended to picture the witches as being carried by demons in the form of animals such as goats.

References to specific instances of witch flight in the period of the witch-hunt almost always come from the confessions of accused witches or of those, usually children, who claimed that the witches had carried them to the sabbat. Few nonwitches claim to have actually seen a witch flying, although they sometimes claimed to have seen them appearing rapidly in distant places, implying some form of supernaturally swift movement. Witch flight is often associated with the use of ointments, usually compounded from various ingredients and applied either to the utensil on which the witch planned to fly or to the body of the witch herself. The presence of belladonna or other hallucinogenic herbs in the formulae for some of these ointments has raised the question of whether the subjective experience of witch flight is a product of chemically induced hallucination. The venom of toads, animals frequently associated with witches, can also cause hallucinations. This is clearly not a universally valid explanation for belief in witch flight. Many of the formulae have no psychoactive component, and some witches were said to fly without using an ointment.

REFERENCES: Robin Briggs. *Witches and Neighbors: The Social and Cultural Context of European Witchcraft*. New York: Penguin, 1996; Norman Cohn. *Europe's Inner Demons: The Demonization of Christians in Medieval Christendom*. Rev. ed. Chicago: University of Chicago Press, 2000; Brian P. Levack. *The Witch-Hunt in Early Modern Europe*. London and New York: Longman, 1987; Jeffrey Burton Russell. *Witchcraft in the Middle Ages*. Ithaca: Cornell University Press, 1972.

FRANCE, WITCH-HUNTING IN

In many ways, France was the cradle of the European witch-hunt. Some of the earliest political sorcery cases, such as those of the **Templars** and **Guichard de Troyes,** were promoted by the French monarchy. The decree of the University of Paris in 1398 was a milestone in the criminalization of **magic.** A great witch-hunt in the Dauphiné from 1428 to 1447 made use of the **sabbat** theory to claim 167 victims and was the source of the witch-hunting experience of the magistrate-demonologist Claude **Tholosan.** It was followed by those of Guillame **Adeline** in 1453 and the **Arras witches** in 1459. Early modern French witch-hunting, however, was usually relatively mild, like that of **England.** In considering French witch-hunting, it is important to distinguish between that region of Europe in which the French language and French culture predominated, and the Kingdom of France. Some of the most active witch-hunting regions in French-speaking Europe, such as **Lorraine** and **Franche-Comte,** were outside France for most of this period. (The town of Avignon, where 18 witches were burned in 1582 by the inquisitor Sebastian Michaelis, was under the jurisdiction of the pope, even though geographically located within the borders of France.) Even within France, there were huge regional variations in witch-hunting, caused both by cultural and legal differences. The kingdom was divided into judicial districts of various sizes overseen by assemblies of magis-

Saint Louis IX, king of France, meets the four witches and his vision of punishment by devils to blasphemers from the manuscript of *Voyage of King or Saint Louis IX of France into Purgatory of Saint Patrick,* fourteenth century. © The Art Archive/Museo Correr Venice/Dagli Orti (A).

trates called parlements. These secular courts, and not ecclesiastical justice, which hardly existed in France, took the lead in witch-hunting. The parlements took vastly different attitudes toward witches in their jurisdictions. Generally, parlements tended to work with panels of judges rather than single magistrates, so zealous witch-hunters working outside the consensus of the magistracy were constrained by their peers.

The Parlement of Paris was the most powerful and prestigious body in the French legal system and the court of appeal for most of the northern half of France. As such, its attitude toward witchcraft was central in shaping the overall French response. This attitude was skeptical—not of witchcraft itself, but of the possibility of proving it to an adequate legal standard. There were members of the Parlement who supported more vigorous action against witches, but they were usually overruled by the majority, who often disdained the provincial courts as witch-obsessed. In dealing with criminal appeals, the general tendency of the Parlement was toward mercy, but this was most marked in the case of witchcraft, in which more than 75 percent of the death sentences in the period 1565–1640 were commuted or dismissed on appeal to the Parlement. More than 90 percent of the non-death sentences were commuted in some form. For a death sentence, the Parlement required either a truly voluntary confession made without **torture,** tangible evidence, such as an actual contract with the Devil, or a respectable eyewitness to an actual magical act. This was the same type of evidence required for most other criminal convictions, and the Parlement stuck to it despite pressure from intellectuals such as the magistrate of the lower court of Laon, Jean **Bodin,** to lower the standard required in witchcraft and sorcery investigations in view of the danger witches posed to the kingdom. Alfred Soman, the leading modern scholar of the Parlement's response to witch cases, claims that of 1,272 witch defendants brought before the Parlement from 1565 to 1670, only 103 were condemned to death.

The Parlement of Paris did not employ **flotation tests,** which it found beneath its dignity, and forbade the use of flotation tests by lower courts in 1601 as part of a crackdown on irregularities in local courts. The use of torture at Paris was also mild and often ineffective in gaining convictions, often merely a sort of show where the accused witch was brought into the torture chamber and the instruments displayed. The last known appearance of torture in a witch case conducted by the Parlement was in 1593. Parisian investigators were more interested in *maleficium* than **satanic pact** or attendance at the sabbat. The record of appeals to the Parlement shows that France had an unusually high proportion of male witches, slightly over half the total, although it is possible that women's cases were less likely to be appealed. French witch-hunting was also a rural rather than an urban phenomenon.

The most active French witch-hunters generally were uneducated local magistrates and members of religious orders. In the late sixteenth century, dominated by the fierce conflicts of Calvinists and Catholics in the French Wars of Religion, the keenest supporters of witch-hunting were the supporters of the Catholic League, the ultra-Catholic party whose goal was the purification of the realm from heresy, with or without the collaboration of the French government. The political leaders of the league, however, were not usually supporters of witch-hunting. A fierce witch-hunt in the province of Champagne in 1587, led by local league supporters using flotation tests, was suppressed by the Parlement in cooperation with one of the league's leaders, Louis of Lorraine, the cardinal of Guise (1554–1588). This seems to have sparked the Parlement's concerns with lower-court abuses in witchcraft and sorcery trials.

Much demonology coming from league supporters, such as the Spanish Jesuit and Parisian professor Juan **Maldonado,** strongly identified sorcery with heresy, endorsing a witch-hunt as complementary to a campaign to eradicate Protestant heresy. Even Catholics who opposed the League, such as Queen Catherine de Medici (1519–1589) and King Henri III (r. 1574–1589), were often portrayed as demonic witches. (Italians such as Catherine, numerous and unpopular in France, were also frequent targets of witchcraft **accusations.**) The only major sixteenth-century French demonologists to stand outside this tradition were France's only Protestant demonologist, Lambert **Daneau,** and Bodin, who despite his promotion of witch-hunting did not identify witches and Protestants. *Politique* Catholics who opposed the eradication of Protestantism if it meant civil war were much less keen on witch-hunting. This group included most of the leaders of the various parlements, and the essayist Michel de Montaigne (1533–1592), whose essay "On the Lame" showed sympathy with accused witches and skepticism about their crimes. (Montaigne was actually related to two major demonologists, de **Lancre**, who defended him, and Martin **del Rio,** who denounced him.)

Leaguer demonology was strongly connected to another characteristic of French witch-hunting: the spectacular cases of demonic **possession** that became more and more closely entwined with witchcraft. These possessions originally were promoted vigorously as anti-Protestant propaganda. The first, that of Nicole **Obry** in 1564 and 1565, had relatively little to do with witchcraft, but the second celebrated demoniac, Marthe **Brossier,** claimed that a witch had caused her possession. By the early seventeenth century, with **confessional** conflict relatively cooled down, witches moved much more to the fore. The **Gaufridi** case in 1611, the case of the possessed noblewoman Serene de Bajamont in 1617, and the famous cases of possessed nuns at **Loudun** in 1633 and Louviers in 1643 all saw the punishment of clerical witches.

The parlements tightened their grip on witch-hunting in the seventeenth century, continuing to investigate lower-court judges and executioners suspected of using corrupt or improper methods in investigation, or of blocking appeals to the Parlement. A classic example is the Parlement of Paris's ending of the reign of terror of the executioner of Rocroi, Jean Minard. Minard had been operating as a well-paid witch-pricker in the far north of France and the southern Spanish Netherlands. By the summer of 1601, he claimed to have been instrumental in the **execution** of 274 witches. Even though only eight were French subjects, the Parlement had Minard arrested and sent to the galleys that November. In 1624, after a witch-hunt had broken out in Champagne the previous year, the Parlement decreed that all witchcraft convictions in its jurisdiction would be automatically appealed to Paris. This followed and expanded on earlier impositions of similar requirements on areas where judicial abuses had taken place and gave a lead to the French courts to bring far fewer witchcraft cases (particularly because the district court bore the expense of sending the appellant and the case records to Paris). The last witch executed in the jurisdiction of the Parlement of Paris by regular legal processes for several decades was Catherine Bouillon, in 1625.

A wave of witch-hunts spread over several regions of France in 1643 and 1644, precipitated by bad weather, the suffering of the country due to the Thirty Years' War, and the activities of professional witch-finders. Areas affected included the Pyrenees, the Toulouse area, Burgundy and Champagne. The most vigorous seventeenth-century witch-hunts usually took place in areas outside the jurisdiction of the Parlement of Paris, notably in the territories of the Parlement of Bordeaux in the south and the Parlement of Rouen in Normandy, which relative to its size had more executions for witchcraft than any other Parlement. The territories of the Parlement of Bordeaux, which included much of France's **Basque** population, saw the spectacular witch-hunt of Maldonado's student Pierre de Lancre.

Normandy had a unique witch-hunting culture, combined with a Parlement that jealously defended its privileges against what its magistrates viewed as Parisian interference. Norman witch-hunting was endemic, rather than concentrated in spectacular hunts. The Parlement upheld death sentences at an exceptionally high rate, upholding the death penalty in 93 cases of 202 appeals from 1564 to 1659. Normandy was one of the few areas where most suspected witches were men, and other areas that shared this pattern, such as **Iceland** and **Estonia,** were on the far northern fringes of the European world. William Monter states that of 380 known witchcraft defendants in Normandy, nearly three-quarters were men. The occupational groups that dominated Norman witch-hunting were shepherds, followed by priests and blacksmiths. Although the concepts of the sabbat, the satanic pact and the **Devil's mark** were known and employed, Norman witch-hunters were mainly interested in *maleficia,* specifically the possession of toads to make poison and the use of the Eucharist for magical purposes.

Normandy, along with Béarn and Guyenne, was the center of the last great French witch-hunt, which occurred around 1670. It was precipitated by **witch-finders,** and vigorously supported by the Parlement of Rouen. This provoked Royal intervention, leading to a much harder line against witch-hunting from the central government. The **Affair of the Poisons,** in which allegations of diabolical witchcraft touched the court itself, also put witchcraft on the central government's agenda. Louis XIV's (r. 1643–1715) proclamation of 1682, prompted by a recent Norman witch-hunt and the Affair of the Poisons, redefined the offense of witchcraft as poisoning or sacrilege rather than *maleficium* or demonic activity. This did not end witch-hunting, and persons continued to be punished, sometimes with death, as in the case of two shepherds judged guilty of "so-called witchcraft" by the Parlement of Paris for the use of the Eucharist for magic in 1661. The last death sentence approved by the Parlement of Rouen took place two years later and was inflicted on a shepherd and his wife. Witch-hunting slowly died out, however, and persons attacked by their neighbors as being witches had more frequent recourse to the law in self-defense. One important milestone in the decline of the French witch-hunt was the last great possession case, that of Marie Catherine Cadière in 1731, in which accusations of witchcraft were not sustained by the Parlement of Aix. The crime of witchcraft was finally eliminated from French law after the French Revolution. The new penal code the Constituent Assembly promulgated in 1791 omitted it, along with other "imaginary crimes" such as heresy.

REFERENCES: Ian Bostridge. *Witchcraft and Its Transformations, c. 1650–c. 1750.* Oxford: Clarendon Press, 1997; Robin Briggs. *Witches and Neighbors: The Social and Cultural Context of European Witchcraft.* New York: Penguin, 1996; Richard Kieckhefer. *European Witch Trials: Their Foundations in Popular and Learned Culture, 1300–1500.* Berkeley: University of California Press, 1976; Emmanuel Le Roy Ladurie. *Jasmin's Witch.* Trans. Brian Pearce. New York: George Braziller, 1987; Brian P. Levack. *The Witch-Hunt in Early Modern Europe.* London and New York: Longman, 1987; William Monter. "Toads and Eucharists: The Male Witches of Normandy, 1564–1660." *French Historical Studies* 20 (1997): 563–595; Robert Muchembled. *Popular Culture and Elite Culture in France 1400–1750.* Trans. Lydia Cochrane. Baton Rouge and London: Louisiana State University Press, 1985; Jonathan L. Pearl. *The Crime of Crimes: Demonology and Politics in France, 1560–1620.* Waterloo, Ontario: Wilfrid Laurier University Press, 1999; Alfred Soman. "Decriminalizing Witchcraft: Does the French

Experience Provide a European Model?" *Criminal Justice History* 10 (1989): 1–22; Alfred Soman. "The Parlement of Paris and the Great Witch Hunt (1565–1640)." *The Sixteenth Century Journal* 9 (1978): 31–44; Charlotte Wells. "Leeches on the Body Politic: Xenophobia and Witchcraft in Early Modern French Political Thought." *French Historical Studies* 22 (1999): 351–377.

FRANCESCO, MATTEUCCIA DI (D. 1428)

The trial of the Italian **cunning** woman Matteuccia di Francesco or Francisci of Todi in 1428 is one of the best documented early-fifteenth-century witch trials. Matteuccia had been practicing as a cunning woman for several years before the trial, serving a predominantly female clientele. She performed **counter-magic** for those who thought themselves bewitched and advised the concubine of a priest to drink the ashes of a female mule's hoof mixed with wine as a contraceptive. In addition to providing **magical** remedies for persons with physical injuries, aches and affliction by spirits, Matteuccia also aided many women who were beaten by their husbands or lovers. She seems to have been a victim of a shift in attitudes in Todi related to the visit of the preaching friar **Bernardino of Siena,** a fierce hater of witches, in early 1426. That March, the town adopted a new and stricter law against witchcraft, providing for **execution** by burning.

The persecution of Matteuccia was carried out by the Court of Malefactors of Todi and marked a dramatic shift. For most of the trial, the offenses to which Matteuccia confessed were the ordinary activities of a cunning woman. Toward the end of her interrogation, probably under the threat of **torture,** she began to confess to frankly diabolic activities, connected to the emerging stereotype of the witch as set forth by Bernardino and others. These activities included sucking the blood out of babies, making an ointment out of their fat, calling up a demon in the form of a goat, and **flying** to a **sabbat**-like gathering of witches at a walnut tree in Benevento. This is among the earliest appearances of the sabbat in a trial. On March 20, Matteuccia's hands were tied behind her back, and she was placed on the back of a donkey, taken to the place of execution and burned at the stake.

REFERENCES: Richard Kieckhefer. *Magic in the Middle Ages.* Cambridge: Cambridge University Press, 1989; Franco Mormando. *The Preacher's Demons: Bernardino of Siena and the Social Underworld of Early Renaissance Italy.* Chicago and London: University of Chicago Press, 1999.

FRANCHE-COMTE, WITCH-HUNTING IN

Franche-Comte, now part of eastern **France** on the Swiss border, was part of the Holy Roman Empire until France annexed it in 1674. Its immediate sovereign before the French conquest was the king of Spain, as duke of Burgundy, although sometimes it was governed from Brussels in the Spanish Netherlands by the king's representatives. Culturally, however, it was always French, and the supreme court of appeal for the province was a French-style parlement, seated in Dôle. Witchcraft in Franche-Comte, like that of France, was strongly connected to demonic **possession,** particularly because the territory possessed the relics of the famous wonderworker Saint Claude, who specialized in curing cases of possession and attracted many possessed people from Savoy and elsewhere. Franche-Comte did not produce the dramatic political possession cases centered in convents that France did. Another common type of witch activity in Franche-Comte was lycanthropy. In 1573, the Parlement of Dôle gave permission for villagers to carry weapons when hunting a **werewolf,** and the **execution** the following year of the werewolf Gilles Garnier, who confessed to having killed and eaten children, attracted a great deal of attention. Franche-Comte witchcraft remained mostly a phenomenon of the rural poor.

There were few witch executions in Franche-Comte until the late sixteenth century. Several developments contributed to an increase at this time. Secular justice took over from the Inquisition in 1599, and the famous witch-hunting magistrate and demonologist Henri **Boguet** was appointed chief judge of the lands of the Abbey of Saint Claude in 1596. The key factor in the spread of witch-hunting was a 1604 decree from Brussels giving seignorial courts, those maintained by feudal lords, the power to execute for witchcraft. Severe witch-hunting continued until 1611–1612, when the Parlement began to ease. Boguet had three convictions overruled by the Parlement in 1612.

The next witch-hunt in Franche-Comte occurred from 1628–1629, after a series of poor harvests in the northern half of the district. The ravages of the Thirty Years' War, which raged in Franche-Comte from 1635 to 1644, reduced witch-hunting in the area to practically nothing. The greatest witch-hunt in the history of the province occurred, from 1657 to 1659, only after it had largely recovered from the ravages of the war. The moving force was a zealous inquisitor, Father Symard, who centralized the witch-hunting effort with a call in every parish for information from those who thought themselves bewitched or knew of witches. A local chronicler claimed that in the first year of the witch-hunt, more than one hundred witches had been arrested, although of course not all of these were convicted. About 22 were executed. The witch-hunt provoked a response from Francois Bouvot, a **physician** in Besancon, a Free Imperial city in Franche-Comte. Bouvot published a French translation of Friedrich von **Spee's** classic indictment of witch-hunting, *Warning to Prosecutors*, in 1660, with much additional material reflecting local conditions. Likely more effective in ending the witch-hunt was the appeal of a conviction to Rome. When the **Roman Inquisition,** famously cautious in witch cases, heard of Symard's methods, they had him removed from the Franche-Comte Inquisition, bringing about the end of witch-hunting in that province.

REFERENCES: William Monter. *Witchcraft in France and Switzerland: The Borderlands during the Reformation*. Ithaca and London: Cornell University Press, 1976; Alfred Soman. "Decriminalizing Witchcraft: Does the French Experience Provide a European model?" *Criminal Justice History* 10 (1989): 1–22.

FRANCISCAN ORDER

See Bernardino of Siena; Sinistrari, Lodovico Maria.

G

GALIS, RICHARD

Richard Galis wrote the first English work recounting a witchcraft case from the point of view of a bewitched person, *A Brief Treatise conteyning the most Strange and Horrible Crueltye of Elizabeth Stile alias Bockingham & her Confederates executed at Abingdon upon Richard Galis* (1579). His work also displays more literary polish and ambition than other contemporary English witch narratives.

The case of Stile and the other Abingdon witches was already widely known. The witches had been accused of murdering Galis's father, also Richard Galis, and several other people by making wax images of them. The case had attracted the attention of the Privy Council and had also been the subject of an earlier pamphlet, *A Rehearsall both Straung and True, of Hainous and Horrible Actes committed by Elizabeth Style, alias Rockingham, Mother Dutten, Mother Devell, Mother Margaret, Fower Notorious Witches, apprehended at Windsor in the Countie of Barks. and at Abbington arraigned, condemned, and executed, on the 26. day of February laste Anno 1579* (1579). Galis presented his account as one supplementing *A Rehearsall* (which does not mention him), particularly focusing on the harms done to himself and his family. Galis did not provide an explanation for why he had attracted the witches' wrath. He presented himself as a completely innocent victim of a number of diabolical assaults, including turning his friends against him and procuring his imprisonment. He described himself as a godly Protestant responding to these attacks through prayer and **Bible** reading. Galis also criticized the negligence of magistrates who permitted the witches to carry on their diabolical activities. On several occasions, he described himself as taking violent action against the witches, at one point tying Stiles by a cart-rope around her waist and dragging her before a magistrate. On a subsequent occasion, he attempted to blow up Mother Dutton's house. This kind of behavior led one reader of his pamphlet, the witch-hunting opponent Reginald **Scot,** to describe Galis as a madman. However violent, these attacks were ineffectual, and the witches were tried and executed only after Galis left town.

REFERENCE: Marion Gibson, ed. *Early Modern Witches: Witchcraft Cases in Contemporary Writing*. London and New York: Routledge, 2000.

GAUFRIDI, LOUIS (D. 1611)

Louis Gaufridi was a French Catholic priest executed as a witch in 1611. Gaufridi was a popular confessor of many women in Marseilles, including a girl from a noble family named Madeline de Demandolx de la Palud (1593–1670). To destroy what was perceived as a dangerous intimacy between Madeline and Gaufridi, her parents sent her to a convent of Ursuline nuns in Aix-in-Provence. There her confessor was a priest named Jean-Baptiste Romillon, known to be concerned over the poor sexual morals of French clergy. Romillon diagnosed convulsions de Demandolx had been having as demonic **possession,** encouraging her to denounce Gaufridi as the cause of her torments. A nun at the convent, Louise Capeau, also claimed Gaufridi had seduced her and was now causing demons to torment her. Romillon failed in his exorcisms and passed de Demandolx and Capeau on to the great exorcist Sebastian Michaelis at the convent of Saint Maximin, where the exorcisms became a public spectacle.

Gaufridi denied everything and even attempted to have the nuns silenced, but Romillon and his allies in the church succeeded in having him brought before the Parlement, or law court, of Aix on charges of witchcraft. Madeline put on quite a show before the Parlement, alternately accusing Gaufridi of witchcraft, mocking him, declaring her love for him and making the motions of **sex.** The **accusations** went beyond mere possession. Gaufridi was charged with having forced her to make a **satanic pact** with her own blood and then having sex with her. Madeline claimed that Gaufridi had baptized her in the name of Lucifer and taken her to **sabbats,** where she engaged in sexual practices including sodomy (on Thursdays) and bestiality (on Saturdays). He had given her a demon named Beezelbub (Capeau's demon was named Verrine). These were dangerous claims for Madeline to make, because she was admitting to being a witch. Under the pressure of **torture** and imprisonment, Gaufridi eventually confessed to being a leading witch and attending the sabbat. Gaufridi was executed April 30, 1611. Before being burned, he was first put through extreme torture, including strappado and squassado, to make him divulge the names of accomplices, which he refused to do. He also refused to incriminate Madeline, which helped her escape trial as a witch herself. Gaufridi was mercifully strangled before being burned. Madeline was cured the next day, although Capeau continued to be possessed and procured the death of another witch, a blind girl.

The Gaufridi case attracted international publicity. Michaelis published an account, *The Admirable History of the Possession and Conversion of a Penitent* (1613), and the lead **physician** involved, J. Fontaine, published a study of its medical aspects. Possessed nuns at a Brigidine convent in the Spanish Nether-lands later described Gaufridi as a leader at sabbats, and an account of his trial was translated into English as evidence of the low fortunes of Catholicism. Madeline, expelled from the Ursulines, went on to live a life of self-denial, ritual self-abasement such as encouraging people to spit in her face, and the teaching of young girls. But she never lost her reputation for witchcraft. By 1653, Made-line was left unprotected from legal attack because of the death of her parents and some of the ecclesiastical establishment of Marseilles, where she then lived. A girl fell ill after visiting her chapel, and when she began vomiting pins, feath-ers and a piece of paper with the word "Arabie" on it, the case was identified as one of demonic possession. Exorcism revealed that Madeline's demon was Beezelbub, who now claimed that Madeline was his wife and that she had bewitched the girl. In the resulting trial, Madeline denied ever having a close relationship with Gaufridi or having attended the sabbat, but the written record of the previous trial was against her. She was convicted and sentenced to life imprisonment but released after 18 months. She lived out the rest of her days in extreme poverty, on a small country estate belonging to a distant relative.

REFERENCES: Joseph Klaits. *Servants of Satan: The Age of the Witch Hunts.* Bloom-ington: Indiana University Press, 1985; Michelle Marshman. "Exorcism as Empower-ment: A New Idiom." *Journal of Religious History* 23 (1999): 265–281; Anita M. Walker and Edmund H. Dickermann. "A Notorious Woman: Possession, Witchcraft and Sex-uality in Seventeenth-Century Provence." *Historical Reflections/Reflexions Historiques* 27 (2001): 1–26.

GEILER VON KAYSERSBERG, JOHANN (1445–1510)

Johann Geiler von Kaysersberg, a cathedral preacher at Strasbourg, preached a series of sermons for Lent in 1508 that were published after his death as *The Ant-Hill* (1516), a title derived from Johannes **Nider's** Latin *Formicarius.* Twenty-six of the sermons discuss witchcraft. Geiler von Kaysersberg was a preacher, addressing a large audience in German, not a scholar writing a formal treatise, and his approach to witchcraft is not always internally consistent. At one point, he is skeptical of witch's flight, arguing that it is a demonic delusion, but elsewhere he suggests that witch flight is not beyond the power of demons and that they move women riding on pitchforks. He also denied the reality of **transformations.** Whatever their powers, Geiler von Kaysarsberg suggested that witches be put to death. He firmly identified witches as female, suggesting that 10 women were burned as witches for every man and attributing women's greater susceptibility to their weakness, their talkativeness and their greater facility for being understood by demons. His work appeared with woodcut illus-trations, some possibly by Hans **Baldung Grien.**

REFERENCE: Alan Charles Kors and Edward Peters, eds. *Witchcraft in Europe 400–1700: A Documentary History.* 2d ed. Revised by Edward Peters. Philadelphia: University of Pennsylvania Press, 2001.

GENDER

One indisputable fact about the European witch-hunt is that a large majority of its victims were women. Although the exact proportion will never be known, the most common estimate is that 80 percent of executed witches were women. This overall figure conceals great regional variation, ranging from areas such as **England, the northern Netherlands** and **Hungary,** where 90 percent or more of convicted witches were women, to a few areas such as **Iceland** or Normandy where the majority of victims were men. The reasons for the female preponderance are disputed, and as with many broad, general questions about the European witch-hunt, the answers are hard to apply to the whole phenomenon, over five centuries and many cultures and confessions.

One suggestion is that the witch-hunt was an expression of misogyny. Some of the earliest **feminist** historians working in the field put forth this argument, and it continues to find supporters today. Certainly there is no difficulty in finding misogyny in trial records and demonological texts, the most notorious example being Heinrich **Kramer'**s *Malleus Maleficarum* (1486). The *Malleus* includes a famous and frequently quoted passage attacking women's weakness and insatiable sexual lusts, qualities that made them far more vulnerable to **Satan.** Kramer and Sprenger went so far as to construct a false etymology for the Latin word *femina,* woman, as based on the phrase *fe minus,* less faith. Women's greater vulnerability to Satan's temptation to become witches was linked by theoreticians with Eve's vulnerability to the serpent, which had caused the Fall from the garden. On the level of the actual trials, there is some evidence that women outside male control, such as singlewomen and widows, were more likely to be accused, and that many women accused of witchcraft were viewed as assertive women, "shrews," lacking in the proper feminine submissiveness. In this context, it can be misleading to look simply at trials and the proportion of female victims, because **accusations** of witchcraft that never made it to trial, or even the threat of accusation, could function as a way of asserting male social control.

Many feminist and feminist-influenced historians have identified the early modern period generally as one of increased misogyny, accompanied by women's increasing economic marginalization. Early feminist historians produced romanticized portraits of "wise women," purportedly skilled in herbal healing and women's health, who were driven out violently by witch-hunters, acting as agents for patriarchy in the state, church and medical profession. Most scholars have abandoned this position, but there is some evidence that economically independent women were more likely targets of accusation. Carol F. Karlsen has identified a pattern in **New England** in which women with the prospect of inheriting land outright were more likely to be targeted for accusation and explained the phenomenon by the patriarchal rulers' fear of land being removed from male control. This pattern does not seem to have held elsewhere, however, and of course many accused witches were too poor for control of property to have been an issue.

There are several problems with using misogyny as an explanation for the witch-hunt. It fails to explain why men were witch-hunted at all, and the very universality of misogyny makes it less useful as an explanation. There is little evidence that areas of moderate, low and no witch-hunting were less misogynistic than areas of high witch-hunting. Even in demonology, many opponents of the witch-hunt, including Johann **Weyer,** Reginald **Scot** and Friedrich von **Spee,** were misogynists, although they emphasized feminine weakness and stupidity rather than insatiable sexuality. By contrast, some supporters of the witch-hunt, such as Jean **Bodin** and Francesco Maria **Guazzo,** devoted little attention to gender questions. No demonologist or European legal code identified witchcraft as a solely female offense. By contrast, those punished for non-witchcraft-related **infanticide,** another crime increasingly prosecuted in the early modern period, were virtually 100 percent women.

An alternative way to connect witches and women is to ask not which qualities of women made them liable to be suspect as witches, but which qualities of witches made them more likely to be thought female. Some have pointed to a contrast between men's and women's ways of harming their enemies. Men were thought more likely to use physical violence, whereas women were thought more likely to use words, as well as subtle methods such as poison. This kind of hostility could be easily assimilated to witchcraft, for which accusations of *maleficia* often turned on words and substances. Even in places where both could be suspected of witchcraft, men's and women's witchcraft could be conceptualized differently. One common pattern was for women's witchcraft to be seen as directed against people, causing sickness and death, whereas male witchcraft was directed against livestock and other property. Another was for wealthy and powerful men who had risen socially to be suspected of having prospered through witchcraft.

A classic objection to the theory of the witch-hunt as based on gender conflict was the prominence of women as accusers of other women. This has been modified by scholars, such as Clive Holmes in the case of England, who have pointed out that in trials, women accusers often acted under the direction of powerful men. Others, however, such as Robin Briggs, have expanded the argument about women accusers to claim that allegations of witchcraft could emerge within communities of women and that a woman's reputation for witchcraft could first be established among her fellow women before being known among men. Many women accused of witchcraft were charged by other women with offenses dating back for decades, and women's gossip communities could create and spread reputations for witchcraft, particularly because so much socializing in early modern communities was done in monogendered settings. The initiative passed from women to men, often the husbands of the gossiping women, when hostility to the accused witch took the form of legal proceedings.

Witchcraft was also connected to women's bodies. Many fluids produced by women, such as menstrual blood and milk, were viewed as having **magical** properties. (One witch claimed her pact with the Devil was written in her own menstrual blood.) Areas particularly identified with women, such as **sex,** conception, pregnancy and birth, were also frequently involved in witchcraft accusations. Men feared female witches' ability to afflict them with impotence, or imagined the relationship between the Devil and female witches as a sexual one. **Familiars** were pictured as nourishing themselves on the **witch's mark** acting out a distorted parody of motherhood. Lyndal Roper, in examining a series of trials in the imperial city of Augsburg, has identified a pattern in which recently delivered mothers accused "lying-in maids," older women who saw to the needs of the household and baby while the mother was recovering from the delivery, of witchcraft. A **psychoanalytically** influenced historian, Roper analyzes the pattern in terms of the mother's projection of her anxieties over the child's future—infant mortality was common in early modern Europe—onto her rival, the lying-in maid.

Increasingly, scholars are examining women in the witch-hunt not solely in terms of victimization but in terms of strategies of empowerment. This could take many forms. Becoming feared as a witch could be a calculated risk for a woman. Many persons suspected of being witches were never subject to judicial punishment, and in the meantime a reputation as a witch could inspire fear in other people, leading to gifts of food, for example. Women could also be empowered as accusers, and witchcraft's status as a *crimen exceptum* meant that women's testimony in court was more highly valued in witchcraft cases than in other legal matters. The most flagrant display of female power in witchcraft cases were those of the possessed women, usually young, in spectacular cases such as **Loudun** and **Salem.** These women made of their usually marginalized role, not only as women but as young women, a role of great power, whether exercised against men or women.

REFERENCES: Anne Llewellyn Barstow. *Witchcraze: A New History of the European Witch Hunts*. San Francisco: Pandora, 1994; Willem de Blécourt. "The Making of the Female Witch: Reflections on Witchcraft and Gender in the Early Modern Period." *Gender and History* 12 (2000): 287–309; Sigrid Brauner. *Fearless Wives and Frightened Shrews: The Construction of the Witch in Early Modern Germany*. Amherst: University of Massachusetts Press, 1995; Robin Briggs. *Witches and Neighbors: The Social and Cultural Context of European Witchcraft*. New York: Penguin, 1996; Marianne Hester. *Lewd Women and Wicked Witches: A Study in the Dynamics of Male Domination*. London and New York: Routledge, 1992; Clive Holmes. "Women: Witches and Witnesses." *Past and Present* 140 (1993): 45–78; Carol F. Karlsen. *The Devil in the Shape of a Woman: Witchcraft in Colonial New England*. New York: Norton, 1987; Lyndal Roper. *Oedipus and the Devil: Witchcraft, Sexuality and Religion in Early Modern Europe*. New York: Routledge, 1994; Deborah Willis. *Malevolent Nurture: Witch-Hunting and Maternal Power in Early Modern England*. Ithaca: Cornell University Press, 1995.

GENEVA, WITCH-HUNTING IN

Geneva, now part of **Switzerland,** was an independent city-state in the early modern period. The religious reformer John Calvin (1509–1564) lived there and dominated the city's religious and political life from 1541 until his death.

Geneva was also adjacent to the Italian territory of Savoy, famed from ancient times for its many witches. As such, Geneva was an active persecutor of witches but milder than many other states in similar circumstances. Calvin endorsed the persecution of witches but was not particularly interested in the subject, and the Calvinist clergy did not usually fan the flames of persecution.

Witch-hunting in Geneva is often confused with a similar but distinct phenomenon, the persecution of *engraisseurs*—"greasers"—accused of spreading an ointment that caused plague. The persecutions of *engraisseurs*, usually poor people and immigrants employed to fumigate houses and clear away the bodies of the dead, initially did not involve **accusations** of supernatural or diabolic crime, but rather the use of naturally acting poisons motivated by greed—the *engraisseurs* needed plague victims to keep their jobs, their pay and the opportunities for pilfering they provided. Only 1 of the 65 persons accused of plague spreading in 1545–1546 was also convicted of witchcraft, Pernette Marca, and the crime in which the magistrates took the greatest interest, eventually leading to her **execution,** was plague spreading, not witchcraft. A witch-hunt, centering in two villages outside Geneva, Peney and Satigny, also took place in 1545. It involved more than a dozen accused witches, most of whom were punished with fines or banishment, (one, Morys of Satigny, was executed). This witch-hunt, although a topic of public concern, was not viewed as connected with the plague-spreading conspiracy.

The situation was quite different after the late-sixteenth-century revival of witch-hunting. The city had been suffering plague since 1567, and in 1571 the largest witch-hunt in its history targeted plague-spreaders as witches. At least 29 accused witches were executed and many others banished in a witch-hunt that combined charges of "greasing" with such classic demonological ideas as the **sabbat** and **satanic pact.**

There are about five hundred recorded witch trials in the 150 years after Calvin's arrival in Geneva. Given the high rate of survival of Genevan records, this probably represents the majority of cases that occurred. The witch-hunt in Geneva peaked relatively early, in the 1560s and early 1570s. The records show that, outside the witch-hunt of 1571, Geneva had one of the lowest rates of execution in Europe, about 20%. Geneva magistrates seem to have used banishment as an alternative to execution in cases where the guilt or innocence of the subject was in doubt, rather than following the practice of other areas which simply tortured until a confession was obtained. The relatively mild **torture** practiced by the Genevans kept individual witch cases from developing into large hunts, and in some cases the magistrates were uninterested in following up accusations even when an accused witch named others. Witchcraft in Geneva as elsewhere was associated with the rural population. The rural areas attached to the city, which contained about one-fifth its population, accounted for approximately half of the witch cases. The last execution of a witch in Geneva was that of Michée Chauderon in 1652, and the last witch trial was in 1680–1681.

REFERENCES: Robin Briggs. *Witches and Neighbors: The Social and Cultural Context of European Witchcraft.* New York: Penguin, 1996; William Monter. *Witchcraft in France and Switzerland: The Borderlands during the Reformation*. Ithaca and London: Cornell University Press, 1976; William G. Naphy. *Plagues, Poisons and Potions: Plague-Spreading Conspiracies in the Western Alps c. 1530–1640*. Manchester and New York: Manchester University Press, 2002.

GERMANY, WITCH-HUNTING IN

The German lands of the Holy Roman Empire were the center of the European witch-hunt, persecuting with a ferocity almost unknown elsewhere. Brian Levack estimates the total number of witch trials in the German-speaking lands of the empire as at least 30,000 and probably much more—more than half of the European total. The number of deaths is unknown but is undoubtedly a majority of the total European figure. The German lands were also the home of a large number of influential demonologists, both supporters and opponents of witch-hunting. The reasons for this German preeminence are many, but foremost among them seems to be the patchwork of small territories covering much of the country, particularly in the west and southwest. Northern and Eastern Germany, dominated by larger and more centralized political units, saw relatively little witch-hunting (with the exception of the Duchy of Mecklenburg). Even in the west, the Palatinate, a centralized Calvinist territory for much of the witch-hunt period, saw few trials and no witch **executions,** and large, centralized Catholic **Bavaria** proportionately had many fewer than smaller Catholic territories. The great German witch-hunts are virtually all associated with small, independent principalities, particularly those ruled by officials of the Catholic Church. A local witch-hunt in one of these territories could rage unchecked by any central legal authority comparable to the Parlement of Paris in **France** or the English assize judges. The imperial court at Speyer could exercise little authority in most German territories. Authorities in these small principalities were also more vulnerable to popular pressure for witch-hunts than were mighty potentates like the emperor or the electors of Bavaria and Saxony.

Germany was not prominent in the early phases of the witch-hunt but began to emerge into a central position with the career of the German Dominican inquisitors Johann Sprenger (1436–1495) and Heinrich **Kramer**. Kramer was the author of the *Malleus Maleficarum* (1486), a text more closely associated with actual witch-hunting in Germany than elsewhere—the majority of its editions were German. There was a steady drizzle of cases involving individuals, couples and small groups in the fourteenth and most of the fifteenth century, but the scale of German witch-hunting increased with Kramer's persecution from 1482 to 1486, in the area near Constance. This involved 48 defendants and some executions, although the number is unclear. Kramer's promotion of witch-hunting in Germany was not unopposed, and he frequently complained of the opposition offered by church and civil authorities. Although Kramer's attempt to launch a witch-hunt in **Innsbruck** in 1485 was unsuccessful, mostly because of opposition by ecclesiastical authorities, large-

A portion of a newsletter about the infernal deeds and the execution of the witch Anna Eber-lehrin, printed by Elias Wellhöffe, Ausburg, 1669. © Dover Pictorial Archive.

scale witch-hunting seems to be have become more common thereafter, particularly in the Rhineland.

The intense witch-hunting characteristic of some areas of Germany in the late fifteenth century gave way to a pronounced lull in the early sixteenth century. Despite the lack of actual persecutions, awareness of witches and their importance did not greatly diminish—they were frequently mentioned by both Catholic and Protestant preachers and polemicists in the debates of the early Reformation, and Hans **Baldung Grien,** Albrecht Dürer (1471–1528) and a host of lesser lights produced memorable witch **art.** Witch images generally circulated more widely in Germany than elsewhere.

Witch-hunting began to revive after midcentury with the **Weisensteig** witch-hunt claiming 63 victims in 1562 and 1563. (Ironically, the greatest and most thoroughgoing attack on witch-hunting and witch belief produced by a German was the **physician** Johann **Weyer's** *On the Tricks of Demons,* published in 1563, at the beginning of the revival of German witch-hunting.) This revival seems to have been connected with climactic deterioration and possibly to a slackening in the conflict between Catholics and Protestants that had absorbed a great deal of German persecuting zeal in the preceding years of the sixteenth century. Witch-hunting intensified after 1570, and the German witch-hunt reached its first peak in the late 1580s and 1590s. Particularly intense witch-hunts in the late sixteenth century include the **Wiesensteig** and **Obermachthal** hunts, that in the archbishopric of Trier, where nearly four hundred witches were burned between 1587 and 1593, and that of the territory of the Convent of Quedlinburg, where 133 witches burned in a single day in 1589. The most significant demonologist to emerge from the German witch-hunt in this period, Peter **Binsfeld,** was suffragan (or assistant) bishop of Trier, and his *Treatise on the Confessions of Evildoers and Witches* (1591) took a tough line. The Trier witch-hunt is also noteworthy for its persecution of child witches, which would become a major feature of witch-hunting in Germany and elsewhere. Generally speaking, witch persecution in this period and later was often seen as part of a general project of moral reform, and witches usually had more to fear from zealous followers of the Protestant Reformation or Catholic Counter-Reformation than from more easygoing or corrupt rulers.

The law governing witchcraft in Germany during the late sixteenth century was supposed to that of the Holy Roman Empire, particularly the *Carolina,* the code of criminal law proclaimed by Charles V (Holy Roman Emperor, 1519–1556) in 1532. Article 109 of the *Carolina* dealt with witchcraft but did so in a way that was not informed by demonology. The *Carolina,* proclaimed at a low point in German witch-hunting, provided for the punishment of witches by burning, but only for those witches who used **magic** to cause harm. Witch-craft that did not cause harm, whether or not directly connected to the Devil, was not to be punished with death, but with other punishments at the discre-tion of the judge. This mild law, which also limited the amount of **torture** that could be applied to a criminal suspect, had little effect in many parts of Ger-many; however, as many jurisdictions retained the right to legislate for them-selves. The influential 1572 Criminal Constitutions of Electoral Saxony defined **satanic pact** or dealings with the Devil, with or without *maleficia,* as punishable by death by burning, and the Bavarian Mandate against Supersti-tion, Magic and Witchcraft of 1612 took a similar hard line.

Another unique characteristic of the German legal system was the promi-nent role of university law faculties, which fulfilled many of the functions of appellate courts. Judges were frequently required by imperial and local law to consult with law professors, particularly in witchcraft cases. The role of univer-sities in German witch-hunting seldom led to a moderating effect, however. Because universities in Germany, like all European universities, were church institutions (whether Catholic or Protestant) their law faculties often inter-preted witchcraft theologically, as a matter of satanic pact rather than *maleficia.* Involvement of university scholars was one route by which demonological notions of pact and **sabbat** entered the German legal system. German magis-trates desiring professorial approval for witch-hunting and torture also were sometimes not above "university shopping"—trying different law faculties until they found a congenial one.

Lack of central judicial supervision also explains another factor tending to magnify witch-hunting in Germany—the enthusiastic and unrestrained use of torture. The *Carolina's* limits were often ignored, and some accused German witches were tortured dozens of times. German torturers, a profession usually combined with executioner, were also known for their creativity in devising new techniques for the infliction of pain.

German witches themselves resembled witches elsewhere—about 80 to 90 percent were women, fitting the usual pattern, and most were poor, old and rural. The German construction of the evil female witch went along with a construction of the "good woman," identified with the Virgin Mary in Catholic areas and with the pious housewife and mother in Protestant ones, and defined by domesticity and subservience. German witches were often single women who had a reputation for lack of subservience to men and authority generally, although in a large German witch-hunt virtually any woman, and many men, were vulnerable to **accusation.** Despite the prominent role of courts and authorities in German witch-hunts, they were not unpopular—in many areas witch-hunts were actively demanded by ordinary Germans, particularly in times of bad weather and widespread crop failure—and the period from 1560 to 1630, the height of the central European witch-hunt, was one marked by increased cold, glacial advance and climactic deterioration. Much of Germany combined a high population density with backward and undiversified agriculture, making it particularly vulnerable to bad weather and climactic change. Witches were often blamed for these phenomena, and ordinary Germans were capable of taking a great deal of initiative in these matters. The great witch-hunt in the archbishopric of Trier in the early 1590s saw local village committees, established to fight witches, temporarily wresting judicial authority from the Bishop's administrators. In 1588, after a severe hailstorm, the poor peasants of the town of Schwabsoien in the Bishopric of Augsburg expressed a willingness to sell the communal forest to pay for the services of the torturer and witch-hunter Hans **Vollmair,** the "Master of Biberach." The focus of these "village inquisitions," however, remained *maleficia* rather than satanic pact or sabbat attendance.

Some German theologians attacked people who blamed bad weather and other disasters on witches, holding that this infringed on the power of God and that a community would do better to consider which of its own sins God was punishing rather than look for witches in their midst. The early-sixteenth-century Catholic theologian Martin **Plantsch** was a prominent supporter of this theory, but it was particularly marked among sixteenth-century Lutheran theologians, although other Lutherans strongly backed witch-hunting.

German witch-beliefs included a common description of witches in the "Wild Hunt." The leader, often identified by learned writers as the pagan goddess **Diana,** was referred to by Germans as Holda or Perchta. Certain mountains, such as the Heuberg in Swabia, were identified as gathering places of the witches.

After a brief lull in the early seventeenth century, German witch-hunting became active again around 1611 with the beginnings of the persecutions at **Ellwangen.** The wave of persecutions culminating in the late 1620s and concentrated, although not exclusively, in Catholic ecclesiastical territories in the Rhineland and Franconia is the most severe in European history. In addition to the Ellwangen persecution, it included massive persecutions in **Offenburg, Baden-Baden, Eichstätt, Mergentheim, Würzburg, Bamberg** and Schwabisch Gmund as well as many other territories. The period actually saw something like the creation of a civil service devoted specifically to witch-hunting. Rulers established special witch prisons and witch-commissions to oversee witch-hunting in their territories, and recruited specialist witch-hunters who moved from territory to territory applying their expertise.

The great Franconian persecutions involving hundreds of suspects mostly ended around 1630. The immediate cause was the Imperial Diet at Regensburg in 1630, which saw a concerted effort to halt the persecutions in the Catholic ecclesiastical territories, which had begun to affect members of the social elite. There are also indications that in some territories the hunts were falling apart for internal reasons, because the social tensions they created were becoming unbearable and some magistrates had begun to doubt their mission. The long-term cause for the decline in German witch-hunting was an improvement in climactic conditions beginning around 1630, which made German life slightly less precarious. Another factor was the publication of the German Jesuit Friedrich von **Spee's** anonymous *Warning to Prosecutors* (1631). Unlike Weyer, Spee did not deny the existence of witches, but focused on the Achilles's heel of German witch-hunting: its dependence on irregular judicial proceedings and evidence gained by torture. Another vulnerability was the increasingly common reliance on the testimony of children.

Although many German princes and university faculties withdrew their approval from witch-hunting and even began to work against it in the ensuing decades, 1630 did not mark the end of the German witch-hunt by any means. The focus of witch-hunting shifted from Franconia to the Electorate of Cologne, where as many as two thousand witches died during the 1630s under the rule of the Archbishop-Elector Ferdinand von Wittelsbach (1577–1650), of the ducal house of Bavaria. The actual witch-hunt was carried out by specially commissioned magistrates, including the loutish Franz Buirmann and the scholarly Heinrich von Schultheis, who wrote a response to Spee, *Detailed Instructions on how to proceed against the horrid vice of Witchcraft* (1634). This was the last really large-scale witch-hunt in Germany.

Smaller, local hunts persisted into the second half of the seventeenth century. A zealous magistrate, George Ludwig Geisz, ran a witch-hunt in the small town of Lindheim in 1661. There were 30 executions before escaped prisoners, appealing to the imperial court at Speyer, forced a halt to the trials. (Geisz had to leave town to avoid retribution.) A major witch-hunt, although not on the scale of the hunts of the 1620s, took place in the independent Protestant town of **Esslingen,** until then largely free of persecution, from 1662 to 1666. About three dozen were executed. A much larger hunt was the **Zaubererjackl** series of trials in the archbishopric of Salzburg from 1675 to 1690. This persecution took at least two hundred lives and was the last witch-hunt anywhere in Europe to involve hundreds of victims. It marked a temporary shift from the image of the witch as a poor rural woman to that of an urban beggar, often a boy or young man.

Witch-hunting proceeded at a moderate pace in eighteenth-century Germany. Large-scale witch-hunts were ended, but individuals and small groups were still vulnerable despite the efforts of German witch-hunt opponents such as Christian **Thomasius.** Children continued to be targets. The imperial city of Augsburg, which had seen little witch-hunting, imprisoned about 20 children on witchcraft charges during a witch-hunt beginning in 1723. None were executed, although the last child was not released until 1729. (Conditions were so bad that four children petitioned the town council to be allowed to die.) The case of the aged nun, Sister Maria Renata Sanger von Mossau, executed near Würzburg in 1749 for causing the **possession** of other nuns at her convent attracted much publicity and controversy. The case employed the classical theory of demonological witchcraft, including the sabbat and satanic pact, indicating the continued vitality of these ideas. Father Ferdinand **Sterzinger's** speech before the Bavarian Academy of Sciences in 1766 denouncing witch-hunting set off a major controversy in Catholic Germany in which many defended traditional witch beliefs. The last witch executed in the German lands was a poor, mentally disturbed woman, Anna Maria Schwägel, killed in the prince-abbacy of Kempten in 1775.

REFERENCES: Wolfgang Behringer. "Weather, Hunger and Fear: Origins of the European Witch-Hunts in Climate, Society and Mentality." Translated by David Lederer. *German History* 13 (1995): 1–27; Wolfgang Behringer. *Witchcraft Persecutions in Bavaria: Popular Magic, Religious Zealotry, and Reason of State in Early Modern Europe.* Translated by J. C. Grayson and David Lederer. Cambridge: Cambridge University Press, 1997; Sigrid Brauner. *Fearless Wives and Frightened Shrews: The Construction of the Witch in Early Modern Germany.* Amherst: University of Massachusetts Press, 1995; Robin Briggs. *Witches and Neighbors: The Social and Cultural Context of European Witchcraft.* New York: Penguin, 1996; Brian P. Levack. *The Witch-Hunt in Early Modern Europe.* London and New York: Longman, 1987; H. C. Erik Midelfort. "Heartland of the Witchcraze." *History Today* 31 (1981): 27–36; H. C. Erik Midelfort. *Witch Hunting in Southwestern Germany, 1562–1684.* Stanford: Stanford University Press, 1972; Lyndal Roper. " 'Evil Imaginings and Fantasies': Child Witches and the End of the Witch Craze." *Past and Present* 167 (May 2000): 107–139; Lyndal Roper. *Oedipus and the Devil: Witchcraft, Sexuality and Religion in Early Modern Europe.* New York: Routledge, 1994; Robert S. Walinski-Kiehl. "The Devil's Children: Child Witch-Trials in Early Modern Germany." *Continuity and Change* 11 (1996): 171–189; Robert S. Walinski-Kiehl. " 'Godly States,' Confessional Conflict and Witch-Hunting in Early Modern Germany." *Mentalities* 5 (1988): 13–25.

GIFFORD, GEORGE (D. 1620)

George Gifford, an Elizabethan Puritan minister, published two works on witchcraft showing remarkable awareness of the village milieu in which witchcraft **accusations** arose. Gifford's well-written books, *A Discourse of the Subtill Practises of Devilles by Witches and Sorcerers* (1587) and *A Dialogue Concerning Witches and Witchcraftes* (1593) emerged from his experience as a preacher in Maldon, Essex. Essex was the English county that saw by far the largest number of indictments and prosecutions for witchcraft during the witch-hunt. Gifford was the second demonological writer in English (the first was Reginald **Scot**) and the first to base his work primarily on English sources. He recounts several witch cases, emphasizing the complex personal interrelationships between witches, victims and accusers that led to accusations. Gifford recounts several instances of the popular witchcraft story where the denial of charity to an old woman is followed by personal disaster, leading to an accusation of witchcraft. His works are also sources for popular beliefs about witches, such as the belief that a way to defend oneself from a witch was to draw blood from her. Gifford thought that the fundamental error that many people made was to ascribe power to the witch herself, or even to the Devil, rather than to God, who is the ultimate source of the evils.

Gifford believed in the existence of witches and endorsed the biblical death penalty for them, but he recommended that magistrates and investigators proceed with caution. As a preacher, he believed that it was necessary to teach those who believed themselves harmed by witchcraft to bear their sufferings with patience, knowing that it was God's will that they be afflicted. The real menace in Gifford's eyes was not the wicked witch, but the **cunning** man or woman who often was the first recourse of those who believed themselves to have been afflicted by witchcraft or other misfortune. By using powers diabolical in origin to benefit people, the cunning folk posed a far greater threat to their souls than did the wicked witches. Recourse to cunning folk also served people as a substitute for the prayer and repentance that Gifford believed was the only proper response to affliction.

Gifford's *Dialogue* was republished once, in 1603, and was cited in other English demonological writings such as Richard **Bernard's** *Guide to Grand Jury Men* (1627). Despite Gifford's belief in witches, his work was one source for Thomas **Ady's** skeptical *A Candle in the Dark* (1656). His work also influenced the development of the modern **community-based** interpretation of witch-hunting.

REFERENCES: Alan Macfarlane. "A Tudor Anthropologist: George Gifford's *Discourse* and *Dialogue*." In *The Damned Art: Essays in the Literature of Witchcraft*, ed. Sydney Anglo, 140–155. Boston: Routledge and Kegan Paul, 1977; James Sharpe. *Instruments of Darkness: Witchcraft in Early Modern England*. Philadelphia: University of Pennsylvania Press, 1996.

GIORDANO DA BERGAMO

Giordano da Bergamo, an Italian Dominican theologian, wrote a Latin *Inquiry of Witches* around 1470. The work, which was not printed until modern times, drew on Giordano's personal experiences with witches. Giordano took a compromise position between the developing witch stereotype and the **Canon Episcopi**. He argued that demons could deceive witches, whether awake or asleep, into thinking they traveled when they actually remained at home physically, a position consistent with the *Canon*, but that demons also could actually physically transport witches, the position more commonly upheld by fifteenth-century writers. A given case of witch transport could have either explanation. Giordano denied the possibility of witch **transformations,** always a demonic illusion, and was skeptical about the **Devil's mark.** He also endorsed the prevalence of human-demon **sex** and was one of the few early witchcraft theorists to devote as much effort to the question of men's intercourse with demons in female guise than women's intercourse with a demon in male guise. Giordano was also one of the earliest writers to state that holding correct beliefs about witches was a matter of Christian faith.

REFERENCES: Jeffrey Burton Russell. *Witchcraft in the Middle Ages*. Ithaca, Cornell University Press, 1972; Walter Stephens. *Demon Lovers: Witchcraft, Sex, and the Crisis of Belief*. Chicago and London: University of Chicago Press, 2002.

GLANVILL, JOSEPH (1636–1680)

Like his friends and fellow late-seventeenth-century English witch believers Henry More (1614–1687) and Richard Baxter (1615–1691), the Anglican clergyman Joseph Glanvill was a leader in applying empirical techniques to the spiritual world to prove its reality and confute atheists. His work on the reality of witches and supernatural phenomena was first published in 1666 as *A Philosophical Endeavour towards the Defense of the Being of Witches and Apparitions*. This edition was mostly destroyed in the Great Fire of London in 1666, but two subsequent editions appeared in 1667, the second under the title *Some Philosophical Considerations Touching the Being of Witches* and the third as *A Blow at Modern Sadducism*. The third edition included the famous case of the phantom drummer at the house of a Mr. Mompesson in Tedworth, Wiltshire, which Glanvill visited in 1663. The work was posthumously published with material added by More and Anthony Horneck (1641–1697), who contributed an account of the **Mora** witches in **Sweden,** as *Sadducismus Triumphatus* (1681). Throughout his intellectual engagement with witchcraft, Glanvill's primary concern was not witchcraft and witches but the reality of the spiritual world and its interaction with the material world. Glanvill was devoted to the struggle against atheism, which, like other Christian apologists of the time, he associated with the materialistic doctrines of the philosopher Thomas Hobbes (1588–1679). "Sadducism," closely allied to atheism and materialism, was the doctrine of the ancient Jewish Sadducees, who had denied the reality and immortality of the soul. Glanvill's work was part of a refocusing of demonology in the time of the decline of actual persecution. The enemy against whom his writings were directed was no longer primarily the witch herself, but the atheist who denied the reality of the spiritual world.

Glanvill was a member and polemical defender of the Royal Society for the Advancing of Natural Knowledge, Restoration **England's** foremost scientific organization, and many have found Glanvill's philosophical skepticism and role as a defender of natural philosophy incompatible with his belief in the reality of witchcraft. There was no incompatibility between the two positions during his time, however. Glanvill attempted to rebut atheist and Sadducist assaults on the reality of the spiritual world empirically through the compilation of supernatural anecdotes, including witch stories. Because it was necessary for these stories to be veracious, Glanvill was careful to credit witnesses and recount his own investigations of the phenomena, as in the case of the Drummer of Tedworth. His compilations of witchcraft and other supernatural stories can be seen as models of empiricism.

Glanvill became identified as England's foremost defender of the reality of witchcraft through his debate with the **physician** John **Webster,** author of *The Displaying of Supposed Witchcraft* (1677). Webster claimed that although evil spirits existed, God prevented them from entering into compacts with witches. Recognizing Glanvill as his principal opponent, Webster made him in particular the target of his attacks. Glanvill responded in *Sadducismus Triumphatus*. He asserted that in arguing against the belief in demonic **possession** by claiming that demonic spirits were "subtle bodies" unable to occupy the same space as other bodies, Webster, despite his proclaimed piety, was playing into the hands of Hobbesian materialism with its denial of a spiritual world. Glanvill was considered by most judges to have vanquished Webster, and after his death, he continued to be seen in England, **New England** and Europe (a German translation of *Sadducismus Triumphatus* was published in 1701) as a leading champions of belief in witches. *Sadducismus Triumphatus* went through several editions through the first quarter of the eighteenth century and greatly influenced subsequent demonologists in the English-speaking word, including Baxter, whose *The Certainty of the World of Spirits* (1691) is heavily indebted to Glanvill's work. Other demonologists drawing on Glanvill were Richard **Bovet,** George **Sinclair** and **Cotton Mather.**

REFERENCE: Ian Bostridge. *Witchcraft and Its Transformations, c. 1650–c. 1750.* Oxford: Clarendon Press, 1997.

GLOVER, MARY

In April 1602, Mary Glover, the 14-year-old daughter of a prosperous London shopkeeper, quarreled with an old woman named Elizabeth Jackson. A few days later, she fell ill, eventually accruing a number of dramatic, if intermittent, symptoms, including muteness, blindness and a swelling in the throat that made it impossible for her to eat. Glover attributed these symptoms to bewitchment by Jackson, murmuring "hang her" whenever Jackson was brought into her presence. Glover was visited by large numbers of people on her sickbed, and the question of whether her illness was natural or demonic divided London's religious, medical and legal establishments. The most prestigious members of the London College of **Physician**s, in alliance with the bishop of London, Richard Bancroft (1544–1610), held that her illness was natural or fraudulent. Bancroft was particularly suspicious of the Glover family's Puritanism.

Jackson was indicted on December 1, 1602. Unfortunately for her, the judge presiding over the trial was the lord chief justice of the Court of Common Pleas, Sir Edmund **Anderson,** a zealous witch-hunter. Anderson demolished attempts to explain Glover's illness medically, and his charge to the jury virtually ordered conviction. Jackson failed some of the common tests for witch-craft, such as the ability to recite the Lord's Prayer (this is the first recorded use of this test in a court of law) and was convicted and sentenced to a year in prison. This was the maximum sentence available under the Witchcraft Act of 1563 for a witch who had not killed anyone. She did not serve the sentence, however, but was released shortly afterward, probably due to Bancroft's intervention. Glover was exorcised on December 14 by a group of Puritan clergy and pious laymen. Bancroft later arrested and imprisoned several of them, he was highly suspicious of all exorcising activities since the John **Darrell** affair.

Intellectually, the most important result of Glover's case was a work by one of the physicians who had ineffectually testified in Jackson's favor at the trial, Edward Jorden (1569–1632). Jorden's *A Briefe Discourse of a Disease Called the Suffocation of the Mother* (1603) ascribed Glover's illness to "hysteria," a disease caused by the displacement of the uterus. This was an unusual stance for him to take. The usual disease to which symptoms resembling bewitchment was ascribed was melancholy, not hysteria, a diagnosis that had little currency in **England** (Jorden's was the first book in English on the subject). It was also unusual to ascribe hysteria to a woman as young as Glover, as it was usually associated with sexually mature women. Jorden dealt with this objection by broadening the concept of hysteria to assert that it could be caused by problems in the brain as well as the female reproductive system. Jorden placed his writing in the tradition of opposition to witchcraft belief, drawing several examples from Reginald **Scot's** *The Discoverie of Witchcraft* (1584)—a very bold move given Scot's bad religious reputation. Jorden would go on to testify for the defense in the Anne **Gunter** case, another case of alleged **possession** through witchcraft. Despite the intellectual quality of his work, it was not reprinted until the twentieth century, and melancholy continued to be the most common medical diagnosis for symptoms resembling bewitchment.

REFERENCE: Michael MacDonald, ed. *Witchcraft and Hysteria in Elizabethan London: Edward Jorden and the Mary Glover Case.* London and New York: Tavistock/Routledge, 1991.

GOATS

See Animals.

GRENIER, JEAN

Jean Grenier was among the most famous French **werewolves.** In February 1603, Grenier, then 14 years old, ran away from home after his father, Pierre, had beaten him for breaking the Lenten fast. Grenier got a job as a cowherd in the village of Paulet. One of his fellow cowherds was a 13-year-old girl named Marguerite Poirier. Three days before Grenier's arrival on the scene, Poirier had been attacked by a large, wolflike animal, whom she beat off with a stick. When he heard of this, Grenier boasted of having turned into a wolf by means of a skin given him by a dark man named Pierre Labourant, of having attacked Poirier and of having killed and eaten children—a standard feature of lycanthropy cases. A local magistrate heard of Grenier's repeated boasting and associated him with attacks on children that had been taking place in the area. Grenier was taken in and closely questioned, eventually breaking down and describing how the dark man, who he now referred to as the Lord of the Forest, had given him a wolfskin and special ointment in return for his service. He also implicated his father and a friend of his from back home, Pierre du Tillaire. Grenier was also found to have a **Devil's mark.**

The local court of Coutras, which had jurisdiction over Grenier's home, had Pierre Grenier and Pierre du Tillaire arrested. In a confrontation with his son, Pierre claimed that Jean was an idiot who could be easily convinced to say anything. Jean revoked his **accusation** of Pierre, then reinstated it. A search of the Grenier house found neither wolfskin nor ointment. The local court condemned Jean Grenier to be hanged and burned, and the two others to be tortured. Although not legally obliged to refer death sentences to the Parlement of Bordeaux, which had jurisdiction over this part of **France,** the Coutras court customarily did so, so everyone went to Bordeaux. Some of the magistrates of the Parlement may have doubted the evidence of Jean Grenier's having been a witch, whereas others may have regarded him, with his obvious mental impairments and a record of having been beaten and neglected by his family, as an appropriate object of judicial mercy. The court ordered that Jean Grenier be held for life in a local monastery, where he had been staying during the trial. Pierre Grenier and Pierre du Tillaire were released pending further investigation, and disappear from the record. The witch-hunter Pierre de **Lancre** interviewed Jean Grenier in 1610 at the monastery and reported that he was sticking to his story of having been a werewolf and of his accusation of his father, whom he hated. He also reported that Grenier had a remarkable ability to run around on his hands and legs. Grenier died shortly thereafter.

REFERENCE: Caroline Oates. "The Trial of a Teenage Werewolf, Bordeaux, 1603." *Criminal Justice History* 9 (1988): 1–29.

GRILLANDUS, PAULUS

Paulo Grillando, a papal judge active in witch trials in the south of **Italy** in the early sixteenth century, Latininized his name to publish a treatise on witchcraft and the law, *Treatise on Heretics and Sorcerers* (1524). It contains a detailed description of the **sabbat,** and many anecdotes, some of which seem derived from folktales about witches who had attended sabbats at Benevento. Grillandus also recounted his own judicial experiences. Unlike many of his Italian contemporaries and successors, Grillandus fully accepted the witch stereotype, including *maleficia*, sexual intercourse with demons, the satanic pact and the sabbat. The influence of his work was not immediate—Grillandus was publishing at the end of the first wave of witch-hunting, and his *Treatise* was the last significant demonology to be published for decades. It was reprinted in 1546, however, and had a great effect on Catholic demonology, being extensively quarried by Jean **Bodin,** Francesco Maria **Guazzo,** Pierre de **Lancre** and Martin **del Rio.**

REFERENCE: Julio Caro Baroja. *The World of the Witches.* Translated by O. N. V. Glendinning. Chicago: University of Chicago Press, 1965.

GUAZZO, FRANCESCO MARIA

Francesco Maria Guazzo was the author of an influential demonology, *Compendium Maleficarum*, published in 1608 and reprinted with additions in 1626. A monk of the small, Milan-based order of the Ambrosians, Guazzo was present in 1605 at the court of Duke William of Julich-Cleves, a German principality then undergoing a witch-hunt at which Guazzo assisted. Although, unlike many other demonologists, he did not often bring personal experience into his writings, he did recount the suicide of a 90-year-old sorcerer charged with bewitching the duke. During his time in **Germany,** he claimed, he began work on the *Compendium*. The influence of Guazzo's German experience may be seen in the fact that he was the only Italian writer after the

Frontispiece from the *Compendium Malleficarum* (1626) by Francesco Maria Guazzo, Italian demonologist. © The Art Archive/Dagli Orti (A).

mid–sixteenth century to accept fully the theory of diabolical witchcraft with the **sabbat** and satanic pact. The *Compendium* is not particularly original, and most of it is made up of passages taken from the works of other authors. It does show a wide range of reading in both general and demonological literature. Among demonologists, Guazzo's principal source was Nicholas **Remy,** but he also drew on the work of Martin **del Rio and** Johannes **Nider,** as well as Heinrich **Kramer's** *Malleus Maleficarum* (1486), among other Catholic authorities. Guazzo saw witchcraft as a global phenomenon and includes stories of Catholic missionaries and converts and their struggles against demons in the far-flung fields of Japan, Mexico and Peru. He covers such standard demonological topics as the sabbat, the heritability of witchcraft, the powers of witches, various forms of *maleficium*, demonic **possession** and the sexuality of witches. The *Compendium*'s discussion of witches and **sex** had a particularly great influence on Lodovico Maria **Sinistrari's** treatment of the subject. The *Compendium* also contains many illustrations of typical activities of witches and the Devil.

Guazzo considered Protestants his enemy nearly as much as witches. One of his principal goals was demonstrating the efficacy of Catholic practices, such as the use of relics, holy water and the sound of church bells, against demons and witches. Protestants, by contrast, were utterly powerless against witches and demons, and Guazzo repeated a story that demons had abandoned possessed persons to attend the funeral of Martin Luther (1483–1546).

REFERENCE: Francesco Maria Guazzo. *Compendium Maleficarum*. Ed. Montague Summers, trans. E. A. Ashwin. 1929. Reprint, New York: Dover Press, 1988.

GUICHARD OF TROYES

The case of Guichard of Troyes was one of the earliest political prosecutions of a magician in late medieval Europe. Guichard, a churchman who had come from obscure origins to be bishop of Troyes and one of the richest and most powerful prelates in **France,** was a classic target of a sorcery **accusation** in the fourteenth century—the person of low birth whose meteoric rise, to many, could only be explained by the power of the Devil. He rebuffed one attack in 1307, when Pope Clement V (pope, 1305–1314) declared him innocent of charges of corruption. The next year, a hermit named Reynaud of Langres claimed before the archbishop of Sens and royal officials that he had witnessed Guichard performing **magical** acts at night, accompanied by a local witch, around the time of the death of Queen Jeanne of Navarre (1273–1305), Guichard's one-time patron who had become his enemy. Reynaud of Langres also claimed that he had refused Guichard's plea to poison the brother and children of the king of France, Philip IV (r. 1285–1314). Word soon reached the king, who took up the case as he would later take up posthumous charges of sorcery against Pope Boniface VIII (pope, 1294–1303) to pressure Clement to let the king have his way over the **Templars.** The king declared that if the pope did not institute an enquiry into the bishop's actions, the king would do so himself. Clement yielded and charged the archbishop of Sens to arrest Guichard on charges of *maleficia* and poisoning, as well as other unspecified crimes. By adding unspecified crimes to the list of charges, Clement gave Philip's officials *carte blanche* to make any other charge against Guichard they thought would be effective. The royal officials took no chances, actually abducting Guichard from the archbishop's prison.

The formal enquiry began in October 1308. Guichard was charged before a tribunal consisting of the archbishop and two other bishops with having invoked the Devil with the aid of a local fortuneteller and sorceress, Margueronne de Bellevillette, and a Dominican priest, Jean de Fay. After Guichard did homage to the Devil, **Satan** instructed him in how to destroy the queen using **image magic.** The story was laid out by Reynaud of Langres, by Guichard's chamberlain, who was tortured until he agreed to tell the story the royal officials wanted told, and by Margueronne, who agreed to do so after being threatened with **torture** and allowed to present herself as a horrified witness of Guichard's diabolic dealings rather than an accomplice. After a four-month adjournment, royal officials came back with more witnesses and more charges, beginning with one that Guichard was himself the son of an incubus demon who his mother had invoked to overcome her sterility. Twenty-seven witnesses provided details of this story. Guichard was also charged with dealings with demons throughout his life. It was claimed that he kept in a glass flask a demon with whom he had frequent conversations and who spied on members of his household for him. Guichard was charged with responsibility for a number of murders and with preparing a special poison out of adders, scorpions, toads and spiders to be administered to the royal princes. The net result of all this was anticlimactic. The enquiry spun out for years, and once Clement had agreed to Philip's plans for the destruction of the Templars in 1311, the king lost interest in the Guichard case. Guichard was transferred from royal to papal custody and set free in 1314. His reputation was restored to the degree that the pope appointed him to a church position in **Germany,** and subsequent fourteenth-century writers treated the affair as an attempt to frame him.

REFERENCE: Norman Cohn. *Europe's Inner Demons: The Demonization of Christians in Medieval Christendom*. Rev. ed. Chicago: University of Chicago Press, 2000.

GUNTER, ANNE

The case of Anne Gunter was one of the best-known and best-documented examples of fraudulent claims of bewitchment and diabolical **possession** in seventeenth-century **England.** It is also a classic example of how village feuding could erupt into witchcraft **accusation.** The prime mover in the affair was Brian Gunter (1540?–1628), Anne's father, a gentleman who lived in the village of North Moreton, close to Oxford. Gunter was a violent and contentious man, not popular in the village, and had a particularly nasty feud with the Gregory family, a clan of yeomen of which two members Gunter had killed years earlier in violence related to a football match. Anne's illness appeared in the fall of 1604. **Countermagic** and consultation with local **physicians** and **cunning folk** led to accusations against three local women, Elizabeth Gregory, Agnes Pepwell and Mary Pepwell, as having bewitched her. The Pepwells were standard examples of the kind of women who were vulnerable to witchcraft accusations—a mother and her illegitimate daughter, poor and marginal in village society, they already had reputations as witches. They were probably added to the list of accused to strengthen the credibility of the charge against Gregory, Brian Gunter's real target.

Anne's sufferings attracted wide interest both from local people and outside the village as far as Oxford, where the Gunters had family connections. Many came to see her fits. Anne and Brian, with the help of recently published accounts of such witchcraft cases as that of the witches of **Warboys,** added to the credibility of the accusation by having Anne ostensibly vomit pins as well as emit them from other orifices of her body. Brian also gave her a potion of "sack and salad oil" to encourage vomiting. Anne's sufferings were not convincing to all who viewed her, however.

The climax of the case's first phase was a trial of Elizabeth Gregory and Mary Pepwell (Agnes had not been taken into custody) at the Assizes in Abingdon, one of the first witchcraft trials under the Statute of 1604. The efforts of a local gentleman, Thomas Hinton, who was skeptical of Anne's story, contributed to an acquittal. But Brian Gunter, a man of immense stubbornness, was not about to give up. Anne continued to exhibit symptoms of bewitchment and demonic possession, and Brian Gunter determined to bring her before King **James I** on his visit to Oxford in the summer of 1605. He could hardly have chosen a worse tactic, although it was not without reason. In the early part of James's reign, not only Gunter but many of his English subjects overestimated his interest in witch-hunting. James in fact prided himself on his ability to see through deceptions like Anne's, and the clergy with whom he surrounded himself in England, such as Richard Bancroft (1544–1610) and Samuel Harsnett (1561–1631), had become hardened skeptics of claims of possession after the cases of John **Darrell** and Mary **Glover.** (It may have been from Harsnett's pamphlet attacking Catholic exorcisms, *A Declaration of Egregious Popish Impostures* [1603], that Brian Gunter got the idea of feeding his daughter sack and salad oil to induce vomiting). Furthermore, Anne was growing weary of the charade. James took custody of Anne, passing her on to Bancroft and then to Harsnett. Isolated from her father, Anne quickly recanted her story, explaining how she had come to fake her "demonic" symptoms. Lengthy proceedings were brought against the Gunters in the court of Star Chamber, which accounts for the voluminous documentation of the case, exceeding that of any other English witch case. Brian Gunter was imprisoned, but the ultimate judgment against him is unknown, as is Anne's fate.

REFERENCE: James Sharpe. *The Bewitching of Anne Gunter: A Horrible and True Story of Deception, Witchcraft, Murder and the King of England.* New York: Routledge, 2000.

H

HAIZMANN, JOHANN CHRISTOPH (1652–1700)

On August 29, 1677, in the **Austrian** village of Pottebrun, Johann Christoph Haizmann, a painter from **Bavaria,** working in the local castele, fell into convulsions and exhibited the symptoms of bewitchment. Haizmann's case took a peculiar turn when he spontaneously confessed to having signed a **satanic pact** nine years earlier. A Pottenbrun magistrate questioned him as to whether he was a witch, but the local authorities treated him as a demonically possessed person rather than a witch. The peak of the witch-hunt had long passed in the area, and the treatment of Haizmann's case indicates that the categories of the witch and the possessed person were becoming less distinct. The local Catholic priest, Leopold Braun, took pity on Haizmann, whom he described as a miserable man, and wrote to the nearby Abbey of Mariazell for help. In early September, Haizmann arrived at Mariazell, where he underwent severe exorcisms. On September 8, the Feast of the Nativity of the Virgin, Haizmann had a vision of the Devil in the form of a winged dragon. He seized the contract, written in his own blood, from the Devil's grip. Over the course of the next three weeks, he was apparently cured of his demonic affliction. This was a great triumph for Mariazell, publicized in the form of a ballad. Haizmann painted a triptych for the altar, showing himself and the Devil, the latter in the form of an old gentleman, concluding a preliminary agreement in 1668, written in ink, to make a pact the next year. The second panel showed **Satan,** in the form of a monstrous hairy man, and Haizmann making the formal pact in blood in 1669. The center panel showed the Virgin delivering Haizmann from the Devil, this time shown as a winged dragon. Eight paintings that Haizmann did of the Devil also show him growing progressively more monstrous. Haizmann's relationship with the Devil was curiously one sided—he agreed to be the Devil's bodily son but the pact did not obligate Satan in any way. Haizmann claimed that he had been seeking relief from the poverty, depression and bad luck that had dogged him and to have refused specific offers of gold and **magic** books from the Devil.

Shortly after his cure, Haizmann went to live with his married sister in Vienna. There he joined a religious group for laymen, the Brotherhood of the Holy Cross. It turned out the Devil had not finished with him yet, and Haizmann slipped back into torments, this time caused by the still-outstanding preliminary agreement of 1668. He kept a diary during this time, the remaining portion of which shows the Devil, in the form of a cavalier, tempting Haizmann with wine, gold and beautiful women, interspersed with descriptions of angels calling him to a devout religious life. Returning to Mariazell in the spring, Haizmann was again intensely exorcised, and on May 9, 1678, Satan was obliged to return the first pact. The pacts and other items associated with the exorcisms were kept at Mariazell, as memorials of the great triumph over the Devil. Haizmann himself seems to have found peace after this episode. He became a lay brother of the abbey under the name Brother Chrysostom, and by the time he died, he had a reputation for holiness. Despite his striking story and the artifacts left behind at Mariazell, Haizmann was mostly forgotten in the following centuries. The story reemerged when Sigmund Freud (1856–1939), founder of **psychoanalysis,** drew on materials recently rediscovered by an Austrian archivist to write a long essay on the case. Freud argued that Haizmann, whose "parent," according to his diary, had died shortly before he made his first pact with the Devil, saw Satan as a substitute father, and that the pact was linked to Haizmann's unresolved Oedipal feelings. Although this interpretation is not accepted by modern students of the case, it helped establish psychoanalytic interpretation of early modern witchcraft and demonology.

REFERENCES: Sigmund Freud. "A Seventeenth-Century Demonological Neurosis." In *The Standard Edition of the Complete Psychological Works of Sigmund Freud, Volume 19,* ed. James Strachey, 67–105. London: Hogarth Press, 1961; Ida Macalpine and Richard A. Hunter. *Schizophrenia 1677: A Psychiatric Study of an Illustrated Autobiographical Record of Demonic Possession.* London: William Dawson and Sons, 1956; H. C. Erik Midelfort. "Catholic and Lutheran Reactions to Demon Possession in the Late Seventeenth Century: Two Case Histories." *Daphnis* 15 (1986): 623–648.

HALE, JOHN (1636–1700)

The reverend John Hale of Beverley, Massachusetts, along with **Increase Mather, Cotton Mather** and Robert **Calef,** was one of the most important contemporary chroniclers of the **Salem** witch-hunt and **New England** witch-hunting in general. By the Salem trials, Hale was a long-time student of witchcraft whose life spans virtually the entire history of New England witchcraft persecutions. As a boy of 12, he attended the hanging of one of the first witches to be executed, Margaret Jones of Charlestown, Massachusetts—an event he vividly remembered 50 years later. Hale was close by during the Salem witch-hunt, Beverly being immediately north of Salem Town. Although he lacked an official role in the Salem investigation, he did question some of the accusers and suspects and volunteered testimony against three of the accused. Hale encouraged active persecution until he found himself more personally involved in the Salem affair. This occurred when a young woman named Mary Herrick claimed to have been afflicted by the specter of Hale's own wife. Although Mrs. Hale suffered no legal harm, this **accusation** does seem to have caused Hale to question the legal proceedings. Hale's chronicle of New England witchcraft and Salem, *A Modest Enquiry into the Nature of Witchcraft,* was published only posthumously in 1702 (with an introduction by another minister, John Higginson of Salem Town), about five years after it was written. It is the most extreme published statement of the shocking effects that the Salem trials had had on a firm supporter of the idea of the existence of witches. As Hale stated, "I have been from my Youth trained up in the knowledge and belief of most of those principles I here question as unsafe to be used." Unlike those, like Cotton Mather, who focused on possible irregularities in the Salem trials only, Hale considered the entire witch persecution in both New England and **England** to be discredited by the Salem events. His narrative emphasized the conscientiousness and thoroughness of the investigating magistrates not only to defend them personally, but to suggest that the problem was not technically "bad" but technically "good" witch-

The title page of *A Modest Inquiry into the Nature of Witchcraft* by John Hale, 1702. © Corbis.

hunting. Hale doubted the efficacy of many traditional procedures for the persecution of what he called the "malefick" witches accused of evil acts, but like many writers in the Puritan tradition going back to George **Gifford** and William **Perkins,** he called for increased vigilance against the **cunning** folk and the workers of beneficent **magic** and divination.

REFERENCES: George Lincoln Burr. *Narratives of the Witchcraft Cases, 1648–1706.* New York: Charles Scribner's Sons, 1914; Richard Weisman. *Witchcraft, Magic and Religion in 17th-Century Massachusetts.* Amhurst: University of Massachusett's Press, 1984.

HALLUCINOGENS

See Medical Interpretations.

HAND OF GLORY

One of the most common kinds of **magic** using corpses involved hands, particularly the hands of unbaptized or unborn children, executed people or murderers. This was the "hand of glory," belief in which went back to the Middle Ages and was particularly strong in Germanic Europe. It was believed that candles on the fingers of the dead hand would never burn out (unless extinguished with milk) and that if an intruder held one, the inhabitants of a house would not wake up while it was burning—an alternative term was "thieves' candle." (If someone in the house was not asleep when the candle was lit, a candle on one of the fingers would not burn.) The use of such magic was also associated with poisoners, who poured poison into the throats of sleeping people whom the candle prevented from waking up. Some magical books contained elaborate formulae for the preparation of a hand of glory, but magic using corpse hands was also practiced—or thought to be practiced—by illiterate witches. Procurement of unborn children's hands often meant killing and mutilating pregnant women. The charge of murder to procure infant's hands for magical purposes dominated the early phases of the **Pappenheimer** witch trial.

REFERENCES: Francesco Maria Guazzo. *Compendium Maleficarum*. Ed. Montague Summers, trans. E. A. Ashwin. 1929. Reprint, New York: Dover Press, 1988; Michael Kunze. *Highroad to the Stake: A Tale of Witchcraft*. Translated by William E. Yuill. Chicago and London: University of Chicago Press, 1987.

HARES

See Animals.

HARKETT, MARGARET

A short and rare anonymous pamphlet of 1585, *The Severall Factes of Witchcrafte*, tells the story of Margaret Harkett, a widow more than 60 years old who lived in Stanmore in Middlesex. Harkett was a poor woman and petty thief who cursed those who caught her stealing or denied her charity. Harkett's greatest crime was the murder of John Frynde, who had refused to buy a pair of shoes from her at Harkett's price, so she cursed him. Shortly afterward, Frynde fell from a pear tree and hurt his testicles. Harkett, claims the pamphlet, spread the rumor that Frynde's condition was actually caused by his having caught a sexually transmitted disease from a prostitute. Frynde confronted Harkett about these lies, and she cursed him again. Frynde took sick soon afterward and died a horrible death when his rotting guts burst out of his belly, claiming all the while that Harkett had bewitched him. This emphasis on the horror caused by a witch's curse would grow to play an even more important role in subsequent pamphlets. No trial record survives for Harkett, but the pamphlet claims she was hanged at Tyburn, the place where London and Middlesex felons were publicly executed.

REFERENCE: Marion Gibson, ed. *Early Modern Witches: Witchcraft Cases in Contemporary Writing*. London and New York: Routledge, 2000.

HEREDITABILITY

A belief common among both magistrates and ordinary people was that witches' children, whether or not they had actually been conceived by human-demon **sex,** were more likely than the general population to become witches themselves. It was common for entire family groups, such as the **Pappenheimers,** to be charged with witchcraft. Witches were widely believed to pass on their diabolical knowledge and power to their children, and, in **England,** where the belief in **familiars** was strongest, familiars were also described as passed down from mother to child. This idea made sense to early modern Europeans, living in a society in which most people followed their parent's professions. It also fit the idea of **Satan** using his grip on one member of a family to satisfy his lust for the destruction of the other members' souls. Confessing witches frequently claimed to have learned witchcraft from a (usually female) parent, although sometimes this seems to be a way to shift blame. Statements during trials frequently asserted that an accused witch's parents had been witches as evidence of guilt. In its widest dimensions, the idea of hereditary witchcraft informed the conception of a massive, organized sect of witches. This can be seen in Pierre de **Lancre**'s writings on the **Basque** witches whom he persecuted, which elaborately describe the stages by which witches' children were initiated into the Devil's service. De Lancre and other demonologists, such as Francesco Maria **Guazzo,** who believed that having witch parents was certain proof of accused witch's guilt, described how parents introduced their children to the Devil, offered themselves sexually to the Devil in the child's presence, encouraged the child to have sex with the Devil, married the child off to a demon or took the child with them to **sabbats.** Even in the absence of belief in a large-scale, organized witch-cult, the children of witches were more suspect than were others. This could become a self-fulfilling prophecy, because the shunned child turned to cursing and threatening members of the community, thus confirming their belief that she was a witch.

REFERENCES: Robin Briggs. *Witches and Neighbors: The Social and Cultural Context of European Witchcraft*. New York: Penguin, 1996; Francesco Maria Guazzo. *Compendium Maleficarum*. Ed. Montague Summers, trans. E. A. Ashwin. 1929. Reprint, New York: Dover Press, 1988.

HOLLAND

See Northern Netherlands.

HOLLAND, ROBERT (1557–1622?)

The only work of demonology in Welsh is a dialogue, *Tudor and Gronow*. The author was a Puritan English clergyman with a Welsh parish, Robert Holland. *Tudor and Gronow* was probably published in or near 1595, but the first edition was entirely lost, and it was not reprinted until 1681. Holland concentrated the attack on folk **magic** and superstitious practices, widespread in **Wales,** and, in Holland's opinion, diabolical. His work resembles that of his fellow-Puritan parish clergyman, George **Gifford.** *Tudor and Gronow* begins with an explication of the common Welsh saying, "to cast a cat unto the devil." Holland identifies magic as popular among all classes in Wales, and frequently involving animal sacrifice, which arouses Holland's horror as the person sacrificed to could only be the Devil. He also lamented the bad job the Church of **England** was doing in Wales, where there were few clergymen, and those that were there were incompetent and ignorant of the Welsh language.

Holland's brother Henry Holland (d. 1603) was also a demonologist. He wrote one major work, A *Treatise against Witchcraft* (1590), one of several produced in the last decade of the sixteenth century and the first decade of the next, also including those of William **Perkins** and King **James VI** of **Scotland.** All were intended to introduce more sophisticated Continental demonology into Britain.

REFERENCE: Stuart Clark and P. T. J. Morgan. "Religion and Magic in Elizabethan Wales: Robert Holland's Dialogue on Witchcraft." *Journal of Ecclesiastical History* 27 (1976): 31–46.

HOLY ROMAN EMPIRE

See Austria and Bohemia; Franche-Comte; Germany; Lorraine; Switzerland.

HOPKINS, MATTHEW

Matthew Hopkins, a member of the minor Puritan gentry of East Anglia, was the leading spirit behind what was by far the largest witch persecution in English history (1645–1646). Hopkins, who lived in the Essex village of Manningtree, is a mysterious figure. In the winter of 1644–1645, during the English Civil War between the Royalist supporters of King Charles I (r. 1625–1649) and the English Parliament with its Puritan supporters, Hopkins became concerned about witches. The Hopkins phenomenon is only understandable in the civil war context. The war led to an upswing in witch persecution in many parts of **England,** after the quiescence of the 1630s. Essex was a firmly Parliamentarian county and not as yet a battlefield, but the authority of central government and particularly of the judicial system there had virtually collapsed. Areas suffering the stress of war but not engaged in actual battle were common locations for witch-hunts throughout the period. Hopkins's ally, the clergyman John Stearne, spoke of their campaign against the witches in language analogous to that of Parliamentarian soldiers, and the feeling of many Puritans that they were engaged in a struggle against the Satanic evil of their opponents was easily adaptable to witch-hunting.

Hopkins's first victim was an elderly, one-legged widow of Manningtree, Elizabeth Clarke, accused in early 1645. A confession was procured by "watching the witch," a process in which the accused was kept awake for days, in the hope that she will be visited by her **familiars.** This kind of **torture,** keeping people awake or compelling them into unending physical exertions such as running or walking, as opposed to the Continental use of instruments of torture such as racks, would be characteristic of the Hopkins persecutions—and quite effective in procuring confessions. Another form of investigation, practiced on nearly every accused witch, involved stripping them naked to search for **witch's marks,** often carried out by another of Hopkins's associates, the **midwife** Mary Phillips. This was a ritual of public humiliation, undoubtedly psychologically effective in destroying an accused witches defenses. The confessions, encouraged by leading questions from Hopkins, led to the naming of more witches and thus the witch-hunt continued. By summer it had spread to the neighboring county of Suffolk. It is impossible to know the full extent of the persecution because the surviving records are incomplete. What is known is that in its course, at least two hundred witches were tried, of whom about half were executed. The largest group of people executed at one time in the entire history of English witch-hunting were probably the 19 sentenced to be executed at **Chelmsford** in the fall of 1645. Hopkins became a consultant, brought in by local authorities desiring the services of an expert investigator of witches, and started referring to himself as "witch-finder general." Hopkins, even with the help of Stearne, Phillips and other assistants, could not have done it all himself, and authorities' support of him and emulation of his methods were central to the persecution.

Although this scale of witch-hunting was unprecedented in England, the type of charges made against witches were not. The persecuted witches were about 90 percent female, as was usual in England, and, again typically, from the poorest classes and possessing a long-standing reputation for witchcraft. Unlike many of the large German hunts, the later stages of the Hopkins hunt did not see deviation from the stereotypical norm of accused witches with many **accusations** against men and people from the upper classes. The charges were usually of *maleficium* of the standard kind, such as causing the death of children or livestock. The theory that Hopkins brought Continental ideas, such as the **sabbat,** into English witch-persecution is now discredited among scholars. The sources of Hopkins's and Stearne's demonology were English—Thomas Pott's pamphlet on the **Lancashire** witches and other trial reports, King **James's** writings and Richard **Bernard's** *Guide to Grand Jury Men.* What was unusual was the tendency of accused witches to speak of personal encounters with the Devil, including (usually unpleasant) **sex.** The importance of sexuality in these confessions may reflect Hopkins's obsessions, although it is not without precedent in English witch beliefs.

The Civil War meant that the normal checks preventing witch persecutions from becoming massive crazes, notably the early intervention of assize judges as agents of the central government, were not operating. It is not altogether clear what brought the persecutions to an end. Coverage by the London-based Parliamentary press was not always favorable, and one local clergyman, John Gaule, preached against Hopkins and the hunt in April 1646, becoming embroiled in a pamphlet controversy with Hopkins as a result. In its course, some of Hopkins's questionable methods, such as torture, became more widely known. Another factor may have been the exhaustion of the supply of women with previous reputations for witchcraft. Hopkins himself was ill and retired to Manningtree in the summer of 1646, dying about a year later of tuberculosis. The legend that he was tried and condemned as a witch rests on no seventeenth-century evidence.

REFERENCES: Diane Purkiss. "Desire and Its Deformities: Fantasies of Witchcraft in the English Civil War." *The Journal of Medieval and Early Modern Studies* (1997): 103–132; James Sharpe. *Instruments of Darkness: Witchcraft in Early Modern England.* Philadelphia: University of Pennsylvania Press, 1996.

HUNGARY, WITCH-HUNTING IN

Hungary, one of Europe's great cultural crossroads and melting pots, was remarkable in the chronological pattern of its witch-hunting, which reached its peak late in comparison to other countries, in the second and third decades of the eighteenth century. Hungary was a meeting place for the folklore and demonology of the Hungarians, the Roma (or Gypsys, then as now often credited with supernatural power), the Slavic peoples to the North and South, the Romanians to the East and German settlers and soldiers. Religiously, the picture was just as diverse, with Hungarian Catholics, Calvinists and Unitarians as well as German Lutherans and Catholics, and Muslim Turkish rulers in southern and central Hungary from the early sixteenth to the late seventeenth centuries. The first recorded witch trials emerged in the 1560s, in the mixed German and Hungarian city of Koloszvar. In the ensuing decades witch-hunting steadily increased. Notable political witch-trials occurred in the early seventeenth century in the Principality of Transylvania in Eastern Hungary, the only independent portion of the country (the rest was divided between the Ottoman Turkish Empire and the **Austrian** Habsburgs). Powerful aristocratic women seen as threats to the ruling house, the best known being the infamous "blood countess," Elizabeth Bathory, who was tried during 1609–1611, were accused of witchcraft or of hiring lower-class female witches to perform evil deeds, along with a number of other crimes such as murder or poisoning. Another important Transylvanian political trial, with more than 20 accused, occurred in 1679–1686 when Prince Michael Apafi (1632–1690) accused a political rival's wife of bewitching his own wife, Anne Bornemisza (1630–1688). What really accelerated the pace of Hungarian witch-hunting, however, was the imposition of Habsburg rule over the entire country in the late seventeenth century. Although witchcraft **accusations** stemming from Turkish territory were occasionally tried in courts in other parts of Hungary, the Turks had kept witch-hunting out of the Hungarian territory they ruled (as was true throughout the Ottoman possessions in southeastern Europe). With their expulsion in 1686, the former Ottoman territories moved to the front among active witch-hunting provinces. The imposition by the Habsburg authorities in 1696 of the law code *Practica Rerum Criminalium*, ultimately based on the work of the early-seventeenth-century Saxon demonological jurist Benedict Carpzov (1595–1666), also encouraged accusations and trials.

The peak of Hungarian witch-hunting was in the period 1710–1730, following the suppression of the last significant noble revolt against Habsburg rule in 1711. More than two hundred were accused and more than 60 sentenced to death in each of those decades. The most significant and famous of the Hungarian trials of the early eighteenth century occurred in the Szeged region in 1728 and 1729. Fourteen people, including a former chief judge of the city, were executed in the Szeged trials, a high total for Hungary, which saw no massive witch-hunts on the German model. This followed a series of natural disasters, including a severe drought in 1728 (witches were charged with having sold the rain to the Turks). It was also linked to factional struggles between a Hungarian-dominated group supporting local autonomy and German settlers. Witch-hunting continued through the midcentury, with German Habsburg soldiers stationed in Hungary often serving as **witch-finders.** What eventually brought Hungarian witch-hunting to an end was the intervention of the Habsburg government, under the rule of the Empress Maria Theresa (1717–1780). The attack on witch-hunting and other popular **magical** beliefs began in 1756 when the empress reserved all pending witch-trials in local courts to courts of appeal, which abandoned them. A series of legal changes culminating in 1768 theoretically abolished witch-hunting in Hungary, stating that nearly all witchcraft cases were the result of superstition and delusion and reserving those rare cases of demonic magic, if they existed at all, to the sovereign. The abandonment of witch-hunting in Hungary is often associated with the empress's Dutch **physician** and adviser, Gerard van Swieten (1700–1772). Van Swieten was a supporter of the Enlightenment and an opponent of all sorts of supernatural belief, including belief in both witches and vampires (the celebrated 1755 case of the "vampire" Rosina Polakin, whose body was actually exhumed, attracted a great deal of notice and ridicule of Hungarian "superstition" throughout Europe). Embarrassment over the case seems to have been a major motivation for the Habsburg government's clamp down on Hungarian witch-hunting. The Hungarian aristocracy's fierce localism and suspicion of Habsburg authority delayed the abandonment of witch-hunting. The last witch **execution** occurred in 1777.

The chronology of the Hungarian witch-hunt is unusual (although it can be viewed as an extreme case of the process whereby witch-hunting moved from the center to the periphery of European civilization), but the witch-hunts themselves were not very different from those that occurred elsewhere. About two thousand witch trials are known from the documentary record, resulting in 449 known death sentences. This may be half the total number that actually occurred. About 90 percent of the accused were women, high but not unparalleled in the European context. Trials were carried out by civil rather than ecclesiastical authorities, and **torture** was employed both to elicit confessions and to force convicted witches to name others. One unique feature of Hungarian witchcraft in the presence of a shamanistic figure from Hungarian folklore known as the *taltos*. Not unlike the **benandanti** of Friuli, the *taltos* were supposed to be organized in military units that battled witches in dreams and visions but was increasingly defined by legal tribunals as a witch. Most Hungarian trials emerged from accusations of *maleficia*, and the **sabbat** played only a minor role, most prominent in areas of German settlement. Hungarian trials were not greatly influenced by learned demonology, and the country produced few demonological writers, none of particular note.

REFERENCES: Gabor Klaniczay. "Hungary: The Accusations and the Universe of Popular Magic." In *Early Modern European Witchcraft: Centres and Peripheries*, ed. Bengt Ankarloo and Gustav Henningsen, 219–256. Oxford: Clarendon Press, 1990; Gabor Klaniczay. *The Uses of Supernatural Power: The Transformation of Popular Religion in Medieval and Early Modern Europe*. Trans. Susan Singerman, ed. Karen Marsolis. Princeton: Princeton University Press, 1990.

HUTCHINSON, FRANCIS (1660–1739)

In 1718, Frances Hutchinson, a Church of **England** clergyman, published *A Historical Essay concerning Witchcraft. With Observations of Matters of Fact, tending to Clear the Texts of the Sacred Scriptures, and Confute the Vulgar Errors about that Point.* This was one of the first attempts at a scholarly history of the witch craze but was primarily motivated not by scholarship but a desire to attack witch-hunting and advance Hutchinson's own career. Hutchinson, vicar of a church in the major seventeenth-century witch-hunting center of Bury Saint Edmunds, had been collecting materials for the book since the dawn of the eighteenth century but had run into trouble with higher authorities in the church who feared controversy and prevented publication. Hutchinson's interest in publishing peaked again in 1712, the year of the Jane **Wenham** trial, when witchcraft was a "hot" subject but still too controversial for the cautious and careerist Hutchinson. What eventually precipitated Hutchinson's publication was the work of Richard Boulton, **physician,** defender of witch-hunting and author of *A Compleat History of Magick, Sorcery and Witchcraft* (1715).

The *Historical Essay* recounts a number of major witchcraft trials, pointing out the violence and illegality used by many witch-hunters. It contains significant original research carried out over many years, including discussions with people who remembered the Matthew **Hopkins** witch-hunts in Suffolk (for which Hutchinson's work remains an important source) and a visit to Wenham. The *Historical Essay* also rehearses well-worn arguments against identifying the witches mentioned in the **Bible** with modern witches. Hutchinson's most important ideological move was to link disbelief in witches with the progress of **science** and natural philosophy. He was a friend of Hans Sloane (1660–1753), a physician and future president of the Royal Society, and wrapped his denial of witchcraft in the methods of experimental science. (Interestingly, Boulton, who had published a four-volume abridgement of the works of the great seventeenth-century scientist Robert Boyle [1627–1691], also associated his diametrically opposed position on the witch-hunt with modern science.) True reasoning preserved the enquirer from vulgar error— Hutchinson associated witchcraft belief with the superstitions of the common people. Given the abuses inseparable from witch-hunting, it threatened the security and property of English people that it was the function of the social and legal system to uphold. Although Boulton responded to Hutchinson's attacks on demonology in *The Possibility of Magick, Sorcery, and Witchcraft demonstrated. Or, a Vindication of a compleat History of Magick, Sorcery and Witchcraft. In Answer to Dr. Hutchinson's Historical Essay* (1722) this work was largely ignored. Hutchinson's *Essay* essentially marked the end of the debate on witchcraft among the English elite. Hutchinson ended his career as bishop of Down and Connor in **Ireland.**

REFERENCES: Ian Bostridge *Witchcraft and Its Transformations, c. 1650–c. 1750.* Oxford: Clarendon Press, 1997; James Sharpe. *Instruments of Darkness: Witchcraft in Early Modern England.* Philadelphia: University of Pennsylvania Press, 1996.

I

ICELAND, WITCH-HUNTING IN

On the fringe of European civilization, the Danish-ruled island of Iceland came to witch-hunting very late. The first Icelander to be burned as a witch was Jon Rognvaldsson, charged with having raised a ghost to cause harm to people and livestock and with the possession of a sheet of runes found in his house. The extremely poor society of Iceland offered plenty of scope for **accusations** of *maleficia*, and these dominated all Icelandic trials. (So poor was Iceland that the community did not want to be responsible for the fuel to burn a witch, and witches were often burned on a pile of their own household goods.) **Satanic pact** played an extremely minor role, and the **sabbat** or **sex** with the Devil none at all. Searches for **Devil's marks** and **flotation tests** were not used. Some European-educated Icelandic Lutheran pastors attempted to bring more advanced demonology to Iceland, but their works circulated only in manuscript and had little effect on popular attitudes.

The principal peculiarity of the Icelandic witch-hunt was the strong majority of men among the accused and executed. Of the approximately 120 trials in the 50 years after Jon Rognvaldsson's burning, only 10 involved women, and of the 22 Icelanders burned as witches, only 1 was a woman. There are several possible reasons for this deviation from the standard European pattern. One is the unique structure of Icelandic society, in which the kind of poor, single or widowed woman living alone who furnished so many accused witches elsewhere simply did not exist. There were no village communities in Iceland, only scattered farmsteads. Everyone was required to be part of a large household, and given the cramped conditions of these environments—only the very wealthy could afford a private bedroom for the heads of household, let alone anyone else—social isolation was simply impossible. Another reason for the peculiar **gender** pattern was the importance of pre-Christian **magical** traditions in Iceland. Effective use of magic, which was usually envisioned as the manipulation of the spoken or written word, like Jon Rognvaldsson's runes, rather than the use of herbs, for example, was associated with the learned, who were assumed to be men. The most powerful magicians wielded too much social influence to be condemned as witches. Jon Gudmundsson (1574?–1658), widely credited with having turned a Turkish slave-raiding ship away from Iceland by the power of his poetry, was in and out of trouble for witchcraft in the 1630s but suffered only a short period of exile. The clergyman who brought witchcraft charges against him was defrocked for acting out of malice.

Although the king of **Denmark's** decree against witchcraft of 1617 was read in the Allthing, the Icelandic popular assembly, in 1630, it was not immediately followed by a spate of witch-hunting. There were some cases in the 1650s and then a burst in the 1670s and early 1680s. It was difficult to get a conviction, partly because Iceland did not permit **torture,** although there are some cases where it was used illegally. Iceland also preserved compurgation, an ancient practice abandoned elsewhere in Europe, which allowed for acquittal based on 12 people who knew the accused swearing to his or her innocence. Accused witches occasionally used compurgation successfully.

The last case of an Icelander burned as a witch occurred in 1685. The victim was Halldor Finnbogasson, a somewhat deranged man who claimed to have made a **satanic pact.** Interestingly, the sentence indicated that the court had its doubts as to whether Halldor, who was not charged with *maleficium*, was even a witch. The next year appeals to the Royal Court in Denmark were made obligatory in all capital cases, and this seems to have ended Icelandic interest in witch-hunting.

REFERENCES: R. C. Ellis. "The Kirkjubold Affair: A Seventeenth-Century Icelandic Witchcraft Case Analyzed." *The Seventeenth Century* 8 (1993): 217–241; Kirsten Hastrup. "Iceland: Sorcerors and Paganism." In *Early Modern European Witchcraft: Centres and Peripheries,* ed. Bengt Ankarloo and Gustav Henningsen, 383–401. Oxford: Clarendon Press, 1990.

IMAGE MAGIC

A common *maleficium* was working harm to a person by manipulating a small image of him or her. Image magic had a long history by the early modern period, as was used in the learned magical tradition as well as the practices of uneducated witches and **cunning folk.** A Latin manual of explicitly demonic ritual magic dating from the fifteenth century and probably written by a clergyman explained how a magician could win a woman's love by drawing the figure of a naked woman with the blood of a dove on the skin of a bitch as well as other uses of images. Images could be made of many substances, including wax, parchment, clay, wood, straw or rags. The "puppets," made of rags and stuffed with goat hair found in the house of a poor Massachusetts Irish woman, Goody Glover, in 1688. **Cotton Mather,** in his *Memorable Providences, Relating to Witchcrafts and Possessions* (1689), described how by wetting her finger with her spittle and stroking the images, Glover caused the children of the Goodwin family to writhe in pain. In his interrogation, the English cunning man John **Walsh** described a complicated formula for making images out of the earth of a new grave, ashes from a human rib, a spider, the inner pith of an elder-tree and water in which toad **familiars** had been washed. Although Walsh denied ever making such an image, he claimed that by sticking pins in particular areas of the image, affliction would be caused in that part of the victim's body; a pin in the heart would cause death in nine days.

Images could be prepared for magical operations by being baptized, a misuse of a sacrament that aroused the particular ire of church authorities. Images were also made more potent by incorporating a piece of the victim's body, bodily excrements such as spittle, or clothing. Operations performed on them included burning, burying, stroking and piercing with pins or thorns. Some Scottish witches shot at clay images with neolithic flint arrowheads, called "elf-bolts" and believed to be the work of the fairies.

The greatest in the land could view themselves as vulnerable to the image magic of ordinary people, and the finding of a small image of the monarch in unusual circumstances was taken seriously by political authorities. One charge against the **North Berwick** witches was making a wax image of **James VI** in order to melt it in a fire, supposedly causing the king to waste away and die. Image magic could also be used as **countermagic,** with the witch's victim sticking pins into a small image of the witch.

REFERENCES: Marion Gibson, ed. *Early Modern Witches: Witchcraft Cases in Contemporary Writing.* London and New York: Routledge, 2000; Richard Kieckhefer. *Magic in the Middle Ages.* Cambridge: Cambridge University Press, 1989; P. G. Maxwell-Stuart. *Satan's Conspiracy: Magic and Witchcraft in Sixteenth-Century Scotland.* East Lothian, Scotland: Tuckwell Press, 2001.

IMPOTENCE

See Ligature.

INFANTICIDE

Witches were frequently accused of infanticide, often accompanied by cannibalism by the use of the body parts in **magic. Accusations** of secret child murder have a long history in Western culture. In the Middle Ages, the most frequent targets of such accusations were the Jews, charged with using the blood of Christian children to make matzos. The libel was applied to witches in the fifteenth century, with the development of the European witch stereotype. Such early works as the **Errores Gazariorum** and Johannes **Nider's** *Formicarius* speak of the murder and devouring of children, either the witch's own or another's, and their sacrifice to the Devil. Infanticide could take place in many ways. Witches were frequently described in both popular culture and learned demonology as transforming themselves into cats (or taking on their semblance) to make their way into houses and kill infants by draining their blood.

A witch sacrifices a child over the naked body of her client who wishes to revive the flagging ardor of her lover. Illustration from Michelet, *La Sorciere*, ca. 1600. © Mary Evans Picture Library.

Ritual murder of children as a sacrifice to the Devil was usually associated with the **sabbat** and played a smaller role in those territories, such as **England,** where the sabbat was not a standard feature of the witch stereotype. Murdered children at the sabbat were usually devoured, their remains used for magical purpose; the fat of murdered children is often referred to as an ingredient in magical ointments for purposes such as **flying,** and murdered children could be cooked in a pot and the broth drunk by witches to obtain magical power and knowledge. Demonologists disagreed on whether witches and devils particularly desired to kill unbaptized children, thus procuring the loss of a soul before it could be cleansed of original sin by baptism, or baptized children, whose purity enraged them. Usually, unbaptized children, whose bodies could be thought of as reservoirs of the evil power of original sin, were thought of as particularly vulnerable to being kidnapped, killed and used by witches. (Baptism was in part a rite of exorcism, freeing the child from **possession** by demons.) On a more mundane level, sometimes a family that had lost a child blamed a suspected witch for having caused the child's death by *maleficium,* as in the case of the **Flower witches** and the earl of Rutland's son. Rutland is discussed in the "Flower Witches" article.

Accusations of magical infanticide took place in a context of growing hostility to infanticide in general, in a culture in which the death of babies and children was a common experience. Many European jurisdictions were tightening their infanticide laws and more actively prosecuting suspects. Infanticide even more than witchcraft was seen as a woman's crime, with virtually 100 percent of the accused being female. Both the female infanticide and the usually female infanticidal witch inverted the cultural expectations of motherhood. Cases in which women did undoubtedly kill their children, because of what today would be called postpartum psychosis, were often interpreted as yielding to diabolical temptation. In those infrequent cases in which midwives were accused of witchcraft, they were usually charged with having abused their position to kill the children whose lives they were supposed to preserve.

REFERENCES: Louise Jackson. "Witches, Wives and Mothers: Witchcraft Persecution and Women's Confessions in Seventeenth-Century England." In *The Witchcraft Reader*, ed. Darren Oldridge, 353–366. London and New York: Routledge, 2002; Jeffrey Burton Russell. *Witchcraft in the Middle Ages*. Ithaca: Cornell University Press, 1972; Walter Stephens. *Demon Lovers: Witchcraft, Sex, and the Crisis of Belief*. Chicago and London: University of Chicago Press, 2002. María Tausiet. "Witchcraft as Metaphor: Infanticide and Its Translations in Aragon in the Sixteenth and Seventeenth Centuries." In *Languages of Witchcraft: Narrative, Ideology and Meaning in Early Modern Culture*, ed. Stuart Clark, 179–195. New York: St. Martin's Press, 2001.

INNSBRUCK WITCH-HUNT

The witch-hunt in the small town of Innsbruck in the German Tyrol in 1485 is one of two documented witch-hunts carried out by the author of the *Malleus Maleficarum* (1486), the Dominican friar Heinrich **Kramer,** also known as Institoris. It was the only one carried out with the authority Kramer received from the papal bull **Summis Desiderantes Affectibus** (1484). The course of events reveal that even a fanatical witch-hunter like Kramer with papal backing could make little headway against a reluctant local leadership. Innsbruck lay under the temporal jurisdiction of the Archduke Sigismund of **Austria** and spiritually in the diocese of Brixen, headed by bishop Georg Golser. The witch-hunt's origins are obscure, but Kramer had arrived in the village by July, and on the 23rd Golser granted a 40-day dispensation to all who complied with Kramer's efforts. Hearings lasted from August 9 to September 14. The depositions Kramer collected reveal a huge range of **magical accusations,** mostly directed at women—there were only 2 men among the 50 accused—and at the peasantry and lower class in the towns. Witnesses, from all social strata, claimed to have been bewitched by hairs, threads from altar cloths, the bones of unbaptized babies, dead mice and dung taken from the Jewish quarter. Witches were accused of practicing **image magic,** love magic and magic to cause impotence, among many other practices. The accusers seldom mentioned the Devil, although one claimed that magic was caused by diabolic invocation. Kramer's commentary on the depositions, several of which were later included in his *Malleus Maleficarum*, played up the diabolic element whenever possible. The **sabbat** played no role in the Innsbruck witch-hunt.

The scope of Kramer's investigation was arousing Golser's concern. Golser viewed most witch activity as simply a matter of demonic illusion, something not best dealt with by mass trials and executions. On September 21, he sent a letter to Sigismund, requesting that he limit Kramer's activities to cases in which significant bodily harm had been caused by *maleficium* and cases of blasphemy. Golser sent a similar letter to Kramer. This seems to have had little effect, because in early October Kramer brought charges against seven local women. From October 4 to October 21, 30 interrogatory sessions took place involving **torture.** Golser and Sigismund continued to be concerned with

Kramer's methods. The archduke requested that Golser appoint a commissioner to advise Kramer and oversee the investigation, and Sigmund Saumer, a parish priest, commenced activities as Golser's commissioner on October 14. On October 29, in front of the tribunal (on which Kramer sat as one of the seven judges as well as prosecutor). Kramer interrogated one of the accused, Helena Scheuberin, on her sexual behavior, hoping to establish a link between Scheuberin's sexual immorality and her practice of witchcraft. This connection obsessed the misogynist Kramer. At this point some of the other commissioners intervened, asserting that this line of questioning was irrelevant. Saumer, also sitting on the commission, procured a short recess, and when the tribunal reconvened, the accused had a defense lawyer, procured by Golser's agents. Johann Merwais was a tough, wily canon lawyer who proved more than a match for Kramer. He effectively put the Dominican on trial, moving to declare the entire proceeding null and void for gross procedural irregularities, such as Kramer's not having a notary approved by the bishop present during questioning of the accused under torture. This was a questionable argument—having a notary was not a requirement mentioned in *Summis Desiderantes Affectibus*. Merwais's call for the release of the prisoners and the imprisonment of Kramer was not immediately effective, but the trial's momentum had clearly shifted.

On a subsequent session on October 31, Merwais demanded an appeal to Rome, but settled for suspension of the trial while the commissioners reviewed Kramer's actions. The president of the tribunal, Christian Turner, declared the proceedings invalid and ordered that the prisoners be released on their promise to appear at a future trial. This was probably merely pro forma, as shortly afterward Archduke Sigismund stated that he would not fund another trial. Despite hints from Golser that it would be better if he left Innsbruck before a riot broke out, Kramer stayed in the area until early February, when Golser ordered him to leave, hinting that old age had robbed Kramer of his mental powers. Kramer's experience affected him deeply. In addition to the Innsbruck depositions included in *Malleus Maleficarum*, many of its suggestions for **trial procedure** are designed to frustrate the skeptical churchmen and aggressive defense lawyers he had met at Innsbruck.

REFERENCES: Richard Kieckhefer. *European Witch Trials: Their Foundations in Popular and Learned Culture, 1300–1500*. Berkeley: University of California Press, 1976; Eric Wilson. "Institoris at Innsbruck: Heinrich Institoris, the *Summis Desiderantes*, and the Brixen Witch-Trial of 1485." In *Popular Religion in Germany and Central Europe, 1400–1800*, ed. Bob Scribner and Trevor Johnson, 87–100. New York: St. Martin's Press, 1996.

INSTITORIS

See Kramer, Heinrich.

IRELAND, WITCH-HUNTING IN

Despite the fact that one of the earliest witch trials, that of Alice **Kyteler,** took place in Ireland, the island saw remarkably little witch-hunting during the early modern period. This is probably due to Ireland's legal and political situation from the mid–sixteenth century on. During this time, the island was ruled by the English, whose administrative and judicial system almost completely excluded the native Irish Catholic population. The lack of a legal framework in the early sixteenth century also hindered witch-hunting, although it was not an insuperable obstacle. In 1578, English authorities in Kilkenny executed three witches, including a "blackamoor," claiming the authority of the natural law in the lack of a statute. The Protestant-dominated Irish Parliament remedied this awkward situation by enacting the English witchcraft statute of 1563 into Irish law in 1586. The statute did not promote witch-hunting in Ireland as it did in **England,** however The Irish population deeply mistrusted the English judiciary and did not accuse each other before it. Without **accusations,** there was nothing to generate witchcraft cases. The English, unlike the rulers of **Spanish America,** did not identify natives resisting their rule as witches, possibly because they identified Irish rebelliousness with Catholicism rather than paganism. The Irish did have the concept of witchcraft but seem to have viewed protection by either religious or folk countermagic sufficient. A horseshoe hung up in a house was considered protection against witches and was frequently encountered among ordinary Irish people.

The early modern period also saw English and Scottish Protestants settle in Ireland, bringing their witchcraft beliefs with them and generating witchcraft accusations and witch cases. Every known witchcraft trial in early modern Ireland after 1578 involved Protestants accusing other Protestants. The procedures followed generally were those of England, although the English statute of 1604 never became law in Ireland. The best-known seventeenth-century case was that of Florence Newton, the "Witch of Youghal" in 1661, accused of bewitching a young girl, Mary Longdon, and then of causing the death of one of her guards in jail, David Jones. Her final fate is unknown. The last Irish witchcraft case, that of the Island Magee witches, occurred in 1711. Mary Dunbar, a young servant woman, accused seven local Presbyterian women of bewitching her. Dunbar displayed classic symptoms of **possession,** such as vomiting strange objects and falling into fits. Despite the urgings of the judge, the seven women were convicted of witchcraft and sentenced to spend a year in jail and stand in the pillory four times during the year. The Irish witchcraft statute, long a dead letter, was finally repealed in 1821 as part of a general reform of Irish law.

REFERENCES: Elwyn C. Lapoint. "Irish Immunity to Witch-Hunting, 1534–1711." *Eire/Ireland* 27 (1992): 76–92; St. John D. Seymour. *Irish Witchcraft and Demonology*. Dublin: Hodges, Figgis, 1913.

ITALY, WITCH-HUNTING IN

Despite being the location of some of the earliest **sabbat**-based witch trials and producing a host of demonologists, Italy never saw a major witch-hunt. Italy's rich tradition of popular **magic** and sorcery, including diviners, healers, makers of love potions and those claiming the ability to locate buried treasure,

Seventeenth-century Italian painting of Saint Charles Borromeo (1538–1584). © The Art Archive/Museo Storico Aloisiano Castiglione delle Stiviere/Dagli Orti.

began to be seen as diabolical witchcraft in the fifteenth century, partly through the efforts of preaching friars led by **Bernardino of Siena.** One of the earliest appearances of the sabbat in a witch trial anywhere was in the case of Matteucia **di Francesco** of Todi in 1428. Di Francesco was tried by a secular court, but the secular courts were gradually losing control over witchcraft to the church courts. In 1410, the great council of Venice promulgated a law declaring that cases of sacrament desecration were properly handled by church courts, but all other magical offenses were to be handled by secular courts. The trend continued, however. The usual place for alleged sabbats and gatherings of witches in Italy was the "walnut tree of Benevento," which had in fact been chopped down centuries earlier. References to it persisted into the eighteenth century.

Fifteenth-century Italy saw a number of witch trials, usually carried out by Dominican inquisitors and involving individual witches or small groups. One exception is a trial at Bormio, a small town in the Alps, in 1485, known from references in Heinrich **Kramer's** *Malleus Maleficarum* (1486). There the Inquisition had 41 witches executed. In the late fifteenth and early sixteenth centuries, Italy had many important demonologists, mostly supporters of witch-hunting such as **Giordano da Bergamo,** Bartolommeo **Spina,** Silvestro **Mazzolini,** Girolamo **Visconti** and Gianfrancesco **Pico della Mirandola.** The leading Italian opponent was Gianfrancesco **Ponzinibio.** The supporters could reckon on the support of the papacy, (Mazzolini and Spina were papal officials), which usually relied on inquisitors to attack groups of witches and magicians in a tradition going back to **John XXII** in the early fourteenth century. (In Rome itself, however, day-to-day antimagical law enforcement was carried out mostly by secular magistrates of the papal government by the early sixteenth century.) After *Summis Desiderantes Affectibus* in 1484, the next important antimagical decree was Alexander VI's (pope, 1492–1503) *Cum Acceperimus* (1501) giving authority to a papal inquisitor in Lombardy to hunt out and prosecute witches and poisoners. In 1521, Leo X (pope, 1513–1521) ordered the Venetian bishops to proceed against witches and to ignore the protests of the secular authorities. Two years later, Adrian VI (pope, 1522–1523) addressed an antiwitch decree to Modesto of Vincenza. The antimagical papal decrees culminated in Sixtus V's (pope, 1585–1590) 1585 *Coeli et Terrae,* directed more against learned magicians than witches.

In 1542, Paul III (pope, 1534–1549) founded the centralized **Roman Inquisition** to replace the ad hoc Inquisitions that had persecuted witches and heretics in Italy and Europe. With jurisdiction extending through the entire peninsula, including the Spanish-ruled south (where it was required to work through episcopal courts), the Roman Inquisition controlled the identification and prosecution of magical offenses. The Inquisition's moderation spared Italy the full horrors of the witch-hunt, to the degree that secular governments wanting a more thoroughgoing persecution sometimes attempted to prod the Inquisition into action or even take over witch-hunting themselves. Italy during the period of the Roman Inquisition was not completely free from witch-hunts and witch burnings, however, particularly before the Inquisition had established full control by the end of the sixteenth century. Charles Borromeo (1538–1584), when archbishop of Milan, was responsible for the burning of some witches in the territory surrounding the city in the early 1580s, and there was a sabbat-based witch-hunt at Lucca in 1589.

The most common magical crimes that the Roman Inquisition and other Italian authorities dealt with remained traditional sorcery rather than diabolical witchcraft. The practitioners were mostly women and mostly poor. (The exception was learned magic using books, which remained an exclusively male offense, associated with the upper classes and priests.) Many of the women called before the Inquisition in Italian cities were prostitutes, who employed love magic to attract or keep men or to harm their rivals. Foreign women, particularly Greeks, were often thought to have magical powers or expertise. Italian authorities usually identified the cause of women's greater likelihood to be witches or use magic as their weakness and ignorance rather than their lust and malevolence, and if a woman admitted her fault and was sufficiently deferential, she often received a mild penalty. Unlike the French, the Italians usually managed to keep their numerous cases of demonic **possession** separate from witchcraft offenses.

The Inquisition's relative lack of interest in diabolical witchcraft was reflected in Italian intellectual life, in which the lack of interest in demonology in the late sixteenth and seventeenth centuries contrasts with the activity of the fifteenth and early sixteenth centuries. The only significant Italian demonologist accepting the full range of the witch stereotype during the second phase of intense witch-hunting was Francesco Maria **Guazzo,** much of whose experience was outside Italy.

The Inquisition never seriously threatened traditional sorcery, although there are indications that some Italians began to think such magic sinful. Even on an individual level, the campaign against magic was marked by some spectacular failures. The healer, diviner and **cunning** woman Laura Malpiero, identified in 1648 as the most famous witch (*strega*)" in Venice, died peacefully a free woman in 1660, despite harassment by the Inquisition. Although interest in persecuting magic users and witches was fading by the second half of the seventeenth century, it did not disappear entirely, and patterns varied greatly in various regions of Italy. In the Otranto diocese of Oria, for example, more than half of the few cases of diabolical witchcraft that occurred in the early modern period happened during the episcopate of Giovanni Labanchi from 1720 to 1746, although the accused witches were treated leniently. Eighteenth-century

Italy did produce one important writer against witch-hunting, Girolamo Tartarotti (1706–1761), author of *Nocturnal Meetings of Witches* (1749). Tartarotti was answered by the Franciscan Benedetto Bonelli, author of *Critical Animadversions on the Nocturnal Meetings of Witches* (1751).

REFERENCES: Thomas V. Cohen and Elizabeth S. Cohen. *Words and Deeds in Renaissance Rome: Trials before the Papal Magistrates.* Toronto: University of Toronto Press, 1993; Thomas Deutscher. "The Role of the Episcopal Tribunal of Novara in the Suppression of Heresy and Witchcraft 1563–1615." *Catholic Historical Review* 77 (1991): 403–421; David Gentilcore. *From Bishop to Witch: The System of the Sacred in Early Modern Terra d'Otranto.* Manchester and New York: Manchester University Press, 1992; Brian P. Levack. *The Witch-Hunt in Early Modern Europe.* London and New York: Longman, 1987; Christine Meek. "Men, Women, and Magic: Some Cases from Late Medieval Lucca." In *Women in Renaissance and Early Modern Europe*, ed. Christine Meek, 43–66. Dublin: Four Courts Press, 2000; Franco Mormando. *The Preacher's Demons: Bernardino of Siena and the Social Underworld of Early Renaissance Italy.* Chicago and London: University of Chicago Press, 1999; Guido Ruggiero. *Binding Passions: Tales of Magic, Marriage and Power at the End of the Renaissance.* New York and Oxford: Oxford University Press, 199; Anne Jacobson Schutte. *Aspiring Saints: Pretense of Holiness, Inquisition, and Gender in the Republic of Venice, 1618–1750.* Baltimore and London: Johns Hopkins University Press, 2001; Anne Jacobson Schutte. " 'Saints' and 'Witches' in Early Modern Italy: Stepsisters or Strangers." In *Time, Space, and Women's Lives in Early Modern Europe*, ed. Anne Jacobson Schutte, Thomas Kuehn and Silvana Seidel Menchi, 153–164. Vol. 53 of *Sixteenth Century Essays and Studies.* Kirksville, Mo., Truman State University Press, 2001; Sally Scully. "Marriage or a Career: Witchcraft as an Alternative in Seventeenth-Century Venice." *Journal of Social History* 28 (1995): 857–876.

J

JACQUIER, NICHOLAS (D. 1472)

Nicholas Jacquier was a Dominican inquisitor who worked in northern France and Bohemia. In 1458, he wrote the Latin *A Scourge for Heretical Witches*, one of the first works devoted entirely to expounding the new witch stereotype. Jacquier's principal concern, shared by many other mid-fifteenth-century demonologists, was to demonstrate the irrelevance of the **Canon Episcopi**'s denial of the possibility of witches' flight to modern heretical witches. Jacquier argued that modern witches differed from those of the *Canon* by including men and members of the clergy, rather than being only foolish old women. Modern witches also denied God and paid homage to the Devil, and their meetings differed from those in the *Canon*. Because modern witches engaged in sexual acts at their meetings, acts that Jacquier claimed could leave them exhausted for days afterward, their meetings, contrary to the *Canon*, could not be illusory.

Jacquier also attacked those skeptical of witches' guilt. Addressing these questions led him into a number of other aspects of the developing witch stereotype, including the **sabbat, infanticide** and the desecration of the cross. Jacquier was one of the first demonologists to mention the **Devil's mark.** He claimed that witches were the worst of all heretics, because their heresy was taught and led directly by the Devil rather than by humans. Witches, unlike other heretics, knowingly and deliberately denied God. The mere exercise of any **magic** power was proof of a pact with the Devil. Jacquier drew on his own experiences as an inquisitor as well as recent witch cases such as that of Guillame **Adeline** and urged judges to take a tough stance in witchcraft cases. *A Scourge for Heretical Witches* did not appear in print until 1581, when it was published by a German Carmelite friar, Johannes Minzenberg, in a single volume along with a number of fifteenth- and sixteenth-century texts regarding magic and witchcraft.

REFERENCE: Alan Charles Kors and Edward Peters, eds. *Witchcraft in Europe 400–1700: A Documentary History*. 2d ed. Revised by Edward Peters. Philadelphia: University of Pennsylvania Press, 2001.

JAMES VI AND I (1566–1625)

As demonologist, king of **Scotland,** and from 1603 king of **England,** James Stuart played an important role in the witch-hunt. This role was complex, and by focusing on various aspects of his career, James can be made to appear either as a fanatical witch-burner or as an astute defender of accused witches.

The earliest evidence of James's interest in demonology stems from his visit to the court of the king of **Denmark** in the winter of 1589–1590, to claim his bride Anne of Denmark (1574–1619). While in Denmark, James, a man of many interests, took advantage of the situation to visit theologians and philosophers, including Niels Hemmingsen (1513–1600), a Lutheran professor whose writings James later cited with approbation in his writings on demonology. There is no indication that witchcraft was among the subjects the two discussed, however. On his return to Scotland with his bride, James and his companions ran into severely inclement weather in the North Sea. This led to the **North Berwick** trials of 1590–1592, in which hundreds of accused witches were tried on the charge of treason, having attempted to take the king's life. Their alleged leader was James's political enemy Francis Stewart Hepburn, fifth earl of Bothwel (d. 1624). The king played a key role in keeping the trials going and pushing the juries toward conviction and **execution.** He advised the legal authorities on tactics of **torture** and interrogation. He also promoted the idea that the witches were active devil worshippers. Given James's highly developed sense of self-preservation and his sincere belief in the divine status of kingship, the fact that the witches were allegedly trying to kill him (by burning waxen images and poisoning his sheets) accounts for a great deal of his enthusiasm for persecution. He also seems to have been genuinely impressed by the ability of a witch to tell him what conversation had passed between him and his wife on their wedding night. James's anti-witchcraft stance could also help him politically. James had long been looking toward the English throne he would eventually inherit in 1603, and one English pamphlet on the North Berwick trials, *News from Scotland* (1591), had used the king's self-presentation as a great enemy of witches and **Satan** to flatter England's future monarch.

James's participation in the North Berwick trials was followed by his publication of *Daemonologie* in 1697. This relatively brief work is not an original contribution to demonology but is extremely important as the first presentation of sophisticated Continental demonological theory, based on the **satanic pact,** in English. It was directed against two skeptics, Johann **Weyer** and Reginald **Scot,** whose *Discoverie of Witchcraft* (1584) had not yet been refuted in English. Its linguistic accessibility, and the prestige it gained from having been written by a king, long made *Daemonologie* a frequently invoked and influential source for English and Scottish demonologists. For example, there are indications that

James's approval of **flotation tests** in the *Daemonologie* was responsible for their later introduction into English witch trials. *Daemonologie* was twice printed in London in 1603, the year James acceded to the English throne, and Dutch, Latin and French translations appeared in subsequent years. *Daemonologie* marked the peak of the king's interest in witch-hunting, however, and the same year James began to moderate the witch-hunt in Scotland.

James's arrival as king of England in 1603 did not, contrary to what is often asserted, result in an intensification of witch persecution. (The story that he ordered all copies of Scot's *Discoverie* to be burned is also without contemporary evidence.) However, regardless of James's move to moderation in Scotland, many of his new English subjects regarded him as an avid witch-hunter, or at least as someone passionately interested in the subject. Both William Shakespeare's witch-filled Scottish play, **Macbeth**, first performed in 1605 or 1606, and the witchcraft act of 1604, which for the first time made dealings with **familiar** spirits, as opposed to **maleficium**, a crime, can be seen as English efforts to please their rather puzzling new monarch.

Whatever the English expected, James's most heavily publicized actions in England in regard to witchcraft were not those of a persecutor or promoter of persecution (in fact, prosecutions declined in his reign from their Elizabethan peak) but of a skeptically minded investigator of alleged crimes by alleged witches. James was proud of his intelligence, identifying himself with the biblical King Solomon. Perhaps more than any other early modern monarch, he saw himself as a teacher of his people, a role that could encompass introducing new demonological ideas into Scotland, or revealing the tricks and frauds of feigned victims of witchcraft in England. Cases in which James was involved in the role of exposer of fraudulent claims of victimhood and demonic **possession** include those of Anne **Gunter** (1605); John Smith, the "Leicester Boy" (1616), in which James's intervention saved the lives of several accused witches; and Katherine Malpas (1621). This skeptical attitude in individual cases should not be confused with rejecting the tenets of orthodox demonology including the satanic pact, which there is no sign James ever did, or with a refusal to take seriously what was for James always the most important and quintessentially diabolical form of witchcraft, that which was directed at him personally. In 1620, a man named Peacock was accused of plotting against James by witchcraft, and sent to the Tower of London, where he was tortured. (Witches were not usually tortured in England. Peacock was not tortured as part of a judicial process, but as a matter of state security.)

The reasons for James's change of heart, to the extent that it was real, are unclear, although the prevalence of skepticism about individual witchcraft cases in the highest circles of the English church and court may have influenced it. Samuel Harsnett (1561–1631), the exposer of fraudulent claims of demonic possession and exorcism, was a close associate of the king. James and his English courtiers seem to have often joked about witchcraft. The fact that little English witchcraft was directed at the royal person probably eased James's tensions, particularly because his hatred of potential regicides was redirected at

Roman Catholics and Jesuits after the failure of the Catholic Gunpowder Plot to blow up the king and both houses of Parliament in 1605. James's attempts to cool England's religious divisions might also have made him reluctant to portray the kingdom as actively besieged by Satan, instead emphasizing the harmony and peace enjoyed during his reign.

REFERENCES: Stuart Clark. "King James's *Daemonologie*: Witchcraft and Kingcraft." In *The Damned Art: Essays in the Literature of Witchcraft*, ed. Sydney Anglo, 156–181. Boston: Routledge and Kegan Paul, 1977; Christina Larner. "James VI and I and Witchcraft." In *Witchcraft and Religion: The Politics of Popular Belief*, 3–22. Oxford: Basil Blackwell, 1984; Lawrence Normand and Gareth Roberts, eds. *Witchcraft in Early Modern Scotland: James VI's Demonology and the North Berwick Witches*. Exeter, England: University of Exeter Press, 2000; James Sharpe. *The Bewitching of Anne Gunter: A Horrible and True Story of Deception, Witchcraft, Murder and the King of England*. New York: Routledge, 2000; Jenny Wormald. "The Witches, the Devil and the King." In *Freedom and Authority, Scotland c. 1050–c. 1650: Historical and Historiographical Essays presented to Grant G. Simpson*, ed. Terry Brotherstone and David Ditchburne, 165–180. East Lothian, Scotland: Tuckwell Press, 2000.

JESUIT ORDER

See Maldonado, Juan; del Rio, Martin; von Spee, Friedrich.

JOAN OF ARC

See Darc, Jehanne.

JOAN OF NAVARRE (1370?–1437)

In September 1419, Joan of Navarre, Queen Dowager of **England,** was charged with plotting to murder her stepson King Henry V (r. 1413–1422) by sorcery. The charges seem to have originated with Joan's Franciscan confessor, John Randolf. Her property was confiscated and she imprisoned. Although no evidence other than Randolf's charges was ever presented, it is possible that there had already been rumors about Joan—as a foreigner, she was unpopular in England, and her father, King Charles the Bad of Navarre, had an evil reputation as a sorcerer. The charges against Joan were not of the kind that would be made later, with the full development of the witch stereotype. They focused on the causing of harm through sorcery, rather than dealings with **Satan.** Joan was never put on trial, and once she was imprisoned, no further action on the charges was ever taken. In captivity, Joan was maintained with a great deal of luxury, including a large personal staff. Leading people in the English realm, including the archbishop of Canterbury and the bishop of Winchester, were guests at her table. The real purpose of holding her prisoner was to divert the revenue from her dowry into the empty coffers of King Henry, currently fighting expensive wars in **France.** On his deathbed in 1422, Henry ordered Joan released, and she was, although the charges were never formally dropped. John

Randolf was not so lucky; he was held prisoner in the Tower of London and died in a brawl there in 1429.

REFERENCE: A. R. Myers. "The Captivity of a Royal Witch: The Household Accounts of Queen Joan of Navarre, 1419–21." *Bulletin of the John Rylands Library Manchester* 24 (1940): 263–284.

JOHN XXII, POPE 1316–1334

No medieval pope did more to promote the idea of the menace of devil-worshipping magicians than did the French lawyer Jacques Duése, who took the style of John XXII on being made pope in the southern French city of Avignon, then the headquarters of the papacy. John had dealt with at least one case of sorcery as a judge before becoming pope, and he feared attempts on his life by the use of poison and sorcery. His pontificate was marked by a flurry of antisorcerous activities. In 1317, John had the bishop of Cahors, Hughes Geraud, arrested for trying to kill him by sorcery and poison. The unfortunate bishop was tortured and burned at the stake. In 1318, the Archbishop of Aix, Robert Mauvoisin, was charged, although not convicted, for **magical** practices, and the pope condemned several priests at Avignon for possessing and using magical books and artifacts. Another person at the papal court, Bernard Delicieux, was tried and convicted for possessing magical books in 1319.

As can be seen from the emphasis on books and artifacts in John's attacks on sorcery, the objects of the pope's fears were not witches as they later became known, but learned ritual magicians. He issued a bull, *Super illius specula*, against magicians and sorcerous practices such as sacrifice to demons and the making of magic talismans in 1326 or 1327. *Super illius specula* enunciated no new principles not found in the antimagical decrees of previous popes, but it expressed the pope's opinion that the antimagical campaign was among the most pressing tasks of the Church. John was a highly authoritarian pope who made extensive use of the Inquisition, the jurisdiction of which over magicians he reaffirmed, and he continued throughout his papacy to charge his opponents with magic and devil worship. The pope's example was important; it was during John's pontificate that the trial of Alice **Kyteler** in **Ireland** was carried out by one his appointees. Another significant case during John's reign was the burning of the university teacher and astrologer Cecco d'Ascoli by the Florentine Inquisition in 1327, the first **execution** of an academic for practicing magic. The flurry of antimagical activity associated with John ended shortly after his death, however.

REFERENCES: Norman Cohn. *Europe's Inner Demons: The Demonization of Christians in Medieval Christendom*. Rev. ed. Chicago: University of Chicago Press, 2000; Edward Peters. *The Magician, the Witch and the Law*. Philadelphia: University of Pennsylvania Press, 1978.

JUNIUS, JOHANNES

Johannes Junius, a burgomaster of the German city of **Bamberg,** was among the hundreds of victims of the persecutions carried out under the witch-bishop

Johann Georg Fuchs von Dornheim (r. 1623–1633). The Bamberg and other Franconian persecutions were unusual in reaching into the upper classes, and Junius was one of several Bamberg burgomasters to be tried and executed. Junius initially denied any connection with witchcraft when confronted with witnesses claiming to have seen him at **sabbats** and other witch gatherings. He continued to deny any connection with witchcraft after being tortured with thumbscrews and leg screws. After he had been stripped and searched for the **Devil's mark** (a bluish mark in the shape of a clover leaf was found and pricked), he was tortured again with strappado, still refusing to confess. He confessed, however (according to the documents of the persecutors), without **torture,** but under the threat of more torture. Junius's confession tells how he was in financial difficulties, and a demon in the guise of a beautiful woman seduced him. The demon then turned into a goat, and after some reluctance on Junius's part forced him to deny God and accept the Devil as lord. He was welcomed into the company of witches, receiving the name Krix. The demon, referred to as his "paramour" was named Vixen. He told how Vixen had unsuccessfully urged him to kill his children, and how he had seen other leaders of Bamberg at witch gatherings. He claimed that he had ridden a flying black dog to the sabbats. Junius confirmed his confession before the court. He was burned in 1628, following by the burning of his wife within a few months.

Junius's principal significance for the history of the witch-hunt is his authorship of a remarkable letter, addressed to his daughter and smuggled out of prison. Such were the mutilations of his hands that it took him several days to write the letter. In it he reaffirmed his innocence, and explained why, under severe torture, he not only confessed to all sorts of diabolic activity but implicated others as well. He described his confession as a complete lie and recounted how the torturers had forced him to give them the names of accused witches by going over Bamberg street by street. The letter claims that the jailer advised him to confess as the only way to avoid further torture, because ultimately confession was inevitable. A Catholic, Junius was denied the ministrations of a priest. He also described how he and those he had named as witches, who had also named him during their interrogations, had forgiven each other.

REFERENCES: Joseph Klaits. *Servants of Satan: The Age of the Witch Hunts.* Bloomington: Indiana University Press, 1985; Alan Charles Kors and Edward Peters, eds. *Witchcraft in Europe 400–1700: A Documentary History.* 2d ed. Revised by Edward Peters. Philadelphia: University of Pennsylvania Press, 2001.

K

KEPLER, KATHARINA (D. 1621)

The persecution and trial of the German accused witch Katharina Kepler is principally known for the involvement of her son Johannes Kepler (1571–1630), the great astronomer. Katharina Kepler, a widow, lived in the town of Leonberg in Württemburg, a place of active witch-hunting. Her troubles began when a former friend, Ursula Reinbold, accused Kepler of poisoning her. Legal proceedings began in August 1615, when Reinbold's brother, Urban Krautlin, mentioned the Kepler matter to a lower magistrate, Luther Einhorn. Krautlin was a man of some influence as barber to Prince Achilles of Württemburg. Krautlin and Einhorn brought Kepler to court and demanded she use **magic** to cure Reinbold of the sickness she had caused. This was meant as a legal trap—if Kepler had used **countermagic,** that would have been justification for **torture.** Kepler refused to use countermagic or in any way take responsibility for Reinbold's sickness, although Krautlin carried persuasion to the point of touching Kepler with his sword. Kepler also responded by a countersuit for defamation in the city court of Leonberg.

Johannes Kepler, then in the town of Linz, heard of the case at the end of the year in a letter. Any **accusation** of witchcraft was particularly threatening to Johannes, a former court astrologer for the magic-obsessed Holy Roman Emperor Rudolf II (r. 1576–1611) and himself sometimes accused of sorcery or witchcraft. He responded by an indignant letter to the court supporting his mother. The defamation suit proceeded slowly, and the witchcraft charges against Katharina Kepler were revived in October 1616, when she brushed against some girls in a field. One 12-year-old girl in the party claimed that Kepler had struck her, causing pain and paralysis in the arms. The magistrate threatened to inform the ducal council of the matter, and Kepler made the mistake of trying to bribe him with a silver cup to drop the affair. The magistrate refused the bribe and informed the ducal council of Kepler's actions. Kepler hurriedly departed to Johannes Kepler in Linz, and the ducal council ordered that she be arrested on sight. Johannes Kepler requested that the defamation suit be allowed to continue even in Katharina Kepler's absence. In October 1617, Katharina Kepler returned to Württemburg. The following May, the defamation suit was resolved in Kepler's favor because of Reinbold's bad reputation—years ago, she had been convicted of prostitution.

The witch trial of Katharina Kepler, however, continued, with the presentation of a massive 49-count indictment. The accusations focused on **maleficia**. A tailor, Daniel Schmid, accused her of having caused the deaths of his two children by coming into their house unannounced and saying a blessing over them. She was accused of harming livestock, and it was claimed that she had grown up in the house of kinswoman who was a witch. In July 1620, the council ordered that she be arrested, questioned and confronted with witnesses. If after that she refused to confess, she was to be tortured. Kepler still refused to confess, but the intervention of Johannes Kepler with the duke won a five- to six-week respite before torture. Katharina Kepler's other son, Christoph, a Leonberg tinsmith, was able to have the trial moved from Leonberg, claiming that his mother's troubles were harming his own reputation, to the small town of Guglingen. The trial began September 1620 before the Guglingen magistrate Johann Ulrich Aulber. Kepler enjoyed the support of Johannes Kepler and defense lawyer Johannes Rueff. The documents of the case were sent to the law faculty of the University of Tübingen, which was given the responsibility to decide whether Kepler would be tortured. Johannes Kepler, a Tübingen graduate, was friends with a jurist there, Christoph Besold (1577–1638). Whatever influences were brought to bear, the Tübingen faculty issued a compromise decision, claiming that the evidence was insufficient for either torture or acquittal. Instead, Katharina Kepler was to be questioned again, in the presence of the instruments of torture. This was done, but as she had done throughout the entire proceedings, Kepler stoutly maintained her complete innocence. She was exonerated and set free in November, dying the following April. The affair may have had a legacy in the writings of Johannes Kepler. His *Somnium*, published posthumously in 1634, is a fantasy about an Icelandic youth modeled on Kepler himself who journeys to the moon by magic. The hero's mother is portrayed as having a longstanding relationship with good spirits similar to the relationship a witch has with evil ones.

REFERENCE: Max Caspar. *Kepler*. Trans. and ed. C. Doris Hellman. London and New York: Abelard-Schuman, 1959.

KISS

The idea that witches kissed and were kissed by the devil in an obscene and degrading manner had deep roots, descending to the witch-hunt from the literature of medieval heretic hunters. A description of secret gatherings of heretics kissing a demonic black cat on the feet, under the tail and on the genitals occurs in a twelfth-century account. The medieval Scholastic philosopher and

The ritual kiss of the sabbat to Satan by sorcerers and witches. From the *Compendium Malleficarum* (1626) by Francesco Maria Guazzo, Italian demonologist. © The Art Archive/Dagli Orti (A).

theologian William of Auvergne (c. 1180–1249) described demon worshipping heretics as kissing cats and toads, really demons in animal form, on the mouth and buttocks. The "kiss of infamy" (*osculum infame*) played a prominent role in the trial of the **Templars,** who were charged with requiring their initiates to kiss the mouth, navel and buttocks of the prior. This differed from most of the previous associations of kissing with heresy by having the kiss bestowed on a human rather than a demon and may have been connected to the charges of homosexuality made against the Templars. Charges of kissing the devil show up fairly often in fifteenth-century trials, although it was not mentioned in Heinrich **Kramer's** *Malleus Maleficarum.* This kind of kissing was a diabolical parody of the kiss of peace and also referred to the use of kissing in feudal ceremonies of homage; by making this degrading kiss, the witch initiate was accepting the **Satan** as his or her lord.

During the early modern witch-hunt, kissing the Devil was often associated with the making of the satanic pact as a way of sealing the bargain and showing the witch's submission. Kissing the Devil's anus or buttocks also often featured prominently in descriptions of the **sabbat.** Young **Basque** witches, for example, when being initiated into the witch-cult were described as kissing the Devil on his genitals and under his tail.

REFERENCES: Brian P. Levack. *The Witch-Hunt in Early Modern Europe.* London and New York: Longman 1987; Jeffrey Burton Russell. *Witchcraft in the Middle Ages.* Ithaca: Cornell University Press, 1972.

KRAMER, HEINRICH (INSTITORIS) (1430?–1505)

The fifteenth-century German Dominican inquisitor Heinrich Kramer, also known by the Latin version of his name, Institoris, was a leading demonologist and witch-hunter in late medieval **Germany.** His classic treatise of 1486 (written with another Dominican, Johann Sprenger [1436–1495], although Kramer was by far the dominant partner), *Malleus Maleficarum* (Hammer of Witches) is the best known of all witch-hunting manuals. Kramer was appointed inquisitor of south Germany in 1474. (Sprenger, a theology professor at Cologne, had already been appointed inquisitor for the Rhineland in 1470.) Records of Kramer's and Sprenger's early witch-hunts have disappeared, but they seem to have been frustrated by lack of cooperation from the political and ecclesiastical authorities of southern and western Germany.

Their response to this foot-dragging was to go over the heads of the local authorities to the pope, from whom they procured the bull **Summis Desiderantes Affectibus** in 1484. This decree seemingly empowered Kramer and Sprenger over the local authorities, but in practice it did not do so. The two cases in which Kramer's carrying out witch trials are recorded in local documents, as opposed to his own claims in the *Malleus*, were in Ravensburg in October 1484, before the bull was promulgated, and in **Innsbruck** the following year, where Kramer specifically claimed authority based on the bull. The Ravensburg affair was a moderate success for Kramer, and he procured the **execution** of two women, Anna of Mindelhym and Agnes Baderin, out of at least eight suspects. Innsbruck was by contrast a complete fiasco; resistance from the bishop, George Golser, and local authorities blocked Kramer from executing even one of the 50 accused witches. Kramer's frustration contributed to the writing of *Malleus Maleficarum* the next year.

Malleus is a treatise in the Scholastic manner, using the objection-and-response format employed by medieval philosophers and theologians. It is longer, more wide-ranging and systematic than previous demonologies. It incorporates material from the Innsbruck trials and is prefaced with *Summis Desiderantes Affectibus*, as well as in later additions an approbation from the theology faculty of Cologne. (Kramer had forged the approbation.) Although self-contradictory in many places, it is a work of some learning, drawing on a range of classical and medieval sources, of which the most important are the **Bible,** Aristotle (384–322 B.C.), Augustine (354–430), and Thomas Aquinas (1222–1274). It also drew from Johannes **Nider's** work. *Malleus* synthesizes many of the elements of the witch literature as it had been developing over the course of the fifteenth century, although it omits the **sabbat,** the **kiss** and the **Devil's mark.** It does include *maleficia*, **infanticide** and an explicitly **satanic pact.** Kramer and Sprenger identify witchcraft as heresy and apostasy, deserving of the severest penalties from the magistrate; in fact, they do not so much as discuss penalties less than death for convicted witches and state that those accused witches judged innocent should not to get off scot-free. Like most demonologists of their time, they distinguish modern witchcraft from that described in the **Canon Episcopi.**

Frustrated by the impediments society presented to witch-hunting, Kramer and Sprenger encouraged judicial activism, suggesting that the rumor of witches in a given area alone is a proper cause for judicial investigation. Judges may take the evidence of all sorts of persons in a witchcraft case. One problem in the Innsbruck investigation had been the witches' aggressive defense lawyer, Johann Merwais, and *Malleus Maleficarum* supports severe limits on the actions of defense lawyers, pointing out that too vigorous a defense renders the lawyer himself suspect of heresy. The identity of accusers should be withheld from witches and their counsel, thus preventing one common defense tactic, claiming that **accusations** were motivated by personal enmity. Kramer and Sprenger endorsed deception and **torture** to win confessions from accused witches, pointing out that God would never allow an innocent person to be convicted.

Kramer identified witches as a vast and growing conspiracy headed by **Satan** and directed against the church and all faithful people. He emphasized that the evil actions of witches and the Devil could only take place by the permission of God, but that they also angered God, thus causing him to punish humanity by granting even more power to the Devil and witches. Only vigorous persecution, if that, could break this vicious cycle. Another defense is ecclesiastic countermagic such as exorcism, making the sign of the cross and the wearing of religious amulets, about which Kramer is much more enthusiastic than later demonologists would be. The existence of witches is not merely beyond question, it is a positive article of faith, so that those who deny their existence are not merely wrong but heretics.

One element distinguishing *Malleus Maleficarum* from other demonologies is its obsessive hatred of women and **sex,** which seems to reflect Kramer's own twisted psyche. (He had been criticized for his lengthy interrogations of accused female witches at Innsbruck over their sexual histories.) The very title of *Malleus Maleficarum* reflects Kramer's misogyny, as *Maleficarum* is a Latin female collective plural, rather than the masculine one, *maleficiorum*, which would be used to denominate a mixed-**gender** group. Kramer's interpretation of why women were more likely to be witches also differed somewhat from the standard. Kramer did accept the standard argument of misogynist demonologists that the female propensity for witchcraft was in part due to female weakness. He even derived the Latin word for woman, *femina*, from *fe minus*—"less in faith." He placed more emphasis on supposedly insatiable female sexuality than on female weakness, however. Kramer saw sex as the root of all sin, as that for which Adam and Eve originally fell. Sexuality was also particularly vulnerable to attack by witches, demons or Satan. Kramer endorsed the idea that devils begat children on human witches by first assuming female form to have sex with human men, preserving the semen, and then taking male form to impregnate women. He also suspected that the reluctance of many great ones in the land to persecute witches was caused by their reception of demonic sexual favors. Kramer also discussed witch-caused impotence at length, going so far as to claim that witches had the ability to steal men's penises through illusion. In one of the most bizarre images in the entire demonological literature, he asserted that people often found 20 or 30 penises together like a birds nest, crawling around and being fed on grain. These were not actual, but illusionary penises.

One of the most vexed questions in the entire historiography of witchcraft is the extent of the influence of the *Malleus Maleficarum*. Certain facts are not disputed. It was an extraordinarily popular text in its time, reprinted 14 times by 1520, benefiting from the recent invention of printing, although it does not seem to have revived Kramer's witch-hunting career. (The Nuremburg city council did appeal to him for an expert opinion on witch **trial procedure** in 1491, however.) Corresponding with the mid-sixteenth-century lull in witch-hunting, it was not reprinted until the 1570s, after which it received many more editions until the late seventeenth century. Unlike other witchcraft treatises, however, it was not translated from Latin into major vernacular languages. The ready availability of the *Malleus* in modern translation and the extreme—and highly quotable—nature of its statements on witches and women have made it a major source for witchcraft historians. Generally, **liberals** and **feminists** have used it most, the former stressing Kramer's fanaticism and scorn for legal safeguards, the latter his misogyny. More detailed study has indicated that the *Malleus* had limited effect on actual witch trials. The great Inquisitions of the Mediterranean world—the Spanish, Roman and Portugese—did not treat it as an authority, preferring **Eymeric,** a much more legally learned and better-organized text. Protestants, although drawing on many ideas put forth in the *Malleus,* found it too mired in Catholicism to be a safe guide. In the Catholic world, the works of Nicholas **Remy** and Martin **del Rio** replaced the *Malleus* as a theoretical authority in the late sixteenth century. Its ubiquity, however, must have made it an important contributor to the ideas that many educated people held of witches and the proper way to deal with them.

REFERENCES: P. G. Maxwell-Stuart. *Witchcraft in Europe and the New World, 1400–1800.* Houndsmills, England and New York: Palgrave, 2001; Walter Stephens. *Demon Lovers: Witchcraft, Sex, and the Crisis of Belief.* Chicago and London: University of Chicago Press, 2002; Eric Wilson. "Institoris at Innsbruck: Heinrich Institoris, the *Summis Desiderantes,* and the Brixen Witch-Trial of 1485." In *Popular Religion in Germany and Central Europe, 1400–1800,* ed. Bob Scribner and Trevor Johnson, 87–100. New York: St. Martin's Press, 1996.

KYTELER, ALICE

The trial of the Irish noblewoman Alice Kyteler in 1324 was one of the first, along with the trial of the **Templars,** to use such concepts of witchcraft persecution as demon worship and **sex** with devils. Kyteler, of Flemish descent, had survived three husbands and was currently married to a fourth. She had accumulated much wealth as their legatee and through her own business dealings.

After her death, most would go to her son by her first husband and only recorded child, William Outlaw. The children of her subsequent husbands, all of whom she had married as widowers, wanted a greater share of the estate. They accused her and eleven others, four men and seven women, in Kilkenny before the bishop, Richard Ledrede of Ossory of having bewitched her husbands and murdered them by sorcery and of poisoning her current husband, Sir John Le Poer, who was in truth very ill. Ledrede, an Englishman currently conducting an aggressive antiheresy drive, condemned Kyteler as a heretic and sorcerer. Confessions obtained under **torture** showed that Kyteler had renounced Christ and the Church, sacrificed to demons and had a devil called Robert Artisson as a **familiar.** She was alleged to have had sexual relations with him and to have prepared **magical** ointments under demonic instruction. These were all themes with little immediate precedent that would become prominent in the later witch craze. Their appearance in **Ireland,** a place largely spared witch trials and witch-hunts, at this early date remains mysterious, although Ledrede had studied in **France** during a period in which early witch trials had taken place and was a client of pope **John XXII,** famous for his opposition to sorcery. Unlike the later witches, though, Kyteler was portrayed as a powerful magician rather than as a wretched slave of **Satan.** A woman attendant on Kyteler, Petronilla of Meath, was flogged and burned at the stake for her role as a go-between between Kyteler and Robert Artisson. Outlaw received a severe penance for abetting heresy, and Kyteler fled to **England.** Her ultimate fate remains unknown, although a local legend links a witch named "Alice Ketyll" with Clapdale Castle in Clapham, Yorkshire.

REFERENCES: Jeffrey Burton Russell. *Witchcraft in the Middle Ages.* Ithaca: Cornell University Press, 1972; Bernadette Williams. " 'She was usually placed with the great men and leaders of the land in the public assemblies'—Alice Kyteler: A woman of considerable power." In *Women in Renaissance and Early Modern Europe,* ed. Christine Meek, 67–83. Dublin: Four Courts Press, 2000.

L

LADIES FROM OUTSIDE

From the late fifteenth to the late eighteenth centuries, cases of heresy and witchcraft in Sicily fell under the jurisdiction of the **Spanish Inquisition.** Punishments for witches were relatively light—usually amounting to banishment, or, for men, a term at the galleys. From 1579 to 1651, the Inquisition dealt with a series of cases involving 57 women and 8 men, all poor people, who identified themselves as members of a group called the Ladies from Outside. (The belief can be traced back to the mid–fifteenth century.) This term had two meanings, one referring to a group of supernatural beings like fairies, the other to their human associates. The human ladies from outside, often claiming a "sweet blood" that gave them the power to heal supernaturally caused afflictions, journeyed in spirit on Tuesday, Thursday and Saturday nights to revel in meetings presided over by a goddess called the "Queen of the Fairies," the "Greek Lady," the "wise Sybil" or several other names. The gatherings were pleasant, with fine food, music and enjoyable **sex.** The fairies resembled humans, except in having hands and feet like **animals.** The ladies from outside claimed to be organized in companies and to have the ability to heal those diseases in humans or animals caused by the fairies. The cult was widely known; members discussed it openly, and the Inquisition never had trouble finding witnesses.

The inquisitors attempted to deal with the ladies from outside by explaining to them that their meetings were really **sabbats,** presided over by the Devil. They may have been successful in convincing individuals, but the Sicilians as a whole never viewed the cult, which survived to modern times, as diabolical. This failure contrasts with the **Roman Inquisition's** success against the *benandanti*. Gustav Hennigsen has suggested that the reason for this failure is that the Sicilians, unlike peninsular Italians, lacked the concept of evil witches who caused harm. Another possibility is the cultural and ethnic gap between Spanish inquisitors and Sicilians.

REFERENCE: Gustave Hennigsen. "The Ladies from Outside: An Archaic Pattern of the Witches' Sabbath." In *Early Modern European Witchcraft: Centres and Peripheries,* ed. Bengt Ankarloo and Gustav Henningsen, 191–215. Oxford: Clarendon Press, 1990.

LAMBE, JOHN

The case of the Englishman Dr. John Lambe indicates the often permeable nature of the boundary between the learned magician and the witch. Lambe was a disreputable character who had been a tutor to noblemen's sons and then a medical student, fortuneteller and sorcerer. He was twice indicted and twice convicted of witchcraft in 1608, under the statute of 1604 but escaped **execution,** being confined to the prison of King's Bench in London. He reemerged into prominence as friend, **physician** and **magical** adviser to the most powerful English politician of the 1620s, George Villiers, first duke of Buckingham (1592–1628), a favorite of King **James I.** Buckingham's favor protected Lambe after he was convicted of the rape of an eleven-year-old girl in 1623, and his favor continued even after examination by the London College of Physicians revealed him to be ignorant of the astrology he professed to practice. Nick-named "the duke's Devil," Lambe shared in Buckingham's growing unpopularity in the latter half of the decade and was murdered by a London mob in 1628, a few months before Buckingham was assassinated. The occasion was the subject of a pamphlet, *A Briefe Description of the Notorious Life of John Lambe, otherwise called Doctor Lambe, together with his ignominious Death* (1628).

English demonological writers such as Richard Baxter (1615–1691) continued to tell stories of Lambe and his magical powers in the seventeenth century. A servant of Lambe's, Anne Bodenham, known as "Dr. Lambe's darling," was supposed to have learned various magical processes such as divination from him, and she practiced as a **cunning** woman and seller of magical charms. Among other things, she was accused of having advised a young woman with fits to pray to the planet Jupiter for relief. Bodenham was convicted of witchcraft and hanged in Salisbury in 1653. While being walked to the gallows, she demanded beer and announced her intention to die drunk. Her career was the subject of another pamphlet, by Edmund Bower, *Dr. Lamb Revived* (1653), based on his interviews with Bodenham in her cell and his attendance at her trial.

REFERENCES: James Sharpe. *Instruments of Darkness: Witchcraft in Early Modern England.* Philadelphia: University of Pennsylvania Press, 199; Keith Thomas. *Religion and the Decline of Magic.* New York: Charles Scribner's Sons, 1971.

LAMOTHE-LANGON, ETIENNE-LEON

The nineteenth-century French hack writer Etienne-Léon Lamothe created a series of forgeries that bedeviled scholarly historians of the witch-hunt for well over a century. Son of a Toulouse magistrate guillotined during the French Revolution, Lamothe was a graphomaniac from an early age, publishing a five-volume novel on medieval troubadours, along with three other novels, by the age of 22. What really turned Lamothe to writing, however, was the defeat of Napoleon at Waterloo in 1815. Lamothe had served Napoleon loyally as an administrator, and his adherence to the Bonapartist cause meant that he had no possibility of employment by the new French regime of Louis XVIII. Lamothe became a full-time writer. After churning out a series of Gothic novels, he turned his hand to a history of the Inquisition of Toulouse. His three-volume *History of the Inquisition* appeared in 1829, the same year as 20 other volumes from his hand reached print. The work was inspired by the commercial success of the *History of the Spanish Inquisition* by the Italian scholar Giovanni Antonio de Llorente (1756–1823).

Lamothe endorsed and embroidered a fraudulent story from a fifteenth-century chronicle of a Toulousaine woman named Angela de la Barthe who was supposedly executed in 1275 for dealings with the Devil, but his principal forgery was out of whole cloth. This was a series of trials and mass burnings of witches numbering in the hundreds in the south of **France** in the fourteenth century. In addition to the creation of the trials and **executions** out of his own imagination, Lamothe also misled witch-hunt historians in two more subtle ways. The first is that he applied the stereotype of the **sabbat**-attending, orgy-participating, devil-worshipping witch, essentially an early modern creation, to the late Middle Ages. The accounts of the sabbat that he published, claiming to be transcribing the inquisitorial documents, are actually based on the early-seventeenth-century work of Pierre de **Lancre.** The other distortion is more subtle. Lamothe's emphasis on the south of France led him to associate the beginnings of the witch-hunt with the inquisitorial persecution of the Cathar heresy. The Cathars were members of a medieval Dualist church whose beliefs were parallel to those of the ancient Manicheans. They saw good and evil as coequal powers and spurned the material world as innately corrupting, the domain of the lord of evil. Lamothe ascribed beliefs about the equality of God and the Devil, drawing on Cathar dualism, to his alleged late medieval witches.

Despite Lamothe's hopes, *History of the Inquisition in France* was a commercial failure, and he turned his hand from inquisitorial studies to the composition of spurious memoirs of historical figures including Louis XVIII and Napoleon. In France, where his reputation was not that of a historian, his work had no impact on Inquisition history. It entered the mainstream of witchcraft history through **Germany,** where its author was unknown. Lamothe's imaginary trials were briefly mentioned in Wilhelm Gottlieb Soldan's *History of the Witch-Hunt* (1843), along with the equally imaginary work of Giovanni Battista **Piotto.** They were extensively discussed in the great German scholar Joseph Hansen's *Inquisition and Witch-Hunt in the Middle Ages* (1900). From here they entered the mainstream of witch-hunt historiography, accepted in Rossell Hope Robbins's (b. 1912) *summa* of the **liberal** tradition in witchcraft studies, *The Encyclopedia of Witchcraft and Demonology* (1959) and as late as Jeffrey Burton Russell's *Witchcraft in the Middle Ages* (1972), much of whose argument concerning the continuity of medieval heresy and late medieval witchcraft rests on uncritical acceptance of Lamothe's forgeries. Shortly after Russell's work, the forged trials were exposed by two scholars working independently, the Briton Norman Cohn and the American Richard Kieckhefer.

REFERENCES: Norman Cohn. *Europe's Inner Demons: The Demonization of Christians in Medieval Christendom*. Rev. ed. Chicago: University of Chicago Press, 2000; Richard Kieckhefer. *European Witch Trials: Their Foundations in Popular and Learned Culture, 1300–1500*. Berkeley: University of California Press, 1976; Rossell Hope Robbins. *The Encyclopedia of Witchcraft and Demonology*. New York: Crown, 195; Jeffrey Burton Russell. *Witchcraft in the Middle Ages*. Ithaca: Cornell University Press, 1972.

LANCASHIRE WITCH-HUNT

The 1612 Assizes at Lancaster in Lancashire produced the largest number of witches hanged at one time in **England** before the Matthew **Hopkins** witch-hunt. The most important case began in a region known as the Pendle Forest, where two families, that of Anne Whittle, known as "Old Chattox," and that of Elizabeth Southern, "Old Demdike," had long-established reputations as witches. The affair began with an encounter between "old Demdike's" grand-daughter Alizon Device, and a peddler, John Law. She asked to purchase some needles from him, and he refused on the grounds that he did not want to undo his pack. Shortly after the two parted on unfriendly terms, John Law had a stroke. Although Alizon begged and received John Law's forgiveness, his son, Abraham Law, brought an action against her for witchcraft.

The initial judge in the case was a local justice of the peace, Roger Nowell (1551–1623). Alizon Device confessed to Nowell that she had been initiated into witchcraft by her grandmother, Old Demdike and also accused Old Chattox of witchcraft and *maleficia*. Alizon's mother, Elizabeth Device, was found to have a **witch's mark,** and both Demdike and Chattox confessed to witchcraft. Demdike claimed to have a **familiar** named Tibb, while Chattox confessed to having murdered a father and son, Christopher and Robert Nutter, in 1595. This had clearly expanded far out of the ability of one local magistrate to handle, and Nowell sent Demdike, Chattox, Chattox's daughter Anne Redfearne, and Alizon Device to Lancaster for the next Assizes.

Two factors enabled Nowell's investigation into the case of Alizon Device to become a full-fledged witch-hunt. One was an unusually cooperative witness, Alizon's nine-year-old sister Jennet Device. The other was a meeting of the families of the accused and some other people in the area at Malkin Tower, Demdike's home. The meeting was held on Good Friday, a day of fasting among Christians but allegedly marked by the witches with a feast. It was charged that the attendees planned to blow up the castle where the prisoners were being held. Although the meeting was not a **sabbat,** it gave the investigation a similar dynamic, and identifying and charging those who attended the meeting became a central goal. With the help of Jennet and her somewhat slow-witted brother James, magistrates compiled a list of attendees. Old Demdike died in jail, but the rest survived for the assizes, which began August 17 under the assize judges Sir James Altham and Sir Edward Bromley, of whom Bromley was the more active in witchcraft cases. The cases involved all the standard appurtenances of English witchcraft cases, including familiars, **image magic,** charms and *maleficia* against humans and livestock. Ten witches were sentenced to be hanged, including Chattox, Redfearne, Elizabeth Device, Alizon Device, James Device and four other witches whom had been identified by James and Jennet Device as having attended the meeting, and whom subsequent investigations had revealed to be wielders of harmful or fatal **magic.** A 10th witch, Isobel Roby, whose case was unconnected with the Pendle Forest witches, was also hanged. Finally, a Yorkshire witch who had attended the Malkin Tower meeting, Jennet Preston, had already been hanged at Yorkshire Assizes.

The other major witchcraft case that was being handled at the Lancashire Assizes was that of the Salmesbury witches, a group of three women accused by a 14-year-old girl named Grace Sowerbutts. This case collapsed when Sowerbutts confessed in the courtroom that she had been coached by a Catholic priest, Christopher Southworth.

The court clerk Thomas Potts was the author of *The Wonderful Discoverie of Witches in the Countie of Lancaster* (1612), a collection

The Lancashire Witches: The young witch Jennet urges her familiar, the cat Tib, to attack her victim. An illustration by John Gilbert in Harrison Ainsworth's *The Lancashire Witches*, 1612. © Mary Evans Picture Library.

of legal documents with commentary and the sole surviving document on the cases. *The Wonderful Discoverie* was the longest and most detailed of English witchcraft narratives. Pott was much more familiar with the legal process than most writers of witchcraft pamphlets. Whereas most English witchcraft pamphlets were hurriedly produced in a catch-as-catch-can manner, Potts was commissioned by the judges to produce a substantial narrative of the cases. For his part, Bromley wrote a preface in which he claimed to have revised the text to render it scrupulously accurate. One of Potts's and Bromely's principal goals was to vindicate the judges and the judicial system in general. Therefore, every action of the court, whether in convicting or acquitting a witch, was shown to be right. The pamphlet is not a literal record, however. For example, Potts inserted written depositions into the record of the actual court proceedings, representing them as oral testimony, and omitted several stages in the legal process. The documents are reproduced with commentary praising the judges and vehemently abusing witches and

Roman Catholics. The only work of demonology Potts showed any familiarity with was King **James's** *Daemonologie*, which he praised lavishly—not surprisingly, considering the author was occupying the English throne at the time. English demonologists including Richard **Bernard** would use Potts's work.

The affair had a sequel in 1633, when a Pendle Forest boy named Edmund Robinson claimed to have been kidnapped by witches and taken to a sabbat. Promoted as a **witch-finder** by his father and uncle, Edmund was taken around the area identifying witches. In the capacity, he encountered the future witch-hunt opponent John **Webster,** serving as a curate of a church that Robinson visited. Seventeen witches, including Jennet Device, were convicted on Robinson's charges, but the affair attracted the interest of the Privy Council, the members of which demanded that some of the prisoners and Robinson be sent to London. Examination involving, among others, Charles II and his **physician** William Harvey (1578–1657) discovered no **witch's marks** or other conclusive evidence, and the convictions were overturned, although some of the accused were still being held in jail several years later. The affair was the subject of a play by Thomas Heywood (1575?–1650?) and Richard Brome (1590–1652), *The Late Lancashire Witches* (1634), which assumed the witches' guilt. Lancashire witchcraft was also the subject of Thomas Shadwell's (1642?–1692) play *The Lancashire Witches* (1682), drawing on both the 1612 and 1633 affairs, presenting witchcraft as real while ridiculing the excessively credulous.

REFERENCES: Laird H. Barber. *An Edition of the Late Lancashire Witches by Thomas Heywoid and Richard Brome*. New York and London: Garland, 1979; Marion Gibson, ed. *Early Modern Witches: Witchcraft Cases in Contemporary Writing*. London and New York: Routledge, 2000; Edgar Peel and Pat Southern. *The Trials of the Lancashire Witches: A Study of Seventeenth-Century Witchcraft*. New York: Taplinger, 1969.

LANCRE, PIERRE DE (1553?–1630)

Pierre de Lancre carried out the only official witch-hunt with mass **executions** in the history of early modern **France.** De Lancre was a native of Bordeaux, from a magisterial family. He attended Juan **Maldonado's** lectures on demonology and witchcraft at the College of Clermont, and joined the Parlement (law court) of Bordeaux in 1582. De Lancre was a devout Catholic of the French Counter-Reformation, an ideological position compatible with witch-hunting. His first book, *Tableau of the Inconstancy and Instability of All Things* (1607), does not deal with witches directly but points toward his later demonological works in its intense misogyny. De Lancre described women as more vulnerable to the devil both through their frailty and weakness and through their insatiable sexual desires.

In 1609, King Henri IV (r. 1589–1610) appointed de Lancre and the president of the Parlement of Bordeaux, Jean d'Espagnet, to investigate witches in the Pays de Labourd, a territory in the far southwest of France with a large **Basque** population. (The Parlement resisted this appointment, objecting to the idea that a two-judge panel, rather than the whole Parlement, was to be empowered to inflict **torture** and capital punishment. Their objection was overruled by the king.) De Lancre was much the dominant personality of the two, and d'Espagnet may not even have accompanied him. De Lancre's tour of the area took about four months, in which time he probably procured the burning of around 80 witches. Many others were sent back to Bordeaux, where their final fate remains unknown. (The Parlement did have a reputation for leniency in witch trials.)

De Lancre's efforts in the Pays de Labourd were recounted in his *Description of the Inconstancy of Bad Angels and Demons* (1612) and its augmented second edition in 1613. De Lancre's writings give an anthropological analysis of the role of diabolism and witchcraft in a society that he clearly loathed. As a patriotic Frenchman, convinced of the superiority of the French monarchy, French justice and the French language, de Lancre found the mixture of French, Spanish and Basque cultural elements in the Pays de Labourd highly suspicious. As a Counter-Reformation Catholic, he was appalled at the low state of the Catholic Church in the area, declaring that many priests were witches. A patriarchal misogynist, he was particularly upset at the prominent role that women played in the region. The principal industry was deep-sea fishing, and the men would be away for six months out of the year. During that time, women had a great deal of independence, which de Lancre believed they used to attend **sabbats** and worship the Devil. De Lancre was a strong believer in actual sabbats, which appeared often in the confessions made to him. The description of the sabbat in his works are among the most elaborate and influential to appear in the literature. De Lancre argued that the **Canon Episcopi** no longer applied to modern witches. If the sabbat was only a dream, he argued, why would the details of different accounts so often agree? He also believed in the **Devil's mark,** claiming the ability to see it even in a witch's eye. De Lancre strongly associated witchcraft with women—not with old women, however, but with young and pretty ones, whose beauty, frequently described in glowing terms, made them all the more useful tools of **Satan** for working his evil purposes. The language de Lancre used to describe the Basques resembled that that writers of travel literature used to describe Native Americans, and de Lancre claimed that devils driven away from the Americas and Asia by the activities of missionaries and exorcists had come to Europe to promote witchcraft.

De Lancre's witch-hunt relied on prolonged interrogation, torture and the use of child witnesses. (He was greatly dependent on an interpreter, Lorenzo de Hualde, because he spoke no Basque. De Hualde went on to become a witch-hunter on the Spanish side of the Pyrenees.) So great was the terror de Lancre inspired that many Basques fled across the Pyrenees to Spain, helping to precipitate the **Zugurramurdi** witch-hunt. His witch-hunt ended because of the expiration of his commission, as well as the combined action of the bishop of Bayonne, Bernard d'Eschaux, who refused to hand over priests accused of witchcraft to de Lancre, and the Parlement of Bordeaux, to whom, along with the king, d'Eschaux appealed to rein in the socially disruptive witch-hunt.

Conscious of a job well done, de Lancre went on a pilgrimage to Loreto and began work on *Description of the Inconstancy of Bad Angels and Demons*. He was made a state councilor in Paris.

De Lancre wrote two other demonological works, both aimed at combating what he saw as a dangerous tendency toward laxity on witchcraft issues on the part of French judges. (Witchcraft persecution was indeed declining in France during this period.) His encyclopedic *Incredulity and Misbelief in Sorcery Plainly confuted* (1622), dedicated to Louis XIII (r. 1610–1643), was unusual in including a denunciation of the Jews and their alleged satanic practices. Demonological works did not usually treat anti-Semitism as a central issue. It drew a skeptical response from the humanist Gabriel Naudé (1600–1653), *Apology for all the Great People who have been Falsely Suspected of Magic* (1625). De Lancre responded in *On Sorcery* (1627). As a demonologist, de Lancre's principal influences were Martin **del Rio** and the Francophone magisterial tradition of demonology—Jean **Bodin,** Henri **Boguet** and Nicholas **Remy.** His work was the last major defense of classic witchcraft belief and witch persecution to appear in France, although it failed to reverse the decline of French witch-hunting.

REFERENCES: Julio Caro Baroja. *The World of the Witches*. Trans. O. N. V. Glendinning. Chicago: University of Chicago Press, 1965; Margaret M. McGowan. "Pierre de Lancre's *Tableau de l'Inconstance des Mauvais Anges et Demons:* The Sabbat Sensationalized." In *The Damned Art: Essays in the Literature of Witchcraft*, ed. Sydney Anglo, 182–201. Boston: Routledge and Kegan Paul, 1977; Jonathan L. Pearl. *The Crime of Crimes: Demonology and Politics in France, 1560–1620*. Waterloo, Ontario: Wilfrid Laurier University Press, 1999; Gerhild Scholz Williams. *Defining Dominion: The Discourses of Witchcraft and Magic in Early Modern France and Germany*. Ann Arbor: University of Michigan Press, 1995.

LAWSON, DEODAT

Deodat Lawson was the author of the first printed account of **Salem** Village witchcraft, *A Brief and True Narrative of Some Remarkable Passages Relating to Sundry Persons Afflicted by Witchcraft, At Salem Village, Which Happened from the Nineteenth of March, to the Fifth of April, 1692* (1692). Lawson's involvement with Salem stemmed from the fact that he had served the village as its minister from 1684 to 1688, when he left after a dispute as to whether he should be fully ordained. Lawson took a position at another church in the area but remained an ally of the Salem Village faction driving on the witch-hunt, the Putnam family and the minister Samuel Parris (1653–1720). Some blamed the deaths of Lawson's wife and daughter in 1689 on witches. Lawson visited Salem Village shortly after the outbreak of bewitchments that began the witch-hunt, and his narrative is basically an account of the bewitchments and **accusations** of witches by the bewitched girls that he had witnessed or of which he received accounts from "persons of undoubted reputation and credit"—Salem Village members of the Putnam faction. While in the village, he also preached a sermon, published as *Christ's Fidelity the Only Shield Against Satan's Malignity* (1693), putting the witch attacks in the context of **Satan's** struggle against

New England, and urging the magistrates to vigorous action while expressing the hope that the attack would not divide the village against itself. Like many New England clergy, Lawson also expressed skepticism over spectral evidence—the bewitched claiming to see phantoms of the witches that were harming them. He pointed out that the Devil could use such counterfeits to turn Christians against each other. In 1696, Lawson returned to **England,** from where he had originally immigrated to Massachusetts. He died in poverty and obscurity many years later.

REFERENCE: Frances Hill, ed. *The Salem Witch Trials Reader.* N.p.: Da Capo Press, 2000.

LE FRANC, MARTIN (D. 1461)

Martin Le Franc, a poet and papal official from Normandy, was the author of a long French poem about women, *The Defender of Ladies,* probably written in 1442. *The Defender of Ladies* was a contribution to a debate about women that had been going on since the appearance of Jean de Meung's misogynist *Romance of the Rose* in the fourteenth century. It takes the form of a dialogue in which one male speaker attacks women and the other defends them—the defender, representing Le Franc's view, consistently getting the better of the argument. Le Franc devoted several hundred lines (out of more than 24,000) to the charge that women were more likely to become witches. In this discussion, he mentioned several ideas characteristic of the new image of the witch, such as **satanic pact,** the **sabbat, kissing** and **sex** between witches and the devil and witch flight, all of which he ridiculed. In the tradition of the *Canon Episcopi,* Le Franc identified witchcraft as principally a product of satanic delusion and called for the clergy to combat superstition rather than witches. One of the earliest defenses of accused witches, *The Defender of Ladies* was published in 1485.

REFERENCE: Alan Charles Kors and Edward Peters, eds. *Witchcraft in Europe 400–1700: A Documentary History.* 2d ed. Revised by Edward Peters. Philadelphia: University of Pennsylvania Press, 2001.

LIBERAL HISTORIOGRAPHY

From the beginning of the serious scholarship of the history of the European witch-hunt, beginning while it was still going on in the work of Christian **Thomasius** and Frances **Hutchinson,** a dominant school of interpretation has been that loosely described as liberal. Liberal historians write from a position of strong opposition to witch-hunting and tend to view it as a phenomenon imposed on innocent victims by powerful hierarchies in church and state. Liberal historians are usually anticlerical and tend to portray religious institutions, rather than state institutions, as the driving force behind the witch-hunt. Many liberal historians are Protestants, and focus on the witch-hunting misdeeds of the Catholic Church, although other Protestant and Catholic liberal historians are more evenhanded. In Protestantism, liberals sometimes exaggerated the responsibility of those Protestants whom they particularly disliked, such as the Calvinists.

Significant liberal historians in the nineteenth century, who established the textual foundation for modern studies of the witch-hunt, include Jacobus Scheltema (1767–1835) in Holland, Wilhelm Gottlieb Soldan (1803–1869) and Joseph Hansen (1862–1943) in **Germany** and Henry Charles Lea (1825–1909) in the United States. The tradition was carried on in the twentieth century by Wallace Notestein (1878–1969); George Lincoln Burr (1857–1938), who along with Andrew Dickson White (1831–1914) built the great collection of witch-hunt materials at the Cornell University Library; and Rossel Hope Robbins (b. 1912), among many others.

At its best, liberal historiography combined a strong moral passion with keen awareness of the institutional and legal contexts of the witch-hunt. Its weaknesses included the tendency to caricature witch-hunters as fanatics or monsters of greed attempting to enrich themselves by confiscating the wealth of accused witches. The heroes of the liberal school, however, are not usually the victims of the witch-hunt, often seen as merely passive, but those few skeptics who spoke out against witch-hunting, notably Johann **Weyer,** Reginald **Scot** and Friderich von **Spee.** The attitude of liberal historians to victims of witch-hunting was particularly condescending when the victims were uneducated and female—articulate male victims, such as Johannes **Junius** and Dietrich **Flade,** received far more respect.

Optimistic liberals saw witch-hunting as a superstition that had been happily overcome by reason and progress; while pessimistic liberals, whose position became dominant in the twentieth century, saw it as an expression of an impulse to persecute inherent in human society, leading to the atrocities of the twentieth century (hence the term "witch-hunt" was used to describe the persecution of accused communists during the American McCarthy era). Arthur Miller's play *The Crucible*, an artistic work deeply influenced by the liberal view of the witch-hunt, was written and produced as a response to McCarthyism and continued to influence popular views of the **Salem** witch-hunt long after.

Liberal historiography faced few serious intellectual challenges through the mid–twentieth century. **Psychoanalytic** interpretations and the **Murray thesis,** however influential in the culture at large, attracted little notice from witchcraft historians. The one challenge that attracted much notice was mounted by the highly eccentric British Catholic, the Reverend Montague Summers (1880–1948). For Summers, witch-hunters, at least Catholic witch-hunters, were noble heroes, and witches wretched and malevolent slaves of the Devil. Although Summers was a learned man responsible for the publication of English translations of some key demonological works, including Heinrich **Kramer's** *Malleus Malleficarum* (1486), his views were too eccentric for him to found an effective antiliberal school.

Effective challenges to liberalism came later, with the rise of **feminist** and **community-based** interpretations. Feminists inherited the moral passion characteristic of the liberal school but directed it at patriarchy rather than superstition or repressive church institutions. **Gender** had only minor importance for most liberals, who tended to see the witch-hunt as a conflict between male witch-hunters and male protoliberals like Scot, whereas feminists saw it as a struggle between men and women and were much more interested in the women, who comprised a large majority of the victims, than the liberals had been. Community-based historians challenged liberalism's top-down picture of witch-hunting by emphasizing the way that witch-hunts emerged out of divisions among common people, rather than being imposed by authorities. Few historians of witchcraft today can be described as traditional members of the liberal school, but all owe it a debt for establishing this perspective of the subject.

REFERENCES: *George Lincoln Burr: His Life by Roland Bainton: Selections from His Writings Edited by Lois Oliphant Gibbons.* Ithaca and New York: Cornell University Press, 1943; Henry Charles Lea. *Materials Toward a History of Witchcraft.* New York and London: Thomas Yoseloff, 1957; Wallace Notestein. *A History of Witchcraft in England from 1558 to 1718.* Washington, D.C.: American Historical Association, 1911; Rossell Hope Robbins. *The Encyclopedia of Witchcraft and Demonology.* New York: Crown, 1959.

LIGATURE

The ligature, or *aiguilette,* was a commonly used **magical** technique to procure the impotence or sterility of a male enemy. In its simplest form, it worked by tying a knot in a lace, preferably at the wedding ceremony. This was an idea that went back to classical antiquity. It remained widespread throughout the Middle Ages; most of the discussion of magic among medieval lawyers and theologians up until the thirteenth century was in the context of magically procured impotence and its effects on the status of a marriage. The ligature and other impotence-causing magic was not necessarily a specialty of witches but seems to have been widely used in Continental Europe (in the British Isles, impotence, like sexuality generally, was much less likely to be related to magic and witchcraft) by disappointed rivals of the bride or others who had reason to wish the groom or the couple ill. In the west of **France,** Catholic priests were often believed to practice magic to procure the impotence of young grooms, a superstition expanded to include Calvinist pastors, when they began to arrive in the area in the sixteenth century. Impotence magic could be foiled by a secret marriage and consummation before the magical practitioner could intervene or by the use of **countermagic;** in one area of France, the mother of the groom put a coin in the shoes of the bride and groom to foil any attempts to prevent consummation.

Witches were often charged with procuring impotence, whether through ligature or other means, and demonologists discussed it and recounted stories of witches who had practiced it in their treatises. Francesco Maria **Guazzo,** for example, drew on previous sources to discuss seven ways that witches prevent conception. Heinrich **Kramer's** *Malleus Maleficarum* (1486), the most misogynist of demonological texts, holds that it is within the power of witches—and also their frequent practice—to remove penises from men entirely, although this never became mainstream demonological opinion. (The *Malleus* granted that such acts were illusions, but portrayed them in highly "realist" terms.) Most demonologists discouraged attempts to remedy magical impotence through countermagic, such as the practice of urinating through a wedding ring, recommending prayer instead. **Physicians,** more skeptical of the ligature, often ascribed its effectiveness to the power of the imagination and endorsed countermagic not for its innate efficacy, but as a way of restoring a man's sexual confidence.

REFERENCES: Robin Briggs. *Witches and Neighbors: The Social and Cultural Context of European Witchcraft.* New York: Penguin, 1996; Kevin C. Robbins. "Magical Emasculation, Popular Anticlericalism, and the Limits of the Reformation in Western France circa 1590." *Journal of Social History* 31 (1997): 61–83.

LÖHER, HERMANN

Hermann Löher was a businessman and minor magistrate in the town of Rheinbach in the Electorate of Cologne. During the Cologne witch-hunt of the 1630s, Rheinbach fell under the jurisdiction of the fearsome witch judge Franz Buirmann, whose two visits in 1631 and 1636 resulted in the deaths of 150 people. In 1636, Löher, an opponent of Buirmann, fled for his life with his family to Amsterdam in the Dutch Republic, a territory free of witch-hunting. Many years later, in 1676, he published *The most Pressing Humble Complaint of Pious Innocents.* Although Löher drew on Freidrich von **Spee,** Reginald **Scot** (in Dutch translation) and the obscure Catholic priest Michael Stapirius, whose work is known only through Löher's use of it, the most prominent sections of his book come from his own experience. He vividly describes the procedures of a German witch-court, with its bullying and extensive use of **torture.** Although the kind of witch-hunting he described had ceased in **Germany** by the time he published his book, he makes suggestions for the reform of the process, including giving control over trials to local magistrates rather than iterant specialists like Buirmann. Löher did not deny the existence of witches but clearly thought the vast majority of accused people were innocent. Only one copy of his book survives.

REFERENCE: Lois Oliphant Gibbons. "A Seventeenth Century Humanitarian: Hermann Löher." In *Persecution and Liberty: Essays in Honor of George Lincoln Burr,* 338–359. New York: Century, 1931.

LORRAINE, WITCH-HUNTING IN

The Duchy of Lorraine, French-speaking but part of the Holy Roman Empire rather than the Kingdom of **France,** was an area of severe witch-hunting in the late sixteenth and early seventeenth centuries. Evidence is incomplete, but Robin Briggs, the foremost scholar of Lorraine witch-hunting, estimates approximately three thousand dead in the period 1580–1630, although there are records of trials going back to the 1450s. The severity of Lorraine witch-hunting is explained by its unusual judicial structure, where local courts operated with essentially no supervision. Lorraine witch-hunting was entirely carried out by secular courts, and Catholic priests seem rarely to have been involved in the cases, even as witnesses. Local secular courts, sometimes run by illiterate judges, were free to try and execute witches without oversight by a parlement, as was the case in France or **Franche-Comte.** In 1569, the duke required the local courts to submit their handling of serious cases to the central tribunal in Nancy for approval, but if the local courts disregarded the advice of the Nancy tribunal, which at that time was usually in the direction of greater leniency, nothing was done. The conviction rate in local courts was high, around 90 percent. **Torture** was commonly used, mostly thumbscrews and racks, with the *tornille,* the twisting of ropes around the upper arms, and the strappado, suspension by the arms, used more rarely. The local nature of the judicial system also meant that Lorraine witch-hunting never developed into massive witch panics, because this would have required some central authority to coordinate it. Witch-hunting in Lorraine was endemic rather than epidemic. It almost completely ceased after 1632, when the area became a battleground in the Thirty Years' War, and the population of the duchy as a whole diminished by more than half.

Lorraine witches were mostly women—those for about three-quarters of whom records survive—and overwhelmingly poor. Most had built up a reputation for witchcraft before being accused or were members of families with bad reputations. Local feuding often continued for years before resulting in witch **accusations.** Lorraine people's ideas about witchcraft incorporated *maleficia,* the **satanic pact** and the **sabbat,** which was frequently described in confessions obtained without the use of torture. Given that the officials to whom they were confessing were often more closely allied with popular demonology than with learned ideas, Lorraine's version of the sabbat lacks many of the developed features of the sabbat more generally. Sexual orgies were rare, and dancing much more common. Cannibalism and **infanticide** were also rarely mentioned. The sabbat was often described as rather tedious, and some Lorraine witches claimed that they paid the devil a chicken every year to be released from the obligation to attend. Approximately one-quarter of Lorraine witch accusations began with a witch claiming to have seen another person at the sabbat, but sabbats did not lead to massive witch-hunts.

Lorraine did produce one significant witch-hunter and demonologist, Nicholas **Remy,** a ducal official from 1575, appointed as duumvir of the Nancy tribunal in 1576 (leading to the Nancy tribunal taking a harder line against witches) and eventually elevated to the rank of procurer-general in 1591. His *Demonolatry* (1595) draws heavily on his experiences as a Lorraine witch-hunter, but his claim of having burned nine hundred witches is probably exaggerated.

REFERENCES: Robin Briggs. *Communities of Belief: Cultural and Social Tension in Early Modern France.* Oxford: Clarendon Press, 1989; Robin Briggs. *Witches and Neighbors: The Social and Cultural Context of European Witchcraft.* New York: Penguin, 1996.

LOUDUN WITCH-HUNT

Few early modern witch cases have attracted more attention, then or since, than the **execution** of Father Urbain Grandier in the small French town of Loudun in 1634. Grandier's case provides an excellent example of how local and national politics could combine with the actions of individuals to produce a witch trial. Loudun was a town divided between Protestants and a growing Catholic community, and under pressure from the central government to demolish its historic fortifications. Grandier, of bourgeois origin and Jesuit education, had arrived in Loudun in 1617 as parish priest in the Jesuit-controlled living of Saint Pierre du Marche. Grandier was a highly intelligent man and charismatic preacher, but also a man of strong sexual drives, who engaged in semi-open affairs with Loudun women. In 1629, Grandier was charged with responsibility for the pregnancy of Phillippe Trincant, the daughter of a local magistrate, Louis Trincant. Formerly a friend and ally of Grandier, Louis Trincant became his bitterest enemy. Trincant's persecution of Grandier as a seducer led to a spell of imprisonment for Grandier and temporary suspension from the functions of the priesthood, but the sentence was reversed and Grandier freed by the civil court of Poitiers.

Two factors precipitated Grandier's doom. One was the crisis of the city walls. Cardinal Richelieu (1585–1642), the effective ruler of **France** under King Louis XIII (r. 1610–1643), followed a determined policy of leveling all fortifications outside immediate royal control to prevent them from being used by rebels. Grandier's patron, the governor of Loudun, Jean d'Armagnac, wanted to keep the walls, particularly those of the inner keep or donjon. In this he was supported by a diverse faction, including Protestants and Catholics. Others, including the Trincants, were "cardinalists," supporters of Richelieu and of tearing down the walls. In 1631, a trusted agent of Richelieu, Jean Martin, baron of Laubardemont, was sent to Loudun to oversee the tearing down of the walls. Laubardemont, who had already overseen a witch-hunt in Bearn, was to become the most effective of Grandier's persecutors. The other was an epidemic of bewitchments and **possessions** among the cloistered Ursuline nuns of Loudun. (The Ursuline convent had been established in 1622.) As often happened, this followed a devastating outbreak of the plague, which in the summer of 1632 killed 20 to 25 percent of the town's population. The outbreak began September 21, 1632, with the appearance of the specter of a man in clerical garb to Sister Marthe, but quickly the major figure in the possessions became the prioress or mother superior of the convent, Jeanne des Anges (1605–1655).

Jeanne des Anges was young and inexperienced for a convent ruler. She allowed and encouraged more nuns to claim visions and bewitchments and brought in exorcists. Eventually the nuns began to identify the person responsible for their bewitchment as Grandier. This was curious, because none of them had ever met or seen him. Jeanne des Anges accused Grandier of having passed demons into the convent along with some roses and of having used love magic on the nuns. The convent's confessor, Father Mignon, a nephew of Louis

Trincant, compared the events to the case of
another witch-priest, Louis **Gaufridi.** Ecclesiastical proceedings commenced against
Grandier, who responded by using the civil
courts to block the church. Grandier was
opposed by his ecclesiastical superior, Henri
Chasteignier de la Rocheposay, bishop of
Provence, but supported by Rocheposay's
superior, Archbishop of Bordeaux Henri
d'Escoubleau de Sourdis. De Sourdis intervened in late December, ordering a vigorous
inquiry into the reality of the possessions,
with medical advice. This was followed by a
hiatus in the proceedings of about a year.

What reignited the case was Laubardemont's arrival in September 1633 to supervise
the last stage in the destruction of the fortifications, that of the donjon. Laubardemont
charged Grandier with writing an anti-
Richelieu tract, *Letter from the Queen Mother's
Shoemaker to M. de Baradat.* Grandier and
Richelieu had been enemies since 1618, when
they had quarreled over who had the right to
go first in a religious procession in Loudun. In
November, Laubardemont was commissioned
to arrest Grandier and investigate his involvement with the possessions. Investigation of

The public burning of Father Grandier for signing a pact
with the Devil. From a contemporary drawing, Loudon,
1634. © Dover Pictorial Archive.

Grandier's household revealed a tract he had written supporting priestly marriage, which led to his identification as a heretic. Laubardemont also encouraged the nuns to revive their charges against Grandier. In retaliation, Grandier's
family attempted to involve the Parlement of Paris, which had jurisdiction over
Loudun and was notoriously skeptical of witchcraft charges. Richelieu stymied
them by obtaining an order from the Council of State forbidding the Parlement's involvement.

Laubardemont sponsored public exorcisms of the nuns, who put on spectacular displays of fits, physical contortions and sexual acting out. (The nuns'
behavior is often explained as a product of sexual repression. This diagnosis was
made at the time as well as in later centuries.) Most of the exorcists were members of the Capuchin order, who endorsed the idea that devils under exorcism
were compelled to speak the truth. This idea was vigorously promoted in
preaching, and the exorcisms were used both to attack Grandier and to discredit the Protestants. On April 29, 1634, Jeanne des Anges vomited out a pact
between **Satan** and Grandier, supposedly signed in Grandier's own blood. On
June 23, Grandier attempted the exorcism of the nuns. His attempts to clear
his name, such as addressing the nuns in Greek, a language none of them

spoke, although presumably demons did, were frustrated. A commission of magistrates from the area around Loudun, chosen by Laubardemont, began to try the case and met for the first time on July 26. They heard 72 witnesses against Grandier. On August 18, Grandier was sentenced to death by burning, preceded by ordinary and extraordinary **torture.**

Judicial torture in Loudun at the time consisted of a procedure known as the "laced boots." The victim was strapped on a wooden pallet, and each leg was individually bound by a board on either side. The two boards on each side of the leg were tied together tightly, and wedges—four for ordinary torture, eight for extraordinary—were driven between the board and the leg, with the purpose of breaking the joints of knee and ankle. Grandier refused to confess or name accomplices, even though 10 wedges were administered. The last wedges were driven in by priests in attendance, a truly shocking violation of the protocols relating to torture and the priesthood. Laubardemont promised Grandier the mercy of preliminary strangulation before burning if he confessed, but he continued to refuse. On the way to the execution, Capuchin friars forbade the large crowds in attendance from praying for the condemned man. Grandier was burned alive.

The killing of Grandier produced a large literature, with more than a dozen tracts for and against his guilt published in 1634 alone, and many more in succeeding years. (The case has also inspired films, most notably Ken Russell's *The Devils* of 1971.) The possessions and exorcisms continued until 1638. Jeanne des Anges eventually switched from claiming demonic possession to claiming that the saints had appeared to her and granted her miraculous healing powers, and by the time of her death she was revered as a living saint.

REFERENCES: Michel de Certeau. *The Possession at Loudun.* Trans. Michael B. Smith. Chicago and London: University of Chicago Press, 2000; Robert Rapley. *A Case of Witchcraft: The Trial of Urbain Grandier.* Montreal and Kingston: McGill-Queens University Press, 1998.

LOWESTOFT WITCH-HUNT

A small witch-hunt in the English town of Lowestoft in 1662 is noteworthy for the involvement of two leading seventeenth-century English intellectuals, the judge Sir Matthew Hale (1609–1676) and the **physician** Sir Thomas Browne (1605–1682), as well as its influence on the subsequent literature. The two women accused, Amy Denny (often referred to in later literature as Amy Duny) and Rose Cullender, were elderly widows, poor but not beggars or dependent on charity. The **accusations** were of *maleficia*, and notions of satanic **magic** or pact played no role. Denny was the main target. Samuel Pacy accused her of bewitching his two daughters, 11-year-old Elizabeth and 9-year-old Deborah. The split between Denny and the Pacy family had allegedly begun when Deborah Pacy refused to sell Denny some herring. Denny was also accused of causing the death of a young woman, Elizabeth Durrant, and attempting to kill her baby brother William. Cullender was also accused of bewitching young girls and women as well as minor *maleficia* such as causing carts to stick and afflicting a man with huge lice. Possibly due to the weaker evidence against Cullender, she, but not Denny, was examined by a jury of women, including the mother of one of the afflicted girls, for **witch's marks.** Four were found. After being brought before a local justice of the peace, the two were held over for an assize judge.

The assize judge at the trial in Bury Saint Edmunds was Hale, a judge widely respected for his deep learning in the law and his personal piety. Hale was a convinced believer in the reality of witchcraft who had presided over the condemnation of another witch, Judith Sawkins of Aylesford, in 1658. Dramatic moments included the occasion when Amy Denny was brought before a blindfolded Elizabeth Pacy, who sprung at her and scratched her forehead until it bled. (On another occasion, when a blindfolded girl was touched by a third party after being told it was Denny, she had much the same reaction, but Samuel Pacy, present at the occasion, prevented this from resulting in the acquittal of the women by means that remain unclear.) Another magistrate present on the occasion, Sir John Keeling, an old enemy of Hale's, questioned the evidence. This may have been influenced by Keeling's staunch Anglican Royalism, because the Pacy family were Protestant Dissenters. The testimony of Browne, a leading scientific and religious writer as well as a physician, was to establish that the girls were genuinely bewitched. He claimed that **Satan** had heightened a natural "fit of the Mother," or hysteria. Browne's testimony was to establish the girls' bewitchment, rather than the evidence against Denny and Cullender.

Hale's summing up to the jury endorsed the reality of witchcraft, and most scholars view it as pushing the jury toward conviction. The two women were indeed convicted and then executed by hanging. The pronouncement of sentence, according to contemporary accounts, cured Elizabeth Durrant's stepmother, Dorothy Durrant, of a lameness. The Lowestoft case had a long-term influence, particularly because Hale was held in great respect by lawyers, Puritans and moderate Anglicans. It was described in a substantial, although misdated, pamphlet, *A Tryal of Witches at the Assizes Held at Bury St. Edmunds for the County of Suffolk on the tenth day of March 1664 before Sir Matthew Hale Kt then Lord Chief Baron of his Majesties Court of Exchequer* (1684). Hale's meditations on witchcraft, allegedly inspired by the trial although not discussing it, were published along with a grab bag of other material in *A Collection of Modern Relations of Matter of Fact Concerning Witches & Witchcraft upon the Persons of People* (1693). Accounts of the trial figure in Hale's friend and admirer Richard Baxter's (1615–1691) *The Certainty of the World of Spirits* (1691) and **Cotton Mather's** *Wonders of the Invisible World* (1693). The trial account was devastatingly dissected in Francis **Hutchinson's** *A Historical Essay concerning Witchcraft. With Observations of Matters of Fact, tending to Clear the Texts of the Sacred Scriptures, and Confute the Vulgar Errors about that Point* (1718).

REFERENCE: Gilbert Geis and Ivan Bunn. *A Trial of Witches: A Seventeenth-Century Witchcraft Persecution.* London and New York: Routledge, 1997.

M

MACBETH

Although William Shakespeare (1564–1616) used witch characters and witch imagery in many of his plays, the one most associated with witches is unquestionably *Macbeth*. The witches open the play in its first scene, and by suggesting to Macbeth that he will one day be king of **Scotland,** they precipitate its action. *Macbeth* was probably written in 1606 and performed during the Christmas season at the end of that year and early in 1607. This was a time when Shakespeare, like many other Englishmen, was aware that the new monarch, **James I,** was particularly interested in witches. Shakespeare did not invent the three prophesying women and their relevance to the story of Macbeth's rise to the kingship of Scotland, but he did invent the idea of making them witches. In the source on which he based *Macbeth*, Rafael Holinshed's narrative of Macbeth's reign in *Chronicles of England, Scotland, and Ireland*, the three women who prophesy Macbeth's ascension to the throne are described as "goddesses of destiny" like the three fates of Greek mythology or the Norns of northern mythology, "or else some nymphs or fairies," but not witches. Shakespeare's decision to make them witches enhances the connection between Macbeth's evil and **Satan's,** making Macbeth a deliberate chooser of evil rather than a helpless pawn of destiny. Shakespeare did not originate the connection between rebellion and witchcraft. It went back to the biblical book of I Samuel and the verse, "Rebellion is as the sin of witchcraft." The rebels that plotted to blow up the houses of Parliament and the king in 1605, the Gunpowder Plotters, were often described as witches or likened to them, so the connection was very present in English culture in the time Shakespeare wrote *Macbeth*. Several other plays written and performed around the same time—Thomas Dekker's *The Whore of Babylon*, John Marston's *Sophonisba*, and Barnabe Barnes's *The Devil's Charter*—link the destruction of kingdoms to plotters and witches.

Macbeth's witches are composite figures, but the largest element in their makeup is the early modern English witch stereotype. They are hideous old women. They

Macbeth and three witches. From N. Rowe, first illustrated edition of *William Shakespeare's Works*, printed by Tonson London 1709. © The Art Archive/The Art Archive.

have **familiars** in the form of **animals,** named "Paddock" and "Graymalkin." They spend their efforts performing harm to others and avenging the denial of charity. Their frequent use of dead body parts in their **magic**—it is probably this that originally draws them to the battlefield, a rich source—was specifically made a capital offence in the English witchcraft act of 1604, just two years before the play's composition. The power of prophecy *Macbeth*'s witches possess, however, has less to do with English witches than with the witches of the classical world. The language in which Macbeth addresses them refers to the powers of witches in classical literature, such as the power to control the winds. The witches' gatherings, while sharing some features of the **sabbat,** are presided over not by Satan but by the classical goddess of witches, Hecate (whose scenes were added to the play in a revision sometime after the original performance). The witches also sometimes appear to be ritual magicians, in the drawing of circles and the invocation of the spirits that prophesy to Macbeth. By participating in the necromantic ceremony and forcing the spirits to answer his questions, Macbeth, who earlier spoke of having given the "eternal jewel" of his soul to the "common enemy of man" becomes a witch. Like all witches, he eventually finds that the bargain with the Devil is a trap.

REFERENCES: Peter Stallybrass. "*Macbeth* and Witchcraft." In *Focus on Macbeth*, ed. John Russell Brown, 189–209. London: Routledge and Kegan Paul, 1982; Garry Wills. *Witches and Jesuits: Shakespeare's Macbeth*. New York and Oxford: New York Public Library and Oxford University Press, 1995.

MAGIC

By the time of the witch-hunt, Europe possessed a rich magical tradition drawing on Greek, Mesopotamian, Jewish, Egyptian, Arabic and indigenous European elements. Magic existed in highly elitist forms relying on the knowledge of learned languages such as Greek or Hebrew and in the common charms of the village witch or **cunning** man. Although witches were always accused of practicing magic, not all magicians were considered witches, and the relation

Scenes of cabbala and alchemy including the search and manufacture of the philosopher's stone, which turns base materials into silver and gold. *Phase I* from Stephan Michel Spacherus *Cabala Speculum Artis*, 1677. © The Art Archive/Biblioteca Bertoliana Vicenza/Dagli Orti (A).

between learned magicians—always men—and the predominantly female witches was a complex one. During the Middle Ages, the principal focus of opposition to magic had been the learned magician, or "necromancer," rather than the uneducated and illiterate witch. The doctrine of the "implicit pact," made with **Satan** for success in magical activities, was developed to deal with learned magicians rather than witches. The learned magicians, however, presented themselves either as not dealing with demons at all or as masters rather than slaves of the demons. They also presented their magic as text based, requiring literacy in several languages, whereas witch magic was simply a matter of the power of the demons exercised through the witches, requiring no special knowledge on the part of the witch.

As practiced, early modern European magic was divided into theoretical, or "high" magic, and applied or practical forms. High magic was revived during the Renaissance by humanists such as the Florentine Giovanni **Pico della Mirandola** (1463–1494), with the rediscovery of ancient Neoplatonic texts such as the writings ascribed to Hermes Trismegistus, the "Hermetic Corpus." The Jewish Kabbalah also became much more generally known and practiced among Christian scholars at this time. High magic generally involved mystic contemplation and harmony with the divine. The operation of high magic usually involved the performance of elaborate and precise rituals. Hermeticism, Kabbalah and some forms of alchemy emphasized carrying on magical rituals as a form of spiritual improvement. High magic required the magician to be a certain kind of person, pious and virtuous, and also ritually pure in the sense of avoiding certain foods and maintaining sexual moderation. High magic was elitist—high magicians often claimed that their knowledge was not for the vulgar. The goal of high magic was the magical mastery of the forces of the universe for the betterment of both the magician and the universe. High magicians insisted that the spirits they worked with were good spirits, but neither the Church nor the common people always accepted high magicians as different from witches and demonic magicians. The library of the English high magician John Dee (1527–1608), who claimed to converse with angels through a crystal ball, was ransacked by local people convinced that he dealt with demons. Magicians replied to the charges against them by arguing that magic was a higher or more perfect form of Christianity, emphasizing the process of personal purification which serious magic required, and even suggesting that magic could reconcile the differences between Catholics and Protestants.

Many high magicians, such as Heinrich Cornelius **Agrippa,** also practiced practical magic, but Europe was full of practical magicians who did not concern themselves with theory. Practical magic had much closer affinities to the type of magic with which early modern witches were charged. The goal of practical magicians was to advance their own interests by manipulation of magical forces. Astrologers and alchemists, although their practices were frowned upon by some churchmen, were found all over Europe, including the courts of its rulers who valued the astrologers' claims to know the future or the alchemist's claims to make gold. The finding of buried treasure was another activity frequently associated with practical magicians such as those involved in the **Morosini** case. Practical magicians presented their rituals as efficacious for locating the treasure and disarming any magical guardians it might have, whether they sincerely believed their magic worked or whether they made grandiose and fraudulent claims to attract money from investors. The personal qualities of the magical practitioner were usually less important for practical magicians than for high magicians. Practical magicians were less elitist than high magicians, and some published manuals in vernacular languages aimed at a wide audience. The lower ranks of practical magicians blended into the cunning folk, some of whom used books and claimed their magic was part of a learned tradition.

Learned magic, whether high or practical, was frequently charged with Satanism. Magicians had been the target of denunciations as idolatrous and heretical by Christian theologians and Church leaders since the age of the Church Fathers, and most of the decrees against magic issued by medieval popes were aimed against ritual magicians rather then devil-worshipping witches. Penalties against magicians continued in both church and secular legal codes during the early modern period and even grew harsher in that time. Jurists such as Jean **Bodin** and theologians such as Martin **del Rio** treated learned magicians as witches, essentially denying that there was any difference between the learned man with his books and talismans and the village witch. Bodin used the same French word, *sorcier,* to describe magicians, witches and all other magical practitioners. Penalties against magicians were not enforced as often nor were they usually as severe as those against witches.

The blending of ideas about ritual magic and witchcraft in the early modern period can be seen in the **Faust legend,** a German story of a magician who sold his soul to the devil to gain knowledge, thus becoming a witch. The story originated in the legend of an actual sixteenth-century ritual magician, Georg Faust, and was transmitted to a number of European cultures. To degree that "Faustian" ritual magic based on calling up and questioning of demons or dead spirits actually existed, it was the province of charlatans or the deluded. But it was often believed to be widely practiced, even by those skeptical of the existence of witches. Johann **Weyer** believed that witches, as deranged old women deluded by demons, should not be punished by the law, but like his adversary Bodin he also believed that learned magicians should be treated much more harshly—with the death penalty.

REFERENCES: Richard Kieckhefer. *Magic in the Middle Ages*. Cambridge: Cambridge University Press, 1989; Edward Peters. *The Magician, the Witch and the Law*. Philadelphia: University of Pennsylvania Press, 1978; Geoffrey Scarre. *Witchcraft and Magic in Sixteenth- and Seventeenth-Century Europe*. London: Macmillan Education, 1987; D. P. Walker. *Spiritual and Demonic Magic from Ficino to Campanella*. London: Warburg Institute, University of London, 1958.

MAGISTERIAL IMMUNITY

The belief that magistrates and other servants of justice in the performance of their official duties were immune from the attacks of witches was widely held—by demonologists, magistrates themselves, and even by witches. One of the earliest works on witch-hunting, Johannes **Nider's** early-fifteenth-century *Formicarius*, strongly endorses the theory, drawing on the experience of the

Swiss magistrate Peter von Greyerz. It appeared in many demonological works, including Heinrich **Kramer's** *Malleus Maleficarum* (1486) and the writings of Martin **del Rio.** Demonologists who were also magistrates, such as Jean **Bodin,** Henri **Boguet** and Nicholas **Remy,** were enthusiastic supporters, and it also appeared in the juristic literature. Belief in magisterial immunity was compatible with a sacralized view of the magistrates function, particularly insofar as the magistrate was conceived as partaking of the power of the monarch. Bodin and another supporter of the doctrine, **James VI and I,** connected the magistrate's immunity with his share in the monarch's Divine Right to rule. Del Rio contrasted the witches, the Devil's servants, with the magistrates, God's servants. On the Catholic side, belief in magisterial immunity grew stronger during the course of the witch-hunt. The *Malleus* had combined its endorsement of the doctrine with the recommendation that the magistrate take precautions, such as avoiding touching the witch. Del Rio ridiculed the necessity of such things.

The **execution** of justice was often held to end a witch's *maleficia* and to render **Satan** powerless to protect her. Witches are recorded as admitting that their arrest had taken away their powers to do supernatural harm. Some Protestant demonologists were suspicious of the supernatural power ascribed to magistrates and judicial proceedings by magisterial immunity, as absolute magisterial immunity would limit the power of God. The usual solution was to suggest that magisterial immunity depended on the magistrate carrying out the divine purpose by acting vigorously against witches.

REFERENCE: Stuart Clark. *Thinking with Demons: The Idea of Witchcraft in Early Modern Europe*. Oxford: Clarendon Press, 1997.

MALDONADO, JUAN (1534–1583)

Juan Maldonado, a Spanish Jesuit, was appointed in 1565 to the chair of theology at the College of Clermont, a recently founded Jesuit institution in Paris. (He is often referred to by the French version of his name, Jean Maldonat.) In the academic year 1571–1572, Maldonado gave a series of lectures on demons. These lectures were given on Sundays and holidays to maximize attendance and employed a simple Latin so that more people could understand them. Maldonado presented demonology in terms of the religious struggle between Catholics and Calvinists then convulsing **France,** emphasizing the connections between heretics, witches and demons. He drew upon the recent case of Nicole **Obry.** In his discussion of witchcraft itself, Maldonado drew on Heinrich **Kramer's** *Malleus Maleficarum* (1486) and endorsed the reality of witches' **flying** and the **sabbat,** suggesting that Protestant heretics denied the possibility of such things as part of their heresy. He claimed that women were more likely to become witches because of their greater curiosity. Like many Catholic demonologists, Maldonado endorsed religious **countermagic,** such as holy water and the sign of the cross.

Maldonado's lectures were not printed at the time, but they were quite popular. Two of the most important Catholic demonologists, Martin **del Rio** and the witch-hunting magistrate Pierre de **Lancre,** were among Maldonado's auditors, and both drew heavily on his work in their own demonologies. Lecture notes taken from Maldonado were published in a French version by the priest Francois de la Borie in 1605, as *Treatise on Angels and Demons*.

REFERENCE: Jonathan L. Pearl. *The Crime of Crimes: Demonology and Politics in France, 1560–1620*. Waterloo, Ontario: Wilfrid Laurier University Press, 1999.

MALEFICIA

Maleficia was the Latin term for a witch's evil acts (although in Roman law it originally meant evil acts in general). The technical definition of "witch" employed by most demonologists over the course of the witch-hunt was increasingly based on the **satanic pact,** but in the minds of most ordinary people and many secular magistrates, it was *maleficia* that made the witch. The Latin term for witch, as can be seen in such works as Heinrich **Kramer**'s *Malleus Maleficarum* (Hammer of the Witches) and Francesco Maria **Guazzo**'s *Compendium Maleficarum* (Treasury of the Witches) emphasized evil deeds rather than a personal relationship with **Satan.** On the popular level, witch **accusations** nearly always originated in accusations of *maleficium*. Pact and *maleficia* were not competing but complimentary ideas, however. One of the most common benefits sought by a witch and granted by the devil in a pact was the ability to inflict harm on others, and unlike the promises of wealth and power he may have made, on this part of the promise Satan always delivered. Learned demonologists, in fact, treated the power behind *maleficia* as purely demonic, the witch having no independent power of her own, whereas ordinary people were more likely to see the power as inhering in the witch herself.

Maleficia took nearly infinite forms. One of the most common was disease, inflicted either on people, or, nearly as threateningly, on livestock. Given the lack of learned **physicians** in most parts of rural Europe, disease remained equally open to being explained in medical terms or in supernatural ones. In many areas, one of the first questions asked about a sickness would be whether it was natural or caused by a witch. Animal diseases were even more open to being interpreted as **magical** in origin, because there was little knowledge of the nature of animal disease and no veterinary profession to speak of. Domestic livestock played a key role in the economy of most European households, and a sudden or unexplained sickness or death of an animal could wreak havoc. Animals were also an appropriate target for *maleficia* because they were always straying onto other people's property, thereby precipitating quarrels. Both humans and animals could be damaged by accidents, which could easily be blamed on a witch, and given the close quarters in which many early modern people lived, the malice of one person toward another was often obvious and could cause psychosomatic illness. Demonic **possession,** if caused by a witch, was also a *maleficium*.

Maleficia did not have to strike at individual or family survival; they could be quite trivial. The early modern rural household depended on a number of processes, the chemical nature of which was not understood. The failure of bread to rise, of butter to turn and of beer to brew could all be *maleficia*. At the other end of the scale was the large-scale *maleficium*, such as interference with the weather to cause famine or plague. This was more likely to be blamed on a group of witches working together at a **sabbat** than on an individual witch. Some confessions of accused witches portray debate between rich and poor witches over the infliction of famine, with the rich witches, knowing that their **social class** will not suffer, advocating it and the poor witches arguing against it. Maritime communities could blame groups of witches for storms at sea or the sinking of ships. The most famous example of this sort of *maleficium* was the storms that assaulted **James VI** of **Scotland** on his return from **Denmark.**

There were regional variations in *maleficia*. Some were obviously caused by the varying situations of different areas; for example, witches were associated with the sinking of ships in areas such as Scandinavia where seagoing was common. Others are more related to basic cultural differences. Witches were frequently blamed for male impotence on the European continent, but only rarely in the British Isles. In **England,** an area where witches were seldom thought to gather at **sabbats** or work together in large groups, they were not often blamed for large-scale catastrophes such as plagues and famines, whereas on the Continent they were more likely to be blamed for these misfortunes. Others varied by **gender**—interference with childbirth or the drying up of milk in a mother's breast was hardly ever blamed on a male witch, childbirth and nursing being female preserves.

Not every misfortune was blamed on a witch, even in areas with a high degree of awareness of witchcraft and many witch accusations and witch trials. Early modern people had a variety of explanatory schemes available and were aware that misfortunes could have non-supernatural causes—or nondemonic supernatural ones. God, for example, might send a misfortune as punishment for sin or as an opportunity to demonstrate one's faith.

Means of performing *maleficia* were also various. Simple touching or cursing were common, but there was also the possibility of using the **evil eye** or ointments or powders, whether prepared by the witch or given to her by demons or **familiars.** Rituals or aids, such as **image magic,** could also be employed, although these practices were more often associated with **cunning folk** than with witches.

One motive for *maleficium* was individual vengeance. A common narrative, particularly in English cases, is that of the denial of charity—an act of *maleficium* frequently directed against livestock and performed after a person denied a beggar charity. The beggar, usually an old woman, is then revealed as a witch and takes revenge. Another common pattern is for a harmful act to follow the kind of quarrel that was endemic in early modern village life—between two women over a place in the line for the communal oven, for example. But *maleficia* could also be performed for no individual motive, and Satan or demons are sometimes portrayed in witch confessions as requiring the witch to perform a certain amount of harm to others and punishing at the sabbat those witches who fail to meet their quota.

Some demonologists fought the emphasis on *maleficia* in popular perceptions of the witch, which they sought to replace with a model whereby an act was to be judged by its satanic or demonic origin, rather than its practical result. This argument would place the *maleficia* of the witch and the helpful spells and charms of the cunning folk in the same category, as morally indistinguishable acts of demonic magic. This idea never caught on—neither among ordinary people or lay magistrates, who despite many of the clergy's urging hardly ever persecuted those who used magic for solely benevolent ends. Although the great witch crazes relied on ideas about the sabbat and the satanic pact, charges of *maleficium* always played an important role. Even after the witch-hunt was long over, belief in the danger of occult *maleficium* remained common in many areas of rural Europe.

REFERENCES: Edward Bevers. "Witchcraft Fears and Psychosocial Factors in Disease." *Journal of Interdisciplinary History* 30 (2000): 573–590; Robin Briggs. *Witches and Neighbors: The Social and Cultural Context of European Witchcraft*. New York: Penguin, 1996; Keith Thomas. *Religion and the Decline of Magic*. New York: Charles Scribner's Sons, 1971.

MALLEUS MALEFICARUM

See Kramer, Heinrich.

MARYLAND AND VIRGINIA, WITCH-HUNTING IN

The southern British colonies saw far less witch-hunting than **New England,** but English laws against witchcraft did apply and occasionally led to proceedings. The earliest on record is a case against a Virginia witch, Joan Wright, in 1626. There is no record of a trial or verdict.

There was a slight peak in witch-related activity associated with the period of the English Civil War and Interregnum, with three cases of witches being lynched on ships approaching the southern colonies from **England** and several cases of accused witches filing civil actions against their accusers for defamation. The only witch **execution** in either colony occurred in 1685, when Rebecca Fowler of Maryland was convicted and hanged for bewitching Francis Sandsbury and others. Virginia saw a well-publicized case in 1706, when Grace Sherwood was tried in a case including searches for the **witch's mark** by juries of women and **flotation tests.** This was the culmination of years of charges, suits and countersuits by Sherwood and her neighbors. Sherwood was jailed, but the case seems to have ended without a verdict. The last witch trial of the region occurred in Maryland in 1712, when Virtue Violl was acquitted of charges of bewitching Elinor Moore.

REFERENCES: Richard Beale Davis. "The Devil in Virginia in the Seventeenth Century." *The Virginia Magazine of History and Biography* 65 (1957): 131–149; Francis Neale Parke. "Witchcraft in Maryland." *Maryland Historical Magazine* 31 (1936): 271–298.

MATHER, COTTON (1663–1728)

The Massachusetts minister Cotton Mather was **New England's** leading demonologist, retaining seventeenth-century witch beliefs into the early Enlightenment. Mather, a descendant of two distinguished families of New England ministers (his father **Increase Mather** was New England's first important demonologist), saw the society of his day as besieged by **Satan** and grievously falling off from the relatively pure society of the first New England settlers. The fierce diabolic assault heralded the quickly approaching end of the world. Witchcraft was only one form of diabolic assault. (The growing willingness of some New Englanders, such as Mather's enemy Robert **Calef,** to deny the power of witches and devils was another.) Mather's first direct encounter with witchcraft occurred in 1688, when the children of John Goodwin, a mason and a layman in Mather's congregation, claimed to be possessed. Mather believed their claims, which eventually led to the **execution** of their neighbor, Goody Glover, an old, illiterate Irish woman, as a witch. Mather invited one of the most severely afflicted children, the thirteen-year-old Martha Goodwin, to stay at his house for intense treatment by prayer and **Bible** reading—a course of action he always emphasized over judicial proceedings. The story of Glover and the Goodwin children was prominently featured in Mather's *Memorable Providences, Relating to Witchcrafts and Possessions* (1689). Mather's purpose in writing this work was not merely asserting the existence of witches and demons, but turning Satan's works against him by showing how his defeat could lead to religious revival. The work was explicitly aimed at an uneducated audience, impatient with theological argument but willing to be absorbed in narrative. It contained an elaborate description of the Kingdom of Hell, in whose courts demons, rather like New England attorneys, sought to win judgments against particular sinners. Despite his position on the margin of the European world (unlike his father, he never visited Europe), Mather was able to draw on demonological literature beyond his own immediate surroundings, such as the Swedish **Mora** trials and the work of the Englishman Joseph **Glanvill.** *Memorable Providences* had influence beyond New England. It was published in London in 1691, with a preface by the great English Presbyterian divine Richard Baxter (1615–1691).

Mather's best-known work on witchcraft was a product of the **Salem** trials of 1692. His position on the Salem cases was ambivalent. He generally approved of the persecution of witches and intervened against the accused witch George Burroughs (1650–1692). Mather's acceptance of the reality of Salem witchcraft can be seen in his belief that witches were responsible for the death of his infant son immediately after the trial. Despite his acceptance of the witches' guilt, Mather was concerned that the persecution was getting out of hand, affecting the innocent as well as the guilty. Like other Boston ministers, Cotton Mather eventually followed the lead of his father Increase in encouraging the end of the persecutions. Cotton Mather's somewhat hastily composed *Wonders of the Invisible World* (1693) was the New England government's official account of the Salem witch-hunt. Like others involved, Mather eventually regretted his participation in the Salem affair, and later in the 1690s he privately interpreted some misfortunes that had befallen his family as God's punishment of him for not having spoken out against the persecutions. In public he defended the actions of the magistrates.

Contemporaneously with the Salem affair, Mather was working on two other possessed women, Mercy Short in 1692 (described in Mather's *A Brand Plucked Out of the Burning*) and Margaret Rule in 1693 (described in *Another Brand Plucked out of the Burning*). Both were young women subject to shrieking fits alternating with periods of depression. Again, he hoped that these incidents would lead to evangelical revival rather than large-scale witch-hunting. Although Short and Rule named specific witches as responsible for their torments, Mather did not follow up these charges legally because of his belief in the weakness of spectral evidence. Mather's connection with the exorcisms of young unmarried women did not go unnoticed, and his relations with these women provided an easy target for Calef's attacks in *More Wonders of the Invisible World* (1700).

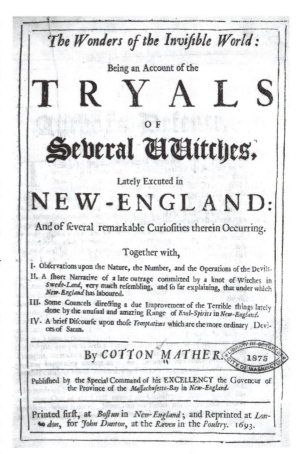

Title page from a second edition of Cotton Mather's witch-hunt pamphlet, reprinted from the Boston edition for John Dunton, London, 1693. © Corbis.

Mather continued to be a target for attacks on traditional witchcraft belief for polemicists in both old and New England. But, possibly influenced by the changing culture of the time, his own position was changing. Although he did not abandon his belief in the possibility of witches and diabolic action, Mather seems to have treated these subjects less confidently in the eighteenth century. His discussion of Biblical passages such as that relating to the Witch of Endor and his writings on New England history, such as his biography of his father, *Parentator* (1724), laid little emphasis on the demonic pact and the witch as a conscious collaborator with Satan, and more on demonic delusion and superstitious foolishness.

REFERENCES: Robert Middlekauf. *The Mathers: Three Generations of Puritan Intellectuals 1596–1728*. New York: Oxford University Press, 1971; Michael P. Winship. *Seers of God: Puritan Providentialism in the Restoration and the Early Enlightenment*. Baltimore: Johns Hopkins University Press, 1996.

MATHER, INCREASE (1639–1723)

The Congregational minister Increase Mather was the first **New England** divine to produce a major treatment of witchcraft. This discussion was part of Mather's *An Essay for the Recording of Illustrious Providences* (1684). In this book, Mather treated witchcraft in the context of the many other supernatural or marvelous wonders through which God providentially governed the world and revealed his presence to humans. As a demonology, *An Essay for the Recording of Illustrious Providences*'s discussion of witchcraft was in the tradition of Joseph **Glanvill.** Mather used the actions of witches to demonstrate the existence of a supernatural world, attacking the standard canon of English anti-witchcraft writers as it had developed by the later seventeenth century, including Reginald **Scot,** Thomas **Ady,** John **Wagstaffe** and John **Webster.**

Mather's second book on witches was *Cases of Conscience concerning Evil Spirits Personating Men* (1693). This work was originally given as a sermon to a group of ministers in Cambridge, Massachusetts (where Mather was president of Harvard), on October 3, 1692. Book and sermon were produced in response to the witch trials and condemnations at **Salem.** Mather had been in **England** representing the interests of Massachusetts when the witch-hunt at Salem broke out, but as the colony's leading minister he was concerned with it immediately on his return. The colony's governor, Sir William Phips, a close political ally, consulted him on the Salem affair. Mather, experienced in dealing with people who believed themselves demonically possessed, did not doubt that witches had indeed afflicted New England and that magistrates had acted properly in response to **accusations,** but he was deeply troubled by the extent of the hunt and by the lack of procedural safeguards. What was particularly problematic for Mather, who believed it was better to let a guilty witch go free than condemn an innocent person for witchcraft, was the use of spectral evidence, where the demonically afflicted person claimed to see the specter of the witch causing the torments. Such sights were used in some of the Salem cases as evidence that the specter seen was actually a witch. To Mather, this fatally underestimated **Satan's** ability and desire to deceive; it was perfectly possible, he believed, for a devil to take the appearance of an innocent person. Mather also repudiated superstitious practices such as **flotation tests** or touching the witch. *Cases of Conscience* upheld a stricter standard of evidence, based on the work of the early-seventeenth-century English demonologists William **Perkins** and Richard **Bernard,** whom Mather praised. He preferred as proof of witchcraft either an unforced confession or the testimony of witnesses to an actual demonic act. Mather's position had influence in bringing the persecution to an end, but he did not blame the magistrates; any condemnation of innocents at Salem was not the fault of the colony's leaders, but of Satan. Mather continued to defend the existence and the **execution** of witches to the end of his long life.

REFERENCES: Robert Middlekauf. *The Mathers: Three Generations of Puritan Intellectuals 1596–1728.* New York: Oxford University Press, 1971; Peter Lockwood Rumsey. *Acts of God and the People, 1620–1730.* Ann Arbor, Michigan: UMI Research Press, 1986.

MAZZOLINI, SILVESTRO (1456–1523)

The Dominican inquisitor and papal official Silvestro Mazzolini was one of the earliest Italian writers to accept the witch stereotype as it had been developed in the fifteenth century. After serving as an inquisitor around Milan between 1508 and 1511, he was summoned to Rome, where he eventually became master of the sacred palace to Pope Leo X (pope, 1513–1521). He published two works discussing witchcraft. One was a theological compilation dedicated to the new pope in 1514, the other a treatise specifically devoted to the subject, *On the Marvels of Witch-sorceresses and Demons* (1521). These are some of the earliest demonologies to show the influence of Heinrich **Kramer's** *Malleus Maleficarum* (1486), but also draw upon the folklore of ordinary Italians. Mazzolini accepted the reality of human-demon **sex,** the **sabbat, infanticide** and witch flight. He described how Inquisitors made children who had attended the sabbat recreate the dances they had done there, and how these dances were so bizarre and different from any known dance that they could only be demonically inspired. Mazzolini was also the teacher of another important Dominican demonologist and witch-hunter, Bartolommeo **Spina,** who succeeded him as master of the sacred palace.

REFERENCE: Walter Stephens. *Demon Lovers: Witchcraft, Sex, and the Crisis of Belief.* Chicago and London: University of Chicago Press, 2002.

MEDICAL INTERPRETATIONS OF WITCHCRAFT AND WITCH-HUNTING

Witchcraft and witch-hunting have been the subject of a number of explanations resting on medical theories. These have generally been the province of persons outside the historical establishment and are often marred by hasty generalizations from a small number of cases. The temptation to expand an explanation of a particular case or a witch-hunt in a particular region into a general theory of witch-hunting is difficult to resist.

Particularly popular in the 1960s and 1970s, a time of widespread academic and cultural interest in hallucinogenic drugs, were explanations for various features of the witch stereotype, notably the **sabbat** and witch flight, as the product of drug-induced states. This interpretation had some precedents during the early modern period, when demonologists and natural magicians, such as Giambattista della Porta (1535–1615), experimented with "witch's salves." Ointments used by witches were identified as containing hallucinogenic plants of the genus *datura,* as well as of the closely related mandrake, henbane and belladonna. Modern experiments with ointments derived from these substances showed that they could produce a sensation of **flying,** along with hallucinations. Many ointment formulae, however, as recorded in early modern texts, rely on substances of presumed **magical** efficacy, such as human fat, rather than of pharmacological potency. Many witches supposedly flew without using any ointment or potion.

Another medicalized theory relies on naturally occurring hallucinogens in grain, produced by a fungus known as ergot. Rye was particularly vulnerable. Ergot contains lysergic acid amide, a substance chemically similar to LSD, and, although much weaker, producing similar delusions. The role of ergot was the subject of a 1976 debate on **Salem** witchcraft between Linnda Caporael, putting forth an ergot-based explanation for the actions of the bewitched girls at Salem, and Nicholas Spanos and Jack Gottlieb. Spanos and Gottlieb pointed out that the girls' diets, rich in vitamin A from milk and seafood, would have protected them from convulsive ergotism and that the symptoms the bewitched persons at Salem manifested did not match up fully with the known symptoms of ergotism, which include vomiting and diarrhea. Spanos and Gottlieb were generally considered to have won the debate, but another, stronger medical explanation of Salem was put forth two decades later by Laurie Winn Carlson, who argued that the actual culprit was an epidemic disease, encephalitis lethargica. Carlson found many similar symptoms manifested by the bewitched at Salem and victims of a worldwide encephalitis epidemic from 1916 to 1930, although her attempts to expand this theory into a generalized explanation of why witch-hunting appeared in certain places in Europe and America and not in others rests on little evidence and is not convincing.

An attempt to medicalize not witchcraft but witch-hunting is the theory of the "syphilitic shock." In the very late fifteenth and early sixteenth centuries, Europe was struck with a new and virulent sexually transmitted disease, either of new world origin or a new variation on a disease endemic to Europe. Many men identified women, particularly prostitutes, as the source of the painful and disfiguring disease and the syphilitic shock theory holds that this increased misogyny led to the witch-hunt. The problem with this theory is that it doesn't fit the chronology well. The most misogynist demonology, Heinrich **Kramer's** *Malleus Maleficarum* (1486), was written and published before the syphilitic shock. The syphilitic shock was still going on at the time of the diminution of European witch-hunting after 1520; the second wave of witch-hunting, beginning around 1560, occurred after the first impact of syphilis had ended, and the disease had become endemic rather than epidemic.

Leland Estes put forth a theory of witch-hunting resting on the overall development of medicine rather than a particular medical phenomenon, suggesting that with the breakup of the Galenic school of medicine that dominated the Middle Ages, early modern **physicians** were more likely to ascribe those diseases they found difficult to explain to witchcraft. This theory does not fit the evidence well and has had little influence on subsequent witchcraft studies.

REFERENCES: Stanislav Andreski. "The Syphilitic Shock." *Encounter* 58 (1982): 7–26; Linnda R. Caporael. "Ergotism: The Satan Loosed in Salem." *Science* 92 (1976): 121–126; Laurie Winn Carlson. *A Fever in Salem: A New Interpretation of the New*

England Witch Trials. Chicago: Ivan R. Dee, 1999; Leland Estes. "The Medical Origins of the European Witchcraze: A Hypothesis." *Journal of Social History* 17 (1983): 271–284; Michael J. Harner. "The Role of Hallucinogenic Plants in European Witchcraft." In *Hallucinogens and Shamanism*, ed. Michael J. Harner, 125–150, New York: Oxford University Press, 1973; Sally Hickey. "Fatal Feeds?: Plants, Livestock Losses, and Witchcraft Accusations in Tudor and Stuart Britain." *Folklore* 101 (1990): 131–142; Eric B. Ross. "Syphilis, Misogyny and Witchcraft in 16th-Century Europe." *Current Anthropology* 36 (1995): 333–337; Nicholas P. Spanos and Jack Gottlieb. "Ergotism and the Salem Village Witch Trials." *Science* 194 (1976): 1390–1394.

MEDIEVAL ORIGINS OF THE WITCH-HUNT

Although the witch-hunt was a product of the early modern period of European history, it drew on a complex intellectual and cultural legacy from the Middle Ages. Medieval theologians and canon lawyers, drawing on early Christian sources, established a link between **magic** and demonic power, and the late medieval persecution of magicians blended imperceptibly into the witch-hunt.

Belief in the power of witches to work ***maleficia*** was common in medieval society, but such offenses were rarely prosecuted in the courts. The accusatorial procedures followed in most medieval secular courts meant that an accuser had to pay a penalty for bringing a false **accusation,** the so-called *lex talionis*. Given the difficulty of actually proving a witchcraft offense, this meant that most violent action against witches was taken outside the legal system, through murder and lynching, in a situation that paralleled that prevalent in late-eighteenth and nineteenth-century Europe after the witch-hunt. Belief in women who transformed themselves into monstrous birds that flew through the air and practiced cannibalism, usually referred to by the Latin term *strigae*, a belief present in both Roman and German cultural traditions, was also common. It was also believed that some women flew by night in groups, accompanied by a pagan goddess referred to by the name of the Roman goddess **Diana,** the biblical character Herodias or the German goddess Holda. To the extent that the church took notice of these common witchcraft beliefs, its main interest was to suppress them as remnants of pagan superstition or delusions fostered by **Satan,** a policy dating back to the early medieval era and embodied in the ninth-century ***Canon Episcopi***. The idea that magic could actually work, and that it should be something of which the church or law took cognizance, was of minor importance in the high medieval period of the twelfth and thirteenth centuries. The classic twelfth-century compiler of the canon law, Gratian, discussed magic in only two places, once to repeat the canon's condemnation of superstitious practices, and once to discuss the question of the impediment to marriage presented by magically caused impotence. For Gratian and subsequent canonists, the penalty for unrepentant magicians was excommunication, not death. The famous biblical passage "Thou shalt not suffer a witch to live" (Exod. 22:18) was not interpreted as literally binding on Christians at this time.

Interest in magic increased in the thirteenth century with the greater circulation of magical texts, many of them derived from the Arabic tradition. Clerics, being Europe's most literate class, were particularly identified with this learned magic. The thirteenth century was also marked by a powerful consciousness of Satan and his never-sleeping malice and hatred of the Christian community. The influential scholastic synthesis of the philosopher and theologian Thomas Aquinas (1224?–1274) included a thorough attack on magic, which he claimed always relied on demonic power. The idea of magic became connected with the idea of heresy, and the pictures presented of the horrible gatherings of heretics, featuring orgies, infamous **kisses** and the presence of Satan provided a prototype for later ideas of the witches' **sabbat.** Pope Gregory IX's (pope, 1227–1241) decree *Vox in Rama* of 1233 gives an elaborate description of heretical gatherings that reads like a description of the sabbat from three centuries later, including such details as the kiss bestowed on the mouth and rear end of a toad. Catholic writers described an essentially imaginary sect of "Luciferians," identified by their belief that Lucifer was the true king of heaven and would reward his faithful followers on earth on his return to his native place, while God and the angels would be cast into hell. In 1258, Alexander IV (pope, 1254–1261) attempted to distinguish between heretical and nonheretical magic, restricting the jurisdiction of the Inquisition to plainly heretical magic involving sacrifice or the invocation of demons or the misuse of the sacraments of the church. The involvement of the Inquisition, with its distinctive procedure, meant that accused magicians no longer had the protection of the *lex talionis* and that the practice of magic, not the working of harm through magic, had become central to defining magical crime. Biblical commentators emphasized the literal reading of Exodus 22:18, and the sense of a life-and-death struggle against heresy so characteristic of the thirteenth century influenced the treatment of magicians as well.

Beginning around 1300, Europe saw a burst of trials for sorcery centered in the French and Papal courts. King Philip IV of **France** (r. 1285–1314) first attacked the military religious order of the **Templars** with charges of sorcery and devil worship, as well as descriptions of orgies deriving from the literature attacking heresy. To pressure the popes to go along with this, Philip tried other churchmen for magical crimes, including bishop **Guichard of Troyes** and a dead pope, Benedict Gaetani, Boniface VIII (pope, 1294–1303). Boniface's pontificate had been marked by a savage struggle with Philip IV, a struggle that broke the pope. Philip's wrath pursued him into the grave. In 1310, he began proceedings against Boniface, charging him with sorcery. Both the Guichard case and the Boniface case fizzled out when Clement bowed to Philip's demands concerning the Templars, but they set a precedent for the use of sorcery charges against one's political opponents that would be followed at the French and Papal courts in the fourteenth century, followed by the English court in the fifteenth century. The most active period of papal persecution of magicians and sorcerers was the pontificate of **John XXII** from 1316–1334. Papal interest died down after that. In **England,** where the use of accusations of sorcery as a political tactic came later, prominent cases include those of **Joan of Navarre** and Eleanor **Cobham**. The fourteenth-century Irish case of Alice **Kyteler** contains many elements later prominent in the great witch-hunt. The classic targets of these late medieval political sorcery allegations were lowborn ministers arising with the favor of royalty, such as Guichard, or women connected with the royal family, but not wives or mothers of the reigning king, such as Joan or Cobham. Both groups had power that did not fit the traditional idea of legitimate political power springing from birth, and sorcery was a concept that rendered this power comprehensible. The initial burst of political cases was over by about 1330.

A group that had more similarities to the later victims of the witch-hunt than the great political figures, few of whom were actually executed for their sorceries, were the lower-class experts who assisted them. These people, for example Cobham's associates Roger Bolingbroke and Margery Jourdemayne, lacked the connections of their employers and were much more likely to be killed. They also provide a link between the court culture and the culture of ordinary people, practitioners of learned and unlearned magic arts. As the century wore on, sorcery cases were increasingly brought against people lower on the social hierarchy than during the great political cases of the early fourteenth century. The inquisitor's manual of Nicholas **Eymeric,** written around 1376, includes an elaborate discussion of the heretical nature of ritual magic and divination, based on Eymeric's extensive experience as an inquisitor. The theology faculty of the University of Paris, the leaders of medieval academic theology, issued an opinion against magicians and the use of magical books and formulae in 1398, claiming that magic is both superstitious and idolatrous. The chancellor of the university and nominalist philosopher Jean Gerson's (1363–1429) 1402 treatise on magic, *The Errors Concerning the Magic Art*, which expanded the 1398 opinion, contains the first recorded use of Exodus 22:18 in a discussion of magic.

During the fourteenth century, some church authorities became more hostile to traditional witch beliefs. Women's beliefs that they followed a goddess in the night were no longer consistently treated as a delusion but were sometimes treated as actual demon worship. Two Milanese women who claimed to be followers of Diana, or "Signora Oriente," were executed in the period 1384–1390. Images associated with the *strigae*, such as cannibalism, were increasingly associated with the women who traveled by night. In the fifteenth century, the ideas of the devil-worshipping magician, the women who rode with Diana, the cannibalistic *strigae*, the heretical gatherings of orgies and devil worship, and the simple village worker of *maleficia* all contributed to the new and powerful concept of the witch.

REFERENCES: Norman Cohn. *Europe's Inner Demons: The Demonization of Christians in Medieval Christendom*. Rev. ed. Chicago: University of Chicago Press, 2000; William R. Jones. "Political Uses of Sorcery in Medieval Europe." *The Historian* 34 (1972): 670–687; Edward Peters. *The Magician, the Witch and the Law*. Philadelphia: University of Pennsylvania Press, 1978; Richard Kieckhefer. *European Witch Trials:*

Their Foundations in Popular and Learned Culture, 1300–1500. Berkeley: University of California Press, 1976; Richard Kieckhefer. *Magic in the Middle Ages.* Cambridge: Cambridge University Press, 1989; Jeffrey Burton Russell. *Witchcraft in the Middle Ages.* Ithaca: Cornell University Press, 1972.

MERGENTHEIM WITCH-HUNT

The small territory of Mergentheim in southwestern **Germany** saw a savage witch-hunt from 1628 to 1631. The district of Mergentheim was about 77 square miles, dominated by the town of the same name, with a population of about two thousand people. It was one of the few remaining territories of the military monastic order of the Teutonic Knights, who lost most of their lands at the Reformation. The witch-hunt began in the spring of 1628, when a young Mergentheim boy named Johann Bernhard Reichardt, who had attended school in the notorious witch-hunting territory of **Würzburg,** was extradited there to face witchcraft charges. In Würzburg, Reichardt confessed to intercourse with the devil (one of the rare admissions of homosexual intercourse with **Satan**) and attendance at the **sabbat,** naming three accomplices. He was burned along with four others in Würzburg on May 9. Suspicion of witch children then moved to Mergentheim, where a group was questioned in July about claiming to have attended the sabbat and gaining secret knowledge from Satan. Most defended themselves by saying that they had only been joking, but one admitted to actual attendance and named others. With what they viewed as a major witch problem on their hands, the authorities who ruled Mergentheim for the knights sought outside help experienced with witch cases. They wrote to the bishop of Würzburg, Phillip Adolf von Ehrenberg (bishop, 1623–1631), and the bishop of **Bamberg,** Gottfried Fuchs von Dornheim (bishop, 1623–1633), two of Germany's most notorious witch-hunters. The Würzburg authorities refused to help, but Fuchs von Dornheim offered the services of an expert witch-hunter, Dr. Ernst Vasolt. Under Vasolt's expensive leadership, arrests were made and lists of accused witches drawn up. Vasolt left shortly after the lists were made, but the Mergentheim officials were now able to carry on the hunt by themselves. The well-maintained and nearly complete Mergentheim records have enabled historians to trace the course of the hunt. October 23, 1628, saw the first burning, of four witches. There were 17 **executions** in 1628. The following year, 91 witches were burned in 23 burnings; 1630 saw a slow decline until the last burning on February 10, 1631. Total deaths in the Mergentheim witch-hunt include 122 executed and 4 who died in prison, probably as a consequence of heavy **torture.** Not everyone on the lists of the denounced was arrested; it usually took three denunciations for a person to be arrested as a witch (although ordinary people's outspoken criticism of the witch-hunt could also get them arrested). The Mergentheim witch-hunt also displayed the characteristic of large German witch-hunts—that men and people from the social elite were not immune. Women, however, were by far the majority of the executed, comprising about 81 percent of the victims.

REFERENCE: H. C. Erik Midelfort. *Witch-Hunting in Southwestern Germany, 1562–1684.* Stanford: Stanford University Press, 1972.

MEXICO

See Queretaro Possession Cases; Spanish America.

MIDWIVES

Although it is sometimes claimed that midwives were disproportionately targeted during witch-hunts, the evidence does not bear this out. Like many misconceptions about witch-hunting, this mistake seems to arise originally from an exaggeration of the significance of Heinrich **Kramer's** *Malleus Maleficarum* (1486) for the actual practice of witch persecution. **Kramer** did discuss midwife-witches and their alleged crimes at great length, concentrating on how midwives could obtain infants to be murdered and subsequently used in **magic.** Succeeding demonologists, including those like Nicholas **Remy** with actual witch-

A pregnant woman sitting in a birthing chair is attended by three midwives, one ready to receive the baby, the second standing behind the chair, and the third standing at the woman's side comforting her. Implements are on a table in background. © National Library of Medicine.

hunting experience, tended to repeat the aspersions cast on midwives by the *Malleus* and Johannes **Nider** rather than adduce further evidence of witch-midwives.

In most early modern communities, midwives were influential and respected figures (midwifery was the closest thing to a learned profession for women) and not the kind of poor and marginal people who made up the majority of accused witches. Some midwives were accused of being witches or even tried and executed for it, but they were a lower proportion of witch suspects than of women as a whole. (One spectacular case was that of Walpurga Hausmännin of Dillingen, executed in 1587, for, among other crimes, murdering 43 unbaptized infants.) One area in which midwives did play an important role in witch-hunts was **England** and the English colonies, where they were normally hunters rather than hunted. Midwives carried out the search of women's bodies for the **"witch's mark,"** the extra nipple or other deformity through which the witch's **familiar** suckled, because they were regarded as experts in the female anatomy.

Likewise, it was considered more socially appropriate for a woman to perform searches of another woman's body than for male medical practitioners to do so.

REFERENCE: David Harley. "Historians as Demonologists: The Myth of the Midwife-Witch." *Social History of Medicine* 3 (1990): 1–26.

MOLITOR, ULRICH

The Swiss lawyer Ulrich Molitor composed one of the first printed demonological treatises, *On Witches and Fortunetelling Women* (1489), written in the form of a dialogue between Ulrich, the archduke of **Austria** and witch persecutor, Sigismund; and Sigismund's secretary, Conrad Sturtzel. The participants refer to recent witch cases in central Europe. The basic question is that of the power of witches and **Satan** to alter physical reality by **flying, transformations, weather witching** and other means. Molitor was much more skeptical of these **magical** feats than his contemporary Heinrich **Kramer,** author of the *Malleus Maleficarum* (1486). Molitor did not believe that the Devil or witches had such powers in the normal course of events. He ascribed witches' belief that they have flown to **sabbats** not to their actual power to fly, but to demonic illusion. The Devil could also use his knowledge of nature to determine when a storm was coming and then delude witches into believing that they had caused it. Despite his skepticism, Molitor advocated a harsh policy toward witches. Whether or not they have actually committed magical *maleficia*, their true crime was giving to the Devil worship and praise rightly belonging only to God. For this crime alone they deserved **execution** by the civil authority. Molitor saw witchcraft as mainly a female practice suggesting that women vanquish the Devil by making the sign of the cross, which he regarded as highly efficacious against Satan and his demons. *On Witches and Fortunetelling Women* also contained the first printed illustrations of witches and their activities. Although crude, these woodcuts were influential in establishing the iconography of the witch.

REFERENCE: P. G. Maxwell-Stuart. *Witchcraft in Europe and the New World, 1400–1800.* Houndsmills, England and New York: Palgrave, 2001.

MORA WITCH-HUNT

The last great witch-hunt involving hundreds of victims took place in northern **Sweden** from 1668 to 1676. This is often referred to as the Mora case, after the parish of Mora where many witches were accused, tried and executed, but it extended over large parts of northern Sweden and even made it as far south as the capital city of Stockholm by the later phases. The principal movers in the early phases were children, who accused adults of the community, mainly women, of kidnapping them and taking them to **sabbats** on Blokulla, an imaginary mountain presided over by the Devil. The Blokulla gatherings resembled traditional sabbats in many ways, but originated in Scandinavian folklore as well as learned demonological theory. The **accusations** emerged from the poor society of northern Sweden but coincided with a drive by Swedish elites against peasant customs. The initial bout of accusations resulted in 18 death sentences. Following standard legal procedure, these sentences were automatically appealed to Stockholm, which upheld 7 of them. The records were sanitized before being sent to Stockholm, with evidence that confessions, necessary for conviction, had been extorted under **torture** removed. The 7 were executed by beheading followed by burning of the body—the standard Swedish way to execute a witch.

The Stockholm authorities may have thought that this **execution** would end the persecution, but they were wrong. The residents of Mora requested a Royal Commission to deal with what they characterized as a plague of witches in their community. A duly appointed commission, mingling officials from Stockholm with local authorities, sentenced 23 to death. There was one catch, which was that to carry out the sentence, a confession was required, and Sweden did not incorporate torture as a normal part of its judicial process. Those witches who steadfastly refused to confess despite heavy psychological pressure were brought to watch the execution of those who did, in hopes that this pressure would produce confession, but this strategy was completely ineffective. Of the 23 cases, 15 were executed, along with 6 from another parish.

Hundreds of accusations in areas of northern Sweden where commissions were operating filled the early 1670s. The principal accusers remained children, some of whom seem to taken up careers as **witch-finders,** supported from parish funds. There were cases of child informers demanding blackmail from peasants, threatening them with accusations. Sometimes large groups of children were held in "witch houses" where they were supposedly kept safe from hostile **magic** by a heavy regimen of prayer and **Bible** reading. This environment enabled the children to coordinate their stories, contributing to the standardized quality of the tales of Blokulla, which impressed the judges.

Despite tensions on the commissions between the local authorities and the Stockholm officials, who were generally more suspicious of the children's tales, safeguards for the accused began to erode. Some witches were being executed without confession, and by 1675, the government sanctioned the use of torture in witch cases. It was in this year that more than a hundred executions, over half of the entire total, took place. The hunt was undone by its own success, however. Witch accusations were creeping southward, reaching Stockholm that year. In the spring of 1676, the court of appeals in Stockholm began investigating cases directly, rather than simply examining the records local officials forwarded. This resulted in the appointment of yet more royal commissions, but these were completely dominated by skeptical Stockholm officials. Turning the pressure on the accusers, the commissions gained several confessions from child accusers stating that they had made the whole thing up. The witch-hunt quickly collapsed, and four accusers, including a boy of 13, were executed.

About two hundred accused witches were executed throughout the entire period. The witch-hunt tilted heavily toward women, particularly older women and widows. About 85 percent of the accused were women, and of the women accused about 15 percent were executed, as opposed to about 5 percent of the men.

Mora left a deadly legacy. An account in Swedish by a convinced believer in the witches' guilt, the pastor Elaus Skragge, was translated into Dutch, German and English and circulated throughout the Protestant world. Skragge's account was incorporated into the English language demonologies of Joseph **Glanvill,** George **Sinclair** and **Cotton Mather** and also figured in Balthasar **Bekker's** polemic against witchcraft belief *The Enchanted World.* The pattern of child accusations was repeated at **Salem,** with direct influence from Mora in the shaping of the accounts.

REFERENCES: Bengt Ankarloo. "Sweden: The Mass Burnings (1668–1676)." In *Early Modern European Witchcraft: Centres and Peripheries,* ed, Bengt Ankarloo, and Gustav Henningsen, 285–317. Oxford: Clarendon Press, 1990; Robin Briggs. *Witches and Neighbors: The Social and Cultural Context of European Witchcraft.* New York: Penguin, 1996.

MOROSINI, GIULIO

Giulio Morosini, a young Venetian nobleman, was the protagonist of one of the most well-publicized investigations into **magic** carried out by the Venetian Inquisition, a unit of the **Roman Inquisition.** Morosini claimed that an Armenian had told him of a vast hidden golden treasure in a cavern in the Veronese mountains, so guarded that whoever took any of it could not find his or her way out until relinquishing the treasure. Morosini assembled a group of five people including himself, of whom the most magically skilled was a priest, Fra Cesare Lanza, and accumulated a number of magical books and manuscripts, including the *Key of Solomon* and Heinrich Cornelius **Agrippa's** *On Occult Philosophy.* The plan, mostly based on the *Key of Solomon,* was to consecrate a book, with prayers and Hebrew words, and then use a magical sword to draw a circle that would invoke spirits that would help the group evade the magical defenses of the treasure. By the rules of ritual magic, the participants had to be pure, chaste and holy, but this was going to be difficult to achieve. Two, Don Gregorio Giordano and Antonio Saldagna, were renegade priests, and along with the fifth, Francesco Oglies, were more interested in sponging off Morosini than in actually finding treasure. Oglies and Saldagna were also known for hanging around outside Venetian convents in hopes of seducing the nuns.

The whole scheme fell apart before the final invocation could occur. (Lanza claimed to the inquisitors that he had been deliberately dragging the process out.) Saldagna and Oglies were picked up by the Inquisition during an investigation into some suspected Judaizers, and the Inquisition found about the treasure hunt. The case lasted from the late summer of 1579 to early 1580. Giordano, who was on the fringes of the scheme, seems to have decided that making a clean breast to the Inquisitors was the best way of saving his own skin and told them everything he knew. The others eventually corroborated his account. All of the conspirators were forced to admit that their magical activity had been formally heretical, in that the spirits they invoked were receiving worship fit only for God. Morosini, Giordano, Saldagna and Oglies were relatively easy to convince—none were tortured—but the priest Lanza was a tougher nut to crack. His involvement was one of the inquisitors' principal concerns, particularly because he had officiated at magical ceremonies in his priestly garb. He at first insisted that he had prayed to God only, although the inquisitors pointed out that his prayers had been for unworthy ends. Three days of intensive questioning, followed by a period of imprisonment, led Lanza to admit that he had sought the aid of spirits and offended God by seeking aid from them and rendering them service due only to God.

The treasure hunters were forced to abjure their heresy at a formal ceremony in the Church of St. Mark, patron saint of the Venetian Republic. All five were sentenced to perpetual imprisonment as heretics, although the next year all sentences were commuted to house arrest, except for Saldagna, who was banished from the city, and Oglies, who was involved in another criminal case with the Venetian secular authorities. The Morosini case occurred as the Inquisition in Venice and elsewhere in **Italy** was turning its attention from Protestant heretics to magicians and witches, and it is part of the background of Sixtus V's (pope, 1585–1590) antimagical bull of 1585, *Coeli et Terrae* (Heaven and Earth).

REFERENCE: Ruth Martin. *Witchcraft and the Inquisition in Venice, 1550–1650.* Oxford: Blackwell, 1989.

MURRAY THESIS

The Murray thesis, originated by the Scottish scholar Margaret Alice Murray (1863–1963), is one of the most influential ideas in the modern historiography of witchcraft and the early modern witch-hunts. Although it has long been rejected in its entirety by serious witchcraft scholars, it continues to play an important role in popular culture and, despite Murray's own rationalism, in the beliefs of modern **feminist,** neopagan and Wiccan groups.

Murray was not a student of European witchcraft but an Egyptologist by profession. Her thesis was influenced by her reading of early anthropology with its emphasis on fertility cults, in particular Sir James Frazer's *The Golden Bough.* Murray's interpretation of European witchcraft was first and most importantly set forth in *The Witch-Cult in Western Europe* (1921) and *The God of the Witches* (1931). Murray believed that witches were practitioners of a widespread European fertility cult based on the worship of a horned god named Dianus. This cult had existed long before Christianity and remained the religion of the European common people long after society had been officially "Christianized." This idea was not original to Murray—indeed, a version of it appears in the ninth-century **Canon Episcopi**—but in her work it was presented for the first time with what appeared to be detailed historical evidence. Murray claimed that the **sabbat,** as described in the writings of early modern demonologists, was really the religious gathering of this cult. The witch-hunt was really an effort by the Christian elite of European society to destroy the religion of the pagan common people, carried out at a new and far greater level of intensity. As such it was connected to the Protestant and Catholic Reformations of the early modern period.

Another Murray innovation based on slender evidence was the concept of the "coven." Covens were groups of 13—12 witches and 1 leader—that Murray portrayed as the basic units of witch-cult organization. The leader was the person referred to as the "Devil" in witch interrogations and wore horns to impersonate the horned god. Murray's desire to make things come out in groups of 13 involved considerable manipulation of the numbers. Murray was open to considerable justified criticism in general on her use of sources, which was highly selective and uncritical, often using isolated details from the confession of one witch to make sweeping generalizations about the "witch-cult." (Murray's discussion of the coven relies particularly heavily on the confession of Isobel Gowdie, a witch executed in the great Scottish persecution of the early 1660s.) She made little use of archival materials, but relied on demonologists' writings, pamphlets and printed accounts of trials. Her writings on the sabbat ignore or minimize those aspects that render it clearly a fantasy, such as the allegations that witches flew to sabbat meetings, often simply skipping over descriptions of flight in the quotations from primary sources she printed.

Murray's development of the thesis grew more fantastic in *The Divine King in England* (1954), where she argued that medieval and early modern English rulers were practitioners of the witch religion, and that the murders of some medieval kings, such as Edward II (r. 1307–1327), were sacrifices to the witches' god. Murray also believed that Thomas Becket (1118?–1170), Jehanne **Darc** and Gilles de Rais were ritual witch sacrifices. This idea was rejected almost universally, but Murray's basic approach to witchcraft as an alternative religion was accepted by a number of reputable European historians, such as Steven Runciman and Christopher Hill. Her views were also spread by her authorship of the *Encyclopedia Britannica* article on witchcraft in 1929. Several of her works, resonating with the feminist and countercultural beliefs of the 1960s, became best-sellers in that era, when there was little scholarly study of witchcraft and the witch-hunt in the English-speaking world. Students of the history of witchcraft, however, as opposed to European historians such as Runciman and Hill who worked in other fields, were suspicious, if not dismissive, of Murray's thesis from the beginning. Despite her presidency of the Folklore Society in 1953, most British folklorists were also suspicious of her thesis. The revival of English-language witchcraft history in the early 1970s with the work of Keith Thomas, Alan MacFarlane and Norman Cohn destroyed the influence of the Murray thesis among academic historians, but it remains widely believed by nonscholars.

REFERENCES: Norman Cohn. *Europe's Inner Demons: An Enquiry Inspired by the Great Witch-Hunt.* Rev. ed. Chicago: University of Chicago Press, 2000; Ronald Hutton. *The Triumph of the Moon: A History of Modern Pagan Witchcraft.* Oxford: Oxford University Press, 1999; Margaret Alice Murray. *The Divine King in England: A Study in*

Anthropology. London: Faber and Faber, 1954; Margaret Alice Murray. *The God of the Witches*. London: Sampson Low, Marston, 1931; Margaret Alice Murray. *The Witch-Cult in Western Europe: A Study in Anthropology*. Oxford: Clarendon Press, 1921; Jacqueline Simpson. "Margaret Murray: Who Believed Her, and Why?" *Folklore* 105 (1994): 89–96.

N

NATIONAL AND REGIONAL VARIATIONS IN WITCH-HUNTING

The witch-hunt did not happen apart from the diverse cultures and institutions of European and colonial regions. Its history is marked by enormous geographical variation, affecting both witchcraft beliefs and the practices by which societies dealt with witches and witch-hunters.

One striking geographical divide was that between Mediterranean Europe—Spain, **Portugal** and **Italy**—and more northern regions. Mediterranean witchcraft beliefs remained focused on *maleficia*, with comparatively little interest in the **sabbat** or the **satanic pact.** More important, legal proceedings against witchcraft were dominated by ecclesiastical rather than secular justice—the **Roman Inquisition,** the Spanish Inquisition and the Portugese Inquisitions applied relatively rigorous standards of evidence, and few large-scale witch-hunts developed in these territories. The exceptions were those frontier areas where Inquisitions came into contact with different cultures, more willing to analyze witchcraft in satanic terms. The practices of rural people in these frontier areas could easily be interpreted as witchcraft, and the credibility of their statements was difficult to evaluate, particularly because they often spoke different languages than the inquisitors. Examples of areas where these cultural contacts produced witch persecution are the **Basque** region of the Spanish Pyrenees; the Slavic and German Friuli region of the Venetian Republic, which produced the *benandanti* cases; and the hill-folk of Savoy, targets of inquisitorial suspicion since the days of the **Waldensians.** The other large area of Mediterranean Europe, Greece and the Balkans, was directly subject to the Muslim Turkish Ottoman Empire and saw no judicial witch-hunting at all.

North of the Alps and Pyrenees lay the heartland of the witch-hunt, continental Western Europe. As many as 75 percent of the total number of **executions** in the witch-hunt may have taken place here, with a preponderance in the area of the Rhine River, an area where centuries of battle had produced myriad small political units. The principal large jurisdictions which practiced persecution in this region were **France,** a pioneer in witch-hunting, the Holy Roman Empire and **Switzerland.** The empire and Switzerland, two of the most decentralized polities in Europe, were particularly vulnerable to witch-hunts launched by zealous local magistrates acting without effective oversight. The Holy Roman Emperor exercised little judicial power in the empire outside the hereditary lands of the Habsburg family in **Austria and Bohemia.** In the empire, the vast majority of executions took place in the relatively small jurisdictions in the south and west of the country, particularly but not exclusively those ruled by Catholic prelates, such as **Ellwangen** and **Eichstätt.** Northern and Eastern **Germany,** mostly parceled out between large principalities such as Saxony and Prussia, saw less persecution. French-speaking areas of the empire, such as **Lorraine** and **Franche-Comte,** had a higher rate of persecution than France itself. Within the boundaries of the French kingdom, witch-hunting tended to be more characteristic of peripheral regions, such as the southwestern Basque region, the arena of Pierre de **Lancre's** famous witch-hunt, than of the heartland of the French monarchy in northern and central France. Most of this area was under the jurisdiction of the Parlement of Paris, which was for much of this period far more skeptical of witchcraft **accusations** than regional Parlements such as that of Rouen or de Lancre's Parlement of Bordeaux. The peculiar religious situation in France from the late sixteenth to the late seventeenth century—a country with an established Catholic church and government and a tolerated Protestant church—was also reflected in the French penchant for spectacular **possession** cases, often manipulated by Catholic priests to demonstrate the demons' friendship with the heretics. The great exception to the correlation of decentralization and witch-hunting in western and central Europe was the Dutch Republic, which was marked by both a high degree of local autonomy and a notably low rate of witch-hunting—the last witch was burned there in 1608. The reason for the low level of witch-hunting is unclear.

The British Isles were an area of comparatively little witch-hunting activity. This is partly because of the different judicial system, the common law, which held sway in **England** and the varying extent of its Irish possessions in this period. The comparative insignificance of **torture** in the English system along with the absence of Inquisitorial **trial procedure** made chain-reaction hunts built on the confessions of witches much more difficult than in those areas following Roman law, such as Germany. Witch trials remained focused on *maleficia* rather than the sabbat, human-demon **sex** or the satanic pact. The high degree of centralization characteristic of the English legal system since the Middle Ages also made it virtually impossible for local magistrates to launch large-scale witch-hunts, with the exception of the time of the English Civil War in the mid–seventeenth century. The Matthew **Hopkins** witch-hunt, by far the largest in English history, took place in conditions of the collapse of central governmental authority. The county of Essex in eastern England, Hopkins's home territory, saw the most persecution of any area in England, a distinction possibly related to its high concentration of Puritans. The comparatively small kingdom of **Scotland,** whose legal system blended English and Continental elements, had from the mid–sixteenth century on a zealous Calvinist clergy intent on creating a godly society. It executed the most witches of any British region. The other British area of high witch-hunting activity was the legally anomalous **Channel islands.**

Scandinavia also saw comparatively little witch-hunting, despite one spectacular episode, the Swedish **Mora witch-hunt** from 1668 to 1674. The most avid persecution was in **Denmark,** where witch-hunting began fairly early. **Sweden, Norway** and the fringes of the Scandinavian world saw considerably less. The deviance of the Scandinavian extremities and their isolation from the main current of witch-hunting can be seen in the fact that **Finland** for most of this period and **Iceland** throughout were among the few areas where most executed witches were male.

The witch-hunt came later to eastern Europe, but when it came it arrived with intensity. Witch-hunting in the eastern territories of the Habsburgs peaked in the late seventeenth century, and in the independent kingdoms of **Poland** and **Hungary** not until the early eighteenth century. Cultural contacts with Germans seem to have been the key conduit for the introduction of witch-hunting and demonological theory—those parts of eastern Europe that were mostly Slavic in culture and orthodox in religion, such as **Russia,** had little witch-hunting. Poland was particularly vulnerable to large-scale witch-hunting because of the extreme weakness of the central monarchy, which enabled witch-hunting local magistrates to operate as they pleased. Lack of mechanisms for law enforcement also meant that a high degree of extralegal violence characterized the Polish witch-hunt. Witch-hunting in the European colonies in the Americas also developed comparatively late. The best-known example, and the only large-scale witch-hunt on American soil, was the **Salem** trials of 1692. **New England,** which alone among European colonies replicated the classic pattern of the European village, was also the only area to see sustained witch-hunting.

REFERENCES: Robin Briggs. *Witches and Neighbors: The Social and Cultural Context of European Witchcraft.* New York: Penguin, 1996; Brian P. Levack. *The Witch-Hunt in Early Modern Europe.* London and New York: Longman, 1987; Geoffrey Scarre. *Witchcraft and Magic in Sixteenth- and Seventeenth-Century Europe.* London: Macmillan Education, 1987.

NEW ENGLAND, WITCH-HUNTING IN

The only areas of English colonization in the New World to see many cases of witchcraft were two provinces of New England, Massachusetts Bay (including modern Maine and New Hampshire) and Connecticut. The third New England province, Rhode Island, known for its **confessional** pluralism and tolerance, saw no witch-hunts at all. New England witch-hunting was based on English witch-hunting but manifested some important differences along with

Punishing the Witch by George H. Walker. © Bettmann/Corbis.

many similarities. The only large-scale witch-hunt in New England history, the **Salem** witch-hunt of 1692, occurred at the end of the period of active witch persecution, but it built on a legacy of witch cases stretching back for decades.

The first few decades of English settlement on the northeastern American coast seem to have produced few witchcraft **accusations,** although a Boston woman named Jane Hawkins was indicted but not tried for witchcraft in 1638. The laws governing witchcraft in New England at the time were based on the laws of **England,** notably the Statute of 1604. In 1641 and 1642, Massachusetts and Connecticut passed local statutes prescribing the death penalty for witches, defined as anyone who "hath or consulteth with a **familiar** spirit." Although similar to the Statute of 1604, these laws were explicitly based on the biblical law of Moses. The first trial, conviction and **execution** of a New England witch, Alice Young of Windsor, Connecticut, took place under the Connecticut statute in 1647, in the wake of a major epidemic. As in England, regardless of the criminalization of dealings with familiar spirits or the Devil, most actual indictments were based on charges of *maleficium*. The most common type of *maleficium* accusation changed in the seventeenth century from harm to health, property or livestock to "bewitchment," the **torture** of the victim, usually a young woman, with pokings, proddings and pinchings from specters invisible to all but the victim herself. Judicial procedures were modeled on the English. New Englanders also believed in the witch's familiar and the **witch's mark,** and the searching of an accused witches body for witch's marks by a jury of matrons was part of the judicial process. Severe judicial torture was not employed, and the only known New England case of "waking the witch," torture by sleep deprivation, occurred in 1648. Executions were by hanging. Counting the 20 of Salem, there were 36 witches known to have been executed in seventeenth-century New England. There are 93 witchcraft-related cases known outside of Salem. The rate of witchcraft accusation in New England was higher than in England, although lower than in many areas of the European continent or **Scotland.**

New England produced some significant demonologists, notably the Puritan ministers John **Hale, Increase Mather** and **Cotton Mather** and the Boston merchant Robert **Calef.** New England witch-hunters mainly drew on theoretical approaches from England, however. Particularly influential in shaping the New England response to witchcraft were legal manuals and the Puritan demonologists William **Perkins** and Richard **Bernard.** By the late seventeenth century, Joseph **Glanvill's** writings also attracted much interest. A local element important in shaping the response to witches was the "New England idea," promoted by ministers and devout lay Puritans, of New England as a separate and holy community. New England's special relationship with God made it particularly subject to the attacks of **Satan.** This sense of besiegement by Satan was powerful—and not merely metaphorical because of the geographic situation of New England. The English colonists believed that before the arrival of European Christians, all of the Americas had been the unchallenged fortress of Satan. Except for those few Native Americans who had accepted Christianity, the English also identified the tribes they fought for possession of the land with the Devil, although they did not accuse them of being witches in the judicial sense. (The most famous Native American witch in New England history, **Tituba** of Salem, was actually a domestic slave and a Christian. She had to be a member of the Christian community before she could be considered a witch.) Witchcraft, in which most Puritan divines were not particularly interested save in times of high excitement such as the Salem trials, fit easily into this picture as one of many means that the Devil employed in his assault on the godly New England community. But the Devil only acted with the permission of God, and a plague of witches was also one of God's many means for punishing the sins of the community. The witch's **satanic pact** was especially important to New England ministers, as it was to other Calvinists, who conceived it as the inverse of the pact made between the elect and God.

As often happened, ministers' conception of witchcraft as first and foremost the acceptance of subordination to Satan coexisted uneasily with lay conceptions based on *maleficium.* The ministers, following the tradition of English Puritan demonology, placed great stress on the iniquity of the **cunning folk** or "white witches," but the legal process ordinarily took no account of their doings, and even relatively devout laypeople, members of their local Congregational Church, were known to respond to witchcraft by resorting to **countermagic.** Nevertheless, the emphasis on Satan in the countless sermons that good New England churchgoers heard did strengthen the association of witches with the Devil.

One mark of Salem's aberrance among New England witch cases was its unique size. All other New England trials involved individuals or small groups. One reason why New England, and not other English colonies such as Virginia, produced multiple witch cases may be that New England colonies was socially much closer to the traditional European village structure which generated so many witchcraft accusations. The most common accused witch in New England was the poor woman, married or less frequently widowed, on the economic margins of the community. All statistics based on surviving records are only approximations of the real totals, because many records have disappeared, but about 80 percent of known New England witchcraft suspects were women—actually a lower percentage than in England. About half of the men charged with witchcraft were husbands or close associates of female witches. Most of the witches were in their 40s and 50s and came from the lower **social classes.** Witches were more likely than women in general to be childless or have few children. Not every woman in this position was likely to be accused as a witch—a sharp-tongued, assertive woman who cursed her enemies was more likely to be, but even then it was not inevitable. Of the women thought to be witches in New England, only a minority were ever brought to court, and many of these were acquitted, including notorious witches like Eunice **Cole.** Accused witches frequently sued their accusers for defamation.

Witchcraft accusations followed a rhythm. They were unlikely to be made at a time when the community was undergoing severe stress, whether external, such as war, or in its internal politics, such as religious controversy. Resolution of these conflicts were often followed by a spate of witchcraft accusations, however. Towns that saw witchcraft accusations and witch trials—and many New England communities saw none during the entire period—tended to be those marked by factionalism and controversy, the most obvious case being Salem Village, where divisions between witches and accusers tended to run along factional lines, particularly in the early stages of the witch-hunt. External conflict, whether with Native Americans, rival colonial powers such as the French or the Dutch or with the British government, also tended to turn colonists' energies away from witch-hunting. One of the most striking aspects of the Salem trials is that they came on the heels of a long period of quiescence from about 1684 to 1691 as the colonies were preoccupied with their relations with the mother country, which briefly imposed a new and much more centralized colonial system known as the Dominion of New England. The most striking result of the Salem cases was the regret expressed by many who had been leaders in carrying on the persecution and the almost total disappearance of witch-hunting from New England. There were no executions after the last Salem execution, although there were two indictments in 1697. Folk belief in witches continued for centuries, however. Such beliefs, along with the history of the witch trials, deeply influenced the work of later New England writers such as Nathaniel Hawthorne (1804–1864), whose great-great grandfather John Hawthorne had been a leading judge at the Salem trials, as well as John Greenleaf Whittier (1807–1892), H. P. Lovecraft (1890–1937) and John Updike (b. 1932).

REFERENCES: George Lincoln Burr. *Narratives of the Witchcraft Cases, 1648–1706*. New York: Charles Scribner's Sons, 1914; John Putnam Demos. *Entertaining Satan: Witchcraft and the Culture of Early New England*. New York: Oxford University Press, 1982; Richard Weisman. *Witchcraft, Magic and Religion in 17th-Century Massachusetts*. Amhurst: University of Massachusetts Press, 1984.

NEW FRANCE, WITCH-HUNTING IN

The French colony in Canada saw little witch-hunting. One unsuccessful suitor charged with using a **ligature** to spoil the wedding night of a bride and groom was tried in the seignorial court in 1658, receiving a heavy fine and banishment from the colony. There is also some evidence of a possible **execution** of a man for witchcraft and causing the demonic **possession** of a young girl in 1661. New France witch-hunted at a much lower rate than **France**, despite being governed by the same laws and sharing the same beliefs and **magical** practices as the French peasantry from whom most of the colonists were drawn. The different social arrangements of the colony explain this fact. New France was organized not into villages on the European model, which produced so many witchcraft **accusations** but independent farmsteads inhabited by extended families. The colony had a large surplus of men over women, which meant that women were in great demand as marriage partners, and widows had a much easier time remarrying than in Europe. The old widow living alone, who produced so many witch accusations in Europe, was a much rarer figure in New France. The extraordinary fecundity of the people of New France—families of 10 children were not uncommon—meant that old widows were also more likely to be supported by their children rather than having to beg or steal. Despite the absence of persecution, magical beliefs persisted into the modern era. As late as 1776, after the conquest of Quebec by the British, the *Gazette de Quebec* spoke of a **werewolf** in the area.

Catholic missionaries to Native American communities, whose arrival was often accompanied by European diseases, were sometimes tortured or executed as witches or sorcerers by Native Americans, as were Native American converts to Christianity.

REFERENCES: P. G. Maxwell-Stuart. *Witchcraft in Europe and the New World, 1400–1800*. Houndsmills, England and New York: Palgrave, 2001; Jonathan L. Pearl. "Witchcraft in New France in the Seventeenth Century: The Social Aspect." *Historical Reflections* 4 (1977): 191–205.

NEWBURY WITCH

The English Civil War of the 1640s was a time of increased witch-hunting, culminating in the great East Anglian persecution of Matthew **Hopkins** in 1645–1646. One of the earliest incidents took place before the battle of Newbury in 1643 between the Parliamentarian army led by the earl of Essex and King Charles I's Royalists. A contemporary pamphlet, *A Most Certain, Strange,* *and True Discovery of a Witch* (1643) claims that before the battle soldiers from the Parliamentary army had spied a woman crossing a river on a raft, manipulating the raft in such a way that it seemed to move against the current. The soldiers immediately concluded that she was a witch and tried to kill her, but their bullets proved ineffective, actually bouncing off her chest, until one tried a standard **countermagical** practice, scratching the witch's forehead to draw blood. This succeeded, and the witch was then shot to death. (This is a rare example of a witch killed by a bullet.) The pamphlet and other Parliamentarian writings put this story in the context of the English Civil War. The pamphlet asserted that before dying, the witch prophesied that victory would now belong to Essex (as it did, although the battle was inconclusive), and a subsequent writer claimed the witch was a Royalist agent sent to sabotage Essex's army. This is one documented case of an attack made by soldiers on a woman they suspected of both witchcraft and alliance with the enemy; undoubtedly there were many others.

REFERENCE: Diane Purkiss. "Desire and Its Deformities: Fantasies of Witchcraft in the English Civil War." *The Journal of Medieval and Early Modern Studies* (1997): 103–132.

NIDER, JOHANNES (1380?–1438)

Johannes Nider, Dominican friar and professor of theology at the University of Vienna, was the author of a Latin treatise *Formicarius*, probably written between 1435 and 1438, using the model of an anthill to understand human society. Its fifth book discusses witches and magicians under the heading of evildoers and marks an important step towards the full-fledged demonological model of witchcraft. (Nider also discussed **magic** and witchcraft as a violation of the First Commandment in *Preceptor of the Divine Law*, a commentary on the Ten Commandments written around 1440.) Along with several other writers working in the second half of the 1430s—the anonymous author of **Errores Gazariorum**, the French magistrate Claude **Tholosan,** and the chronicler of Valais witchcraft Johann Fründ-Nider introduced the concept of the **sabbat** into European demonology, seeing it as the principal means by which demons transmitted magical knowledge to unlearned witches. (Nider believed that not **Satan** but a lesser demon presided over the sabbat.) He also claimed that sabbat participants engaged in unrestrained **sex** and compared the sabbat to the meetings of heretical sects. Despite his endorsement of the sabbat, Nider did not believe witches got there by **flying,** which, in the tradition of the **Canon Episcopi**, he saw as an illusion.

Nider's work was not merely theoretical but drew on accounts of trials. One of his most important sources was a Bernese magistrate named Peter von Greyerz, who had worked on a series of trials of witches in the Simme Valley during his term as a provincial governor there from 1392 to 1406. Nider recounts the activities of the witches of western **Switzerland,** including the killing and devouring of infants, their own and others', the renunciation of Christ, and the paying of homage to the Devil. He claims that witches cause impotence, sterility and childlessness and that in their malice they used spells to foster hailstorms and bad weather. Nider also stated on the basis of information he had received from a Parisian theologian at the Council of Basel that Jehanne **Darc** had been justly condemned for having a **familiar** spirit. Despite discussing many male witches, Nider identified women as more likely to be witches. His work particularly influenced Heinrich **Kramer,** author of *Malleus Maleficarum* (1486), and **Geiler von Kaysersberg,** and it continued to be an authority throughout the witch-hunt period. *Formicarius* received a printed edition in 1476 and several further editions until its last appearance in 1692.

REFERENCES: Michael Bailey. "The Medieval Concept of the Witches' Sabbath." *Exemplaria: A Journal of Theory in Medieval and Renaissance Studies* 8 (1996): 419–439; Alan Charles Kors and Edward Peters, eds. *Witchcraft in Europe 400–1700: A Documentary History.* 2d ed. Revised by Edward Peters. Philadelphia: University of Pennsylvania Press, 2001.

NORTH BERWICK WITCH-HUNT

One of the most prominent cases of the connection of witch-hunting and high politics was the witch-hunt carried out by the Scottish government, under King **James VI,** from late 1590 to 1593. This was only one part of the major wave of late sixteenth-century Scottish witch-hunting, from 1590 to 1597. The North Berwick cases began with the **accusation** of a servant woman, Geillis Duncan, in November 1590. Duncan had recently been involved in some seemingly **magical** cures of illnesses, and her employer, David Seton, had become suspicious that she was deriving her powers from the Devil. Under severe questioning, which may have included illegal **torture,** Duncan confessed to being a witch and named several others as witches, including a local **midwife, cunning** woman and suspected witch, Agnes Sampson; a schoolmaster, John Fian; and two middle-class Edinburgh women, Barbara Napier and Euphame MacCalzean. She also confessed that the witches were involved in a diabolical plot to kill the king. This brought the case to the attention of the central government. Trials were brief and ended with convictions. John Fian was tried and convicted after he confessed (possibly under torture) in late December, although he was not executed until late January. Agnes Sampson overcame the king's initial skepticism by recounting to him, in private, information about his wedding night with his new bride, Anne of **Denmark** (1574–1619). James believed that this information could only have been obtained by magic.

The interrogations of Fian and Sampson produced an elaborate account of a massive satanic plot against James, described as "the greatest enemy the devil has in the world." The North Berwick trial gains its appellation not from the trials, which were held in Edinburgh, nor from the residences of the witches, none of whom lived in North Berwick, but from large meetings allegedly held in a church at North Berwick, and presided over by the Devil. The Devil as depicted in the witch confessions was not the all-powerful master of evil, but a person who could be argued with and even berated for failing to deliver on his promises. The meetings included political discussion and were referred to as "conventions," a term used in **Scotland** to denote the meetings of political bodies, such as Parliament or the Privy Council. The conventions did not include the more sensational features of the **sabbat,** such as orgies, demonic **sex,** cannibalism or **infanticide.** With the exception of Fian, who claimed to have attended the meetings spiritually while his body lay elsewhere, those who claimed attendance described themselves as getting to the meeting by mundane rather than magical means.

The plots against James had allegedly begun with weather magic, causing the North Sea storms that had afflicted James and Anne, first rendering it impossible for Anne to come over to Scotland in the summer of 1589 and then endangering James and Anne on their coming to Scotland in 1590. A witch-hunt had already broken out in Denmark over the storms, and Duncan described meeting and plotting with a Danish witch. The Scots had not blamed the storms on witchcraft when they had occurred. Further plots against James relied on **image magic** and toad poison.

Part of the background to the trials was the struggle between Reformed Protestantism and Catholicism in lowland Scotland. Sampson's magic was strongly Catholic, involving the use of Catholic prayers like the Ave Maria. Another factor was the unstable Scottish political situation. Sampson and Richie Graham, a sorcerer with a sinister reputation, implicated Francis Stewart Hepburn, fifth earl of Bothwell (d. 1624), one of Scotland's leading magnates, who was known to be feuding with the king's chancellor, John Maitland (1545?–1595). Bothwell was an ambitious, violent and unstable man and carried enough royal blood to have made a plausible claim on the throne if James had died without heirs. It is certainly possible that he had some kind of magical plot going to destroy the king, an action for which there was precedent in Scottish history.

Sampson was executed on January 28, followed by 10 more witches on February 23. On April 15, Bothwell was brought before the king on charges of plotting with Sampson and Graham, and the following day he was committed to Edinburgh Castle. Napier's trial began May 8. At first she was acquitted of the more serious charges and only convicted for consulting with witches. James personally intervened against the jury in a rare but not unprecedented procedure called an "assize of error." He charged, probably with some truth, that the influence of Napier's powerful friends and relatives had procured the lenient verdict. Napier was now convicted of all charges but escaped **execution** by claiming pregnancy. She was eventually released. Much less fortunate was MacCalzean, whose trial began June 9. MacCalzean was a classic example of the assertive, combative, "shrewish" woman who was one common victim of witch-hunting. She was charged with having tried to kill her husband through witchcraft and with having succeeded in killing three of her relations. Unlike Sampson and Fian, who were strangled before being burned, MacCalzean was sentenced to be burned alive, a fate she suffered June 25.

Meanwhile, Bothwell had escaped from Edinburgh Castle and spent the next several years in a series of rebellions and plots against James. He was acquitted of witchcraft by a jury of his peers in August 1593, although eventually he died a poor exile in **Italy.** Graham was not so lucky, being strangled and burned February 29, 1692. The North Berwick affair inspired two major texts. One was James's *Demonology*, which although it makes no direct reference to the cases was in large part inspired by James's experiences. The other was an anonymous pamphlet, probably authored by the Presbyterian minister of Haddington, James Carmichael, *News from Scotland Declaring the Damnable Life of Dr. Fian, a Notable Sorceror* (1591). *News from Scotland* was published in London, where Carmichael had spent some time, and was the first major publication on Scottish witchcraft available to an English audience. James was heir apparent to the English throne he would eventually ascend in 1603, and *News from Scotland* showed him flatteringly to his future subjects.

REFERENCES: P. G. Maxwell-Stuart. *Satan's Conspiracy: Magic and Witchcraft in Sixteenth-Century Scotland*. East Lothian, Scotland: Tuckwell Press, 2001; Lawrence Normand and Gareth Roberts, eds. *Witchcraft in Early Modern Scotland: James VI's* Demonology *and the North Berwick Witches*. Exeter, England: University of Exeter Press, 2000.

NORTHERN NETHERLANDS, WITCH-HUNTING IN

The northern Netherlands began its witch-hunting experience following the usual pattern, but after it established its independence as the Dutch Republic in the late sixteenth century, it deviated sharply, abandoning witch-hunting in the first decade of the seventeenth century. The earliest recorded **execution** of a witch in the area occurred in Maastricht in 1413, when a woman was burned for witchcraft and poisoning. Witch-hunting intensified in the eastern Netherlands in the late fifteenth century, with an influence from Cologne, a center of German witch-hunting, and the backing of the duke of Gelderland, Charles of Egmond (r. 1492–1638). From this base, witch persecution slowly radiated to the rest of the country; a witch was not executed in the most developed province, Holland, until 1542.

Dutch witches were usually charged first with *maleficia* rather than **satanic pact** or attendance at the **sabbat.** Although satanic pact often came into the cases as they were tried, neither sabbat nor human-demon **sex** played a major role in most Dutch witch cases, and witch flight did not appear at all. In dairy-rich areas, witches were frequently charged with spoiling milk or butter—"milk-witch" was a common epithet. **Countermagic** practices included burying a herb called "devil's-dung" (asfetida) at one's threshold to protect the house from witches. If actually attacked by a witch, Dutch people could boil needles in the bewitched person's urine or boil milk from the bewitched cow. Trials of witches often included **torture,** including the rack and "waking the witch." Execution was by burning, usually preceded by strangulation. Perhaps because of the neglect of the sabbat, few trials involved large numbers or executions. Three exceptions were the trials at the Groninger Ommelanden in 1547, with 20 executions, the trials in Peelande in 1595, with 19 victims, and the 40 death sentences at Roermond in Spanish Limburg in 1613. Excluding the deaths in Spanish Limburg, which did not become part of the Dutch Republic until the mid–seventeenth century, the total number of executions was around 150, of whom 90 to 95 percent were women, one of the highest such ratios in Europe. There were great local variations—the province of Friesland saw almost no witch-hunting, possibly because of its centralized judiciary, whereas Groningen saw the most, and male witches were restricted to the eastern part of the country.

The war that established the northern Netherlands's independence from the Spanish monarchy in the late sixteenth century eventually led to the diminution of witch-hunting. The Calvinist clergy of the Dutch Republic's officially sanctioned church had little interest in witch-hunting—their church courts were more concerned with assigning penances to those who sought the aid of **cunning folk** or spread rumors about their neighbors being witches. Although all three of the major northern Netherlands witch-hunts took place at times and places where Catholics were dominant, the Catholic clergy was not full of enthusiastic witch-hunters—the Peelande witch-hunt, carried out by secular magistrates, was opposed by local Catholic priests. In 1594, the faculty of the University of Leiden gave an opinion against the use of **flotation tests,** and 1608 saw the last witch execution in the Dutch Republic. This may be connected with the unusually high degree of religious toleration that marked the Republic.

The end of witch-hunting was marked by little debate, but later in the seventeenth century it became a source of pride for Dutch legal writers, who liked to contrast the enlightened Republic with the nightmarish witch-hunts of **Germany.** Friedrich von **Spee's** *Warning to Prosecutors*, translated into Dutch in 1657 by Nicholas Borremans, was a favorite source of horror stories. Dutch demonology was marked by a strong preponderance of witchcraft skepticism, extending to all points in the religious spectrum, from the Catholic priest Jacob **Vallick,** to the Mennonite Abraham Palinghe, author of *Witchcraft Unmasked* (1659), to Balthasar **Bekker.** Two Dutchmen who made their careers in Germany, Johann **Weyer** and Cornelis Loos (1546–1595), were also opponents of persecution. Despite the predominance of skepticism in the Dutch elite, murders and assaults on persons suspected of witchcraft continued in the absence of official persecution, as did slander suits brought by those accused of witchcraft against their accusers. One unique feature of the Dutch Republic after the persecutions ended was the "weighing house" of the town of Oudewater, where for the payment of a small fee persons could clear themselves of witchcraft **accusations** by being weighed. If the Oudewater authorities certified that the person's weight was appropriate for their height and girth, this was considered exculpatory, as it was believed that witches were lighter. There are records of 13 visitors to Oudewater for this procedure, beginning in 1644 and extending into the eighteenth century. Most were from the eastern and southern regions of the Republic.

REFERENCES: Willem de Blécourt. "The Making of the Female Witch: Reflections on Witchcraft and Gender in the Early Modern Period." *Gender and History* 12

(2000): 287–309; Marijke Gijswit-Hofstra and Willem Frijhoff, eds. *Witchcraft in the Netherlands from the Fourteenth to the Twentieth Century.* Rotterdam: Universitaire Pers Rotterdam, 1991.

NORWAY, WITCH-HUNTING IN

Norway saw one of the first witch trials associating *maleficia* and diabolism, that of Ragnhildr Tregagas of Bergen in 1325, but nearly all of its known witch-hunting took place after the Protestant Reformation. Tregagas was accused of renouncing God and using **magic** to prevent her cousin, who was also her lover, from consummating his marriage. She was tried in an ecclesiastical court and punished with penances rather than burning. This was the last known witch case in Norway until the sixteenth century, at which time it was not a separate country but a province of the Danish monarchy. Its witch-hunt pattern displays similarities and differences from that of **Denmark.** As in Denmark, the initial lead was taken by Lutheran ecclesiastics, although this occurred several decades later in Norway. The bishop of Stavanger, Jorgen Eriksson, appealed to the Danish king for a decree making benevolent sorcery—"white witchcraft"—a capital offense in his diocese. This was granted in 1584, and extended to the whole country in 1593. The Danish witchcraft decree of 1617 distinguished between benevolent and demonic magic, making only the latter capital, but this law was widely disregarded in Norway.

There are 730 known witch trials in Norway, with 280 **executions.** Hans Eyvind Naess, a leading scholar of the Norwegian witch-hunt, extrapolates a total of around 1,400 trials, with about 350 executions. The area that saw the highest rate of witch-hunting was the one most remote from central judicial institutions, Finnmark in the far north. With about 1.5 percent of the Norwegian population, this area saw about a third of the known witchcraft **accusations.** These accusations did not focus on the Lapp population, with its reputation for sorcery, but poor fishing communities of Norwegian descent. About 80 percent of the accused witches in Norway were women, and a large majority from the poorest classes, which were increasing rapidly in number at the time. **Trial procedure** was accusatorial rather than inquisitorial, and nearly all cases began with accusations of *maleficium.* Norway differed from other areas of Europe in that accusations of harming livestock were less common, and accusations of causing harm to boats much more common. The **sabbat** and **satanic pact** were introduced to trials by local government officials, powerful in Norway, and Lutheran pastors, who played a central role in investigations. **Torture** was employed more commonly than in Denmark, although less so than in **Germany.** The rack was the most frequently used torture. Boiling sulfur was also poured on the breasts of accused witches. Although the evidence of criminals, including witches and sorcerers, was supposed to be disregarded when they accused others, this was frequently ignored. **Flotation tests** were also common, although technically prohibited.

The witch-hunt in Norway extended from approximately 1560 to approximately 1700, with its peak between 1610 and 1660. Disillusionment with witch-hunting on the part of central judicial authorities, beginning in the early 1650s, seems to have been the most important factor in bringing the hunt to an end.

REFERENCES: Stephen Mitchell. "Nordic Witchcraft in Transition: Impotence, Heresy and Diabolism in 14th-Century Bergen." *Scandia* 63 (1997): 17–33; E. William Monter. "Scandinavian Witchcraft in Anglo-American Perspective." In *Early Modern European Witchcraft: Centres and Peripheries*, ed. Bengt Ankarloo and Gustav Henningsen, 425–434. Oxford: Clarendon Press, 1990; Hans Eyvind Naess. "Norway: The Criminological Context." In *Early Modern European Witchcraft: Centres and Peripheries*, ed. Bengt Ankarloo and Gustav Henningsen, 367–382. Oxford: Clarendon Press, 1990.

NUMBERS OF VICTIMS

The number of persons killed in the European witch-hunt will never be known and has been subject to wildly varying estimates. The problems in coming up with a number are many. Records are incomplete, in some places virtually nonexistent. Witch-hunters such as Nicolas **Remy** seemed to have exaggerated the numbers of their victims. Other problems are caused by the fuzziness of the categories. Many people died for witchcraft who were not judicially executed—they died (or killed themselves) in the unhealthy conditions of early modern jails or as a result of **torture.** Some were killed outside the judicial process entirely, as a result of lynching or murder. This kind of killing seldom left much of a documentary record.

The tendency in witch-hunt historiography has been for the estimates of the dead to decrease. In the early days of the **liberal** school, many archives remained unknown, and the most extreme witch-hunts, such as the **Bamberg** and **Würzburg** witch-hunts, were often taken as much closer to the norm than they actually were. The belief that the prescriptions of Heinrich **Kramer's** *Malleus Maleficarum,* (1486) which would have made any result of a trial other than **execution** virtually impossible, were literally put into practice also led to overestimation of the number of the dead. Historians exaggerated the numbers of persons arrested for witchcraft and unduly diminished the number who were acquitted or let off with sentences less stringent than death. The looseness with which many antiwitch laws were written seemed to allow for the arrest of just about anyone, and some historians failed to realize that practice was usually different. A number that still occasionally appears in popular writing, 9 million victims, was originally an estimate by an American liberal **feminist** and freethinker, Matilda Joslyn Gage (1826–1898). Gage was a pioneer in women's history, who wanted to make a point about the enmity of the Church to women. Her figure was not based on research and had no basis in reality. Higher numbers today usually appear in the writings of feminist and neopagan authors aiming at a popular audience.

The consensus estimate of most modern academic scholars of the early modern witch-hunt is that there were about 100,000 persons tried and that 40,000 to 60,000 accused witches died in the course of the witch-hunt, about 80 percent of whom were women. This incorporates a "dark figure" standing for the persons whose records and names have been lost to history. The damage caused by the great witch-hunt cannot be reduced simply to deaths, however. Thousands more people were tortured or had their lives and reputations ruined. Some, particularly children, lost their sanity during long imprisonments. Families lost parents, husbands, wives, parents, children—particularly devastating because of the necessity for many early modern families to work together as an economic unit.

REFERENCES: Robin Briggs. *Witches and Neighbors: The Social and Cultural Context of European Witchcraft.* New York: Penguin, 1996; Diane Purkiss. *The Witch in History: Early Modern and Twentieth-Century Representations.* London and New York: Routledge, 1996.

O

OBERMARCHTHAL WITCH-HUNT

The independent territory of the Premonstratensian Abbey of Obermarchthal in the Holy Roman Empire was the scene of a fierce witch-hunt, concentrated in the years 1586–1588. Obermarchthal covered some 64 square miles and had a population of approximately 700. The first recorded **execution** in the territory occurred in 1581, when a man named Melchior Hurm was executed for witchcraft and murder. This execution found no immediate successors, but large-scale witch-hunting occurred in the summer of 1586, when 15 women and 7 men were executed. Subsequent rounds of execution saw a higher female proportion, as 12 women and 1 man were executed in June 1587, and 11 women and 1 man later in the year. The final executions of the hunt occurred in 1588, when 4 women and 2 men were executed. Executions were by burning.

Although the absolute numbers were not high, compared with other German territories, Obermarchthal's tiny population meant that more than 7 percent of the population fell victim. Although records are incomplete, the hunt seems to have taken a classic form with **torture** to elicit confessions and the names of others seen at the **sabbat.** These others were then tortured in their turn. (The famous torturer Hans **Vollmair** took part in the Obermarchthal witch-hunt.) Confessions of sexual crimes and **infanticide** were also common, which may have reflected the accused witches' own behavior or the interests of the torturers and investigating magistrates. The judge Bernhard Bitterlin appears to have taken a tough line against witches, and also convicted seven people for witchcraft in 1627–1628, during the second peak of the German witch-hunt. Although witch-hunting at Obermarchthal never again reached the peaks of 1586–1588, it continued into the eighteenth century.

REFERENCES: Wolfgang Behringer. *Witchcraft Persecutions in Bavaria: Popular Magic, Religious Zealotry, and Reason of State in Early Modern Europe*. Trans. J. C. Grayson and David Lederer. Cambridge: Cambridge University Press, 1997; H. C. Erik

Midelfort *Witch-Hunting in Southwestern Germany, 1562–1684.* Stanford: Stanford University Press, 1972.

OBRY, NICOLE

Nicole Obry was the first in a long line of French girls and women who claimed to be possessed by demons and whose cases became internationally known. Obry was from the small town of Vervins and born around 1550. In late 1565, the recently married Obry, now dwelling in Laon, claimed to have encountered the spirit of her grandfather, who demanded that members of her family go on pilgrimages to release his soul from purgatory. When this request was not entirely fulfilled, the spirit turned angry, tormenting Obry. A priest identified the spirit as actually a devil, and Obry was publicly exorcised in Laon in late November. The spirit was identified as Beezelbub, who spoke through Obry. The nearly continuous exorcisms spread over two months. They sometimes took place in front of thousands of spectators, once including the king of **France,** Charles IX (r. 1560–1574), who gave Obry 10 gold coins to show his appreciation for her witness to the Catholic faith. Obry was finally freed from Beezelbub on February 8, 1566.

What made Obry's case so important was its connection to the religious controversies dividing France between Catholics like Obry and Protestants, known as Huguenots. Obry, Beezelbub and her exorcists used the occasion for ceaseless denunciations of the Huguenots, whom Beezelbub identified as his closest allies. The most important point dividing Protestants and Catholics in France was transubstantiation, the Catholic doctrine that at the moment of consecration the priest changes the bread and wine into the actual flesh and blood of Christ. Because Huguenots denied this doctrine, the exorcists reaffirmed it by demonstrating how powerful a consecrated Host was against demons. Beezelbub also denounced "secret," that is unconfessed, sins among the thousands of spectators of the exorcisms, including witchcraft. The accounts of Obry's case—the "Miracle of Laon"—published in 1566, 1571, 1573, 1575 and 1578 emphasized the support the case gave to orthodox Catholic doctrine, and it was repeatedly invoked by Catholic preachers and lecturers including Juan **Maldonado.**

Local Huguenots opposed the exorcisms, but Obry's case was controversial even among Catholics. Some, such as Jean **Bodin,** were uneasy at the idea of trusting a devil to speak the truth, even when he supported the Catholic cause by describing the Huguenots as his friends. More pragmatically, others were afraid the case would lead to **confessional** violence and the outbreak of a war of religion. For this reason, Obry was briefly imprisoned after she was exorcised. Obry seems to have liked the publicity—she appeared before the public eye again in 1577 when she claimed to have been cured of a temporary blindness by the head of John the Baptist. Obry was the inspiration for a series of other French demoniacs, including Marthe **Brossier,** and a feast celebrating her final deliverance from the demon was celebrated every year at Laon on February 8 until the French Revolution.

REFERENCES: Moshe Sluhovsky. "A Divine Apparition or Demonic Possession?" *The Sixteenth Century Journal* 27 (1996): 1039–1055; D. P. Walker. *Unclean Spirits: Possession and Exorcism in France and England in the Late Sixteenth and Early Seventeenth Centuries.* Philadelphia: University of Pennsylvania Press, 1981.

OFFENBURG WITCH-HUNT

The free imperial city of Offenburg in the Kinzig valley of **Germany** was the site of a series of witch-hunts from 1627 to 1630, which claimed at least 62 lives and were unusually closely intertwined with local politics. The city had a history of witch trials going back to 1557, when two women were executed, but not of large-scale witch-hunting. The hunt began as an offshoot from a hunt in the nearby territory of Ortenau, as in the fall of 1627 Offenburg officials received a report from Ortenau that two residents of Offenburg, Symon Haller and Catherin Holdermann, had been accused of being witches. The Ortenau officials had taken Haller and questioned him under **torture,** sending a copy of the interrogation to Offenburg. The Offenburg officials tortured Holdermann, who refused to confess. Ortenau then turned Haller over to Offenburg, where he, too, refused to confess. Offenburg then copied an Ortenau innovation in torture, the spiked chair, in which the accused was bound. The "Offenburg chair" could also be heated. Offenburg was Catholic and also employed priests to urge the suspects to admit their crimes during confession. Both Haller and Holdermann now quickly confessed, and denounced others. Twelve in total were executed in this first phase of the Offenburg witch-hunt, which extended into January 1628. One was the wife of a councillor, Stettmeister Megerer, who was fined and barred from leaving the city.

A second series of trials was initiated that summer, when the council received information regarding the children of one of the previously executed witches. This resulted in seven **executions** and one death as a result of torture, which was particularly intense in the Offenburg witch-hunt and frequently applied even after conviction. That winter, trials resumed again and were continuous until the beginning of 1630. Much of the dynamic of the Offenburg trials appears to have been a result of factional struggles on the council, which led councillors to attack each other through the women members of their families. Among others, Councillor Philipp Baur lost his wife and daughter, and Councillor Philipp Beck his wife. The families of convicted witches were also levied to pay for the witches' trials and for the celebrations and banquets for the judges and priests which preceded executions. (Ortenau officials also attempted to profit from the Offenburg witch-hunt by seizing Ortenau property belonging to an Offenburg witch, but were slapped down by a ruling of the court of the Holy Roman Empire.) These celebrations was a feature of the Offenburg witch-hunt with few parallels elsewhere. Another feature of Offenburg witchcraft was the frequent mention in women's confessions of marriage with the Devil.

By the end of the witch-hunt, it had extended to the councillors themselves—Councillor Hans Georg Bauer was executed in late November 1629. This was the last witch execution of an Offenburg citizen, although one man from outside the town was executed in 1630. The case which heralded an end to the persecution occurred shortly after, when a woman named Gotter Ness became the first to endure the chair without confession. The council, which seems to have lost some of the certainty with which it had zealously carried out early interrogations, sent her home. Then it arrested three other women, Ness's daughter Maria, Magdalena Holdermann, and Ursula Burck. All three confessed but then revoked their confessions. After further deliberations, the council let them go. Witch trials continued sporadically in Offenburg to the early 1640s.

REFERENCES: Anne Llewellyn Barstow. *Witchcraze: A New History of the European Witch Hunts.* San Francisco: Pandora, 1994; Brian P. Levack. *The Witch-Hunt in Early Modern Europe.* London and New York: Longman, 1987; H. C. Erik Midelfort *Witch-Hunting in Southwestern Germany, 1562–1684.* Stanford: Stanford University Press, 1972 .

OSBORNE, RUTH (D. 1751)

The case of Ruth Osborne of Tring, Hertfordshire, murdered as a witch in 1751, reveals that early modern witches had more to fear than the state and church. Osborne and her husband, John, had been rumored to be witches and to have performed **maleficia** for many years. The alleged bewitching of a farmer, John Butterfield, and his cattle was the last straw. Butterfield, who on the death of his cattle had given up farming and become an innkeeper, organized a "ducking" of the Osbornes, enlisting aid from the neighboring towns by means of public announcements. Despite protection from the local authorities, the Osbornes were seized by a mob numbering in the thousands, and Ruth was forcibly ducked until she died. The leader of the mob was a butcher named Thomas Colley, who later claimed to have been drunk on beer supplied by Butterfield. In a case that attracted widespread publicity, Colley was taken and tried in Hertfordshire Assizes and condemned to death as a murderer. Rather than following the standard practice of being hanged in Hertford, the place of the assizes, Colley was brought back to the scene of the crime in Tring. The English authorities pressured Colley to renounce and denounce belief in witches and their powers on the scaffold, which he did, possibly hoping to help his family, which was losing its breadwinner. This inverted the witch-hunt pattern—now a murderer of a witch was being punished, and rather than renouncing the pact with **Satan,** he was renouncing witch-belief itself. Despite the efforts of the government and local gentry, many local people supported Colley and what he had done, continuing to believe that Osborne had been a malevolent witch who had suffered appropriate punishment.

REFERENCE: James Sharpe. *Instruments of Darkness: Witchcraft in Early Modern England.* Philadelphia: University of Pennsylvania Press, 1996.

P

PAISLEY WITCHES

The seven Scottish witches executed in Paisley in 1697 were the last case of a mass **execution** in western Europe. The Paisley witch-hunt began with a young girl named Christian Shaw, the daughter of a local landowner. On August 17, 1696, Shaw saw one of the family's maids, an highland woman named Katherine Campbell, take a cup of milk from the Shaw's kitchen and drink it. Shaw threatened to expose Campbell's theft, and Campbell cursed her by wishing that the Devil take her soul, an unusually strong expression for the circumstances. On August 21, Shaw had an encounter with an old woman, Agnes Naismith, who had a reputation as a witch. The next day, Shaw was taken with violent fits accompanied by the vomiting of all sorts of materials, including pins and straw. A visit to a well-known doctor in Glasgow brought only temporary respite, and Shaw' family concluded that she had been struck by witchcraft. Shaw's **accusations** of witchcraft extended past Campbell and Naismith.

The Presbytery of Paisley, the council of Presbyterian clergymen with jurisdiction over the area, took an interest and requested the Scottish Privy Council to issue a commission to try the case, standard procedure in Scottish witch trials but one that had fallen out of use. The first commission to a group of magistrates, landowners and lawyers was granted merely to investigate the case. The accusations, mainly from Shaw and an accused witch turned accuser, Elizabeth Anderson, extended to several dozen people. The picture of witchcraft given by the accusations included the standard features of **sabbat,** *maleficia,* witch flight and **satanic pact.** Shaw, an intelligent child, gave edifying performances during her fits of resisting the Devil's temptation to agree to the pact with imprecations and **Bible** quotations. A second commission, overlapping in personnel with the first, was given the responsibility of actually trying 24 accused witches. The trial featured testimony from the accusers, testing of accused witches by requiring them to say the Lord's Prayer, pricking for the

Devil's mark, another feature of Scottish witch-hunting that had fallen out of use, and a hair-raising sermon to the commissioners from a local minister, James Hutchinson, on Exodus 22.18: "Thou shalt not suffer a witch to live." Three men and four women, including Campbell, Naismith, and a local **midwife,** Margaret Long, were first hanged and then burned June 10. Other accused witches were still being held in jail two years later. Two pamphlets were published about the case in **England** and one in **Scotland.** Christian Shaw fully recovered and went on to found the commercial spinning industry in Paisley.

REFERENCES: Isabel Adam. *Witch Hunt: The Great Scottish Witchcraft Trials of 1697.* London: Macmillan, 1978; James Hutchinson. "A Sermon on Witchcraft in 1697." Ed. George Nielson. *Scottish Historical Review* 7 (1910): 390–399.

PAPPENHEIMER CASE

A vagrant family, the Pappenheimers were the victims of one of the most dramatic and well-publicized witch trials in German history. The Pappenheimers consisted of a father, a mother, two grown sons and one young son. The father, Paulus, assisted by his wife Anna and their sons, eked out a meager living as a traveling emptier of privies. The Pappenheimers were caught up in a drive against vagrants and criminals conducted by the **Bavarian** government when an accused thief named them as associates. The thief accused Pappenheimer's grown sons, Michel and Gumpprecht, of having aided him in the murder of pregnant women and the family of being robbers and murderers. Word went out among the various local officials of the Danubian provinces of Bavaria to be on the lookout for the Pappenheimers, and they were arrested and taken to jail in Altmannstein in February 1600. There they were tortured, confessing to a variety of crimes including witchcraft and the murder of pregnant women to secure the hands of their unborn children for **magical** purposes. The local Altmannstein officials sent word to the duke of Bavaria's capital of Munich, and the Pappenhemiers were transferred to Munich's Falcon Tower.

The Duke's government wanted to make an example of the Pappenheimers, and leading councillors, most importantly the ambitious Johann Sigismund Wagnereckh, conducted the interrogations under **torture.** The torture employed was mostly strappado, the suspension of the victim by the arms, twisted behind the back. Torture began with the youngest Pappenheimer boy, Hansel, considered the most likely to break. Wagnereckh was particularly concerned that the Pappenheimers had murdered children to grind up their hands to make a powder that they would eat to aid them in their murders and robberies. Under torture, eventually the Pappenheimers confessed to this and to a variety of other diabolical actions.

The **execution** of Anna and Paulus Pappenheimer, Michel and Gumpprecht, and two of their associates who had been caught in the investigation in the summer of 1600 is one of the most sickening in the annals of the witch-hunt. The desire to make an example of the family led the Bavarian government to inflict the last measure of cruelty upon them in front of a large crowd. First, all six were ripped, six times apiece, with red hot tongs. Then Anna Pappenheimer's breasts were cut from her body, a punishment seldom inflicted anywhere. The severed breasts were rubbed around Anna's mouth and the mouths of her sons. Then the Pappenheimers and their associates were carried in a wooden cart to the place of execution, where the five males had their arms broken on the wheel. Paulus Pappenheimer, considered the leader of the group, was impaled on a sharp stake rammed into his anus and through his intestines—another punishment usually considered archaic. Finally the victims, without the mercy of preliminary strangulation, were burned alive. Hansel Pappenheimer, forced to watch the agonizing deaths of his entire family, was executed along with more people named by the Pappenheimers in November.

Despite the fact that many accused witches had named others under torture, Wagnereckh's best efforts did not result in the expansion of the Pappenheimer case to a full-fledged witch-hunt. Some Bavarian lawyers and officials were troubled by the use of denunciation under torture to justify torturing the persons denounced, and **accusations** were reaching people higher in the social order who were capable of defending themselves. The persecution came to an end with a decree from the duke denouncing irregularities in the procedure, although no one was punished for these irregularities and Wagnereckh continued to rise in the government hierarchy. The Pappenheimer case and the horror of their execution was publicized throughout **Germany** and was also discussed in the writings of learned demonologists including Martin **del Rio.**

REFERENCES: Wolfgang Behringer. *Witchcraft Persecutions in Bavaria: Popular Magic, Religious Zealotry, and Reason of State in Early Modern Europe.* Trans. J. C. Grayson and David Lederer. Cambridge: Cambridge University Press, 1997; Michael Kunze. *Highroad to the Stake: A Tale of Witchcraft.* Trans. William E. Yuill. Chicago and London: University of Chicago Press, 1987.

PEARSON, ALISON (D. 1588)

The case of the Scottish witch Alison Pearson was bound up in both church politics and fairy beliefs. Pearson first appears in the record as a witch in 1583, when the archbishop of St. Andrews, Patrick Adamson (1537–1592), approached the Kirk session about her while she was in prison. Pearson was believed to be one of several local women healers that Adamson had sought out for treatment for health problems. The principal source for these transactions, a satirical poem by Robert Sempill (1530?–1595) written in 1584, "The Legend of the Bishop of St. Androis" hints that Adamson may have been concerned about failing virility. Sempill, a member of the more radically Protestant Presbyterian faction in the Church of **Scotland,** also linked Adamson's recourse to witches with his endorsement of superstitious practices in the church. Pearson was not condemned in 1583 but was tried in 1588, when Adamson had been defeated by the Presbyterian party and even excommunicated. Pearson was charged with having consulted a devil who took on the appearance of her kinsman, William Simpson. Pearson seems to have understood the spirit to be a fairy and spoke of having lived at the court of the Queen of Elfhame for several years. She also may have been a Catholic. Pearson was condemned by the assizes and executed by strangulation followed by burning. Another witch consulted by Adamson, Agnes Melville, was also tried and condemned the same year.

REFERENCE: P. G. Maxwell-Stuart. *Satan's Conspiracy: Magic and Witchcraft in Sixteenth-Century Scotland*. East Lothian, Scotland: Tuckwell Press, 2001.

PERKINS, WILLIAM (1558–1602)

William Perkins was Elizabethan **England's** leading Calvinist theologian, and his posthumously published A *Discourse on the Damned Art of Witchcraft* (1608) had an unrivalled influence on subsequent Puritan demonologists in old and **New England.** Perkins's approach was intellectually austere. He shunned reference to previous demonologists or actual cases of witchcraft, and based his argument almost entirely on the **Bible,** particularly Exodus 22.18, "Thou shalt not suffer a witch to live." Perkins saw the essential nature of witchcraft as the making of the **satanic pact,** or "covenant," which inverted the covenant relation between God and his elect that was basic to Puritan Calvinist theology. So closely does Perkins relate the witch's contact with the Devil to the good Christian's contact with God that he claims that to deny the possibility of physical contact with devils would be to deny the possibility of covenant with God. Perkins describes the making of the covenant as a simple agreement, without the necessity for the witch to sign in blood or **kiss** or have **sex** with the Devil. Other central aspects to the witch stereotype as the **sabbat** or the **Devil's mark** he also ignored. Even *maleficia* played a minor role. Perkins's principal target was not the maleficent witch, but the "good witch," whom he described over and over as even more worthy of death than the evil witch. Perkins believed that all power to perform "magic" could only come from **Satan.** Thus astrologers, **cunning folk** and even ordinary people who recited charms were requesting power from Satan. By extension, this was also true of their clients. "Good witches" were a serious threat. Perkins described their popularity as exceeding that of their opposites, God's ministers. He may have felt the threat particularly strongly because he had been interested in natural **magic** himself as a young man, before his conversion experience.

Perkins's broad definition of witchcraft, extending to a broad population beyond those most people at the time would have considered witches, may relate to the fact that he showed relatively little interest in **gender** issues. His discussion of why women are more likely to be witches, although conventionally misogynistic, is brief and not strongly related to his main argument.

For Perkins, Satan's goal was not harming people through *maleficia* but procuring the damnation of souls. One common strategy employed by the Devil was first afflicting people through maleficent witches, then tempting them to end their affliction through **countermagic.** Whether carried out by an individual—Perkins used the example of "scratching the witch"—or by a cunning person, countermagic had the same flaw of relying on the power of the Devil rather than God. Perkins also condemned Catholic countermagic, exorcism, the making of the sign of the cross and the use of consecrated substances as essentially an invocation of Satan. (Like many Protestant writers, Perkins also claimed that several popes had been witches.) The only proper response to a witch attack on the part of an individual is prayer and the examination of conscience, to see if there are sins for which one is being punished by God through the medium of the witch. The godly could only be afflicted by witches if God permitted it for their ultimate good. The proper response on society's part was the maintenance of a learned and pious ministry and zealous judicial action against witches. *A Discourse on the Damned Art of Witchcraft,* edited by the Reverend Thomas Pickering, was dedicated to one of **England's** leading jurists and magistrates, Sir Edward Coke (1552–1634). Perkins did not endorse every practice against suspected witches—he condemned those which seemed to rely on magic, and thus ultimately on the Devil, such as **flotation tests.** He did endorse **torture** if suspicion were strong enough. Perkins admitted that no matter what the procedure, not every witch was going to be caught. Some were actually God's elect, whom God would preserve long enough for them to repent and be saved, and others God would allow to act freely so they might more richly deserve damnation.

Perkins dominated subsequent English witchcraft writing, whether the writers were supporters of his position, such as Richard **Bernard,** John Gaule or Thomas Mason, or opponents, such as the anti-Calvinist Robert **Filmer.** His work was also enormously influential in Puritan New England.

REFERENCES: Stuart Clark. *Thinking with Demons: The Idea of Witchcraft in Early Modern Europe.* Oxford: Clarendon Press, 1997; James Sharpe. *Instruments of Darkness: Witchcraft in Early Modern England.* Philadelphia: University of Pennsylvania Press, 1996.

PHYSICIANS

Physicians, university-educated medical men, played many roles in the witch-hunt, although seldom were they its victims. Physicians claimed the ability to distinguish between illnesses of natural diabolical origin, and demonologists, who usually accepted the medical orthodoxy of their time, conceded them this role. Some physicians appear to have ascribed illnesses they could not cure to witchcraft. In addition to difficulty of cure, sudden onset and unusual symptoms were characteristics of witch-caused disease. There were some cases in which physicians accused **cunning folk** or women healers, possible competitors in the medical marketplace, of causing illness through witchcraft, but this does not seem to have been common. The position of the profession as a whole tended to be skeptical, because ascribing too many illnesses to witchcraft would unduly diminish the area of their own claimed competence. Physicians, like other Europeans, were divided on the issue. Some,

Bloodletting, folio 19V of the manuscript *Treatise on Medicine* by Aldebrando di Firenze, 1356. © The Art Archive/Biblioteca d'Ajuda Lisbon/Dagli Orti.

such as Sir Thomas Browne (1605–1682), supported witch-hunting. Browne lent his medical expertise on the prosecution side during the trial of the **Lowestoft** witches. Medical writers often included lycanthropy, witchcraft and demonic **possession** while discussing the kinds of problems a physician would have to deal with in practice, although no one wrote as if such problems were common. Many emphasized that only after possible natural explanations had been ruled out should witchcraft be considered.

Physicians had a potentially authoritative role in squelching witchcraft and possession stories that authorities wanted squelched. The Royal Physician Michael Marescot lent his authority, along with many other Paris doctors, to the discrediting of the French fraudulent demoniac Marthe **Brossier.** William Harvey (1578–1657), another royal physician, played a similar role in the discrediting of the charges of witchcraft made against some **Lancashire** people in 1633. Conversely, a physician could powerfully aid a witch-hunt. Dr. Anthony Randall of **Salem** actually diagnosed the illness of Daniel Wilkins (which eventually led to his death) as witch-caused without having even seen the patient! Physicians were generally not the persons who searched the bodies of accused witches for witch's or **Devil's marks,** leaving that task to lower-ranking persons, such as surgeons, **midwives** or even torturers. Physicians did sometimes supervise sessions of **torture,** although this unpleasant task was usually left to surgeons or in some circumstances dispensed with entirely.

With some exceptions, like Browne and the Italian medical professor Andreas Cesalpino (1519–1603), the intellectual elite of the medical profession opposed witch-hunting. Some of the most prominent opponents of witch-hunting were physicians. The most important and the most radical was Johann **Weyer,** who ascribed the behavior of witches to melancholy, a recognized medical condition involving an excess of humors. Melancholy remained the most common medical diagnosis of witch-related conditions, although Edward Jorden (1569–1632), in his 1603 *A Briefe Discourse of a Disease Called the Suffocation of the Mother,* diagnosed an allegedly bewitched person as suffering from "hysteria," a condition caused by a displacement of the uterus in the body. Seventeenth-century **England** produced a remarkable succession of increasingly radical physician opponents of witch-hunting, including Jorden, John

Cotta (author of *The Triall of Witch-Craft* [1616]), Thomas **Ady** and John **Webster,** although some English physicians, such as Richard Boulton and William Drage, supported witch-hunting. By the eighteenth century, a non-supernatural approach to bodily ailments had become almost universal among physicians. Even in **Germany,** the heartland of the witch-hunt, popular books of medical case histories often unfavorably contrasted the patient's self-diagnosis of attack by a witch or other supernatural force with the physician's diagnosis based on the material condition of the body. Few physicians were willing to diagnose witchcraft, even in the most bizarre situations, and some took the lead in opposing witch-hunting. The empress Maria Theresa's (1717–1780) physician, Gerard van Swieten (1700–1772), was a moving spirit in the mid-eighteenth-century campaign against witch-hunting in the Habsburg Empire.

REFERENCES: Robin Briggs. *Witches and Neighbors: The Social and Cultural Context of European Witchcraft.* New York: Penguin, 1996; Norman Gevirtz. " 'The Devil Hath Laughed at the Physicians': Witchcraft and Medical Practice in Seventeenth-Century New England." *Journal of the History of Medicine* 55 (2000): 5–36; Johanna Geyer-Kordesch. "Whose Enlightenment? Medicine, Witchcraft, Melancholia and Pathology." In *Medicine in the Enlightenment,* ed. Roy Porter, 113–127. Atlanta: Rodopi, 1995; Michael MacDonald, ed. *Witchcraft and Hysteria in Elizabethan London: Edward Jorden and the Mary Glover Case.* London and New York: Tavistock/Routledge, 1991; Garfield Tourney "The Physician and Witchcraft in Restoration England." *Medical History* 16 (1972): 143–154; Gregory Zilboorg. *The Medical Man and the Witch during the Renaissance.* Baltimore: Johns Hopkins Press, 1935.

PICO DELLA MIRANDOLA, GIANFRANCESCO (1469–1533)

Gianfrecesco Pico della Mirandola was the nephew of the famous philosopher Giovanni Pico della Mirandola (1463–1494), and a prolific writer and humanist intellectual in his own right. He was a vehement opponent of both witchcraft and learned **magic,** who, as lord of the small territory of Mirandola, had actively supported a fierce witch-hunt in 1522–1523 that had resulted in the **execution** of seven men (including the ringleader, the priest Don Benedetto Berni) and three women. Pico della Mirandola's *Strix* (the Witch), published in Latin in 1523, drew on his experience at Mirandola. Unlike many demonological classics, *Strix* was not a huge treatise but a relatively brief and elegant humanist dialogue. The discussion takes place between four characters, three investigators and the witch herself, and extends over four days. During this time, the witch is interrogated, and one of the three investigators, a witchcraft skeptic named Apistius, "unbeliever," is converted into an avid believer. In addition to the witch's confession, the characters present evidence for the existence of witchcraft from the **Bible** and classical Greek and Roman writers, the use of which indicates a humanist author addressing a humanist audience. Descriptions of witches and magical actions in Homer, Ovid and Apuleius were all pressed into service. The activities the witch describes include attendance at nocturnal festivities presided over not by **Satan** but, as was frequently the case in medieval descriptions of witch-gatherings, by a lady. The humanist witch-believer in the dialogue, Phronimus, "prudent," identifies the lady as the Roman goddess **Diana,** really a demon, and her attendants as her nymphs. The witch also confesses to *maleficia* including **infanticide,** the use of the blood of murdered children to produce demon-summoning ointment and blasphemous actions. She describes **sex** with a devil named Ludovicus. Unlike most demonological writers, Pico claims that sex with demons is extremely pleasurable. *Strix* was published in Italian translation in 1524 (with Pico's cooperation), 1555 and 1556 and in **Germany** in 1612. In translation it became one of the earliest widely available vernacular demonologies.

REFERENCES: Peter Burke. "Witchcraft and Magic in Renaissance Italy: Gianfrancesco Pico and his *Strix*." In *The Damned Art: Essays in the Literature of Witchcraft,* ed. Sydney Anglo, 32–52. Boston: Routledge and Kegan Paul, 1977; Walter Stephens. *Demon Lovers: Witchcraft, Sex, and the Crisis of Belief.* Chicago and London: University of Chicago Press, 2002.

PIOTTO, GIOVANNI BATTISTA

Along with the nineteenth-century writer Etienne-Leon, Baron de **Lamothe-Langon,** the sixteenth-century Italian jurist Giovanni Battista Piotto is the person most responsible for spreading confusion over the **medieval origins of the witch-hunt.** He did this by including an account of a devil-worshipping witch in the Italian town of Orta and her suggested punishment in a group of forged *consilia,* or legal opinions, he ascribed to the great fourteenth-century jurist Bartolus of Sassoferato. All involved members of the Piotto, or de Plotis, family, and seem to have been produced as jokes or as fictional parodies of legal reasoning. The de Plotis who appears in the story of the witch is the (fictitious) bishop of Novara, Joannes de Plotis, who allegedly appealed to Bartolus for advice on sentencing the witch. Bartolus's advice is that she be burnt unless she confessed. The *consilium* first appeared in a collection of *consilia* from various sources published by Giovanni Battista Ziletti in 1566 and along with Piotto's other forgeries appears in editions of Bartolus from 1590 onward. The story appeared in the early witch-hunt history of Wilhelm Soldan in 1843 and became a favorite of anti-Catholic authors who wished to associate Church authority with witch burning. It also contributed to the tendency to see the full-fledged theory of the devil-worshipping witch as older than it actually was. The spuriousness of the *consilium* was revealed by the British historian Norman Cohn in 1973.

REFERENCE: Norman Cohn. *Europe's Inner Demons: The Demonization of Christians in Medieval Christendom.* Rev. ed. Chicago: University of Chicago Press, 2000.

PLANTSCH, MARTIN (D. 1533)

Martin Plantsch was a professor at the University of Tübingen and a prominent preacher at the church attached to the university. In 1505, the **execution** of a witch at Tübingen attracted great popular interest and concern from the clergy of the area over the extent of popular superstition. Plantsch's sermons were published in an expanded version in 1507, *Opusculum de Sagis Maleficis*. Plantsch was a skilled theologian in the nominalist tradition of Gabriel Biel (c. 1420–1495), under whom he had studied at Tübingen. Nominalists placed great emphasis on the absolute and completely free power of God, and Plantsch emphasized that all actions of witches and the Devil are ultimately the actions of God. He used the Book of Job to make the point that **Satan** was God's instrument, and that God sometimes chose to afflict the good for his own purposes. Instruments used by witches to work ill had absolutely no power of their own but only what God allowed them. Plantsch also denied the ability of the Devil or other demons to beget children through intercourse with witches. Although Plantsch claimed that witches deserved to be punished by death, he did not discuss persecution or any legal process in his book. The proper response to witchcraft was not **accusation** or **countermagic,** but repentance and "sacramentalia"—things blessed by the church, such as holy water and consecrated salt. Plantsch's emphasis on God's providence contributed to a tradition which affected both Catholics and Protestants in southwestern **Germany** in the early sixteenth century, a time when persecution was at a low level.

REFERENCE: Heiko Augustinus Oberman. *Masters of the Reformation: The Emergence of a New Intellectual Climate in Europe.* Trans. Dennis Martin. Cambridge: Cambridge University Press, 1981.

POLAND, WITCH-HUNTING IN

The Kingdom of Poland, geographically one of Europe's largest, had a severe witch-hunt, the peak of which occurred late in the European context, in the last half of the seventeenth century through the early eighteenth century. The survival of the widely dispersed judicial records has been incomplete, making a precise figure impossible. The estimate of about 10,000 trials in Poland in which between 5,000 and 10,000 people were executed as witches found in some of the older literature is probably an exaggeration.

Like other Europeans, early modern Poles had long believed in witches' power to inflict *maleficia*. These acts included injuries to human beings or livestock, causing cow's milk to go dry and interfering with domestic processes such as butter churning. A law of 1543 reserved jurisdiction over witch cases to the church courts, but this law would prove impossible to enforce in Poland, the most decentralized kingdom in Europe. Demonological notions about the relation of witches to the Devil began to enter Poland through its western frontier with the German lands of the Holy Roman Empire in the mid–sixteenth century. (Heinrich **Kramer's** *Malleus Maleficarum* [1486] was available in a Polish translation from the early seventeenth century.) Witch-hunting began in Poland in cities with a large German population or contacts with **Germany.** Although by the seventeenth century it had moved to the rural areas, witch-hunting was always most severe in western as opposed to eastern or southern

Poland. Unlike its neighbors **Russia** and **Hungary,** Poland did not experience high-profile political witchcraft trials at its royal court, although some persons were thought to have used **magic** to rise there.

Most Polish witchcraft cases in the sixteenth and early seventeenth centuries ended with the accused being required to repent and foreswear future magical activity, rather than with **execution.** The relative late start of severe large-scale witch-hunting in seventeenth-century Poland can be ascribed to the devastation that afflicted the kingdom in the earlier part of the century as a consequence of the wars with **Sweden** and Russia and the subsequent devastation known in Polish history as the "deluge." In Poland as elsewhere in Europe, large-scale disaster moderated the pace of witch-hunting while the social disruption that accompanied it laid the groundwork for severe persecution later on. Poland was also unusual in both the late peak of its witch-hunting activity and the late peak of the imposition of Catholic Reformation intolerance. Europe's most tolerant country in the late sixteenth century, Poland was aggressively, although never completely, re-Catholicized in the seventeenth and early eighteenth centuries.

The secular courts of municipalities and districts led the Polish witch-hunt, although witch lynching and the "swimming of witches" also seem to have been common. Despite the best efforts of some church leaders and the support of royal decrees in 1672 and 1713, the church monopoly over witch persecution proved impossible to maintain. More than half of the persecutions of which record survives took place between 1676 and 1725. In the highly decentralized Polish state, central supervision of local courts was virtually impossible, and the local courts were free to use **torture** unsparingly. The combination of inquisitorial **trial procedure** and virtually unrestricted torture proved deadly. The last witch executions in Poland, of dubious legality, were of two women in 1793 in the city of Posen, recently taken over by Prussia after the partition of Poland. This date is often taken for the end of the European witch-hunt.

REFERENCES: Maria Bogucka. "Law and Crime in Poland in Early Modern Times." *Acta Poloniae Historica* 71 (1995): 175–195; Brian P. Levack. *The Witch-Hunt in Early Modern Europe*. London and New York: Longman, 1987.

PONZINIBIO, GIANFRANCESCO

The Italian lawyer Gianfrancesco Ponzinibio wrote one of the earliest systematic attacks on the idea of diabolical witchcraft as it had emerged in the fifteenth century, particularly in Heinrich **Kramer's** *Malleus Maleficarum* (1486). Ponzinibio's *Treatise on Witches* (1520) attacked witch trials both for legal irregularities and because Ponzinibio denied the existence of diabolical witchcraft. Instead, he appealed to the **Canon Episcopi** to assert that witch flight, **sabbat,** and other aspects of the emerging witch stereotype were merely delusions. The predominance of women and rural people among accused witches was explained by their greater mental weakness and vulnerability to delusion. Ponzinibio was vigorously answered by Bartolommeo **Spina,** who devoted three tracts in the 1520s to defending the witch stereotype, as well as accusing Ponzinibio of heresy and sympathy for heretics and calling for him to be put on trial. This reputation for heresy long clung to Ponzinibio's name in the Catholic world. Nevertheless, *Treatise on Witches* was reprinted several times in **Italy** and **Germany** and influenced the debate on witchcraft, particularly among lawyers.

REFERENCE: Julio Caro Baroja. *The World of the Witches*. Trans. O. N. V. Glendinning. Chicago: University of Chicago Press, 1965.

PORTUGAL, WITCH-HUNTING IN

Portugal saw less witch-hunting than any other European kingdom. The Portuguese Inquisition, divided into Lisbon, Evora and Coimbra Inquisitions, was active from 1536–1821 and claimed jurisdiction over cases of witchcraft and sorcery. Like their Roman and Spanish fellows, Portuguese inquisitors took little interest in executing witches. The only known witch **execution** in sixteenth-century Portugal occurred in 1559, when five witches were burned in Rossio Square in Lisbon, and another witch shortly thereafter. This unusual case involved a trial before a secular court rather than the Inquisition. The only known witch execution by the Portugese Inquisition happened in Evora in 1626. The Inquisition's principal interest was not witches but secret Judaizers—Jews forcibly converted to Christianity and their descendants, some of whom clandestinely maintained Jewish practices, such as observation of the Saturday Sabbath. By contrast, the Inquisition treated witches and other **magical** offenders such as **cunning folk** and preparers of love potions somewhat leniently. They were seldom tortured, although the use of **torture** increased in the seventeenth and early eighteenth century. Rather than executing witches, the Inquisition sought to publicly humiliate them with whippings and penances, such as being made to stand in the church door.

Popular belief in Portugal usually credited witches with inborn power rather than that derived from a **satanic pact.** Ideas of the **sabbat** and the pact existed, but the full-fledged European witch stereotype never developed. (Portugese tended to think of the pact as a way for a witch to increase the magical power he or she already possessed.) The peak of the Portuguese Inquisition's activity against magical offenses came in the early to mid–eighteenth century. After about 1760, the Inquisition ignored the **accusations** of *maleficia* that continued to be submitted to it, and inquisitors described belief in the satanic pact or human communication with demons as superstition. Occasional cases appeared in Portugal into the early nineteenth century.

The Lisbon Inquisition also had jurisdiction over the Portuguese colony in Brazil. No Brazilian witches were executed, but there was a steady stream of complaints about witchcraft and magic, and sometimes prisoners were brought from Brazil to face the Inquisition. Brazilian magic cases shifted from European-derived witchcraft and magic in the sixteenth and seventeenth centuries to a focus on African-derived practices in the eighteenth century, the time of the greatest volume of Brazilian magical cases. Inquisitors sought unsuccessfully to assimilate African magical practices to European concepts such as the sabbat.

REFERENCES: Francesco Bethencourt. "Portugal: A Scrupulous Inquisition." *Early Modern European Witchcraft: Centres and Peripheries*, ed. in Bengt Ankarloo and Gustav Henningsen, 403–422. Oxford: Clarendon Press, 1990; Maria Cristina Corrêa de Melo. "Witchcraft in Portugal during the Eighteenth Century, Analysed through the Accusations of the Tribunal do Santo Officio de Evora." In *Transactions of the Eighth International Congress on the Enlightenment* (1992): 573–578; Laura de Mello e Souza. "Witchcraft and Magic Practices in Colonial Brazil: 1580–1770." *Acta Ethnographica Hungarica* 37 (1991/1992): 243–256.

POSSESSION

The belief in possession, the overriding of the will of the possessed by a demon that "possesses" the victim's body, is found in many cultures and is an ancient belief in the history of Christianity. Several of the miracles of Jesus in the Gospel involved the cure of the possessed. There is no necessary connection between possession and witchcraft, nor were possessions usually blamed on witches or on any human intermediary in ancient and medieval Christianity. (Nor are they in modern times.) In the age of the witch-hunts, however, the concepts of witchcraft and demonic possession became inextricably entangled. This actually increased during the course of the early modern witch-hunts, with some of the most dramatic possession cases, such as those of the Swedish **Mora** cases and the **Salem** witch-hunt taking place after the overall decline of European witch-hunting. The reasons for this are not entirely clear, although they may be based on the high-profile witchcraft and witches generally evident at the time.

Not all mental illness or madness was blamed on demonic possession. The symptoms of possession included pain, writhing, the display of unnatural strength and talking in a voice different from that normally used, particularly women's use of deep or masculine voices. The speaking of strange languages or languages unknown to the possessed was also a sign of possession. Vomiting of unusual objects, such as pins, needles and stones, was common. Possession was also strongly gendered and age related. The majority of the possessed, and a large majority of the "star" possessed, or "demoniacs," were women, usually young women and girls. Some historians, often working in the **psychoanalytic** tradition, have ascribed this to sexual frustration, and certainly many possessed women used language and gestures that were erotic. A complementary approach, influenced by **feminist** historiography, emphasizes the powerlessness of young women in early modern society and points out that possession offered them a way to be heard and even to be the center of the attention. The most dramatic and well-publicized possession cases involved large numbers of young women. They were the cases that took place in seventeenth-century French and **southern Netherlands** nunneries, such as those of the **Loudun** and Louviers nuns. Convent life, with its strict routine and repression of sexuality, imposed a heavy psychological burden on young women, many of whom had been placed there for reasons of family economics and lacked religious vocation.

One of the reasons for the popularity of demonic possession in the early modern period was **confessional** conflict. Because both Catholics and Protestants believed in the possibility of demonic possession, they asserted the validity of their different techniques for dealing with it. Here Catholics had the advantage, because exorcism was a ritual of the church and usually believed by Catholics to be efficacious if done properly. Protestants believed that exorcistic rituals were idolatrous and Catholic belief in their efficacy arrogant but could offer nothing better than prayers and **Bible** reading, also not always effective. Those advocating a particular religious position used the possessed to vindicate it. The Frenchwoman Marthe **Brossier** owed much of her fame as a possessed person to the support of Catholic religious orders. Her possessing demon Beezelbub expressed his fear and respect for the powers of Catholic priests and his complementary contempt for Protestant ministers, whom he claimed as allies. In **England,** the puritan exorcist John **Darrell** used the possessed to advocate a more

EXORCISMVS

Virtutis eximię contra dæmoniacos,& ad soluendum omne opus diabolicum,& quofcunq; morbos corpora humana vexantes,siuè sint per facturas:maleficia, & incantationes à Maleficis factos , siue à Dæmonibus intro-ductos .

Per eundem authorem compilatum , & ad infirmorum salutem accommodatum .

EXORCISMVS.

Deus in adiutorium meum intende . Domine ad adiuuandum me festina . Gloria Patri,& Filio,& Spiritui Sancto. Sicut erat in principio, & nunc, & femper, & in fecula feculorum.Amen.

Oratio.

Mnipotens,& clementissime Deus à quo omne bonum fumit initium , & femper ad potiora progrediens percipit incrementum , intercedente gloriofa Virgine Maria , totaq; cœlefti curia:concede quæfumus,vt quod ad gloriam tuam,& dæmonum confufionem inchoare aggredimur, æterno tuæ paternæ fapientiæ munere ad defideratum portum perducamur. Per Chriftum Dominum .

In Nomine Sanctiffimę Trinitatis, Patris † Et filij † Et fpiritus † fancti. Amen . Ego minifter Exorcifta Sanctæ Ecclefiæ Apoftolicæ Romanæ feruus licet indignus, per authoritatem fundatam in paffione,

Frontispiece to chapter on Exorcism. From the *Compendium Malleficarum* (1626) by Francesco Maria Guazzo, Italian demonologist. © The Art Archive/Dagli Orti (A).

Protestant Church of England, eventually causing the leaders of the church to take a much more skeptical view of possession and exorcism in general. The unrestrained drama and the power claimed by the usually young and female demoniacs troubled religious authorities generally, and even in Catholic areas they were declining after the mid–seventeenth century. There were indeed several problems with using possessions in religious controversy. Possessions were notoriously easy to fake, and Brossier, the Englishwoman Anne **Gunter** and many others were eventually revealed as frauds. **Physicians** in particular were skeptical of demonic possession, preferring to blame symptoms on "melancholy," a condition on which they could claim expertise. Even if a given possession was genuine, the extent to which demons could actually be believed was often contested.

Both Protestants and Catholics accepted the linkage of possession to witchcraft, viewing it as the ultimate form of *maleficium*. This linkage was accepted by theologians, although there seems to have been a gap between the position of the theologians, holding that witchcraft was one possible cause of possession, and the popular view that possession was always caused by witchcraft. So strong was the linkage between possession and witchcraft that there were cases in which possessed people were used to identify witches as suspects were brought before them. One advantage with blaming possession on a witch is that it offered a cure for the possession if Catholic exorcism and Protestant prayer failed, the **execution** of the witch. The mere claim of a possessed person that she saw a given individual tormenting her or inflicting demons on her was also suspect, however, because the Devil was a master of deceit and not above framing the innocent.

REFERENCES: Robin Briggs. *Witches and Neighbors: The Social and Cultural Context of European Witchcraft.* New York: Penguin, 1996; D. P. Walker, *Unclean Spirits: Possession and Exorcism in France and England in the Late Sixteenth and Early Seventeenth Centuries,* Philadelphia: University of Philadelphia Press, 1981.

PRAETORIUS, ANTON (1560–1613)

Anton Praetorius, a German Calvinist, wrote a German-language denunciation of witch-hunting published in 1598 under the pseudonym Johann Scultetus, *On Sorcery and Sorcerors.* Praetorius, although not denying witches's existence, used both satirical ridicule and a broad range of knowledge to denounce the practices of witch-hunters. He attacked the common use of **torture** beyond the legal bounds of the Holy Roman Empire's *Carolina* code and the search for the **Devil's mark.** Like many demonologists, Praetorius associated witchcraft with his **confessional** opponents, both Catholics and radical Protestants. He claimed the proper response to witchcraft **accusations** was not judicial, but preaching, teaching and promoting good order in the state, church and household. Praetorius also attacked the double standard by which women's **magic** were treated far more harshly than men's. He alleged that ordinary people were far too apt to blame all of their misfortunes on witches and that the **sabbat** was an illusion. The book was reprinted.

REFERENCES: Stuart Clark. *Thinking with Demons: The Idea of Witchcraft in Early Modern Europe.* Oxford: Clarendon Press, 1997; Gerhild Scholz Williams. *Defining Dominion: The Discourses of Witchcraft and Magic in Early Modern France and Germany.* Ann Arbor, Michigan: University of Michigan Press, 1995.

PSYCHOANALYTIC HISTORIOGRAPHY

Psychoanalytic interpretation of the European witch-hunt began with Sigmund Freud (1856–1939), the founder of psychoanalysis. His interest appears in his correspondence with Dr. Wilhelm Fleiss (1858–1928) in 1897, where he speaks of possessed women, a group he does not clearly distinguish from witches, as suffering from the same syndromes as the neurotic patients he was then treating. Freud speculated that both witches and judges had suffered from childhood abuse and spoke of the "harsh therapy" the judges performed. He wrote to Fleiss about getting a copy of Heinrich **Kramer's** *Malleus Maleficarum* (1486) to study. (Freud's analysis of possessed women as suffering from "hysteria" had a precedent in the witch-hunt period, in Edward Jorden's 1603 book on the **Glover** case.) Freud identified the broomstick on which witches allegedly flew to the **sabbat** as a phallic symbol and speculated that witchcraft was the remnant of a primeval, sexualized devil-worshipping religion. Freud's one study of an individual case from the witch-hunt era is on Johann Christoph **Haizmann,** whom he describes as suffering from an unconscious homosexuality expressing itself in paranoia and identifying **Satan** as a father figure. Freud's interpretation has been contested by Ida Macalpine and Richard A. Hunter, who demonstrate that Freud's reading of Haizmann's autobiographical text is tendentious.

Historians of the witch-hunt were generally unaware or uninterested in the psychoanalytic literature. Like early modern historians generally, they have emphasized the differences in the life courses and psychologies of early modern people rather than their similarities with the twentieth-century people who have been the subject of psychoanalysis. The first major book by a historian integrating psychoanalytic with traditional historical sources was John Putnam Demos's 1982 *Entertaining Satan*. Demos used psychoanalysis as one of several tools to understand **New England** witch-hunting. Like many historians using psychoanalysis, Demos's concern was less to understand the witch, and more to understand the accuser and witch-hunter.

Subsequent uses of psychoanalysis in witch-hunt historiography have been principally the work of **feminist** historians and scholars. The literary scholar Deborah Willis's analysis of English and Scottish witch-hunting draws on Melanie Klein's (1882–1960) theories about the early relations of the infant and the mother, which have been influential among feminist intellectuals. Willis identifies the witch, in the mind of her accuser, as a "bad mother." In her discussion of **James VI** of **Scotland** and the **North Berwick** trials, she focuses on James's problematic relationship with powerful mother figures, his own mother Mary Queen of Scots (1542–1587) and Queen Elizabeth of **England** (r. 1558–1603). James's involvement in witch-hunting gave him the opportunity to exert the masculine power often frustrated in politics. Lyndal Roper, a feminist and psychoanalytic historian of early modern German society, has employed similar concepts to analyze a series of cases of lying-in maids accused of witchcraft in seventeenth-century Augsburg and the relationship with the Devil in the confessions of one accused witch.

A psychoanalyst rather than a historian, Evelyn Heinemann has attempted a psychoanalytic and feminist interpretation not of individuals involved in witch-hunting, but of early modern society itself and of witch-hunting as one process in that society. She also sees the witch as a "bad mother" and locates the witch-hunt as a crucial stage in the development of the modern autonomous superego.

REFERENCES: John Putnam Demos. *Entertaining Satan: Witchcraft and the Culture of Early New England*. New York: Oxford University Press, 1982; Sigmund Freud. *The Complete Letters of Sigmund Freud to Wilhelm Fliess 1887–1904*. Ed. and trans. Jeffrey Moussaief-Masson. Cambridge and London: Belknap Press of Harvard University Press, 1985; Sigmund Freud. "A Seventeenth-Century Demonological Neurosis." In *The Standard Edition of the Complete Psychological Works of Sigmund Freud, Volume 19*, ed. James Strachey, 67–105. 1961; Evelyn Heinemann. *Witches: A Psychoanalytic*

Exploration of the Killing of Women. London and New York: Free Association Books, 2000; Ida Macalpine and Richard A Hunter. *Schizophrenia 1677: A Psychiatric Study of an Illustrated Autobiographical Record of Demonic Possession.* London: William Dawson and Sons, 1956; Diane Purkiss. *The Witch in History: Early Modern and Twentieth-Century Representations.* London and New York: Routledge, 1996; Lyndal Roper. *Oedipus and the Devil: Witchcraft, Sexuality and Religion in Early Modern Europe.* New York: Routledge, 1994; Deborah Willis. *Malevolent Nurture: Witch-Hunting and Maternal Power in Early Modern England.* Ithaca: Cornell University Press, 1995.

Q

QUEBEC

See New France, Witch-Hunting in.

QUERÉTARO POSSESSION CASES

In 1691, the Mexican city of Querétaro was the scene of several cases of allegedly witch-caused demonic **possession.** The possessions were associated with a religious order that had recently established itself in the town, the Franciscans of the Propagation of the Faith, who had founded an institution there in 1683. The Franciscans of the Propagation of the Faith were a rigorously penitential order, whose members abased and humiliated themselves and set themselves against many traditional customs and festivals. Their three-hour-long sermons were particularly popular among the town's women, arousing some resentment among their husbands. The possession cases seem to have started in August, when a woman named Francisca Mejia showed signs of possession. Her jaw was locked shut and could be opened only by the application of relics, which caused her intense pain. On being exorcised, one of the demons revealed that they had been placed there by a group of witches, led by one known as the "mice-sucker." As was common in possession cases, Mejia vomited bizarre objects, including pebbles and a toad. The demons were exorcised, only to return eight days later claiming that the witches had sent them back. Another woman, Juana de los Reyes, showed similar symptoms. The head of the Franciscan College, Fray Pablo Sarmiento, claimed that one of the devils possessing Juana revealed that the mice-sucker had sent the devils because she was jealous of Juana's pretty feet. Exorcism forced Juana to vomit a huge toad, which was killed by Juana's father but retained its shape even after being burned in a hot fire. Juana's exorcisms continued over several months, and it was claimed that the mice-sucker had tried to poison her.

The possessions spread to a number of the townswomen. Orders other than the Franciscans were highly suspicious of them, however, and they remained a solely Franciscan affair. By December a letter from the local representative of the **Spanish Inquisition** to the inquisitors in Mexico City claimed that a new demoniac emerged after every Franciscan sermon. Two January events brought the case to an end. After a series of dramatic physical events, including the expulsion of 20 needles wrapped in a blue paper bag from her vagina, Juana de los Reyes gave birth to a child the night of January 1. The Franciscans tried to claim that her pregnancy had been induced by the devils through the use of incubi, but it brought Juana and the whole business under a cloud of suspicion. The second event was a statement dated January 18 from the Inquisition, influenced by leaders of the other religious orders in Querétaro, that the exorcisms cease and that there be no further mention of the possessions. One Franciscan, Fra Matteo Bonilla, was arrested, and Sarmiento was severely reprimanded. The mice-sucker was never identified or tried, and unlike the contemporary affair at **Salem,** the Querétaro episode never developed into a witch-hunt.

REFERENCE: Fernando Cervantes. *The Devil in the New World: The Impact of Diabolism in New Spain.* New Haven and London: Yale University Press, 1994.

R

REMY, NICOLAS (1530–1612)

The **Lorraine** official Nicolas Remy was both an avid witch-hunter and an influential demonologist. His *Demonolatry* (1595) drew on his extensive experience as a witch-hunter, with the names and cases of many of the Lorraine people he had sent to their deaths. He boasted of being responsible for the death of nine hundred, although this is probably an exaggeration. Remy was born into a Lorraine magisterial family and studied law in **France.** He returned to Lorraine as personal secretary to the Duke Charles III (1543–1608) in 1575 and was appointed a member of the tribunal of Nancy, one of the administrative subdivisions of the duchy, the next year. This was the start of his witch-hunting career, in which he not only carried out persecutions, but intervened to fan the zeal of local courts. Remy's rise in the Lorraine service was dramatic. In 1583, he was raised to the nobility; in 1589, he became councillor of the Privy Council; and in 1591, he was made procurator-general, head of Lorraine's judicial system.

Remy distilled his experience of witch-hunting in *Demonolatry*. Although the book shows wide reading, particularly in classical literature, it makes surprisingly few references to previous demonological writings. (The demonologists to whom Remy does refer include Johannes **Nider,** Ulrich **Molitor,** Heinrich **Kramer,** Paulus **Grillandus** and Jean **Bodin.** He also knew the text of the witch-hunting opponent Johann **Weyer,** who he attacked without naming him.) Instead, Remy concentrated on what he had learned as a witch-hunter, recounting more than a hundred cases in the period 1581 to 1591, mostly from the mid-1580s. In those cases he described where trial records have survived, his account seems basically accurate, making his book a particularly good source for the interaction of folk beliefs and learned demonology. Remy endorsed nearly every aspect of the witch stereotype as it had developed including the **satanic pact,** *maleficia,* human-demon **sex,** witch flight, the **sabbat** (of which he gave an elaborate description), **kissing** the Devil (often on the hairy posteriors of his goat-form), hereditarily transmitted witchcraft and the **Devil's mark.** Remy acknowledged that most witches were women but devoted only perfunctory attention to **gender** questions. He also believed that the vast majority of witches were poor beggars. He denied that devils had the power to work **transformations** but believed that they had the power to work extremely convincing illusions. Demons could make bodies out of condensed matter and take human form, but always had a pronounced stench and something wrong with the appearance of their bodies, such as birdlike claws for hands and feet.

Remy strongly believed in **magisterial immunity,** claiming that magistrates, whose position was sacred, had a particular duty to suppress witches. Judicial procedure, not **countermagic,** which he denounced, was the proper way to deal with witches. Witch cases posed a particular challenge, because the Devil often gave witches the ability to resist **torture** but to neglect to search out and punish witches was to delay the coming of God's kingdom. Despite his occasional use of **eschatology,** Remy had far too much contempt for poor witches and far too much regard for the magistracy to engage in the paranoid rhetoric of the universal witch menace indulged in by other French-language demonologists. *Demonolatry* closes with a denunciation of those magistrates who shirked their duty to suppress witchcraft. It was an influential text, and Remy along with Martin **del Rio** became the leading Catholic authority on witchcraft. *Demonolatry* was published in a German translation the next year and was extensively quarried by subsequent demonologists, such as Francesco Maria **Guazzo.**

REFERENCES: Robin Briggs. *Communities of Belief: Cultural and Social Tension in Early Modern France.* Oxford: Clarendon Press, 1989; Stuart Clark. *Thinking with Demons: The Idea of Witchcraft in Early Modern Europe.* Oxford: Clarendon Press, 1997; Nicolas Remy. *Demonolatry.* Trans. E. A. Ashwin, ed. with an Introduction and Notes by Montague Summers. London: John Rodker, 1930.

RIBERA, LUIS DE

Luis de Ribera, or Rivera, an illiterate Mexican cowboy, was tried by the Inquisition of Mexico City for witchcraft in 1630. His case and confession throw an interesting light on the multicultural nature of witchcraft in **Spanish America.** Ribera was an immigrant from Spain, who claimed to have first learned witchcraft from a Native American, who taught him herbal **magic,** particularly for the purpose of attracting women. Ribera's initiator into demonic magic was an African slave, who Ribera claimed had a tattoo of **Satan** on his foot. The African sold Ribera a book of pictures of demons, in which Ribera wrote his name in blood drawn from his nose. Ribera claimed to have acquired this book in the land of the Chichimecs, an Indian tribe popularly associated with demons and witchcraft. He used his new demonic powers to control herd **animals.**

Ribera's witchcraft was revealed when a wagon train with which he had signed on as a mule driver suffered a stampede. Others in the wagon train speculated that the loss was due to witchcraft, and Ribera broke down and confessed. He was taken in irons to Mexico City, where he threw himself on the mercy of the Inquisition, claiming he now deeply regretted his youthful follies and was tormented by visions of Satan, telling him not to repent. The Inquisition let him off with a penance.

REFERENCES: Fernando Cervantes. *The Devil in the New World: The Impact of Diabolism in New Spain.* New Haven and London: Yale University Press, 1994; Marc Simmons. *Witchcraft in the Southwest: Spanish and Indian Supernaturalism on the Rio Grande.* Flagstaff, Ariz.: Northland Press, 1974.

RIO, MARTIN DEL (1551–1608)

The Jesuit Martin del Rio's *Disquisitions on Magic*, first published in 1599 and 1600, was the most authoritative Catholic treatment of witchcraft and other forms of **magic** for the next century and a half; it proved to have great influence among Protestants as well. Born into a wealthy and noble Spanish family resident in the Spanish Netherlands, del Rio was recognized as a child prodigy and educated in the Netherlands; Paris, where he heard the famous demonological lectures of Juan **Maldonado;** and Spain. He published several learned works on the ancient classics in the early 1570s and served as an official in the Spanish government in the Netherlands. The strain of dealing with government affairs in a province torn by civil war proved too much, and del Rio returned to Spain, where he entered the Jesuit order in 1580. He devoted the rest of his life to learning and scholarship.

Del Rio's interest in magic seems to have begun early in his life. It was sharpened by a particular event, the trial of the Benedictine monk Jean del Vaulx in 1597. Del Vaulx had been accused of causing the death of several of his fellow monks at the Abbey of Stavelot by magic and poisoning. He gave a lengthy and detailed confession, available to del Rio through his friend Pierre Dheure, one of the two judges who sentenced del Vaulx to death by beheading. Del Rio's *Disquisitions on Magic* first appeared in its complete form in two volumes in 1599 and 1600. Its coverage of magic was not limited to witchcraft but attempted to cover the entire realm of magical practice, including alchemy, astrology, the observance of omens and the practices associated with **cunning folk.** Del Rio proclaimed that his work drew equally on law, philosophy and theology. The work was Scholastic in form, posing and answering a series of questions and frequently making fine distinctions.

Del Rio was highly suspicious of magic, claiming that most magical practices relied on an explicit or implicit pact with an evil spirit (even if not necessarily **Satan**). Magic, he asserted, was associated with heretics, bad or lukewarm Catholics and non-Christians (when Muslims ruled Spain, he charged, magic was virtually the only subject taught there). He linked the rise in witchcraft in northern Europe with the coming of Protestantism. Unlike experienced magistrates such as his contemporary Nicholas **Remy,** del Rio was unable to draw much from his own experience of witches and witch trials, although he did make some references to encounters with magic and magicians. He made up for this with the immense breadth of his reading and learning. The Catholic demonologists with whom he engaged included Maldonado, Remy, Ulrich **Molitor,** Johannes **Nider,** Nicholas **Jacquier,** Paulus **Grillandus,** Bartolommeo **Spina,** Johannes Trithemius (1462–1516), Pedro Cirvelo, Jean **Bodin** (about whose religious reliability he had some doubts) and Peter **Binsfeld;** Heinrich **Kramer's** *Malleus Maleficarum* (1486) also provided fodder. He refuted the Catholic opponents of witch-hunting Gianfrancesco **Ponzinibio** and Cornelius Loos (1546–1595). The Protestant demonologists he discussed, mostly to refute them, included Lambert **Daneau,** Johann **Weyer** and the Rostock law professor Johann Goedelmann (1559–1611). The wide range of classical, medieval and Renaissance nondemonological texts del Rio used included poems, legal writings, histories and the writings of Jesuit missionaries from North America to Japan.

Del Rio endorsed much of the witch stereotype as it had developed since the fifteenth century. He believed in witch flight, the **sabbat** and **infanticide.** He denied the reality of **transformations** and did not believe it was possible for humans to have offspring by demons, although the demons could acquire semen from a man and transport it to the womb of a woman. Del Rio described a wide range of *maleficia*, of which he claimed the infliction of impotence and sterility to be the most prevalent. He did believe that false **accusations** were made and described how innocent persons could become suspect. Like many other Catholic demonologists, del Rio emphasized the power of Catholic rituals and sacred entities, such as holy water, against demons and witches—and Protestants' corresponding powerlessness. Much of *Disquisitions on Magic* was addressed to magistrates and concerned legal procedures and proofs of witchcraft. del Rio was skeptical of the **Devil's mark** and the **flotation test,** as used in **Germany,** finding that both relied on beliefs that could not be justified. Satan was perfectly capable of making a witch without a mark or of removing one once placed, nor could such marks be consistently distinguished from natural marks. As for flotation tests, they were simply unreliable. Del Rio endorsed **torture** under limitations, saying that torturers should not employ new or unusual forms of torture and that a suspect should not be tortured more than once a day or three times overall. In practice, however, he was less moderate. Duke Maximilian I of **Bavaria,** at the beginning of a witch persecution, asked del Rio's expert advice and received a reply endorsing unrestricted torture and torture on the basis merely of a person having been accused of being present at a sabbat.

Del Rio continued to revise his book, which came out in its final form in 1608, the year of his death. It went through two dozen editions in all, with the last appearing in 1747. Surprisingly, given del Rio's frequently and sometimes pungently expressed loathing of Protestants, his book influenced Protestants as well as Catholics. The Saxon jurist Benedict Carpzov (1595–1666) drew much from it, as did the Scottish lawyer Sir George Mackenzie (1636–1691). Del Rio was referred to as a legal authority in **Scotland** as late as the **Paisley** witch trial in 1697. On the Catholic side, his authority was unrivalled. Pierre de **Lancre** was only one of many who endorsed him as the greatest demonologist. Del Rio's fellow-Jesuit, the opponent of witch-hunting Friedrich von **Spee,** could not denounce him by name, although Spee's attack on demonologists who theorize in placid remoteness from the grubby reality of witch trials was plainly aimed at him. Nevertheless, del Rio's position as the authority on witches and demons continued into the eighteenth century, and he was quoted as an authority as late as the Bavarian trial of Veronika Zerritsch in 1756.

REFERENCES: Wolfgang Behringer. *Witchcraft Persecutions in Bavaria: Popular Magic, Religious Zealotry, and Reason of State in Early Modern Europe.* Trans. J. C. Grayson and David Lederer. Cambridge: Cambridge University Press, 1997; Martin del Rio. *Investigations into Magic.* Ed. and trans. P. G. Maxwell-Stuart. Manchester, England: Manchester University Press, 2000.

ROMAN INQUISITION

The Roman Inquisition was founded in 1542 by the decree of Pope Paul III (pope, 1534–1549) to systematize the different Inquisitions working throughout **Italy,** to establish Inquisitions in places where they were weak or nonexistent and to bring them under the central supervision of the Congregation of the Holy Office, a group of six cardinals working in Rome. Its model was the **Spanish Inquisition,** and like the Spanish Inquisition it provided a centralized system of justice cutting across the boundaries of different dioceses or secular governments. Its jurisdiction covered the whole of the Italian peninsula and Malta, although it was weaker in the Spanish-ruled south than in central or northern Italy. (The Spanish Inquisition operated in the islands of Sicily and Sardinia.) Inquisitors were Dominican or Franciscan friars, working out of a local Dominican convent. As representatives of the pope, they were considered to share in papal infallibility and could usually count on Papal backing in any conflict with local ecclesiastical or secular authority, although they commonly worked harmoniously with bishops' courts.

The primary mission of the Roman Inquisition at its founding was safeguarding Italy from Protestant heresy. The persecution of witches and magicians, although definitely falling in Inquisition's portfolio, was not originally its central concern. Its concerns with **magic** were those practices defined as heretical. For this reason, inquisitorial courts probed deeper than secular ones, being concerned not only with the actions of the accused, but with what they understood those actions to be. For example, inquisitors distinguished between invoking the aid of demons and actually worshipping them, a distinction sometimes difficult to apply to individual cases. The Inquisition's magical interests were not restricted to witchcraft; most cases of magic before the Inquisition involved practices such as making love potions, divination and magical healing rather than *maleficia*.

One reason a major witch-hunt never broke out in Italy in the early modern period was that the Inquisition procedure worked against the possibility. The

Inquisition's basic manual of operations was Nicholas **Eymeric's** fourteenth-century *Directorium Inquisitorum,* which was reprinted with extensive updates and commentary from the Spanish canon lawyer Francisco Pena in a version meant from the Roman Inquisition in 1578. (Heinrich **Kramer's** *Malleus Maleficarum* was not used.) Loose allegations were not permitted, and all depositions from witnesses had to be taken under oath. Before the proceedings began, the accused was asked to submit a list of enemies so that testimony from them would be strictly evaluated. The accused had the right to an attorney, and the Roman Inquisition was unique among early modern tribunals in actually providing indigent defendants funds to hire one. The accused and his or her attorney was provided with a copy of the trial record. **Torture** was applied only after the defense had made its case and required severe indications that the defendant was not telling the whole truth. When applied, torture was comparatively mild—strappado, the suspension of the victim by the arms, was the standard form, but it was not aggravated by hanging weights from the victim's ankles, as was the practice elsewhere, and there was an absolute time limit of an hour. There are many cases in the history of the Inquisition of suspects enduring torture and sticking to their stories. Torture was rarely applied, and as the Inquisition developed its procedures, there was a growing tendency to appeal for permission from the Congregation of the Holy Office before torturing a suspect. Particularly harsh sentences were also scrutinized by the congregation, whose meetings were often chaired by the pope. As an ecclesiastical court, the first goal of the Inquisition was to procure the repentance of a criminal. Unlike many secular courts, it was lenient on first offenders who repented and usually let them off, no matter what their crime, with a penance and perhaps a fine. Even repeat offenders, if they repented, might get off with a whipping or a prison sentence of a few years.

These procedures applied to all Inquisition cases. Suspected witches in particular benefited from the fact that the Roman Inquisition always consulted **physicians** as to whether a given death or sickness was the result of *maleficium* or natural causes. The Inquisition did not search for the **Devil's mark,** nor did it even consider Devil's marks relevant to the question of an accused witch's guilt. It was reluctant to proceed on **accusations** by persons of little credit, especially witches's accusations of others whom they claimed to have seen at the **sabbat.** The sabbat did not play a major role in most inquisitorial investigations, particularly in the south, more remote from French and German influences. The tight, centralized structure of the Roman Inquisition meant that it offered little scope for individual initiative to initiate a witch-hunt, as an early, less organized Inquisition had done for Heinrich **Kramer** and Johann Sprenger (1436–1495).

The Inquisition's involvement in cases of witchcraft and magic increased in the late sixteenth century, mostly because the Protestant menace had been defeated, and the struggle against heresy on the local level had lost its urgency. Marks of this change in emphasis are the well-publicized **Morosini** case of 1579–1580 in Venice, involving the use of magic to hunt hidden treasure, and the 1585 bull, *Coeli et Terrae* (Heaven and Earth), of Sixtus V (pope, 1585–1590) affirming the Inquisition's struggle against magic while defining it in the traditional way as principally ritual magic rather than using the witch-stereotype of sabbat and **satanic pact.** (Sixtus, then Felice Peretti, had been an inquisitor at Venice in the 1550s.) The fact that inquisitors turned more of their attention to witches and magicians meant they dealt with many more cases, but it did not mean that they grew more hostile to them; the Inquisition won its 70-year campaign against the **benandanti** of Friuli without a single **execution,** and in 1626 the Holy Office actually intervened in Florence to halt a witch-hunt that the secular government was carrying out. By the second half of the seventeenth century, interest in witch-hunting among inquisitors was virtually quiescent.

REFERENCES: Brian P. Levack. *The Witch-Hunt in Early Modern Europe.* London and New York: Longman, 1987; Ruth Martin. *Witchcraft and the Inquisition in Venice, 1550–1650.* Oxford: Blackwell, 1989; Mary O'Neil. "Magical Healing, Love Magic and the Inquisition in Late Sixteenth-Century Modena." In *Inquisition and Society in Early Modern Europe,* ed. Stephen Haliczer, 88–114. London: Croom Helm, 1987; John Tedeschi. "Inquisitorial Law and the Witch." In *Early Modern European Witchcraft: Centres and Peripheries,* ed. Bengt Ankarloo and Gustav Henningsen, 83–118. Oxford: Clarendon, 1990.

RUSSIA, WITCH-HUNTING IN

By the early modern period, Russia had had a long history of witch persecution. Persecutions were usually the result of famines, droughts and other disasters traditionally blamed on witches. The town of Pskov burnt 12 women as witches in 1411, during a plague. There were also cases of political witchcraft in the late fifteenth century, as when Tsar Ivan III "the Great"(r. 1462–1505) charged witches with causing the death of his first wife, Maria of Tver, in 1467. Witch-hunting intensified in the mid–sixteenth century. There were two main reasons for this. The church wanted a campaign against witchcraft as part of a general attack on pagan beliefs among the people. A church council in 1551 asked the Tsar to punish the crime of witchcraft with death. This did not mean that the church viewed witches as endowed with supernatural power; rather the menace of witchcraft was its alliance with pre-Christian belief. Thus, a fraudulent witch was as much of a menace as one with actual powers. The other reason for the increased role of witch-hunting in Russian culture was the policy of Tsar Ivan IV "the Terrible" (r. 1547–1584), who used witchcraft charges against his political opponents to advance his autocratic goals. During the Time of Troubles (1598–1613) that followed Ivan's death, charges of witchcraft and poisoning had become common political currency.

The accession of the Romanov dynasty did not end political witchcraft. On January 8, 1690, a high-ranking military officer, Andrei Beobrazov, was beheaded in Red Square along with male witches he had employed to influence the Tsar. The seventeenth century also saw a stream of imperial decrees against witchcraft and other pagan practices. Orthodox Russia's isolation from the religious currents of Reformation and Counter-Reformation Europe was reflected in the area of witch-hunting, where new European concepts such as the **sabbat** and the **satanic pact** had no impact. Seventeenth-century trials remained focused on individual *maleficia*, among them disease and impotence, rather than dealings with spirits or the natural disasters medieval Russian witches had been accused of causing. Russian witch-hunting remained small-scale, with no parallel for the vast witch-hunts of the west, although the patchy survival of trial records does not allow for an estimation of how many accused Russian witches perished. Another difference from the West was that the Russian trials actually targeted more men than women. A similarity was the widespread use of **torture** to elicit confessions, which replaced medieval Russian reliance on **flotation tests.** Even though the Russian authorities lacked the concept of the sabbat, they did use torture to force accused witches to name accomplices, from whom they had learned witchcraft or obtained **magical** herbs. Russia also resembled the West in punishing convicted witches by burning.

REFERENCE: Russell Zguta. "Witchcraft Trials in Seventeenth-Century Russia." *American Historical Review* 82 (1977): 1187–1207.

S

SABBAT

The concept of the sabbat, a gathering of witches presided over by the Devil, underlay many European witch-hunts. Its origins are one of the most hotly debated questions in witchcraft studies. One basic division is between those who identify it as originating in elite circles and imposed upon ordinary Europeans whose concept of witchcraft was less developed, and those who believe it also had origins within popular culture. The medieval historian Norman Cohn, a leading champion of the former view, has pointed out the similarity between the sabbat and the kind of **accusations** that Greeks and Romans had made against Christians, Jews and other dissidents and that the medieval church had made against heretics. Common features included cannibalism, **infanticide,** group **sex** and the worship of deities or devils in animal form. Some thirteenth-century descriptions of heretical gatherings are almost identical to later descriptions of sabbats, down to such unique features as shameful **kisses** bestowed on the genitals and anuses of devils in the form of cats. Anti-Semitism also contributed to the sabbat mythology, because sabbats were at first often referred to as "synagogues," and the term "sabbat" itself derived from the Jewish Sabbath. The fully developed notion of the sabbat began to appear around the middle of the fifteenth century in the works of demonologists including Johannes **Nider.**

Features of the sabbat stereotype as it developed in the hands of demonologists included feasting on what appeared to be fine food but turned to dung and dross, infanticide and cannibalism, bestowing kisses on the shameful parts of **Satan** or other devils (often in goat, cat or toad form) as a mark of subjection, painful and degrading human-demon sex, planning large-scale *maleficia* and dancing—indeed, in **Germany** dancing became so central to the understanding of the sabbat that it was usually referred to as the "witches' dance." Demonologists varied in the degree that they made use of the sabbat. Heinrich **Kramer's**

Witches's Sabbath by Frans Francken the Younger (1581–1642). © The Art Archive/Victoria and Albert Museum London/Eileen Tweedy.

Malleus Maleficarum (1486), written well after the formation of the sabbat concept, did not mention it at all.

Other scholars, notably Robin Briggs, argue that beliefs about the sabbat were common property of both elite and ordinary Europeans. Accused witches often volunteered descriptions of the sabbat without **torture** or even much prompting. Their views of sabbats also differed from those of the demonologists in that they were much more mundane. Carlo Ginzburg believes that popular ideas about the sabbat emerged from a stratum of ideas about gatherings of people with **magical** powers, such as the Friulian *benandanti*, which witch-hunters then forced into the patterns of demonology. For example, witch-hunters explained, sometimes forcefully, that the often benevolent "**Diana**" who presided over some of these meetings was really a devil or Satan.

Descriptions of the sabbat in witch trials varied greatly. Some of the most unique and elaborate come from the early-seventeenth-century **Basque** country witch-hunts carried out by the **Spanish Inquisition** and Pierre de **Lancre.** By contrast, the few English confessions that refer to anything like the sabbat show an extremely mundane occasion, more like a witches' picnic than a satanic ritual. Sometimes the Devil did not even make an appearance. Witches' confessions sometimes describe the sabbat as replicating the social distinctions of the mundane world, with rich witches lording it over the poor and male witches eating the food while female witches cooked it. Some **Lorraine** witches claimed to have found the sabbat so tedious that they paid the Devil a chicken every year to be excused from attending. In **France,** Spain and **Italy,** sabbats were often described as inversions of the Catholic Mass, with such features as the recitation of the Nicene Creed backwards and the consecration of a Host made of ordure. The "Black Mass" with the use of a woman's naked body as an altar, was not a feature of sabbats in the witch-hunting era, appearing only in the **Affair of the Poisons,** a setting influenced by ritual magic more than witchcraft.

The location and scale of sabbats varied. Some were described as close enough that poor witches walked there and back while the rich road in coaches. Others were far away, attracted many witches, and were generally described as being held only a few times a year. Certain places attracted reputations for holding sabbats. In Italy, a walnut tree near Benevento was frequently described as a meeting place by witches from all over the peninsula and Sicily. Germany had the Heuberg mountain in the south and the Blocksberg mountain in the north, **Norway** the Lyderhorn, and **Sweden** the imaginary Blokulla. It was most commonly believed that witches were physically transported to the sabbat, whether by flight or more mundane means, although some continued to uphold the possibility that they traveled their spiritually while their bodies remained at home.

The importance of the sabbat in the witch-hunt varied tremendously between areas. In some, such as **England, Denmark** or **Hungary,** it played no role or only a minor one. In territories such as Germany, where it was central, its most important function was as a mechanism for expanding the circle of suspects. Most large-scale witch-hunts involved the sabbat. A witch-hunt that began with the identification of an individual witch could quickly expand if the witch, with or without torture, could be induced to claim to have attended sabbats and seen other witches there. This was never certain proof, however, because some pointed out that the Devil could create illusions of people having attended. The sabbat was something of a double-edged sword for witch-hunters, as more extravagant claims made for it could cause a reaction that led people to doubt accused witches' guilt. This seems to have happened to Antonio de **Salazar Frias.**

REFERENCES: Michael Bailey. "The Medieval Concept of the Witches' Sabbath." *Exemplaria: A Journal of Theory in Medieval and Renaissance Studies* 8 (1996): 419–43; Robin Briggs. *Witches and Neighbors: The Social and Cultural Context of European Witchcraft.* New York: Penguin, 1996; Norman Cohn. *Europe's Inner Demons: The Demonization of Christians in Medieval Christendom.* Rev. ed. Chicago: University of Chicago Press, 2000; Carlo Ginzburg. *Ecstacies: Deciphering the Witches's Sabbath.* Trans. Raymond Rosenthal. New York: Pantheon Books, 1991; Brian P. Levack. *The Witch-Hunt in Early Modern Europe.* London and New York: Longman, 1987.

SALAZAR FRIAS, ALONZO DE (1564–1635)

More than any other single individual, the priest Alonzo de Salazar Frias was responsible for the **Spanish Inquisition's** halting of witch-burning in the seventeenth century. Salazar was the youngest and most junior of the three inquisitors assigned to the tribunal at Logroño in northern Spain. He was involved in the first case of the **Zugurramurdi** witches in 1609 and 1610, basically going along despite his doubts of the burning of witches who refused to confess. Following the auto-da-fé of the Zugurramurdi witches in November of 1610, Salazar became more and more obstructionist, opposing the two senior inquisitors, Xavier Becerra and Juan de Alvarado Valle, both of whom wanted to expand the Zugurramurdi and allied persecutions into a major witch-hunt, a Spanish parallel for the massive hunt Pierre de **Lancre** was carrying out on the French side of the border. On March 31, 1611, Salazar was ordered by the inquisitor general at the Inquisition's headquarters in Madrid, Bernardo de Sandoval y Rojas (d. 1618), to undertake a visitation to Zugurramurdi and other **Basque** villages in the Pyrenees. He was to promulgate an "Edict of Grace" a particular measure undertaken by the Inquisition to encourage confession by allowing repentant sinners to avoid inquisitorial punishments and confiscations. Salazar, a longtime associate of the inquisitor general, was specifically ordered to be the one to go on the visitation and was also ordered to go unaccompanied by Becerra or Valle, indicating that Salazar's skepticism was known and to some degree approved of by Sandoval and the Supreme Council of the Inquisition. Salazar left on May 22.

On his journey, Salazar painstakingly collected the witches' confessions that he had been asked to do (this was particularly tedious as Salazar did not speak Basque and usually would have required interpreters). Becerra and Valle attempted to block him from hearing the confessions of alleged witches who wished to retract their previous confessions of witchcraft, but orders from the Supreme Council prevented this. Salazar's investigation involved more than 1,800 interviews and was extraordinarily thorough—one of the most impressive in the entire history of the witch-hunt. Salazar noted contradictions between witches' confessions as to location and attendance at the **sabbat,** and grilled confessed witches on the location of sabbats and their means of transportation, often eliciting contradictions. Powders and ointments supposedly made by accused witches for nefarious purposes were shown to apothecaries; fed to **animals,** they were found to be harmless. Salazar also attempted to calm the areas through which he passed, not encouraging and usually ignoring charges and denunciations against suspected witches. He was particularly skeptical of the accounts of children, which were important in the Basque witch-hunt.

Salazar's position, as expressed in his series of reports to the inquisitor-general, was firm and unambiguous—there was no evidence that even a single act of witchcraft had been committed in the entire area. Salazar did not deny the power of the Devil, but thought that **Satan's** true intentions were to throw the area into chaos through dreams and delusions, rather than to hold sabbats and actually create witches. Transforming a human body or making a witch invisible were simply beyond the Devil's powers. Nor did Salazar deny the existence of witchcraft, whose reality was a matter of church teaching. He recommended, however, that proceedings in such cases be undertaken with great caution.

Salazar's return to Logroño on January 10, 1612, was followed by bitter and protracted struggles with Becerra and Valle, who had spent the intervening period hunting witches in the Logroño area. Becerra and Valle attempted to prevent Salazar from sending his reports until they themselves could compose their opinions and successfully requested that the Supreme Council not read the reports after they arrived until Becerra and Valle had had a chance to study

Salazar's notes and compose their responses. This dragged out for over two years, while the Supreme Council steadily lost patience with the goings-on at Logroño. In March 1614, the council summoned Salazar to Madrid, as well as requesting the papers held at Logroño and asking that two witches be sent to Madrid. The council's deliberations vindicated Salazar, and its letter to the Logroño Inquisition dispatched August 29 leaned heavily on his reports, enjoining caution on taking the confession of accused witches and forbidding further open discussion of witchcraft. Salazar's intervention also aborted a witch-hunt being carried out by the civil authorities in Vizcaya in 1616, where the cases of 289 witches had been prepared for sentencing. Salazar succeeded in having the proceedings transferred to the Inquisition's jurisdiction, where all cases were suspended. Shortly thereafter, the Basque country witch panic dwindled to almost nothing. Salazar's policy, reiterated in another report to the Supreme Council in 1623, effectively became the policy of the Spanish Inquisition as a whole, although because his reports were not published and remained unknown outside the Inquisition, they had no impact on intellectual and legal debates on witchcraft elsewhere in Europe. Salazar continued a highly successful career in the Inquisition, and was promoted to the Supreme Council in 1631.

REFERENCES: Gustav Henningsen. *The Witches' Advocate: Basque Witchcraft and the Spanish Inquisition (1609–1614)*. Reno: University of Nevada Press, 1980; William Monter. *Frontiers of Heresy: The Spanish Inquisition from the Basque Lands to Sicily*. Cambridge: Cambridge University Press, 1990.

SALEM WITCH TRIALS

The Salem Witch trials of 1692 are some of the best-known and best-documented of the entire history of the witch-hunt, definitely far better known than any other witch cases in Puritan **New England.** Yet they are highly untypical in many ways. One is chronological—the Salem cases occurred late in the witch-hunt, and outside Eastern Europe, were the last large scale witch-hunt in the entire period. They are also by far the largest witch-hunt in the history of New England, where most cases, such as that of Eunice **Cole,** involved individual witches or small groups. More than half of the witches executed in the history of New England were executed in the Salem trials.

Misconceptions about Salem start with the name—the cases did not originate in the modern town of Salem but in a small area that later split from Salem in 1752 to form the modern town of Danvers. In 1692, this area was Salem Village—a rural area attached to the commercial metropolis of Salem Town. Tensions between Salem Town and Salem Village would play an important role in the witch-hunt. Salem Village was divided into factions, one looking toward Salem Town and opposing the minister of Salem Village church, the controversial Samuel Parris (1653–1720), and the other led by the Putnam family of local landowners and supporting Parris. The Putnams would take the leading role in the witch-hunt.

Illustration titled "Witchcraft at Salem Village" depicting a girl lying on a courtroom floor. Undated engraving. © Bettmann/Corbis.

The Salem cases began with various forms of divination practiced by a number of Salem Village adolescent girls. This kind of **magic,** by which the girls attempted to answer such questions as the identity of their future husbands, was common in Puritan New England, but theologically suspect. In January, two of the participants, Parris's 9-year-old daughter Betty and his 11-year-old niece Abigail Williams began to show fits, convulsions and various sorts of odd behavior that could be explained easily as caused by demons or witches. (Laurie Winn Carlson has suggested that the bewitched people of Salem and some of their livestock were victims of an epidemic of encephalitis lethargica.) As was often the case, the first remedy to be tried was **countermagic,** the baking of a witch cake by Parris's Indian slaves, John Indian and **Tituba,** along with a neighbor woman, Mary Sibley. This proved unsuccessful and was denounced from the pulpit by Parris a few weeks later. The odd fits spread among the girls and a few young women of Salem, mostly those in households identified with the Putnam-Parris faction. Finally, three local women were held responsible for the fits and denounced as witches: Tituba, Sarah Osborne and Sarah Good. All were marginal members of the community. Sarah Good in particular was the kind of aggressive, hostile beggar always at risk for being thought a witch.

Good and Osborne refused to confess (although Good accused Osborne), but Tituba gave a highly detailed confession that served as the basis for a witch-hunt. Tituba spoke of large meetings of witches and attendants including well-dressed men and women, expanding the scope of the hunt beyond the poor and

The Witch House (Judge Corbin's home) in Salem, Massachusetts. © Library of Congress.

marginal and also beyond the local community of Salem Village. The leader of the accusing girls was now Ann Putnam, the 12-year-old daughter of Thomas Putnam Jr., head of the Putnam family. More witches were accused and imprisoned. Sarah Good's four-year-old daughter, Dorcas Good, was held in chains for several months. The increasing number of accused was straining the capacity of the jail to hold them, for they could not yet be tried. Massachusetts at this time was still suffering the aftereffects of the English Revolution of 1688, which had led to the abolishing of the colony's old government without as yet creating a new one. Nobody in Massachusetts had the authority to set up a court. This anomalous situation ended with the arrival of the colony's new governor, Sir William Phips, with a new charter on May 14. Phips hastily and somewhat irregularly set up a new Court of Oyer and Terminer to try the accused witches.

One June 2, the court began to sit. More than 150 persons were indicted before and during the sitting of the Court of Oyer and Terminer, but only 28 were brought to trial. The first witch to be sentenced to death and executed was Bridget Bishop on June 10. Bishop was a resident of Salem Town who had been accused of witchcraft 10 years before. She and her husband, now deceased, had also been in trouble with the law over domestic conflicts. Five more, including Sarah Good (Sarah Osborne had died in jail and, because Tituba had confessed, she was not tried) were convicted June 29 and executed

July 19. In all, 19 persons would be executed for witchcraft. A 20th, Giles Cory, whose wife Martha had been executed, refused to plead before the court and was tortured to death by the piling of heavy weights on his chest, a procedure known as *peine forte et dure* and required by English law for those refusing to plead. As was often the case in witch panics, later accused persons deviated from the stereotype of the witch as a marginal woman, and **accusations** extended well beyond Salem. The most distinguished person executed was the former Salem Village minister George Burroughs (1650–1692). Burroughs nearly saved himself by flawlessly reciting the Lord's Prayer on the scaffold, but the minister **Cotton Mather,** convinced of Burroughs's guilt, intervened to keep the **execution** moving forward. In all, more than a hundred New Englanders were accused of being witches during the panic, including some of the colony's leading citizens.

The only witches killed were those who refused to confess. This was highly unusual for a witch trial and somewhat paradoxical, because confession was one of the few unquestionable forms of legal evidence of witchcraft. To convict those that refused to confess, the court was forced to rely on more questionable forms of evidence. These included "spectral evidence"—the ability of the afflicted women to recognize the apparitions of the witches who tormented them (although no one was brought to trial or convicted solely on the basis of spectral evidence). Another form of evidence was the touch test; if an accused witch touched an afflicted person, whose sufferings then ceased, this was evidence of witchcraft. The reliance on the afflicted gave them great power.

What eventually ended the persecution was the intervention of leading Massachusetts ministers under the leadership of Cotton's father **Increase Mather,** all increasingly troubled by the witch court's reliance on spectral evidence. The last executions took place on September 22. During the summer, uneasiness with the girls' evidence and the **trial procedure** had been building, and Mather's sermon to a group of New England ministers on October 3 seems to have given New Englanders permission to oppose the trials openly. On October 12, Phips, Mather's ally, informed the Massachusetts Privy Council that he was forbidding all further imprisonments and trials for witchcraft. On October 29, he dissolved the court of Oyer and Terminer, and the whole affair wound down after that. Fourteen years later, on her admission into the Salem Village church, Anne Putnam admitted that, deluded by **Satan,** she had accused and caused the death of innocents. In 1711, the General Court of Massachusetts reversed the attainders against 22 witches and their families, and the governor of Massachusetts allocated 578 pounds and 12 shillings as compensation for the survivors.

REFERENCES: Paul Boyer and Stephen Nissenbaum. *Salem Possessed: The Social Origins of Witchcraft.* Cambridge and London: Harvard University Press, 1974; Elaine G. Breslaw. *Tituba, Reluctant Witch of Salem: Devilish Indians and Puritan Fantasies.* New York and London: New York University Press, 1996; Laurie Winn Carlson. *A Fever in Salem: A New Interpretation of the New England Witch Trials.* Chicago: Ivan R. Dee, 1999; Wendel D. Craker. "Spectral Evidence, Non-Spectral Acts of Witchcraft, and Confession at Salem in 1692." *Historical Journal* 40 (1997): 331–358; Frances Hill, ed. *The Salem Witch Trials Reader.* N.p.: Da Capo Press, 2000; Bernard Rosenthal. *Salem*

Story: Reading the Witch Trials of 1692. Cambridge: Cambridge University Press, 1993; Richard Weisman. *Witchcraft, Magic and Religion in 17th-Century Massachusetts.* Amherst: University of Massachusetts Press, 1984.

SATAN

The witch-hunts were a meeting ground for different conceptions of Satan, both learned and popular. In the early modern period, Satan and his innumerable demonic legions were perceived as a constant and very real presence. Despite their propensity to identify their respective theological opponents with the Devil, Protestant and Catholic thinkers differed little in their interpretation of his nature. Satan was a fallen angel whose principal interest in humanity was procuring the damnation of their souls. Although powerful far beyond any mortal, Satan was strictly held in check by God, acting only with God's permission and ultimately for his purposes. Whether or not the Devil retained truly supernatural power was a question for debate, but all agreed he had unmatched knowledge of the hidden and secret properties of natural things, which he could manipulate to serve his evil will. Satan was not remote and abstract but immediately and physically present. In fact, the Devil-obsessed Martin Luther (1483–1546) claimed that Satan sometimes took up residence in Luther's bowels (an association with a long medieval tradition). Satan was the lord of the world, save for that small part of it redeemed by Christ; non-Christians, such as Native Americans, were often identified as being under the Devil's sway and were frequently claimed to be witches in a general sense for this reason.

According to learned theologians and demonologists, Satan was the power with which witches made an agreement to exchange their souls in return for wealth and the power to do evil. This power was in no way intrinsic to the witch but was specifically given by Satan, sometimes along with a **familiar** demon, for Satan's own purposes. Although Satan may have taken delight in the pain and suffering caused by witches' *maleficia*, these things were separate from his main interest, the damnation of souls. For this reason learned demonologists argued that Satan might be behind the ostensibly benevolent **magic** of **cunning folk.** Satan was also the head of the vast conspiracy of witches to act against Christendom. Satan, or a subordinate demon, was present at the **sabbat** as its leader, often in **animal** form. Satan, and other demons, had **sex** with female witches (curiously, Satan was seldom depicted as sodomizing male witches), although most demonologists described intercourse with Satan as unpleasant because of the coldness of his penis and semen.

The Satan who appears in the confessions of unlearned witches has similarities and differences from the Satan of demonology. This Satan is evil but is more concerned with inflicting harm than damning souls. He sometimes beat or threatened witches if they failed to do sufficient evil. His power was more limited, though, and sometimes witches claimed that they had resisted the Devil's orders to do great harm, inflicting lesser harm instead. Satan is sometimes portrayed as foolish in witch's confessions or as giving long and tedious speeches at the sabbat. Sometimes the Satan described by ordinary people seems a different being entirely from the great Lord of Evil, perhaps a lesser demon. Some Scottish witches claimed that the Satan they met at the sabbat had admitted that his powers did not extend to **England.** Ordinary people, who did agree with the learned demonologists in seeing the Devil as a necessary force in the making of a witch, tended to ascribe more independent power to the witch.

To attack traditional notions of witchcraft meant to attack traditional and orthodox notions of Satan's power. Although the idea that Satan and other demons are in fact impotent to cause material harm (or benefit) goes back at least as far as Reginald **Scot** in the late sixteenth century, its classic statement an anti-witch-hunting writer occurs in *The Enchanted World* (1691) by Balthasar **Bekker.** Bekker claimed that the Devil was chained up in hell, unable to affect our world by making agreements with witches or any other ways. This marginalization of the Devil would proceed apace in the eighteenth-century Enlightenment and would eventually make the world of witches and witch-hunters seem bizarre and irrational.

REFERENCES: Robin Briggs. *Witches and Neighbors: The Social and Cultural Context of European Witchcraft*. New York: Penguin, 1996; Jeffrey Burton Russell. *Mephistopheles: The Devil in the Modern World*. Ithaca and London: Cornell University Press, 1986.

SATANIC PACT

Demonologists, witch-hunters, ordinary people and even accused witches often agreed that the source of a witch's powers was her agreement with **Satan.** The satanic pact is a unique feature of European witchcraft, distinguishing it from witchcraft beliefs that have been found in a huge range of cultures. The concept of the satanic pact existed for centuries in the Christian tradition before it became exclusively identified with ritual magicians and then with witches. Legends concerning the satanic pact, such as that of Theophilus, a clerk who made the pact and was then rescued by the Virgin Mary, first appear in Latin Christendom in the ninth century. The original stories of the pact usually did not restrict Satan's part of the exchange to the granting of **magical** powers, but also spoke of wealth, power, and sometimes access to the body of a desired one. Late antique and early medieval literature, however, did speak of magicians as gaining their powers through alliances with demons, whether or not they used the specific concept of a pact.

The idea of the pact and religious concepts of magical power were more tightly intertwined in the twelfth and thirteenth centuries, when both ritual magic and theological opposition to it were on the rise. Ritual magicians denied that they were in any way contracting with or subordinating themselves to demons, claiming instead that they were commanding them. Theologians replied that any dealings with demons, whether or not the magician explicitly made and exchange with devils, involved an "implicit pact," because demons would not grant powers (certainly not the power to perform ostensibly benevo-

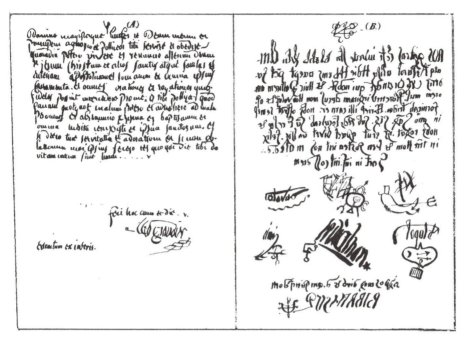

The pact with the infernal powers allegedly signed by Father Urbain Grandier and countersigned by Lucifer, Beelzebub, Satan, Elimi, Leviathan, Asteroth, and Baalbarith, Loudon, 1634. © Dover Pictorial Archive.

lent actions) in exchange for nothing. By contracting with the Devil, the witch or magician was giving him homage due only to God. They enabled the crime of magic to be defined as heresy or idolatry rather than *maleficia*. The mere exercise of any form of magic, claimed some, was proof of satanic pact. However, in the middle ages even theologians and inquisitors who denied that any human had the power to control demons, usually placed the Devil and the magician on a footing of some equality, at least temporarily, until the magician's inevitable death and damnation. This ascription of quasi-equality to magician and demon was seen in the witch-hunt period, during which most versions of the **Faust** legend show the learned male magician Faust commanding devils, although of course he lost everything at the end. By contrast, unlearned female witches were Satan's wretched slaves.

During the witch-hunt, the doctrine of the satanic pact was one way of shifting the definition of the witch away from evil actions, *maleficia* and toward the demonic source of a witch's powers. Any exercise of magical powers, whether or not it caused actual harm, was damnable as demonic. Demonologists who stressed the satanic pact almost invariably called for harsher persecution of **cunning folk** and ritual magicians, whose alliance with the forces of darkness was concealed by the outward benevolence or neutrality of their actions.

Descriptions of the process of making the satanic pact varied greatly. One common element was that it was not merely a prosaic legal contract, but involved paying homage and worshipping the Devil, as well as denying Christ, God and, in Catholic areas, the Virgin Mary and the saints. The witch's agreement to abandon baptism and Christian allegiance could be symbolized by trampling on a cross. The new agreement between the witch and her master was often sealed by the granting of the **Devil's mark** at this time. The homage the witch paid to the Devil was also often seen as particularly humiliating and degrading in comparison to the alliances made by the magician. The witch was often seen as submitting sexually to the Devil or **kissing** his buttocks or anus. The social and **gender** subordination of the typical witch was also reflected in the fact that ordinarily she received very little from the Devil in exchange for her soul and service. Satan or other demons gave witches not vast wealth, but often a single coin that turned to a pebble, leaves or dung. The one thing that the Devil did freely grant in return for service was the ability to perform *maleficia*, often giving the new witch instruments or potions for this purpose. Despite the ability to work revenge through *maleficia*, their performance was often seen merely as one more obligation of the witch to the Devil, and there are stories of witches who had failed to work sufficient harm being punished at the sabbat.

Although homage and adoration could constitute a pact by itself, formal written pacts were often claimed to exist. Johann Christoph **Haizmann,** who believed that he had made a satanic pact, attached great importance to the recovery of the physical documents, which he believed Satan had in his keeping. A written pact between the Devil and Urbain Grandier was also displayed in the **Loudun** case. Written pacts, including Haizmann's, were displayed as trophies of victory over Satan. As can be seen from Haizmann's experience, the satanic pact was never ironclad, although Satan would go to great lengths to keep witches on his side. Some witches told of how Satan prevented them from reconciling themselves with the Church but stories of God's overruling the satanic pact (in Catholic areas, this role was often played by the Virgin Mary) were common.

The theory of the satanic pact was found among demonologists of all religious persuasions, although those Reformed Protestants who conceived of the relation of the elect and God as a "covenant," showed a particular intellectual affinity for its reverse, the "diabolical covenant" between the witch and Satan. The full-fledged theory of the satanic pact was a product of learned demonology. It would be an error, however, to depict it as simply imposed on popular witchcraft beliefs. Belief in an agreement between the witch and Satan could also be found in popular culture. Accused witches sometimes recounted their agreements with Satan in uncoerced testimony. Satan, or a lesser devil, often appeared in these narratives in a moment of depression or despair and offered the witch the ability to gratify her modest desires or revenge herself on her enemies.

Although satanic pact per se did not play the central role in English witch-hunting, it did in the Continent and **Scotland,** the witch's relationship with the **familiar** functioned similarly. Agreements between witches and familiars could be solemnized by the familiar's drinking blood from the witch. The **witch's mark** for suckling the familiar was analogous to the Devil's mark as a sign of the relationship.

REFERENCES: Robin Briggs. *Witches and Neighbors: The Social and Cultural Context of European Witchcraft*. New York: Penguin, 1996; Brian P. Levack. *The Witch-Hunt in Early Modern Europe*. London and New York: Longman, 1987; Edward Peters. *The Magician, the Witch and the Law*. Philadelphia: University of Pennsylvania Press, 1978.

SATTLER, GOTTFRIED

The **Bavarian** witch judge Gottfried Sattler was executed for corruption in the early summer of 1613. This was the culmination of a long struggle in the Bavarian government between the faction supporting a vigorous persecution of witches, headed by the court chancellor, Johann Sigismund Wagnereckh, and the faction opposing it. Sattler had led a persecution in the town of Wemding, an enclave separated from the rest of Bavaria, from 1609 to 1611. Magistrates at the Bavarian capital of Munich opposed to irregular persecution began to investigate Sattler's persecution in the winter of 1611, bringing a number of accused witches to Munich to be questioned. What they found caused a top Bavarian administrator and persecution opponent, Bernhard Barth, to be sent to Wemding. The evidence Barth collected led the Bavarian Court Council to order Sattler's arrest. Investigation showed that Sattler had filed false reports and ordered arrests and **torture** to enrich himself by confiscating victims' property. In September 1612 Sattler experienced torture from the perspective of the victim. Sattler's guilt was clear, but the question of what to do with him led to a struggle between Wagnereckh and opponents of persecution. The law faculty of the University of Ingolstadt, Bavaria's leading university, when appealed to, approved Sattler's **execution.** Wagnereckh tried to get this commuted to exile in the Court Council, but an appeal to the duke of Bavaria, Maximilian I (r. 1597–1651), confirmed Sattler's death sentence.

Sattler's execution was a political defeat for Wagnereckh and the pro-persecution faction, slowing the pace of witch-hunting in Bavaria, and was an example that opponents of persecution in **Germany** frequently appealed to for years. Both the major German Jesuit writers who questioned persecution, Adam Tanner (1572–1632) and Friedrich von **Spee,** adduced the Sattler case as indisputable evidence that witches had been falsely condemned. The evidence Sattler gathered was employed again, however, in the revival of witch persecution in Wemding from 1629 to 1630.

REFERENCE: Wolfgang Behringer. *Witchcraft Persecutions in Bavaria: Popular Magic, Religious Zealotry, and Reason of State in Early Modern Europe*. Trans. J. C. Grayson and David Lederer. Cambridge: Cambridge University Press, 1997.

SAWYER, ELIZABETH

The case of Elizabeth Sawyer in 1621 was among the most well publicized in early-seventeenth-century **England.** The judicial records of her case have been lost, so the main source on the case is the pamphlet by the Reverend Henry Goodcole, which appeared shortly after Sawyer's **execution,** *The Wonderfull*

Discoverie of Elizabeth Sawyer, a Witch (1621). Goodcole was the chaplain of the jail at Newgate, where Sawyer, a Middlesex felon, was being held pending execution. Like many Newgate chaplains, Goodcole supplemented his income with sensational pamphlets based on criminals' confessions. *The Wonderfull Discoverie* was the last in the series of Elizabethan and Jacobean witchcraft pamphlets; the next pamphlet would be published 22 years later, in the vastly different circumstances of the English Civil War.

Goodcole's pamphlet described how Sawyer, who had been suspected to be a witch for a long time, was convicted of the murder of Agnes Ratcleife, who had struck one of Sawyer's sows that was eating her soap. Ratcleife on her deathbed supposedly had charged Sawyer with her murder. The trial included a search for the **witch's mark,** found near Sawyer's anus. The jury of women that found the mark, overcoming resistance by Sawyer that Goodcole did not detail, included two women simply pulled in off the street by court officials. According to Goodcole, the evidence of the witch's mark had a strong effect in swinging the jury to conviction.

The second half of the pamphlet is Sawyer's confession in the form of a dialogue with Goodcole. Goodcole placed great emphasis on Sawyer's penchant for oaths and blasphemies, which provided the Devil with his first access to her. Interestingly, Goodcole allowed Sawyer's denial of having murdered Ratcleife, as well as her admission of another murder of which she had been acquitted, to go uncontradicted. The principal interest of the confession is Sawyer's description of her relationship with the Devil, who had come to her three times a week in the form of a dog, sometimes black and sometimes white. The Devil is described in terms very like a **familiar,** and the pamphlet represents a transitional stage in the English idea of a familiar spirit, as familiars were becoming more diabolical. Because Goodcole, a clergyman, was possibly more familiar than Sawyer with the idea of **Satan** as the cause of witchcraft—he claims his first question to Sawyer was how she came to have familiarity with the Devil—it is not clear how much of this came from Sawyer herself.

Such was the interest in Sawyer and witches that the same year saw the production of a play based loosely on Goodcole's account written collaboratively by William Rowley (1585?–1642?), John Ford (1586–1640?) and Thomas Dekker (1572?–1632), titled *The Witch of Edmonton.*

REFERENCES: Marion Gibson, ed. *Early Modern Witches: Witchcraft Cases in Contemporary Writing.* London and New York: Routledge, 2000; John Ford, Thomas Dekker and William Rowley. *The Witch of Edmonton.* Ed. Peter Corbin and Douglas Sedge. Manchester and New York: Manchester University Press, 1999.

SCIENCE

The age of the witch-hunts was also the age of the scientific revolution, the series of advances in natural knowledge culminating in the establishment of modern science. The relation between the two phenomena was not one of witchcraft and demonology being driven out by science, but a series of attempts to employ science to understand the action of demons and witches. All natural philosophers and demonologists agreed that whatever a witch did by virtue of witchcraft was not performed by her, but by **Satan** or other demons, who were spirits interacting with the material world. Demons had to work through natural causes, as true miracles were reserved for God. Therefore, demons and witches and what they could accomplish were a legitimate topic of enquiry for natural philosophers. Natural philosophers studied questions such as how witches created storms and whether copulation between witches and demons could produce offspring. Demons, particularly Satan, were often portrayed as complete masters of all scientific knowledge, which they employed to carry out their evil deeds. The dominant tradition of natural philosophy in the Renaissance, Aristotelianism, could be interpreted as denying witchcraft and demonic activity, as in the work of the radical philosopher Pietro Pomponazzi (1462–1525), or as supporting it, as in the work of the **physician** and botanist Andrea Cesalpino (1519–1603). Cesalpino's *Aristotelian Investigation of Demons* (1580) was meant to refute the claims of Pomponazzi and others that Aristotle and Aristotelian philosophy offered no support for belief in demons and witches. Cesalpino drew much of his evidence from Heinrich **Kramer's** *Malleus Maleficarum* (1486).

The natural philosopher Francis Bacon (1561–1626) included a call for gathering a history of witchcraft as part of his influential "Baconian" program for the systematic study of nature. Some scholars have attempted to link the scientific revolution and the witch-hunts as complementary parts of a masculine attack on women and the earth, attempting to reduce both to the level of resources, but such connections remain speculative. Witchcraft could touch the lives of early modern scientists directly, as when the great astronomer Johannes Kepler (1571–1630) had to defend his mother Katharina **Kepler** from charges of witchcraft. William Harvey (1578–1657), the scientist who first described the circulation of blood, helped direct a group of **midwives** and surgeons in examining the bodies of accused **Lancashire** witches for **witch's marks** in 1634. The marks were asserted to be natural, and the accused witches were acquitted. The story of Harvey having dissected a witch's **familiar,** a toad, to prove it was nothing more than natural rests on a now-lost manuscript dating from the late 1680s, long after Harvey's death. Interestingly, the recounter of the story, Sir James Long (1613–1692), who was a magistrate, minor natural historian and fellow of the Royal Society for the Advancement of Natural Knowledge, actually used it to criticize Harvey and defend belief in witchcraft, pointing out that familiar spirits used **animals** as their vessels, and dissection could prove nothing relevant to the case.

Contrary to the claims of many older historians, science also had little to do with the decline of large-scale witch persecution in the late seventeenth century. Many natural philosophers, regardless of what they thought of persecution, believed that denying the possibility of witchcraft would lead to materialism and atheism because all were based on a common denial of the power of spirits. Strict insistence on mechanical causation, supported by some early modern scientists, might have led to a denial of the powers of immaterial demons and therefore of witches, but in practice it was seldom applied to the question. One exception was the work of Balthasar **Bekker,** a follower of the philosopher René Descartes (1596–1650). Bekker's *The Enchanted World* (1691) argued that the Devil was bound in hell and unable to affect the natural world. *The Enchanted World* came out nearly a century after the Dutch Republic had actually ceased persecuting witches, so its impact on practices was minimal.

The debate on witchcraft most closely involving early modern science took place in late-seventeenth-century **England,** a time and place of rapid scientific advance in the age of Isaac Newton and Robert Boyle. Joseph **Glanvill,** one of the many English thinkers who rejected mechanical Cartesianism for its materialism, applied Baconian empiricism to the witch question, collecting witch stories with specific names, dates and places to demonstrate empirically the existence and powers of witches and thus the existence of supernatural power. Glanvill's and More's collaborators in the investigation of the powers of witches included such distinguished scientists and fellows of the Royal Society as the Platonic philosopher Henry More, the natural historian Robert Plot (1540–1596), the anatomist Thomas Willis (1621–1675) and Robert Boyle (1627–1691). The relation of the new science to witchcraft could be interpreted in more than one way, however. John **Webster,** author of the skeptical reply to Glanvill, *The Displaying of Supposed Witchcraft* (1677) explained the supposed deeds of witches as natural rather than demonic **magic** credited the experimental natural philosophy of the recently founded Royal Society for combating witchcraft belief. Webster's book was actually licensed to appear in print by the Royal Society, the premier British (and European) scientific organization.. Another skeptic, John **Wagstaffe** (1633–1677), was more conservative in his natural philosophy. In *The Question of Witchcraft Debated* (1669), he asserted that human ignorance of nature was so great that attributing events to demonic rather than natural causes could never be intellectually justified. Despite the radicalism of his anti-demonological position, Wagstaffe's natural philosophy was conservative and Aristotelian. Whatever the actual relation of the scientific revolution and the decline of witch-hunting, by the early eighteenth century they were often claimed to be linked. Both were appealed to as examples of the progress of modern thought in the Enlightenment.

REFERENCES: Stuart Clark. *Thinking with Demons: The Idea of Witchcraft in Early Modern Europe.* Oxford: Clarendon Press, 1997; Cathy Gere. "William Harvey's Weak Experiment: The Archeology of an Anecdote." *History Workshop Journal* 51 (Spring 2001): 19–36; James Sharpe. *Instruments of Darkness: Witchcraft in Early Modern England.* Philadelphia: University of Pennsylvania Press, 1996; Walter Stephens. *Demon Lovers: Witchcraft, Sex, and the Crisis of Belief.* Chicago and London: University of Chicago Press, 2002.

SCOT, REGINALD (1538–1599)

Reginald Scot was the first major English demonological writer and one of the most thoroughgoing skeptics of conventional belief in witchcraft to emerge in the early modern period. Scot was a country gentleman from a leading family of the county of Kent in southeastern **England.** He attended Oxford University without taking a degree and served as a justice of the peace and member of Parliament. His *Discoverie of Witchcraft* (1584) was inspired by his voluminous reading, both in Classical and Continental demonological sources and in accounts of recent English trials, and possibly by his own experience of a witch prosecution in the nearby city of Rochester. Among his continental influences, Heinrich **Kramer's** *Malleus Maleficarum* (1486) and Jean **Bodin's** *On the Demonmania of Sorcerors* (1580) were the chief targets of his attacks, whereas much of his argument drew on Johann **Weyer's** *Of the Tricks of Demons* (1563).

His argument was directed not only at intellectual defenders of witch-hunting, but at popular English witch beliefs as well. Scot drew a picture similar to that of modern social historians of English witchcraft such as Keith Thomas of the witch as an old woman, marginal to her community, who had been denied charity and becomes the focus of resentment after the sudden and unexplained death of a child or of livestock. Scot shared with mainstream demonological writers a rather hostile opinion of the poor old women who made up the bulk of accused witches and believed that in many cases they deserved judicial punishment, but for him they were foolish, malicious and Catholic rather than diabolical.

What makes Scot more radical in his denial of traditional witchcraft belief than Weyer—indeed, more radical than any witchcraft writer before Balthasar **Bekker** at the close of the seventeenth century—is his assertion that there is no supernatural power wielded by humans or demons—by anyone but God. Witchcraft, insofar as it exists at all, is illusionistic, a "cozening art." Any apparently supernatural feat accomplished by a witch can only be done by trickery. (Such was Scot's interest in cozening that he includes a large section, with illustrations, detailing various sleight-of-hand "magic" tricks involving coins and balls and other small objects, having nothing to do with witchcraft.) Both witches and learned magicians were essentially cheats, and Scot demonstrated his contempt for high **magic** by recounting how he had repeated alleged demonic invocations without a devil appearing.

Scot's position was fundamentally religious, albeit rather eccentric (David Wooton has recently argued for Scot's connection to an underground heretical group, the Family of Love) and should not be confused with modern secularism. His robust Protestantism led him to identify "cozening" witchcraft with the Catholicism he despised, for Catholic priests made similar claims to perform miracles through chants and rituals. Yet he also attacked such characteristic doctrines of many Protestant demonologists as the demonic pact. Scot, drawing heavily from Weyer, devotes much of *Discoverie of Witchcraft* to demonstrating that the alleged biblical authorities for witchcraft belief are based on mistranslation of the Hebrew and misunderstanding of the context of such stories as that of the Witch of Endor. His most radical religious position, however, was the denial of any power to affect the physical world on the part of any spirit whatsoever. He did not deny that devils existed and interacted with humans but claimed that they did this in a purely incorporeal way, through temptation and despair.

Scot's influence outside the British Isles was limited by the fact that he wrote in English, and not, as did British writers seeking an international audience, in Latin. His work was translated into Dutch and published in 1609 and 1638, but this was after the end of the Dutch witch-hunt. In England, Scot's work played a marginal role in the demonological controversies of the Elizabethan and early Stuart periods. The witch-hunting opponent Samuel Harsnett (1561–1631) admired the *Discoverie,* and **James VI,** in his *Daemonologie* (1697), blamed Scot for England's allegedly poor record in rooting out witchcraft, which compared so badly with the king's native **Scotland.** (Although James accused Weyer of actually being a witch, he charged Scot only with being a Sadducee, who denied the power of spirits and the immortality of the soul.) The story that James, on acceding to the English throne as James I in 1603, ordered every copy of *Discoverie of Witchcraft* to be burned by the public hangman appears to be without foundation. Scot's work came into its own in England in the second half of the seventeenth century, being reprinted in 1651, 1654 and 1665. The witchcraft skeptics Thomas **Ady** and John **Webster** praised Scot, seeing him as a founder of their position, whereas defenders of witch belief Henry More (1614–1687) and Joseph **Glanvill** attacked Scot's contributions.

REFERENCES: James Sharpe. *Instruments of Darkness: Witchcraft in Early Modern England.* Philadelphia: University of Pennsylvania Press, 1996; Robert H. West. *Reginald Scot and Renaissance Writings on Witchcraft.* Boston: Twayne, 1984; David Wooton. "Reginald Scot/Abraham Fleming/The Family of Love." In *Languages of Witchcraft: Narrative, Ideology and Meaning in Early Modern Culture,* ed. Stuart Clark, 119–138. New York: St. Martin's Press, 2001.

SCOTLAND, WITCH-HUNTING IN

Although serious witch-hunting got underway in Scotland only in the late sixteenth century, the country saw waves of intense persecution alternating with longer periods of relative quiescence into the late seventeenth century. The total number of executed witches in the period was probably between 1,000 and 1,500, a large number for a relatively small kingdom, although not on the scale of the great German persecutions. About 2,000 other people were tried for witchcraft, either being acquitted or receiving a lesser penalty. Women comprised about 85 percent of accused witches in Scotland, somewhat lower than the English percentage but typical for Europe generally.

Scotland had a typical late medieval political trial in 1479, when several witches were executed for having conspired to kill King James III (r. 1460–1488) and another in 1532, when Janet Douglas, Lady Glamis, was burned for attempting to assassinate James V (r. 1513–1542) by witchcraft and poison. There were scattered early-sixteenth-century persecutions carried out under canon law, but the beginning of organized large scale witch-persecution in Scotland can be traced to 1563. That year saw the passage of the Witchcraft Act by the Scottish Parliament, which made witchcraft a criminal offense to be punished by the civil authorities. The state in Scotland was taking over a number of legal responsibilities from the Church courts, in turmoil due to the Scottish Protestant Reformation. The act contrasts with the narrow law passed in **England** the same year by prescribing death for a broad range of **magic** offenses including "witchcraft, sorcery, and necromancy" as well as fraudulent magic and even consulting a magic-user—a clause if put into effect would have resulted in the execution of much of the Scottish population.

The passage of the act was followed by an upswing in persecutions. The largest was a witch-hunt carried out in 1568 in Angus and the Mearns by the Protestant clergyman John Erskine of Dun, with 40 people accused of being witches. Poor survival of records makes it impossible to know how many, if any, were executed. Although some of the Calvinist clergy called for more vigorous state action against witches, witchcraft still had low priority compared with other criminal or moral offenses. The persecutions that were carried out were mostly based on allegations of *maleficia* rather than **satanic pact** or **sabbat** attendance. One particularly dramatic case was the hanging of Sir William **Stewart** in 1568 for witchcraft and treason. In 1573, the Scottish privy council declared witchcraft a *crimen exceptum*, exempting witches from certain pardons and witch judges from the requirement to return confiscated goods. The failure of the broad approach of the 1563 act was acknowledged the same year by the Assembly of the Kirk, which prescribed that those who consulted witches and cunning folk be made to publicly repent in the church, wearing sackcloth.

What radically changed the situation, eventually leading to Scotland's unenviable reputation as a citadel of witch-hunting, were a series of persecutions beginning in 1590 in different parts of the Scottish lowlands. The most famous, although not the first, of these cases was the **North Berwick witch-hunt** of 1590–93, particularly noteworthy for the role played by King **James VI.** James had recently returned from a trip to **Denmark** to fetch his wife Anne of Denmark (1574–1619). James believed that his political enemy, Francis Stewart Hepburn, fifth earl of Bothwell (d. 1624), had used witches both to stir up storms on his voyaging and to threaten his life directly. He took a leading role in the actual carrying out of the persecution of the dangerous North Berwick witches, and thereafter made witch-hunting a major governmental priority. Laws were passed to better enable witch persecution. For example, women, ordinarily barred from testifying in criminal cases, were now allowed to do so in witchcraft cases. The Privy Council commissioned a group of lawyers, ministers and Edinburgh burghers to investigate pending and future witch cases with the use of **torture** and to send these cases to local courts. The resulting persecutions from 1590 to 1597 were among the most severe in Scottish history.

Ironically, in 1597, the same year James published *Daemonologia*, he took action to rein in the witch trials, which seemed to be spreading beyond the control of the central government. James's decree revoked all commissions to investigate witchcraft charges and reserved all witch cases to the central government. Along with treason, witchcraft was now the only crime that could not be judged by the lords of "regalities"—areas of Scotland where the lord was recognized as standing in place of the king in most judicial matters. This centralization was immediately followed by the end of the witch-hunt and an enormous drop in the number of witch cases, although not quite to zero. The next major wave of witch persecutions was not until after James's death, in the period 1628 to 1631, when about 350 witches were tried, as part of a general crackdown on crime by the Scottish Privy Council.

Popular Scottish witch beliefs changed during the witch-hunt, but mostly conformed to the European standard. In the sixteenth century, witchcraft and magic was frequently associated with the fairies or *sithean,* who commanded the belief of many Scottish people. The late sixteenth century saw an ongoing effort by the authorities of church and state to interpret the fairies or ghosts that witches dealt with as **Satan** and his demons. The **Devil's mark,** usually found on the neck, shoulder or arm, started appearing in Scottish witch trials in the late sixteenth century. Belief in sabbats and gatherings of witches was more common and central to the image of the witch than it was in England, but Scottish sabbats, unlike some on the European continent, only rarely featured **sex** with the Devil, **infanticide** and cannibalism. The **satanic pact** seldom appeared in Scottish witch trials until the mid–seventeenth century. When it did appear, it was virtually always in cases of female witches and associated with sex with the Devil.

The typical accused witch in Scotland resembled the typical accused witch elsewhere in Europe, a poor, old woman whose reputation for witchcraft and quarrelsomeness may have been building for decades before she was actually accused. Most male witches were husbands or relatives of female witches. The most widespread type of test to determine whether an accused person was really a witch in Scotland was "witch pricking," the jab of a needle at a point in the body suspected of being a Devil's mark, insensitive to pain. The witch-prickers were almost a professional body in Scotland, some even being brought to towns in the north of England to be employed in witch-hunts there. Because witch-prickers were often paid per witch identified, it was in their interest to spread witch-panics. Torture was part of Scottish witchcraft investigation as it was part of criminal investigation in general, although it is difficult to tell from surviving references how widespread its actual use was. Various instruments, although not the rack, were used, and torture through extended sleep deprivation, known as "waking the witch," was so common as to be treated as routine. **Execution** was by burning, usually preceded by strangulation.

The Scottish state and the Scottish Calvinist Kirk were usually allies in the fight against witchcraft, although Kirk leaders sometimes grumbled at state authorities' lukewarm attitudes. Most charges of witchcraft were first brought before Kirk sessions before being taken to the royal courts. The areas of Scotland that saw significant persecution were those where the central government and the Kirk were strongest, the lowland East of the country. There was little in the Highlands where clan organization was stronger than Kirk or State.

The next major Scottish persecution occurred in 1649, after the execution of King Charles I by the English Parliamentarians. Scotland was at that time ruled by the strongly Calvinist Covenanters, who had a program of moral and spiritual renewal through the vigorous enforcement of morality through law. Witchcraft was particularly important to many Covenanters. The importance of the covenant between God and the elect in Scottish Calvinist theology and of the National Covenant of 1638 and Solemn League and Covenant of 1643 in Scottish Presbyterian politics made the witch's inverted covenant with the Devil particularly horrifying, and the rise of Covenanters is associated with the rise of the satanic pact in witch trials. The witch was the ultimate outsider in the godly national society the Covenanters hoped to build. The year 1649 saw the Scottish Parliament and Privy Council grant hundreds of commissions for local trials.

This persecution tapered off severely in 1650, as the Scottish Parliament took measures to reestablish central control over witch-hunting. What nearly ended persecution entirely was the English occupation of Scotland beginning in 1651. The English disliked the extreme Covenanters and were also disgusted at Scottish judicial methods, including the torture of accused witches. Many witches held pending trial were freed by English authorities. In the later years of the English occupation, however, beginning around 1657, the number of trials began to build up again. There were at least 40 executions in 1658 and 1659, when the trials were again temporarily brought to a halt by the collapse of the Scottish judicial system in the chaos of the last years of the Interregnum.

The persecutions of the late 1650s were a foretaste of the last great Scottish witch-hunt, which followed the Restoration of the monarchy and Scottish legal separation from England in 1660. Between April 1661 and the fall of 1662 there were more than six hundred cases and three hundred executions as the restored Scottish judicial and religious system was free to operate without English control. The campaign began with the denunciation of more than two hundred witches in the areas of Midlothian and East Lothian between April and December 1661. Most of the convictions and executions were carried out by local courts and magistrates acting under commissions given by the Scottish Privy Council to try witches in their area, a form of legal procedure that leaves little documentary trace. The numbers of cases and executions was unquestionably great and provoked a backlash. In April 1662, largely provoked by the witch cases, the Scottish Privy Council proclaimed torture illegal without the express order of the council, although this did not mean its actual use ceased. Witch persecution was also discredited by a scandal in which several witch-prickers, including the celebrated John Kincaid, were revealed to have used fraud to demonstrate the existence of devil's marks. (Two, John Dickson and "Mr. Paterson," were also revealed to be women in disguise.)

Members of the Scottish judiciary, most notably the advocate general, Sir George MacKenzie (1636–1691), a justice deputy during the witch-hunt, were increasingly skeptical of specific witchcraft charges, although no one in Scotland expressed skepticism of witchcraft itself. This attitude was expressed in MacKenzie's influential legal treatise, *The Laws and Customes of Scotland in Matters Criminal* (1678). After the great witch-hunt, magistrates tended to quash witch cases, which were more difficult to bring anyway without sanctioned torture. Although large-scale witch persecution was over in Scotland, local persecutions and even small-scale hunts continued for the rest of the seventeenth century. The execution of seven witches at **Paisley** in 1697 was the last multiple execution for witchcraft in western Europe. The last execution by due process of law in Scotland occurred in Inverness in 1706. Accused witches were killed by a mob at Pittenweem in 1704, and a local court acting illegally without the permission of the central government executed an old Highland woman named Janet Horne as a witch in 1727. This was the last execution of a witch in Scotland.

The Scottish witchcraft act of 1563 was repealed along with the English witchcraft law of 1604 by the Parliament of Great Britain (Scotland and England had merged their parliaments in 1707 by the act of Union) in 1736. Although serious witch persecution in Scotland had ended years before, not all greeted this measure as one of enlightenment. Its English origin, and the fact that the repeal of the Scottish law was basically an afterthought in a measure addressing English law and English concerns, contributed to national resentment. The association of English dominance with toleration of witches in Scottish Presbyterian culture had roots going back to the 1650s. Scotland's increasingly abstract stand against witches had become an aspect of Scottish national identity, increasingly threatened by English dominance of "Great Britain." The repeal's only identifiable opponent in the House of Commons was a Scottish member of Parliament, James Erskine, Lord Grange.

Curiously, for a country with a high rate of witch persecution, Scotland produced little significant demonology. Even the pamphlet literature is limited, and much of our knowledge of Scottish witchcraft comes from pamphlets produced in London for the English market, which tended to exoticize Scottish witches and witch-hunters. Other than James, Scotland's demonologists include John **Bell** and George **Sinclair;** Sinclair's *Satan's Invisible World Discovered* (1685) went through many editions into the eighteenth century.

REFERENCES: George F. Black. "A Calendar of Cases of Witchcraft in Scotland, 1510–1727." *Bulletin of the New York Public Library* 41 (1937): 811–847, 917–936; 42 (1938): 34–74; Ian Bostridge. *Witchcraft and Its Transformations, c. 1650–c. 1750.* Oxford: Clarendon Press, 1997; Julian Goodare. "Women and the Witch-Hunt in Scotland." *Social History* 23 (1998): 288–308; Christina Larner. *Enemies of God: The Witch-Hunt in Scotland.* London: Chatto and Windus, 1981; Christina Larner, *Witchcraft and Religion: The Politics of Popular Belief.* Oxford: Blackwell, 1984; Brian P. Levack. "The Great Scottish Witch Hunt of 1661–1662." *Journal of British Studies* 20 (1980): 90–108; P. G. Maxwell-Stuart. *Satan's Conspiracy: Magic and Witchcraft in Sixteenth-Century Scotland* East Lothian, Scotland: Tuckwell Press, 2001; W. N. Neill. "The Professional Pricker and His Test for Witchcraft." *Scottish Historical Review* 19 (1922): 205–213; Lawrence Normand and Gareth Roberts, eds. *Witchcraft in Early Modern Scotland: James VI's Demonology and the North Berwick Witches.* Exeter, England: University of Exeter Press, 2000.

SEX

Witchcraft was strongly linked with sex, whether actual or theoretical. Sex between humans and demons played a large role in both demonological theory and actual witch trials. It was the ultimate form of physical interaction between the witch and the Devil, whether **Satan** himself or a lesser demon. This immediately brought up the problem of how a material human body could have sex with an immaterial spirit. This question had been answered, ever since Christian theologians in the Middle Ages had elaborated a theory of angels and devils, by claiming that devils, while ultimately spirits, could create a "body" out of compacted air. The artificial nature of the demonic body was particularly useful intellectually in explaining how women could conceive by demons. The standard explanation, going back to Thomas Aquinas (1224?–1274), is that the demon first formed and inhabited a female body as a succubus, had intercourse with a human male, and preserved the semen. It then formed and inhabited a male body as an incubus, ejaculating the preserved semen into a human woman's vagina. Thus, the actual father of the woman's child was a human male. Despite this fact, many argued that the children conceived by demonic intercourse were more likely to become witches, and particularly powerful ones. Toward the end of the witch-hunt, Lodovico Maria **Sinistrari** tried to distinguish between incubi-succubi and demons proper, but his ideas were out of the mainstream and unpublished.

The Devil making love to a witch. From Ulrich Molitor's *Von den Unholden und Hexen*, Constance, 1489. © Dover Pictorial Archive.

Demonic sex played a smaller role in spontaneous confessions by witches than in demonological theory, and when it appeared it was often described in banal terms. Sex was frequently associated with the **satanic pact,** as a way for the Devil to express his new power over the witch, and the witch her subordination. On the popular level, the relationship of spiritual devils to carnal intercourse was not a problem because devils were thought of as material anyway.

One vexed question is whether sexual intercourse with demons brought pleasure to women (no one seems to have questioned that it brought pleasure to men) and whether it was lesser or greater than sex with a human male. The tendency as debate developed was to place more emphasis on the painful and degrading nature of demonic intercourse. (Perhaps demonologists and magistrates feared that emphasizing pleasure made being a witch too attractive to women. There are some cases in which women described the Devil as a better lover than their husbands, although the reverse was more common.) Descriptions of the Devil's penis grew more and more grotesque, emphasizing its incredible size, bizarre conformation and the icy coldness of both penis and ejaculate. Pierre de **Lancre** claimed that the Devil's penis was three-pronged, to simultaneously enter the vagina, anus, and mouth. Sex between devils and female witches was more often conceptualized in bestial terms, with the Devil taking animal form. Children were also more frequently charged with having had sex with the Devil.

The general pattern was for human-demon sex to play less of a role the farther north in Europe the witch-hunt extended (although **Scotland,** where sex between female witches and the Devil frequently accompanied the satanic pact, is an exception). In **England,** demonic sex figured only rarely either in demonological theory or in trial records, with the exception of the Matthew **Hopkins** persecutions. The relationship between the witch and the **familiar,** with the familiar nursing at the **witch's mark,** fulfilled some of the same functions as demonic sexuality in establishing the physical connection of witch and demon.

One curious aspect of human-demon sex as envisioned in early modern Europe was that it was hardly ever same-sex. Heinrich **Kramer,** in fact, emphasized the horror demons felt at the unnatural vice of "sodomy." Although there are scattered incidents of men confessing to having been sodomized by the Devil, it never became a common theme in witch-hunting.

Not all sex engaged in or affected by witchcraft was demonic. Depictions of the **sabbat** often featured promiscuous sex, whether human-demon or human-human. Female witches were sometimes described as promiscuous, and in some regions witchcraft and sexual promiscuity were strongly linked in popular stereotype. Witches were portrayed as having power over sexuality, whether in afflicting men with impotence, a common form of *maleficia*, or in performing love magic, a service of **cunning** women and "professional" witches.

REFERENCES: Robin Briggs. *Witches and Neighbors: The Social and Cultural Context of European Witchcraft*. New York: Penguin, 1996; Walter Stephens. *Demon Lovers: Witchcraft, Sex, and the Crisis of Belief*. Chicago and London: University of Chicago Press, 2002.

SHORE, JANE (1445?–1527?)

Of obscure background, Jane Shore became the mistress of Edward IV, king of England (r. 1461–1483), around 1470. Following Edward's death and the ascent to the Protectorship of his brother, Richard, duke of Gloucester (the future King Richard III), Shore became the mistress of one of the realm's leading aristocrats, William Hastings, Lord Hastings (1430?–1483). At a council meeting Friday, June 13, 1483, Richard (r. 1483–1485), afraid of the potential threat to his rule that Hastings and those associated with the late king represented, accused the king's widow, Elizabeth Woodville (1437?–1492), and Shore of having wasted his body through their sorcery. To demonstrate the fact, Richard displayed his withered left arm, which all present knew had been thus since birth. Hastings, accused of being the leader of the plot, was executed that day. Shore was imprisoned and her property confiscated, but in the end there was no evidence supporting a credible charge of sorcery; instead she was condemned as a harlot to carry a lighted taper through the streets of London—the same penalty another accused sorceress, Eleanor **Cobham,** had suffered 40 years earlier. This seems to have been the end of Shore's legal troubles, but Richard's usurpation of the throne later that month was accompanied by his **accusations** that Woodville and her mother had used sorcery to get Edward IV to marry Woodville.

REFERENCE: Desmond Seward. *Richard III: England's Black Legend*. Rev. ed. London: Penguin, 1997).

SICILY

See Ladies from Outside; Spanish Inquisition.

SINCLAIR, GEORGE (D. 1696)

The Scottish Presbyterian engineer George Sinclair wrote a popular demonology, *Satan's Invisible World Discovered* (1685), which was closely modeled on Joseph **Glanvill's** *Saducismus Triumphatus*. Sinclair fulsomely praised Glanvill's work, sometimes to the point of plagiarism. His own work consisted of a collection of narratives, mostly Scottish, designed to demonstrate the existence of a supernatural world and discourage atheism. Witch stories, including the scandalous story of the Edinburgh siblings Jane and Thomas Weir, executed as witches and incestuous lovers in 1670, comprised about a third of the narratives. The remainder included several stories of ghosts or omens. Some stories were derived from printed sources, but others came directly from Sinclair or his friends and correspondents. (Nonwitch stories included the tale of the Drummer of Tedworth, taken directly from Glanvill.) *Satan's Invisible World Discovered* went through many editions in the eighteenth century, in original, expanded and abridged forms, and was popular among Scottish peasants. It also influenced eighteenth- and nineteenth-century Scottish writers including Robert Burns (1759–1796), Sir Walter Scott (1771–1832) and Robert Louis Stevenson (1850–1894).

REFERENCE: George Sinclair. *Satan's Invisible World Discovered* (1685). A facsimile reproduction with an Introduction by Clement O. Parsons. Gainesville, Fla.: Scholar's Facsimiles & Reprints, 1969.

SINISTRARI, LODOVICO MARIA (1622–1701)

The Franciscan philosopher and consultant to the **Roman Inquisition** Lodovico Maria Sinstrari was the author of *Demoniality*, one of the last major works of demonology in the Scholastic tradition. Its subject was **sex** between humans and spiritual beings. Drawing heavily on Francesco Maria **Guazzo,** Sinistrari endorsed the reality of human-demon sex at the **sabbat,** but that was not his main subject. Most of *Demoniality* is devoted to beings who are not demons, but incubi—a unusual distinction to make. Sinistrari's incubi are beings made of a finer substance than humanity, who occupy a variety of moral positions and can be either saved or damned. Because they are material as well as spiritual, they can have offspring with humans. (Unlike other writers on demonic sexuality, Sinistrari did not believe that incubi must collect semen from male human males to impregnate female human.) He combined Scholastic arguments with those from early modern **science,** frequently referring to recent discoveries made with the microscope. Sinistrari believed that intercourse with actual demons was the greatest of all sins, but intercourse with incubi was in itself a fairly minor one. Nevertheless, if a human involved believed that he or she was having intercourse with a demon, then that person had committed a sin as great as actual demonic intercourse. His work, completed toward the end of his life, was not published until 1875.

REFERENCE: Lodovico Maria Sinistrari. *Demoniality.* Trans. into English from the Latin with Introduction and notes by Montague Summers. London: Fortune Press, n.d.

SOCIAL CLASS

People ranging from popes to poor old women were accused of practicing sorcery and witchcraft, and social class often influenced the pattern of **accusations** and alleged bewitchments. Generally speaking, witchcraft moved down the social ladder in the late medieval and early modern period, beginning with the trials of social leaders such as the **Templar**s, bishop **Guichard of Troyes** and the prosperous landowner Alice **Kyteler** in the early fourteenth century; from the early fifteenth century on, witch-hunts focused more on the poor and socially marginal. The stereotypical witch from the height of the witch-hunt, of course, was a poor old woman, on the economic and social fringes of a village community. Usually accused of having bewitched her social superiors, prosperous villagers, she lacked social defenses better socially placed accused witches could invoke, and thus fell victim to witch-hunting. Many cases did indeed follow this pattern, but many did not.

At the highest social levels were the political sorcery trials, beginning in the late Middle Ages and continuing through the witch-hunt period, with perhaps the most spectacular example being the **Affair of the Poisons** in **France.** These affairs often involved collaboration between high members of the aristocracy or even royalty with lower-class **magical** experts. When magical attempts against monarchs were actually tried, it was the lower-class magicians and witches who were actually condemned to die, while the nobles usually received lighter, although sometimes still harsh, penalties, such as exile or house arrest. Class mobility was a contributing factor to political sorcery accusations, and those who had risen from obscurity to powerful positions at court, usually through the favor of a monarch, were subject to sorcery accusations from members of the established nobility, resentful of newcomers' hold on political power.

A far more common pattern in witch-hunting was for the witch-hunters to come from a higher social class, of bureaucrats and judicial officials, than either the suspected witches or the alleged victims. For much of the sixteenth and seventeenth centuries, various classes in European society had a similar range of beliefs about witchcraft, although the literate were more influenced by demonological texts and developed a more complex picture of it. The sixteenth century, a time of great monetary inflation, was marked by particularly severe class conflict. Peasant rebellion caused real fear among the middle and upper classes in many parts of Europe, given such spectacular episodes as the German Peasant's revolt of 1525 or the French peasant rebellions of the late sixteenth century. Even descriptions of the **sabbat** by poor accused witches reflected their hatred of the rich, as they expressed their resentment of the favor enjoyed by the rich at the sabbat and suggested that rich witches were more likely than poor ones to seek the ruin of the harvest, because this would enable them to manipulate the prices while the poor, witch or not, starved.

A few witch-hunts, such as the **Zaubererjackl trials** of young beggars in Salzburg, can be seen as simple class warfare by the rich and the civic authorities against the poor, but this was exceptional. Another pattern was for witch-hunts to be seen as part of an overall process of social discipline, whereby the manners and mores of the poor were seen as susceptible to improvement by the determined intervention of the authorities of church and state. Campaigns to discipline and reform the peasantry and urban lower classes were often associated with the Protestant Reformation, as in **Scotland,** or the Catholic Reformation, as in **Bavaria.** Witchcraft was associated with the moral backwardness of the poor by many witch-hunters on both sides of the **confessional** line. The poor were viewed as likely to turn to the Devil to better their miserable position, rather than accepting that lot in life to which it had pleased God to assign them. Ironically, by the eighteenth century, not witchcraft but the belief in witchcraft was seen as characteristic of the uncivilized poor, and the resources of church and state were mobilized to fight this.

Despite the existence of the doctrine of "magisterial immunity," which proclaimed that the investigating magistrates were immune from magical attacks by the witches or the Devil, members of the upper classes in European society could not always hold themselves aloof from the actual actions of witches. On many occasions, members of the elite thought themselves, or even more commonly their children, victims. The wrath of a noble who thought his family victimized against an accused witch from the lower classes was nearly impossible to withstand, as in the case of the **Flower witches** executed for killing the child of Francis Manners, earl of Rutland (1578–1632).

Class divisions within the lower classes could lead to witch accusations. Often, initiative for a witch-hunt came from villagers, who sought out the help of magistrates in purging their community of witches. Sometimes vigilante committees of villagers, as in the area around Trier in the great persecution of 1587–1594, acted on their own authority without even seeking the involvement of magistrates. Such committees might become a vehicle for the relatively poor to express their resentment of the more prosperous members of the community by accusing them, and they were eventually suppressed by the authorities. Witch accusations among peasants or ordinary people in the towns could go either up or down the class scale, as relatively well-off people accused servants, beggars or laborers and their families of bewitching them, or as the very poor ascribed the relative prosperity of the village elite to witchcraft. Poor people's demands for charity, particularly when refused by the more prosperous members of the community, could lead to charges of witchcraft from those annoyed by such demands. In many cases, the witch is described as making the **satanic pact** in exchange for a small amount of money from the Devil, an amount that would have real worth only for the very poor. The relatively wealthy accused witches were always better able to defend themselves than the poor.

Most witch-hunts remained restricted to the lower classes, but in the larger hunts, particularly great German witch-hunts such as those of **Bamberg** and **Würzburg,** members of the ruling class could be accused, tried and executed for witchcraft. This was particularly true as the hunt went on and the circle of accusations, usually beginning with lower class people, expanded. Expansion of a witch-hunt to include people from the elite, however, usually signaled its approaching end, as accused witches from the upper classes and their families were better able to manipulate political authority, whether from within or without the area of the witch-hunt, than were the poor. One example is the effort by the family of Dorothea Flockhlin of Bamberg to involve the government of the Holy Roman Empire in preventing her **execution,** which, although it failed to save her, brought the witch-hunt to an end.

REFERENCES: Robin Briggs. *Witches and Neighbors: The Social and Cultural Context of European Witchcraft.* New York: Penguin, 1996; Brian P. Levack. *The Witch-Hunt in Early Modern Europe.* London and New York: Longman, 1987; Geoffrey Scarre. *Witchcraft and Magic in Sixteenth- and Seventeenth-Century Europe.* London: Macmillan Education, 1987.

SOUTHERN NETHERLANDS, WITCH-HUNTING IN

Witch-hunting began relatively late in the southern Netherlands. The earliest demonologists were theologians, including Denis the Carthusian (1402–1471), Hendrik van Gorcum (d. 1431), and Jacob van Hoogstratten, who actually spent most of his career in **Germany.** None accepted the full witch stereotype as it had developed in the fifteenth century, with the **sabbat** and witch flight. Instead, they were concerned with combating superstition and countermagic, viewed as relying on an implicit pact with demons. A more current demonology was espoused by the writers on criminal law, Philips Wielant (1439–1519) and Joost de Damhouder (1507–1581). De Damhouder's *Criminal Practice* (1554) contained an extensive discussion of witchcraft and **magic,** drawing from modern sources including Heinrich **Kramer** and Paulus **Grillandus.** Invoking Exodus 22:18, de Damhouder called for the extirpation of witches.

Campaigns against witches in the southern Netherlands in the late sixteenth century were related to the war between the king of Spain, the sovereign of the Netherlands, and mostly Protestant rebels. The success of the rebellion led to the formation of the independent Dutch Republic in the **northern Netherlands.** The Spanish and their allies in the south promoted aggressive Counter-Reformation Catholicism calling for a reformed Catholic church and purified society. Eliminating witchcraft was part of this vision of a regenerated Catholic Netherlands. In 1570, the duke of Alva (1507–1582), Spanish commander in the Netherlands, issued a Decree on Criminal Justice promising harsher treatment of witches and **cunning folk.** King Philip II (1527–1598) issued a decree against witchcraft, defined in satanic terms, on July 20, 1592. In 1606, the archdukes Albert (1559–1621) and Isabella (1561–1633), who ruled the southern Netherlands as viceroys for Spain, issued another decree.

The first wave of Spanish Netherlands witch-hunts lasted from about 1580 to 1630, followed by a smaller wave from 1650 to 1680. Spanish Netherlands witches were tried in lay rather than ecclesiastical courts, and the judicial system offered a great deal of scope for initiative on the part of local officials. The Council of State at Brussels did sometimes intervene, but it did not exercise the oversight of the French Parlements. The French witch-pricker Jean Minard was principally active in the Spanish Netherlands, but it was the Parlement of Paris, not the Spanish Netherlands authorities, that brought his career to an end. Another who took advantage of the lack of central oversight was Charles van de Camere, the castellan of Bouchain, a district in Hainault. Van de Camere carried on a large witch-hunt in the 1610s, bringing 163 cases from 1610 to 1619. Slightly under half were executed, and only one acquitted—the rest were banished or put into custody. A marked feature of the Bouchain witch-hunt is the presence of child witches; 34 children were tried and 16 executed.

There were great regional variations in Spanish Netherlands witch-hunting. The diocese of Arras was largely free of witch trials, despite bordering on Bouchain. Urban witch trials were more common in the Spanish Netherlands than elsewhere in Europe, and Douai and Dunkerk were centers of urban witch-hunting, but the largest commercial city in the territory, Antwerp, was almost entirely free of it. The south of the Spanish Netherlands was largely French in language and culture, and its witch-hunting history was greatly influenced by other Francophone areas. One of the most spectacular incidents in Netherlands witch-hunting, the Lille **possession** cases of 1613, built on the recent French case of Louis **Gaufridi.** Three nuns from a recently founded Brigidine community were exorcised (one of the exorcists had worked on the Gaufridi case) and revealed they had been bewitched by two nuns in the community, Marie de Sains and Simone Dourlet. De Sains and Dourlet were convicted as witches and burned. The case became well known because of the work of Jean Le Normant, author of *True and Memorable History of the Exorcism of Three Possessed Girls in Flanders* (1623), which contains elaborate descriptions of sabbats presided over by Gaufridi and birthday celebrations for the Antichrist. The possessions were controversial, and some Spanish Netherlands Catholic priests were openly skeptical. However, possession cases continued through midcentury.

Most peasant **accusations** were based on *maleficia*, but the crime was judicially defined in terms of the classical demonological concepts of sabbat, **satanic pact** and human-demon **sex.** (In the southern, French-speaking area of the Spanish Netherlands, it was common for female witches to be accused of having given a pubic hair to the Devil.)

The most important Spanish Netherlands demonologist was the Jesuit Martin **del Rio,** but his audience was principally the learned all over Catholic Europe. His fellow Jesuit Johannes David was the author of a more practical work, the Dutch-language *Sentinel for Guarding Against False Cunning Men and Witches* (1602). David's book recalled the late medieval southern Netherlands demonologists in its emphasis on eschewing countermagic and recourse to **cunning folk.**

REFERENCES: Robin Briggs, *Witches and Neighbors: The Social and Cultural Context of European Witchcraft.* New York: Penguin, 1996; Stuart Clark. *Thinking with Demons: The Idea of Witchcraft in Early Modern Europe.* Oxford: Clarendon Press, 1997; Marijke Gijswit-Hofstra and Willem Frijhoff, eds. *Witchcraft in the Netherlands from the Fourteenth to the Twentieth Century.* Rotterdam: Universitaire Pers Rotterdam, 1991; Robert Muchembled. "Satanic Myths and Cultural Realities." In *Early Modern European Witchcraft: Centres and Peripheries,* ed. Bengt Ankarloo and Gustav Henningsen, 139–160. Oxford: Clarendon Press, 1990; Robert Muchembled. "The Witches of the Cambresis: The Acculturation of the Rural World in the Sixteenth and Seventeenth Centuries." In *Religion and the People, 800–1700,* ed. James Obelkevich, 221–276. Chapel Hill: University of North Carolina Press, 1979.

SPAIN

See Basques; Spanish Inquisition.

SPANISH AMERICA, WITCH-HUNTING IN

Witch-hunting in Spain's New World colonies was a complicated affair drawing on several cultural traditions. These included the witch beliefs the Spanish brought with them from Europe, the belief of many Spanish clergy and officials that the New World gods were actually demons and their cults were witchcraft, the witchcraft beliefs of the native peoples and the beliefs of enslaved Africans and their descendants.

The linkage between the worship of American demon-gods and the European witch cult occurs early in New World Spanish writing. The Franciscan missionary Francisco Andres de Olmos's (d. 1571) *Treatise on Superstitions and Sorceries,* written in the Mexican Indian language of Nahuatl, was closely modeled on the demonology of Martin de **Castañega's** 1529 *Treatise on Superstition and Witchcraft.* De Olmos sought to convince Spanish and Native Americans to treat diabolism principally as deliberate obedience to and worship of devils, rather than *maleficia*—a program with many European parallels. Spanish writers described Native American rites and the use of natural substances for ritual purposes in ways paralleling the **sabbat** and the ointments and potions of European witches. European demonologists outside Spain shared in this conception of American idolatry and European witchcraft as a single system. Pierre de **Lancre** claimed that the spread of Christianity in the New World, by freeing many souls from the Devil's clutches, had forced demons to come to Europe, thus creating a rise in European witchcraft.

The tendency of the Spanish to view Native American religion as demonic, rather than as a perversion of fundamentally good religious impulses, grew with the frustration of missionaries with the stubbornness, as they saw it, with which the Native Americans clung to their religious practices, even while paying lip service to the conquerors' religion. The Spanish often treated Native American men—and even more often women—who claimed healing powers as witches and blamed them for the slow pace of conversions. The Pueblo revolt in northern New Spain in 1680, the most damaging Indian revolt that Spain suffered, was widely blamed on Native American witchcraft.

The identification of Native Americans with witches and sorcerers was a day-to-day reality in the culturally mixed communities of the Spanish Empire. Spanish settlers confessing to witchcraft or demon-worship often identified Native Americans as the Devil's tempters and recruiters or claimed that **Satan** appeared in Native American guise. The superior knowledge of the properties of American plants Native Americans possessed could also appear demonic, and Spanish householders sometimes used their Indian servants as **magical** advisers. The Chichimec Indians of Mexico, who were not entirely subdued, were particularly identified with magical and demonic power. Persecution of witches was more severe and lasted longer in the Andean regions than in Mexico, partly because of the greater resistance of the population to the Spaniards' Christianity.

Francisco de Goya y Lucientes, *Witches' Sabbath: The He-Goat*, 1798. © Giraudon/Art Resource, New York.

Belief in wielders of supernatural power for harm had indigenous roots in Native American cultures, although their evil was not identified with demons or viewed as a threat to society as a whole. Native American witchcraft was also not so strongly identified with women. In the sixteenth century, many Native Americans identified the Devil of Christianity with the evil gods of their own pantheons and saw him as an equally appropriate recipient of sacrifices, sometimes even performed in Christian churches. This type of behavior was characteristic of the Spanish frontier more than central areas of Spanish colonization, which were much more intensively Christianized. Another frontier culture where diabolism and claims to witchery were common was the area of New Spain dominated by cattle herding, particularly the far north. The poor

Spaniards, Indians, mulattos and mestizos of this area, such as Luis de **Ribera,** sometimes claimed to have allied with the Devil for worldly success, sexual conquests or magical powers to control their herds.

Crimes of sorcery and witchcraft theoretically were handled by two court systems after the establishment of the **Spanish Inquisition** in Mexico and Peru in 1571, the Spanish Inquisition and a separate body referred to as the Indian Inquisition, established because of claims that the Indians were too recently Christianized to be under the jurisdiction of the Inquisition proper. (Before 1571, bishops had been given the powers of inquisitors, but the Inquisition had not existed as a separate organization.) The two institutions had a considerable overlap in personnel, however, and the distinction was not always clear in practice. As in Spain, the Inquisition took an interest in cases of magic and witchcraft but usually punished not with **execution** but the infliction of penances. There are even cases in which slaves who confessed to making a **satanic pact** or to other witchlike activity in the hope of receiving better treatment form the Inquisition than they received from their masters. By the late seventeenth century, the period in which the Mexican **Querétaro possession cases** took place, the Inquisition usually treated demonic or witch cases as caused by fraud, superstition or mental derangement rather than by supernatural powers. Much of its interest shifted to the "superstitious" misuse of the rites of the church or sacred objects by folk healers. The idea of the demonic witch as a threat to society as a whole, however, had been internalized by many Native American cultures, and some Native American communities experienced socially divisive witch-hunts even after the disappearance of the Spanish Empire.

A similar situation held in the Spanish colony in the Philippines, although local bishop's courts rather than the Inquisition held sway over magical offenses. A woman was tried for witchcraft there as late as 1808.

REFERENCES: Greg Bankoff. "Devils, Familiars, and Spaniards: Spheres of Power and the Supernatural in the World of Seberina Candelaria and Her Village in Early 19th-Century Philippines." *Journal of Social History* 33 (1999): 37–56; Ruth Behar. "The Visions of a Guachichil Witch in 1599: A Window on the Subjugation of Mexico's Hunter-Gatherers." *Ethnohistory* 34 (1987): 115–138; Fernando Cervantes. *The Devil in the New World: The Impact of Diabolism in New Spain.* New Haven and London: Yale University Press, 1994; Amos Megged. "Magic, Popular Medicine and Gender in Seventeenth-Century Mexico: The Case of Isabel de Montoya." *Social History* 19 (1994): 189–207; Irene Silverblatt. *Moon, Sun, and Witches: Gender Ideologies and Class in Inca and Colonial Peru.* Princeton: Princeton University Press, 1987; Marc Simmons. *Witchcraft in the Southwest: Spanish and Indian Supernaturalism on the Rio Grande.* Flagstaff, Ariz.: Northland Press, 1974; Merry E. Wiesner-Hanks, *Christianity and Sexuality in the Early Modern World: Regulating Desire, Reforming Practice.* London and New York: Routledge, 2000.

SPANISH INQUISITION

Although the Spanish Inquisition never saw witch-hunting as its main mission, focusing instead on heretics and secret Jews and Muslims, witches fell under its jurisdiction. The Inquisition's lack of enthusiasm for witch-hunting

Scene of the Inquisition c.1794, oil on panel. © The Art Archive/Academia BB AA S Fernando Madrid/The Art Archive.

was one reason Spain saw relatively little of it. What there was remained concentrated along the northern border, particularly among the **Basque** population of the Pyrenees mountains. The Inquisition investigated witches specifically as heretics, so devil worship and attendance at **sabbats** were more important than simple *maleficia*. The first documented trial by the Inquisition was that of Narbona Dorcal of the village of Cenorbe in 1498. A trickle of trials continued in the early sixteenth century, mostly of individuals rather than large-scale hunts (although large-scale hunts did take place in the Basque country). Despite its relative insignificance compared with other crimes, the Inquisition dealt with, witchcraft provoked much debate, because many inquisitors questioned witches' ability to **fly** to the sabbat. In 1526, a committee of inquisitors ruled, by a six to four vote, that witches did indeed fly. At the same time they issued a set of guidelines for witch persecution. These guidelines treated witches more gently than other malefactors; witches did not have their property confiscated by the tribunal, nor were they automatically sentenced to death on a second offense. Inquisition policy toward suspected witches remained oriented toward procuring repentance and the next recorded burning of a witch by the Inquisition did not occur until 1535. The Inquisition of Catalonia executed several witches in Barcelona in 1549, but the heads of the Inquisition in Madrid moved in to stop the effort before it grew into a full-scale witch panic. For the next 50 years, there were few cases of witchcraft or even illicit **magic** dealt with by inquisitorial tribunals. The Inquisition of Navarre stepped in when the royal government was conducting a witch-hunt in the Basque country from 1575 to 1577; most of the accused witches were simply let go by the Inquisition.

What temporarily got the Inquisition back into large-scale witch-hunting was the case of the **Zugurramurdi** witches in 1609, caused by the influence of the severe French persecution occurring north of the Pyrenees under Pierre de **Lancre,** an enthusiastically witch-hunting local inquisitor named Juan de Valle Alvarado and lax supervision by inquisitorial leadership preoccupied with the upcoming expulsion of the Morisco (Muslim-descended) population of Aragon. Six witches were burned in an auto-de-fé in Logroño in 1610. The expense of holding the witches, of the trial and of auto-de-fé, as well as the irregularities of the procedure, seem to have soured the Inquisition on witch trials in general. An inquisitor who became skeptical of the witch charges that developed out of the Zugurramurdi hunt, Alonzo de Salazar Frias, also turned the Inquisition away from witch cases. This was not entirely a boon for suspected witches. Witch-hunting continued in seventeenth-century Spain, carried out by local and municipal secular governments, who killed and tortured many more witches and lacked the sophistication, procedural safeguards and moderation in the use of **torture** characteristic of the Inquisition. Some accused witches actually appealed from secular justice to the Inquisition, which continued to claim jurisdiction over witch cases. Those witches who appealed to the Inquisition usually received clemency. Inquisitorial mercy did not mean denial of the existence of witchcraft, and the Inquisition continued to handle occasional witchcraft cases in the eighteenth century. In 1791, long after the witch-hunt had ended elsewhere in western Europe, the Inquisition in Barcelona heard a case against a woman accused of the classic witchcraft crimes of **satanic pact** and attendance at the sabbat.

REFERENCES: Gustav Henningsen. *The Witches' Advocate: Basque Witchcraft and the Spanish Inquisition (1609–1614)*. Reno: University of Nevada Press, 1980; William Monter. *Frontiers of Heresy: The Spanish Inquisition from the Basque Lands to Sicily*. Cambridge: Cambridge University Press, 1990.

SPANISH NETHERLANDS

See Southern Netherlands.

SPEE, FRIEDRICH VON (1591–1635)

The German Jesuit and professor Friedrich von Spee was an influential witch-hunting opponent who limited his attacks to trial irregularities and abuses, rather than attacking the reality of witchcraft. Spee's opposition to witch-hunting had been shaped by his own experience in such centers of persecution as **Würzburg** and Mainz, as a hearer of the confessions of incarcerated witches, and as an observer of trials in the Rhineland. The result of his experience and his reading of predecessors such as Adam Tanner (1572–1632) was the anonymous Latin *Warning to Prosecutors* (1631).

Spee attacked many aspects of the witch-hunt. He believed that ordinary quarrels caused many witchcraft **accusations**. He denounced the irregular use of **torture** and claimed that torture itself was a demonic invention and that no credit could be given to confessions produced by it. Spee repeated, or perhaps invented, the boast of a witch-hunter that given sufficient torture, he could make the pope confess to being a witch. He analyzed the phenomenon by which a tortured witch accused others, who then were tortured to elicit further accusations. Spee claimed, incorrectly, that once this mechanism got started, it could only be stopped by the intervention of a ruler. He criticized the frequent posing of "no-win" dilemmas, as when a woman held for witchcraft showing fear of torture was viewed as having a bad conscience, whereas one showing confidence was hypocritically feigning innocence, and both were presumed witches. Spee generally thought little of the German magistrate class, even suggesting that some were witches, serving **Satan** by protecting the guilty and harming the innocent. He attacked magistrates arrogating to themselves quasi-divine functions and charged them with encouraging persecution to enrich themselves by confiscating the goods of executed witches. He also criticized ignorant and venal priests, who harassed accused witches into confessing.

Spee accepted many of the theories behind the witch-hunt. He agreed that witches did exist and should be punished. He agreed that women's weaknesses—their mental instability, their proneness to delusion and perjury—made them more likely to be accused as witches. His acceptance of the basic principles of witch-hunting, however, may have made him a more effective critic than anti-witch-hunt radicals such as Johann **Weyer** and Reginald **Scot.** There is no question of the popularity of *Warning to Prosecutors*, which went through sixteen editions in the next hundred years and was translated into many European languages including French, Dutch and Polish. There were several German translations, beginning with one in 1632. Spee influenced both Protestants and Catholics—indeed, *Warning to Prosecutors* was so religiously neutral that some suspected its author was a Protestant. (Spee's authorship did not become public knowledge until Christian **Thomasius** revealed it in *Of the Crime of Magic* in 1701.) Subsequent witch-hunt opponents who drew on Spee included Thomasius, the Lutheran Johannes Meyfarht and the Italian Catholic Gironymo Tartarrotti. Spee also directly influenced his friend Johann Philipp von Schonborn (1605–1673), who became bishop of Würzburg in 1642 and archbishop and elector of Mainz in 1647, the same year he issued a decree ending witch-hunts in the electoral territories.

REFERENCES: Julio Caro Baroja. *The World of the Witches.* Trans. O. N. V. Glendinning. Chicago: University of Chicago Press, 1965; Stuart Clark. *Thinking with Demons: The Idea of Witchcraft in Early Modern Europe.* Oxford: Clarendon Press, 1997; H. C. Erik Midelfort. *Witch-Hunting in Southwestern Germany, 1562–1684.* Stanford: Stanford University Press, 1972.

SPINA, BARTOLOMMEO (1475?–1546)

Along with Gianfrancesco **Pico della Mirandola,** who he admired, and his teacher Silvestro **Mazzolini,** the Dominican inquisitor, Bartolommeo Spina, papal official and theologian, was a leading defender of the reality of witchcraft in Renaissance **Italy.** His principal work on witchcraft, *Inquiry on Witches* (1523) was produced in answer to the skeptic Gianfrancesco **Ponzinibio.** Spina accepted *maleficia,* **infanticide, sex** between witches and demons, **magisterial immunity,** the **sabbat** and witches' **flying.** He pointed out that **Satan** had carried Christ to the top of the mountain in the Gospels and claimed that witch flight and the Gospel stood or fell together. Spina tried to reconcile his acceptance of these beliefs about witches with the ***Canon Episcopi*** by distinguishing between the actions of witches and those phenomena that the *Canon* treated. He denied the reality of **transformations,** although he included material about the illusory transformation of witches into cats that harmed children. Spina was disturbed by the growth of Aristotelian naturalism and materialism in the Italian intellectual world and tried to use the evidence of witches' confessions to demonstrate the existence of the soul and spirits, demonic and angelic. His work placed much weight on the intellectual authority of theologians, which he saw as a principal support of witchcraft belief. Although *Inquiry on Witches* is in the form of a Scholastic treatise employing formal argument, it also contains much anecdotal and folkloristic material, some of it drawn from Spina's own experience as an inquisitor and persecutor of witches.

REFERENCE: Walter Stephens. *Demon Lovers: Witchcraft, Sex, and the Crisis of Belief.* Chicago and London: University of Chicago Press, 2002.

STERZINGER, FERDINAND (1721–1786)

On October 13, 1766, 10 years after the last **execution** of a witch in **Bavaria,** a Bavarian priest of the Theatine order, Ferdinand Sterzinger, gave a talk on witchcraft before the Bavarian Academy of Sciences. In a speech that had been secretly approved by leaders of the Bavarian government, Sterzinger treated witch belief as a laughable superstition, while not quite asserting witches to be nonexistent and generally hedging enough to avoid offending church authorities. His speech, swiftly issued in printed form, touched off the Bavarian "witchcraft war," the last major public debate on the subject in early modern Europe.

Sterzinger's work made a great impression throughout the German world, winning approval from champions of the Enlightenment. Many conservative Catholics were not pleased and denounced Sterzinger in sermons and written tracts. (The total number of publications in the "witchcraft war" exceeded 40, mostly anonymous.) South German peasants, most of whom held traditional witchcraft beliefs, also protested. The most important of Sterzinger's early literary opponents was the Augustinian Agnellus Merz, a fellow member of the Bavarian Academy, whose *Urtheil ohne Vorurtheil* was published anonymously in November. Although indicating his doubts over superstitions like the stories of witch flight, Merz argued that the **Bible,** the sayings of the Church Fathers, the traditions of the Church, and the evidence of thousands of confessions all spoke undeniably of the reality of witchcraft. By denying the power of the

Devil, Merz feared, Sterzinger aided those who would deny the power of God. Because the Church had condemned many witches, he also claimed that Sterzinger's arguments posed enormous dangers to its authority. Another opponent from the ranks of the Bavarian Academy, the Benedictine Angelus Marz, was affiliated with the Abbey of Scheyern, which sold thousands of little lead crosses that were supposed to have sovereign efficacy against witches and spells. Afraid for his abbey's commerce, Marz recounted many miracles worked by the "little crosses of Scheyern." Merz and Marz were only two of many champions of witchcraft belief who emerged in the controversy, several of whom expressed regret for the ending of witch trials and hopes for their revival.

Sterzinger's subsequent writings on witchcraft concentrated on the struggle with the learned Merz, focusing on such well-worn issues as the meanings of the Hebrew words the Bible used for witches and the powers of the Devil. Sterzinger's allies, including Catholic priests and members of religious orders, attacked Marz with satires of ignorant and greedy monks.

The witchcraft war was wrapped up in a key issue of Bavarian politics, the possibility of easing the state's fiscal crisis through direct taxation of Bavaria's wealthy abbeys and monasteries. One year after Sterzinger's talk, Councillor Peter von Osterwald gave a talk before the academy, agreeing with Sterzinger and indicating his own belief that the witches killed in the witch-hunt had all been innocent. Osterwald was a leader in the state's campaign to seize monastic wealth, and his association of the monasteries with superstitious and cruel witch-belief was part of the struggle. In the aftermath of the witchcraft war, Sterzinger was appointed director of the historical section of the Bavarian Academy, and several of his allies also received rewards from the government. Sterzinger became a leading opponent of popular superstition in the Holy Roman Empire, and his death was mourned throughout **Germany.**

REFERENCE: Wolfgang Behringer. *Witchcraft Persecutions in Bavaria: Popular Magic, Religious Zealotry, and Reason of State in Early Modern Europe.* Trans. J. C. Grayson and David Lederer. Cambridge: Cambridge University Press, 1997.

STEWART, SIR WILLIAM (D. 1568)

Sir William Stewart, Lyon king of arms, was arrested, tried and executed for witchcraft and treason in the summer of 1568, becoming one of the most powerful victims of the witch-hunt in **Scotland.** The charges against Stewart included calling up a spirit called Obirion, possibly a version of Oberon, king of the fairies, whose picture he inscribed on a lead tablet with the Latin words *servitus pulcher,* "handsome male slave." These summonings, which involved other powerful Scotsmen including the advocate Sir Archibald Napier, were to divine the future course of Scottish politics, then rather uncertain. Stewart used both high learned **magic** and popular divination techniques. In a ceremony involving several others, he used written rituals attributed to **Heinrich Cornelius Agrippa** to summon spirits in an area of Holyrood Park called "Arthur's Seat" outside Edinburgh known as a place for invoking the fairies or *sithean.* He also used the common technique of divination using a sieve and shears, in which his expertise was such that others came to consult him. Stewart did not rely solely on his own divinatory ability, but consulted female witches of considerably lower **social class.** He was convinced from his divinations and consultations that the regent, James, earl of Moray (1531–1570), would die. He also believed that Mary, queen of Scots (1542–1587), who had been forced to abdicate the previous year, would escape from the castle where she was being held, rule Scotland again, and eventually marry and bear the children of Stewart himself. Stewart was executed by hanging rather than burning, indicating that the crime for which he was punished was treason rather than witchcraft.

REFERENCE: P. G. Maxwell-Stuart.*Satan's Conspiracy: Magic and Witchcraft in Sixteenth-Century Scotland.* East Lothian, Scotland: Tuckwell Press, 2001.

STOECKHLIN, CHONRAD

Chonrad Stoeckhlin was both the first accuser of a witch and one of the first two people executed as a witch in a major late-sixteenth-century witch-hunt in the village of Oberstdorf in southwestern **Germany.** A horse herder, Stoeckhlin had a reputation as a **cunning** man and **magical** healer based on his association with the "phantoms of the night," a group of spirits who supposedly flew through the area at night, accompanied by Stoeckhlin. In the summer of 1586, a time when the area was suffering terribly with storms, harvest failure and plague, Stoeckhlin accused a local 60-year-old woman, Anna Enzensbergerin, of being a witch, basing his charge on what he had allegedly been informed by the phantoms. Enzensbergerin fled Oberstdorf, confirming Stoeckhlin's charge in the minds of many villagers. On returning to the village, Enzensbergerin was arrested by the local authorities. They then sent word of their discovery of a witch to the local ruler, the prince-bishop of Augsburg, Marquard vom Berg (bishop, 1576–1591). The government agreed with the local authorities that Enzensbergerin be imprisoned but added that Stoeckhlin should be interrogated as well. The government also began seeking to hire a torturer.

In late July, Stoeckhlin was arrested and taken to a castle, where he was closely questioned by officials of the bishop's government. They refused to believe that the "night phantoms" of which he spoke were good spirits, identifying the gatherings of Stoeckhlin and his phantoms with the witch's **sabbat.** Stoeckhlin at first resisted the questionings and **torture** designed to make him admit the true diabolic nature of the gatherings in which he had participated. He did reaccuse Enzensbergerin and added another local woman, Barbara Luzin, the 80-year-old stepsister of his deceased mother, Ursula Schlederin. Enzensbergerin and Luzin in turn claimed that they had learned their witchcraft from Schlederin. Other accused witches claimed that they had seen Stoeckhlin at the sabbat held at the top of the Heuberg, a mountain in Swabia traditionally associated with witches. As the son of a witch, Stoeckhlin was now even more suspect to the bishop's officials. In December, after severe torture by the notorious Master of Biberach, Hans **Vollmair,** Stoeckhlin confessed to being a witch, to having been taught witchcraft by his mother and to having attended the sabbats on the Heuberg. He also accused a number of other local women, and a few men, as witches. On January 23, 1587, Chonrad Stoeckhlin and a woman named Grethe were burned as witches. Anna Enzensbergerin had already died in captivity, probably as the result of torture. She was condemned as a witch, and her body thrown on the flames. Barbara Luzin was also burned as a witch. In all, the witch-hunt in Oberstdorf resulted in the deaths of about 25 people, all but Stoeckhlin himself women. Many were Stoeckhlin's relatives. This was the first witch-hunt in a series in the lands of the bishop of Augsburg and other territories in south Germany that took hundreds of lives over the next few years.

REFERENCE: Wolfgang Behringer. *Shaman of Oberstdorf: Chonrad Stoeckhlin and the Phantoms of the Night.* Trans. H. C. Erik Midelfort. Charlottesville: University Press of Virginia, 1998.

SUMMIS DESIDERANTES AFFECTIBUS

A papal bull, or decree, was issued by Innocent VIII (pope, 1484–1492) on December 5, 1484, in response to foot-dragging by German ecclesiastical authorities in the Rhineland witch-hunt that had recently been launched by Heinrich **Kramer** and Johann Sprenger (1436–1495). These obstructions caused Kramer and Sprenger to appeal to the pope as the one man who could clear the roadblocks. The bull, part of a long series of decrees on witchcraft and sorcery issued by popes, made it clear that the witch-hunting efforts of Kramer and Sprenger had full papal support even for those areas not named in previous decrees or in those areas that local authorities claimed had no witches. By precluding in advance claims that Kramer and Sprenger were operating outside their jurisdiction, the decree eased the way of the persecutors, although according to records the only time Kramer tried to use it, at **Innsbruck** in 1485, it was not a success. *Summis Desiderantes Affectibus* (With the Highest Fears) broke no new intellectual ground in demonology. It followed in the tradition of previous papal statements in concentrating on heresy, sorcery, *maleficia* and dealings with devils rather than new concepts such as the **sabbat** or **satanic pact.** Despite its conservatism, the bull was a highly influential document in witch-hunting history. It was printed in the first edition of Kramer's *Malleus Maleficarum* (1486) and continued to be printed in each new edition, giving it a permanency that previous bulls lacked, firmly aligning papal authority with witch persecution.

REFERENCES: Eric Wilson. "Institoris at Innsbruck: Heinrich Institoris, the *Summis Desiderantes,* and the Brixen Witch-Trial of 1485." In *Popular Religion in Germany and Central Europe, 1400–1800,* ed. Bob Scribner and Trevor Johnson, 87–100. New York: St. Martin's Press, 1996; Jeffrey Burton Russell. *Witchcraft in the Middle Ages.* Ithaca: Cornell University Press, 1972.

SUTTON WITCHES

A mother and daughter team of witches, Mother Sutton and Mary Sutton of Milton Milles in the county of Bedford, were the subject of an anonymous witchcraft pamphlet of 1613, *Witches Apprehended, Examined and Executed, for notable Villanies by them committed by both Land and Water*. The pamphlet tells of how the Suttons persecuted a local gentleman, Master Enger, causing his livestock to take sick and die, his cart to break down and his servant to sicken. Mary Sutton's witchcraft is portrayed as linked with her sexual promiscuity. The pamphleteer informs the reader that she had three illegitimate children and that the feud between Enger and the Suttons began when Sutton's servant struck one of them, Henry, to punish him for throwing trash into the mill dam. While the servant was lying sick, Mary Sutton appeared to him to tempt him sexually, but God gave him strength to resist. Afterward, the battle between the Suttons and Enger escalated when his seven-year-old son threw stones at Mother Sutton and called her a witch. The Suttons sent two **familiar** spirits, Dicke and Jude, to kill the boy, who died in five days.

The pamphlet describes a **flotation test** that Enger administered to Mary Sutton on the advice of an unknown stranger. (This is the first documented use of a flotation test in **England**.) Enger's men kidnapped Sutton and, when attempting to tie her on the back of a horse, they were all struck lame. Enger beat her until the men were able to move again. They threw her into the mill dam, and when she refused to sink, an examination by women revealed **witch's marks.** After she once again failed to sink, Enger badgered her into a confession. The pamphlet concludes by reporting that both Suttons had been executed at Bedford Assizes on March 31, partly on their own confessions and partly on the evidence of Henry Sutton. Subsequent writers such as Richard **Bernard** would draw upon the Sutton case.

REFERENCE: Marion Gibson. ed., *Early Modern Witches: Witchcraft Cases in Contemporary Writing*. London and New York: Routledge, 2000.

SWEDEN, WITCH-HUNTING IN

Sweden, along with other territories in Europe's far north, had a long literary and cultural association with witches and sorcerers. Swedish law had criminalized **magic** for centuries. New ideas about witch persecution originating further south took a long time to affect Sweden, and the first known witch trial there did not occur until 1471, in Arboga. Secular courts took over witch persecution from ecclesiastical courts at the Reformation, when the Swedish system of ecclesiastical justice collapsed in the transition from Catholicism to Lutheranism. Persecution grew in intensity by a pattern Sweden shared with the rest of sixteenth-century Europe, rising most dramatically at the end of the century. Swedish trials, overwhelmingly in the southern part of the country during the sixteenth century, were usually based on *maleficia*, most commonly harming cattle, bewitching dairy products (cattle and dairy were the economic mainstay of Swedish peasants) and inflicting harm on human beings. Little bags containing hair, nails or other items were commonly believed to be planted for the purpose of magical harm. Swedes also believed in the "milkhare," or "carrier," a small creature a witch created from bits of wood or pieces of old brooms to steal milk. The milkhare took either the form of a hare or of a small grey ball. (Swedes also associated witchcraft with sexual promiscuity—a common term for a brothel was "witch-house.") Sixteenth-century Sweden did not experience large-scale witch-hunting or witch panics, and accused or suspected witches frequently defended themselves with countersuits for slander. **Execution** was usually by beheading followed by burning for women, and breaking on the wheel for men. **Torture** was used infrequently. Local courts were supposed to get permission to torture from higher courts, but this did not always happen.

The seventeenth century saw increased use of the **sabbat** in Swedish witch-hunting, and Sweden eventually became the only Scandinavian country to see large, sabbat-based witch-hunts. The demonological notion of the sabbat blended in Sweden with folklore about gatherings of witches and devils on a mythical mountain called Blokulla. The name appears in the fifteenth century, in northern Sweden, and spread to the south in the following century. It was originally identified with the rocky island of Jungfrau in the southern Baltic, but later it was applied to local hills and mountains. The association of Blokulla with the sabbat first appears in trial records in the late sixteenth century and continued into the eighteenth. Swedish diabolism was strongly gendered; attendance at the Blokulla and other sabbats was overwhelmingly a charge made against women, but the **satanic pact** was almost without exception associated with men.

Witch-hunting was mostly concentrated among the ethnically Swedish population, but there were some persecutions among the Sami or Lapp people of the far north. Persecution of the Sami focused on *maleficia* and superstitious practice rather than diabolical witchcraft. Pre-Christian practices, notably the use of divining drums, were strong among the Sami. Punishment was usually public humiliation and penance, although there were some executions of Sami for "idolatrous" practices. In the eighteenth century, Sami traditional practices were identified as superstition more than idolatry.

A reissuing of the national law code in 1608 called for the death penalty only for those witches who committed murder, but selections from Old Testament biblical law were included in an appendix. Local courts applied the death penalty for a broader range of witchcraft offenses, sometimes claiming to be following biblical authority. Fines were also common, and offenders were frequently sentenced to undergo a public shaming at the church as a penance. In 1614, it was decreed that death sentences applied by local courts be automatically appealed to district courts. Sweden was still a country of moderate witch-hunting, and Swedish troops are sometimes credited with suppressing witch-hunting in the parts of **Germany** they occupied during the Thirty Years' War (1618–1648) (although this phenomenon is greatly exaggerated in older scholarship). Sweden's abdicated queen, Christina (1626–1629), claimed that she had suppressed the death penalty for all nonlethal forms of witchcraft when some trials took place in Verden in 1649, during the Swedish occupation of that territory, but the surviving evidence does not bear this out. By the middle of the seventeenth century, Swedish Lutheran clergy in Sweden were pressing for a more vigorous witch-hunt, based on Exodus 22:18.

The real peak of Swedish witch-hunting occurred late in the overall European witch-hunt, after a 1665 statute assimilated witchcraft and diabolism. The **Mora witch-hunt** in northern Sweden from 1668 to 1676 claimed around two hundred lives. A smaller witch-hunt, but still substantial in the Scandinavian context, took place in the southern region of Bohuslan from 1669–1672. The witch-hunt began when a man named Soren Muremaster blamed an old woman, Anna of Holte, for using magic to make him impotent (impotence **accusations** were rare in Sweden). Anna of Holte, who failed a **flotation test,** then accused another woman, Ragnill Jens Svensis, of being a witch and causing Holte to be accused by her witchcraft. Svensis also failed a flotation test, and Anna of Holte's despairing suicide in jail was regarded as proof of her guilt. The spread of witch-hunting in Bohuslan was facilitated by a zealous judge, Nils Thomesson Feman, and the peculiar legal situation of the territory, which Sweden had only taken from **Denmark** in 1658. Danish law, which placed fewer restrictions on the use of torture, was still in effect. Safeguards provided by Danish law, such as prohibiting basing convictions solely on the testimony of already convicted persons, were ignored, however. The trials were based on accusations of *maleficia* and sabbat attendance, and accusations of **flying** to Blokulla, and child abduction played much less of a role than in the contemporary Mora trials. Flotation tests were also used extensively in the Bohuslan hunt, in which more than a hundred people were accused of being witches: 29 were executed, 15 died as the result of torture or imprisonment under harsh conditions and 2, including Anna, committed suicide.

The period following Mora and Bohuslan saw a decline in Swedish witch-hunting, particularly after 1700. Trials for magic persisted and even increased, but their emphasis changed from *maleficia* to the combating of rural superstition and magical blasphemy, such as the use of church furnishings for magical purposes. Diabolical witchcraft continued to exist as an entity in Swedish law; the Swedish code of 1734 provided for the death penalty for all *maleficia*. An increase in magic-related trials followed, but the death penalty was not enforced. By the time King Gustavus III (r. 1771–1792) abolished the death penalty for witches in 1779, it had already become a dead letter.

REFERENCES: Bengt Ankarloo "Sweden: The Mass Burnings (1668–1676)." In *Early Modern European Witchcraft: Centres and Peripheries,* ed. Bengt Ankarloo and Gustav Henningsen, 285–317. Oxford: Clarendon Press, 1990; Carl-Martin Edsman. "A Manuscript concerning Inquiries into Witchcraft in Swedish Lappland ("Trolldomsrannsakningar i Lappmarken") 1649–1739 by Erik Nordberg." In *Saami Pre-Christian Religion: Studies on the Oldest Traces of Religion among the Saamis,* ed. Louise Backman and Ake Hultkranz, 121–137. Stockholm: Almquist and Wiksell International, 1985; Boldil Nildin-Wall and Jan Wall. "The Witch as Hare or the Witch's Hare: Popular Legends and Beliefs in Nordic Tradition." *Folklore* 104 (1993): 67–76; Per Sorlin.

Wicked Arts: Witchcraft and Magic Trials in Southern Sweden, 1635–1734. Leiden, The Netherlands: Brill, 1999.

"SWIMMING THE WITCH"

See Flotation Tests.

SWITZERLAND, WITCH-HUNTING IN

Switzerland rivaled **Germany** as a center of the witch-hunt. It has been estimated that there were nearly nine thousand trials and more than five thousand **executions** in the Swiss cantons, and Switzerland was both a leader in the early phases of the witch-hunt and the last western European state to execute a witch. (The cantons were legally part of the Holy Roman Empire until the treaty of Westphalia in 1648, but they had de facto independence.) Switzerland's linguistic, cultural, and religious fragmentation makes it difficult to generalize about witches and witch-hunting, and helps explain why Swiss witch-hunting has received less scholarly attention than witch-hunting elsewhere. One safe generalization is that Swiss society was particularly vulnerable to witch-hunting because of its political fragmentation and lack of central judicial institutions. In many parts of Switzerland, a convicted witch had no possibility of appeal to a higher court, whether in Switzerland or in the Holy Roman Empire. About 80 percent of the convicted victims of witch-hunting were women, around the European average. Swiss witch-hunts seldom attained the massive scale of the major German persecutions, typically involving fewer than 10 victims. The cumulative effect of years of small-scale witch-hunting could be devastating, however. The small community of La Neuveville, with a population of under a thousand, executed 60 witches between 1611 and 1667.

Fifteenth-century Swiss witch-hunting was often invoked by historians who traced the origin of the witch-hunt to the cultural differences between lowland Europe, and supposedly "primitive" and only partially Christianized mountain regions. Closer study has revealed that the upland Swiss regions where early witch-hunts took place were closely connected culturally, politically and economically to lowland areas. Nor was the correlation between upland areas and witch-hunting exact. Most trials took place in lowland and urban areas, and the German-speaking upland areas were nearly free of witch-hunting. What is without question is Switzerland's leading role in the early phases of the witch-hunt (although Swiss records for this period have also survived disproportionately). The German word *Hexerei* for "witch" (as opposed to *Zauberer*, "sorceror") is first attested in the Swiss city of Lucerne in 1419. One of the earliest systematic campaigns against witches was launched by a magistrate from Berne, Peter von Greyerz, against witches in the Simme Valley, where he was governor from 1392 to 1406. We know of von Greyerz's witch-hunt because he later recounted it to the demonologist Johannes **Nider,** who incorporated much of the material into his influential *Formicarius*. Von Greyerz's interpreta-

A Swiss woman accused of witchcraft is burnt at the stake. A sketch by an unnamed artist in the *Historic Picturebook for Swiss Youth,* circa 1700. © Mary Evans Picture Library.

tion of the Simme Valley witch-hunt includes many of the elements of the classical witch stereotype. The witches he caught confessed, often after severe **torture,** to *maleficia* including **weather witching, magical** theft of harvests belonging to others, **infanticide** and attendance at **sabbats.** Because Nider's information came from Greyerz, however, and Nider was writing at a later stage of the witch-hunt, it is possible that he exaggerated the conformity of the Simme Valley witch-hunt to the witch stereotype.

Other witch-hunts continued in various regions of Switzerland throughout the fifteenth century, with more than 20 trials between 1400 and 1435. As would be true throughout the Swiss witch-hunt, the leaders of most of these persecutions were lay magistrates—the clergy seems to have been reluctant to cooperate. In a major witch-hunt in the Valais region in 1428 more than a hundred witches were said to have been burnt. The charges included milk theft, destruction of crops, and diabolism. The chronicler Johann Fründ, writing later, described the Valais witch-hunt in terms of the witch stereotype, with the **satanic pact** and witch flight. Survival of the judicial records themselves is fragmentary, but if Fründ's description is accurate, this would be among the first uses of the witch stereotype. Another Valais witch-hunt in 1447 was halted by the intervention of the bishop of Sion. A major wave of Swiss trials from 1477 to 1486 was triggered by agrarian crisis. Crop destruction was a common charge against Swiss witches, reflecting the harsh conditions of many small communities. The Swiss also connected witches to wolves in an unusual way—not as lycanthropes but as wolf riders.

In the early modern period, Swiss jurisdictions were supposed to follow the law code of the Holy Roman Empire, the *Carolina* promulgated in 1532, but the weakness of imperial authority meant that the cantons were free to follow their own ideas. Some, particularly the Catholic cantons, did try to respect the limits on torture set forth in the *Carolina*, but others did not. French-speaking Western Switzerland saw more avid persecution of witches by Protestant than Catholic communities. Like their neigbors in **Geneva,** they persecuted, among other diabolical malefactors, witches who spread poisonous or plague-bearing "grease." Among the most intense witch-hunting regions of Switzerland and all of Europe was the Pays du Vaud, a Catholic area subject to the Protestant Canton of Berne, where the conviction rate of accused witches was more than 90 percent and the total number of victims more than two thousand.

One of the few Swiss demonologists was a Protestant minister in the Pays du Vaud, Francois Perraud. His *Demonology, or a Treatise on Demons and Sorcerers* (1653), was in part devoted to defending Protestantism from Catholic attackers who linked the frequency of witch trials in the Pays du Vaud with its Protestant church. Another important demonologist from Switzerland, although he spent much of his career as a professor at the University of Heidelberg in Germany, was Thomas Erastus (1524–1583). Erastus was a correspondent and opponent of the denier of witchcraft Johann **Weyer,** and the author of *Repetition of the Disputation on Lamiae and Witches* (1578).

After its early start, Switzerland generally followed the chronological pattern of the rest of western European witch-hunting. The frequency of witch-hunting dropped in the early sixteenth century, then picked up again in the second quarter. It began to fall off again after 1650, when persecutors turned their attention away from witchcraft and toward popular superstition. The last Swiss witch execution was also the last in western Europe. In Glarus in 1782, Anne Goldin, a maidservant, was executed for having bewitched Anna Marie Tschudi, a daughter of the family for whom she worked.

REFERENCES: Arno Borst. *Medieval Worlds: Barbarians, Heretics and Artists in the Middle Ages*. Trans. Eric Hansen. Chicago: University of Chicago Press, 1992; Richard Kieckhefer. *European Witch Trials: Their Foundations in Popular and Learned Culture, 1300–1500*. Berkeley: University of California Press, 1976; Brian P. Levack. *The Witch-Hunt in Early Modern Europe*. London and New York: Longman, 1987; E. William Monter. *Witchcraft in France and Switzerland: The Borderlands during the Reformation*. Ithaca and London: Cornell University Press, 1976; William G. Naphy. *Plagues, Poisons and Potions: Plague-Spreading Conspiracies in the Western Alps c. 1530–1640*. Manchester and New York: Manchester University Press, 2002.

SYPHILIS

See Medical Interpretations.

T

TEMPLARS

The destruction of the Order of the Temple by King Philip IV (r. 1285–1314) of **France** in 1307–1308 was an early example of many techniques prominent in the later witch-hunt, such as charging the accused with the worship of demons and obtaining confessions under **torture.** The order was an organization of knights under religious vows, originally founded in the crusader states of the Middle East with the purpose of fighting the Muslims to defend Christian possessions there. With the loss of the last Christian outposts, the order had less justification for its existence, but it remained vastly rich and powerful. Philip's motivation for his attack on the order was in all likelihood simply the seizure of its wealth and the destruction of its political power. In order for the legal assault on a religious order to work, however, Philip claimed to be acting at the behest of an inquisitor, and the charges were that the order had violated its vows. Philip's agents charged the Templars with using an initiation ceremony requiring novices to deny Christ, spit on the cross, strip naked and submit to three **kisses** from the master, on the buttocks, navel and mouth, and sometimes another kiss on the penis (or kiss the master in the same fashion.) The Templars were charged with universal sodomy as well as orgies with female demons and worshipping a idol called Baphomet and a demonic cat. The Templars also confessed to standard charges in attacks on heretical groups, such as anointing their idols with the fat of sacrificed infants. Assent to these charges was won from Templars who were tortured into confession, with use of strappado, the rack, and holding the suspect's feet to a fire. Templars judged guilty were burned at the stake as heretics, 54 of them in one day in 1310. The last commander of the order, Jacques de Molay, was burned in 1314, maintaining his and the order's innocence.

Philip got away with this because the papacy, which was supposed to oversee the Temple (which was exempt from all other jurisdiction), was weak and dependent on French power. The pope, Clement V (pope, 1305–1314) did

A fourteenth-century depiction of the burning of Templar Grand Master Jacques de Molay and Grand Preceptor of Normandy Geoffroy de Charnay, as ordered by Guillaume of Nogaret, March 18, 1314. © Snark/Art Resource, New York.

intervene in 1308 to suspend the proceedings, but French pressure, including the sorcery allegations against bishop **Guichard of Troyes,** forced the pope to dissolve the order in 1612. What made the satanic charges against the Temple different from those made against other groups of medieval heretics is that they were made by the French secular government rather than by the Church. This is the earliest example of a secular government involving itself in such things, setting a precedent for the witch-hunt.

REFERENCES: Malcolm Barber. *The Trial of the Templars* Cambridge: Cambridge University Press, 197; Norman Cohn. *Europe's Inner Demons: The Demonization of Christians in Medieval Christendom.* Rev. ed. Chicago: University of Chicago Press, 2000.

THOLOSAN, CLAUDE

The judge Claude Tholosan was among the first secular magistrates to write of witchcraft, which he did in his brief Latin manuscript treatise, *The Errors of Magicians and Witches*, composed in 1436 or 1437. Tholosan was a senior magistrate in the Dauphiné region of **France,** trained in the Roman law, and had tried more than one hundred witch cases in the Dauphiné, one of the most active witch-hunting centers in the mid–fifteenth century. *The Errors of Magicians and Witches* was among the first demonological writings based on actual firsthand experience hunting witches. Despite his lay status, Tholosan treated witchcraft as basically a religious offence against the canon law, providing a description of the **sabbat** modeled on descriptions of the gatherings of medieval heretics. He included the diabolical **kiss** and the unusual detail of drinking the devil's urine from a vase but denied the reality of witch's **flying.** One of Tholosan's principal concerns was establishing that secular magistrates, as representatives of their prince, have the right and obligation to try and condemn witches, rather than leaving it to ecclesiastical courts. Like many French jurists, he wanted to establish that the king had no earthly superior in his mission to purify society. Tholosan's treatise did not have great influence. It survives in only one copy, was not printed until 1979, and was not referred to by subsequent writers on witches and witch-hunting, but it is historically significant as an early claim to secular jurisdiction in witch cases.

REFERENCES: Alan Charles Kors and Edward Peters, eds. *Witchcraft in Europe 400–1700: A Documentary History.* 2d ed. Revised by Edward Peters. Philadelphia: University of Pennsylvania Press, 2001; P. G. Maxwell-Stuart, *Witchcraft in Europe and the New World, 1400–1800.* Houndsmills, England and New York: Palgrave, 2001.

THOMASIUS, CHRISTIAN (1655–1728)

Christian Thomasius, a jurist and the first head of the University of Halle in Prussia, was one of the leading opponents of witch-hunting in **Germany** during the late seventeenth and early eighteenth centuries. Thomasius came to oppose witch-hunting after careful thought and study. He voted for mild **torture** of an accused witch whose case had been submitted to the law faculty of the university in 1694, but further reflection and examination of the arguments led him to oppose all torture of accused witches and eventually the legal concept of witchcraft. Thomasius's two main works opposing witch persecution were the Latin *Of the Crime of Magic* (1701), a juridical work, and the German *Historical Investigation into the Origins and History of the Inquisitorial Trial* (1712). (Thomasius's willingness to use German in serious scholarly publications, and even to lecture in it, was highly controversial in the conservative German academic culture.) *Of the Crime of Magic* attacked the idea that the Devil had the power to affect the physical world. Thomasius did not deny that there were witches and that they could be justly punished for *maleficia*, even if unsuccessful, but he did deny the central tenets of early modern witchcraft belief, including the **satanic pact,** the **sabbat** and witch flight. Thomasius's Cartesian-influenced skepticism over the possibility of the Devil's action in the material world, similar to Balthasar **Bekker's,** was coupled with juristic skepticism over the validity of confessions extracted by torture. This drew on a German tradition of which the most significant previous exemplar was Friedrich **Spee,** whom Thomasius acknowledged. Thomasius's work widely circulated Gottfried Wilhem Leibniz's (1646–1716) identification of Spee as the author of *Warning to Prosecutors* (1631). Thomasius strongly opposed the use of torture in all judicial processes, not just witchcraft. *Of the Crime of Magic* was published in a German translation by Thomasius's student and fellow opponent of witch persecution Johann Reiche in 1703.

Historical Investigation into the Origins and History of the Inquisitorial Trial included a painstaking study of the origins of witchcraft ideas in the **Bible,** Roman law, the decrees of popes, and the writings of medieval and early modern demonologists. Thomasius took the bold step of describing the witch of Endor as merely a fraudulent ventriloquist. Although a Protestant who attacked witchcraft belief as a papist fraud, Thomasius denounced Protestant as well as Catholic demonologists and witch-hunters. He was the target of heated attacks, and some of his opponents went so far as to call him an atheist. As the leader of the law faculty at Halle, which became one of Germany's leading universities, Thomasius encouraged his students to oppose witch-hunting, and was responsible for German translations of English anti-persecution works by John **Webster** and Francis **Hutchinson.**

REFERENCE: Alan Charles Kors and Edward Peters, eds. *Witchcraft in Europe 400–1700: A Documentary History* 2d ed. Revised by Edward Peters. Philadelphia: University of Pennsylvania Press, 2001.

TITUBA

The native American slave woman Tituba was among the first to be denounced as a witch at **Salem,** and her narrative was one of the most influential in shaping the subsequent course of events. Despite the widespread modern belief that she was of African ancestry, all references to Tituba in her own time classify her as a native American. She was probably born into the Arawak people of northwestern South America, the "Spanish Main." Whatever her origins, Tituba first enters the historical record as a slave in Barbados. There she was exposed to the cultural traditions, including those related to **magic** and witchcraft, of both the English rulers and the Africans who comprised the majority of the slave population. In 1680, Tituba, who had been purchased by the minister Samuel Parris (1653–1720), was brought to **New England.** She served Parris and his family as a household slave, coming to Salem Village with the rest of the Parris household on his being appointed minister there in 1689.

Tituba was involved in the care of the young girls of Parris's family, Betty Parris and Abigail Williams, when they began to show symptoms of bewitchment or demonic **possession,** including inexplicable pains, hallucinations and contortions. Tituba and her husband, another Indian slave of Parris's known as "John Indian," assisted a neighbor, Mary Sibley, in the preparation of a "witch-cake" from the girls' urine and rye meal on February 25, 1692. This was traditional English **countermagic** to discover a witch, and Sibley was the principal, although like many Puritans she may have associated Native Americans with magical power and enlisted their assistance for that reason. For reasons that remain unclear, the girls, who were aware of the witch-cake, shortly afterward named Tituba, along with two English women, Sarah Osborne and Sarah Good, as their tormentors. Tituba was also the recipient of a beating from Parris, who like many ministers viewed countermagic with great suspicion. Tituba was arrested on February 29. On March 1, she confessed to dealing with the devil and tormenting the girls, probably hoping that a show of cooperation would be rewarded with lenient treatment. Tituba's confession, extending over two days, was full of bizarre detail, including the story of a meeting of witches in Boston also attended by demonic **familiars.** In addition to implicating Osborn and Good, poor women, Tituba spoke of unknown men and women wearing fancy clothing, diverting the witch-hunt both outside of Salem, and adding the possibility of male witches and witches from the social elite to the poor women who were the initial suspects. Tituba's placement of the forces that compelled her to undertake the bewitchment of the children in Boston, well away from Salem Village, may reflect her Native American heritage, in which malign supernatural forces were usually viewed as emanating from other communities. Other elements of her story, such as her **satanic pact,** clearly emerge from her experience of English society in Barbados and New England. Tituba's confession provided the basic narrative for witchcraft at Salem.

The magistrates viewed Tituba, unlike Good and Osborne, as cooperative, but she was sent to jail with them in Boston on March 7. Like other Salem witches who confessed, she was not executed, but she was held in jail throughout the witch-hunt. Eventually, during the reaction against the witch trials in the summer and fall, she recanted her confession and blamed Parris for forcing her to admit falsely to being a witch. Parris refused to pay for her board and by jail procedures she could not be released until the costs of holding her, which continued to accumulate, were paid. In April 1693, an unknown person paid Tituba's jail fees, undoubtedly as a way to purchase her as a slave. Tituba then disappears from the historical record.

REFERENCE: Elaine G. Breslaw. *Tituba, Reluctant Witch of Salem: Devilish Indians and Puritan Fantasies*. New York and London: New York University Press, 1996.

TOADS

See Animals.

TORTURE

The investigation of witchcraft in European societies involved the use of physical pain to elicit confessions. In this witchcraft was far from unique—torture was increasingly used in the early modern period and was a recognized part of criminal trials in European countries that used inquisitorial **trial procedure.** Torture could also be used as part of the penalty for a crime, including witchcraft, and the infliction of physical pain was often incorporated into the **execution** process, most dramatically perhaps in the execution of the **Pappenheimer** witches. The use of judicial, or investigative, torture began in Continental Europe during the high Middle Ages, with the influence of Roman law and the greater emphasis on the use of human investigation, as opposed to divine revelation, in distinguishing the truth of a criminal charge. By the early modern period, judicial torture was used in all countries whose legal systems were based on Roman law and employed inquisitorial trial procedure, which was every country except some in northern Europe, most notably **England,** which had its own common law system and retained adversarial procedure. Nonetheless, there were considerable variations in the use of torture between European regions and various courts, and even the English made some use of mild forms of torture in witch cases. The Spanish and **Roman Inquisitions,** in contrast to their reputation, made little use of torture.

As opposed to political torture administered to discover plots by enemies of the state, judicial torture was, always in theory and often in practice, regulated. Torture was only to be administered when there was thought to be evidence of guilt. Its primary purpose was to elicit confession, an important part of the process of convicting a criminal under inquisitorial and Roman law–influenced systems. The difficulty of finding evidence or eyewitnesses in witch cases, however, meant that torture was more frequently used in witch cases than in other criminal trials. This was theoretically justified by the claim that only extreme pain could loosen the Devil's grip on a witch's soul. (Torture's power to release

A pen and charcoal sketch by Domenico Beccafumi of an Inquisition scene: Torture employing strappado. © Réunion des Musées Nationaux/Art Resource, New York.

a witch from **Satan's** power was confirmed in some locations by the blessing of the instruments before a session commenced.) Although it was usually a requirement that confessions made under torture had to be confirmed by the accused after torture, in many cases this safeguard was a mockery, because refusal to confirm the confession would inevitably lead to more torture. Women, with a greater biological ability to resist pain, usually endured torture better than men did, although there was great individual variation.

Torture played a central role in the creation of witch hysteria. Full and detailed confessions to the classical model of learned demonology, with the apparatus of **satanic pact** and attendance at **sabbat,** was almost always wrung from the defendant with torture. Such confessions could then, in a classic circular process, be employed as evidence of the validity of the learned demonological model. Torture was also important in getting the accused witch to name the names of other witches that she knew of or had seen at the sabbat. Safeguards and limitations on the use of torture tended to erode in large-scale witch panics. The *Lex Carolina* of the Holy Roman Empire, for example, limited the amount and duration of torture that could be inflicted on an individual and discouraged the use of torture on those people whose sole evidence of guilt was having been named under torture by an accused witch, but these safeguards were ignored in the great German witch-hunts. By far the greatest witch-hunt in English history, the Matthew **Hopkins** persecutions, also deviated from standard English legal procedure in Hopkins and his associates' extensive use of torture, notably the practice of "waking the witch"—the deprivation of sleep for extended periods of time. (This was a common procedure in Scottish trials as well.) This suggests the connection of torture and large-scale witch-hunting.

Tortures used in Continental witch trials included relatively mild forms, the first degree, such as thumbscrews or the tearing out of fingernails, to more severe forms, the second degree. One common form of the second degree was strappado, or the suspension of the prisoner by his or her arms so that the weight of the body twisted and dislocated the shoulders. Sometimes weights were attached to the prisoner's feet to intensify the agony. Finally the "third degree" included the rack; the "Spanish boot," in which the legs and feet were crushed in a vice; and squassado, an extension of strappado in which the suspended prisoner was repeatedly dropped, always stopping a few inches short of solid ground. These were common procedures, but there were many others used in specific areas or by specific torturers. The great German witch-hunts of the period 1580–1630 led to the introduction of many new devices for the infliction of pain such as the "witch's chair," a metal chair in which the alleged witch was bound while a fire was kept going below. Some witch's chairs were also spiked. The men who carried out these procedures were disdained socially, but essential to the witch-hunt. Some, like the German Hans **Vollmair,** went on to become leading witch-hunters.

The use of torture and evidence from torture was never completely uncontroversial. A popular argument for moderate opponents of witch persecution, such as the German Jesuits Adam Tanner (1572–1632) and Friedrich von **Spee,** was that evidence from torture was unreliable. Growing suspicion of confessions elicited by torture was one reason for the diminishing and eventual cessation of witch-hunting.

REFERENCES: Robin Briggs, *Witches and Neighbors: The Social and Cultural Context of European Witchcraft.* New York: Penguin, 199; Joseph Klaits. *Servants of Satan: The Age of the Witch Hunts.* Bloomington: Indiana University Press, 1985.

TRANSFORMATIONS

A **magical** power commonly associated with witches, although not as commonly as **flying,** was that of transforming themselves or other people into

Witches in the shape of animals. From Ulrich Molitor's *Von den Unholden und Hexen,* Constance, 1489. © Snark/Art Resource, New York.

animals, most notably in the case of **werewolves** and other lycanthropes. This power presented some intellectual problems, however, because many believed that actually altering the substance of a thing, as opposed to working an illusion of change, was beyond the powers of demons or witches. Claims to transform themselves, often to cats, or other people frequently appear in witch confessions, and witch victims sometimes complained of being transformed into animals to ride to the sabbat. One of the common motifs in folk tales of witches is that of the strange animal that is wounded. The wound is later found on the body of an old woman, demonstrating that she and the animal are the same. These kinds of tales often appear in literature and the writings of demonologists, but rarely in actual witch confessions and accounts of witch victims. The belief in transformation was condemned in the ninth-century **Canon Episcopi,** and illusions of transformation were blamed on demons. Unlike the belief in flight, also condemned in the *Canon,* belief in transformation was not accepted by mainstream early modern demonologists, even by those prepared to allow witches a great deal of magical power, such as Heinrich Kramer.

REFERENCES: Robin Briggs. *Witches and Neighbors: The Social and Cultural Context of European Witchcraft* New York: Penguin, 1996; Brian P. Levack. *The Witch-Hunt in Early Modern Europe.* London and New York: Longman, 1987.

Trial of George Jacobs of Salem for witchcraft, Salem, Massachusetts. © Library of Congress.

TRIAL PROCEDURE

A precondition for witch-hunting in most of Europe was the adoption of new judicial methods in the late Middle Ages, the so-called inquisitorial procedure. Before the thirteenth century, the dominant mode of proceeding was adversarial, in which a case before a court was conceptualized as a contest between two private parties. The responsibility for prosecuting a criminal case lay with the alleged victim, rather than a prosecutor who was an agent of the court. In many cases, the cause would be judged ultimately not by a magistrate but by God, with the use of trials by ordeal or by combat. In the thirteenth century, much of Continental Europe, influenced by developments in the Roman and canon law as well as concern with the rise of crime and heresy, adopted the idea that a judicial process was an investigation of a crime against church or state authority, to be judged by magistrates as representatives of that authority. Although cases could still be, and many were, initiated by persons claiming to be victims, they could now also be brought by magistrates themselves, proceeding on the basis of rumor or "common fame." This was particularly dangerous for old women who fit the "witch stereotype." However the case originated, the burden of investigation and prosecution then lay with representatives of church and state. Rather than serving as an impartial arbiter between competing claims, the role of a judge in a criminal case was to find out the truth. The role of the jury, often influential in early medieval cases, dwindled to a merely ornamental one and eventually was eliminated altogether under inquisitorial procedure. Because the magistrates, rather than the victim, were now the principal construc-tors of the case against the accused, the old *lex talionis*, under which the bringer of an **accusation** determined to be false was liable for penalty, was abandoned under the new system. This greatly facilitated bringing witchcraft accusa-tions, as well as those of many other crimes.

The need to find truth in inquisitorial procedure led to a much greater emphasis on winning a confession from the criminal. The law of evidence adopted, referred to as the

Seventeenth century woodcut by an unnamed artist of a trial of a witch by ducking in the mill-stream. © Mary Evans Picture Library.

"romano-canonical" law of proof, held that either a confession or two eye-witnesses were required to prove the commission of a crime. Confession was particularly important in witchcraft cases, because eyewitnesses were hardly ever to be found. Inquisitorial procedure, therefore, went hand in hand with an increased reliance on **torture,** which was supposed to be regulated as to what grounds of suspicion made it acceptable as well as extent and duration. Legisla-tors knew that torture, particularly in the hands of a zealous magistrate, could produce false confessions. Confessions made under torture were supposed to be affirmed by the alleged criminal afterward, but because a torture victim who recanted her confession was often simply tortured again, this was an inadequate safeguard. Another problem for magistrates investigating alleged witch cases was the quality of the witnesses. Inquisitorial procedure lay great stress on the reliability of witnesses, usually excluding the testimony of those who were of ill repute themselves. This was a problem in witch-hunts, which often turned on the testimony of confessed witches as to whom they had seen at the **sabbat** or otherwise knew to be witches. Some jurisdictions also placed less weight on women's testimony than on men's, another problem in making a witchcraft charge effective. The legal unreliability of testimony in witchcraft cases was sometimes circumvented by declaring witchcraft a *crimen exceptum*, to which normal rules of proof and evidence did not entirely apply. This also enabled more free use of torture. Alternatively, zealous witch-hunters could simply ignore procedural safeguards, although this sometimes led to their being over-ruled by remote courts of appeal, such as the Parlement of Paris in the case of northern **France.** Reversals on appeal often came too late for executed witches, however. The courts that most strictly followed legal procedure in the first instance, those of the Roman and **Spanish Inquisitions,** were the ones that executed the fewest witches.

Another problem area was the use of leading questions, designed by the investigating magistrate to elicit a specific response. Many jurisprudents considered this to be improper procedure, but it was common in witch cases. The combination of leading questions and torture often created stereotyped confessions, in which the alleged witches' description of witchery, the sabbat or **Satan** simply conformed to the ideas already held by the judge.

Although early modern trial procedure facilitated witch-hunting in many ways, a strict insistence on proper procedure could also hinder it. Many of the most successful opponents of the witch-hunt, such as Friedrich von **Spee,** focused on the legal difficulties that witchcraft prosecutions produced, rather than making the much more radical argument against the existence of witches. The torture of accused witches—the only evidence of their witchcraft being the accusations of other accused witches under torture—was particularly vulnerable to question by legal authorities.

England, along with its colonial offshoots in **New England** and elsewhere, presents a special case. The English legal system, known as the common law, did not adopt inquisitorial procedure. Juries remained prominent as triers of the fact and also brought indictments in the courts. (In **Scotland,** whose system had features in common with both Continental and English systems, juries were triers of the fact, but had no involvement in the process whereby indictments were brought.) The original complainant was considered the prosecutor of the crime, and the trial retained the form of a contest between two adversaries in which magistrates, at least in theory, adopted the position of impartial referees rather than seekers of truth. The different procedures of English law offered advantages and disadvantages to accused witches. English courts were open to a remarkably broad range of evidence, including hearsay of the type that would not have been accepted as proof of guilt in a continental court. (The English only developed a law of evidence strictly defining what was and what was not admissible in the eighteenth century after witch-hunting in England had ceased.) Because English procedure did not require confession as evidence of guilt, however, torture was not employed, nor were witches usually pressed to name accomplices.

REFERENCE: Brian P. Levack. *The Witch-Hunt in Early Modern Europe.* London and New York: Longman, 1987.

V

VALLICK, JACOB

The Gelderland parish priest Jacob Vallick wrote one of the first works on witchcraft written in Dutch, *Bewitching, what kind of work it is* (1559). It is primarily concerned with pastoral issues and takes the form of a dialogue between two women, Elisabeth and Mechteld. Elisabeth has suffered a string of misfortunes—a sick horse, butter refusing to turn, and an ailing husband—and blames a witch. She plans to use ecclesiastical **countermagic** by getting holy water from a local monastery. Mechteld recommends that they consult the parish priest first. The priest, Vallick's mouthpiece, denounces all countermagic, whether ecclesiastical or otherwise, and suggests that blaming one's problems on witches is a delusion of the Devil, best combated by leading a more pious life. Vallick was acquainted with Johann **Weyer,** whose attitude to witchcraft was similar. Although the original 1559 edition of *Bewitching* is lost, it is known from references by Weyer and Lambert **Daneau.**

REFERENCE: Willem Frijhoff. "Witchcraft and Its Changing Representation in Eastern Gelderland, from the Sixteenth to the Twentieth Centuries." In *Witchcraft in the Netherlands from the Fourteenth to the Twentieth Century*, ed. Marijke Gijswit-Hofstra and Willem Frijhoff, 167–180. Rotterdam: Universitaire Pers Rotterdam, 1991.

VENICE

See Benandanti; Italy; Morosini Case.

VINETI, JEAN

Jean Vineti, a Dominican inquisitor and theology professor at the University of Paris, was the author of *Treatise against the Invokers of Demons*, probably written sometime between 1450 and 1470 but not published until 1483. Vineti's principal concern was establishing the existence and power of demons and their contacts with mortals rather than with witches or magicians per se. His principal source of evidence was **possession** and exorcism, and to a lesser extent ritual **magic,** rather than witchcraft. Much of his treatise was devoted to discrediting alternative natural and astrological explanations for demonic events. He discussed the *Canon Episcopi,* distinguishing between the kind of people about which it was written and modern heretical witches. He drew upon including leading medieval theologians and philosophers, notably Thomas Aquinas (1224?–1274).

REFERENCE: Walter Stephens. *Demon Lovers: Witchcraft, Sex, and the Crisis of Belief.* Chicago and London: University of Chicago Press, 2002.

VIRGINIA

See Maryland and Virginia, Witch-Hunting in.

VISCONTI, GIROLAMO

Girolamo Visconti was a university professor of logic at Milan, and like many fifteenth- and early-sixteenth-century demonologists, he was a Dominican. He was related to the ruling family of Milan. (A distant forebear, Galleazzo Visconti, had been accused of trying to kill Pope **John XXII** by **image magic** in 1320). Girolamo Visconti was the author of two works on witchcraft, written around 1460, *A Small Book Proving Witches are Heretics* and *A Small Book on Lamiae, or Witches.* He endorsed the **sabbat** and sexual orgies between humans and demons taking place there. He also recounted cases of witches misusing the consecrated Host and discussed **infanticide,** explaining how God's permitting the killing of infants was compatible with his goodness. A learned man, Visconti drew on the writings of theologians as well as his own encounters with witches. Like many of the early writers, he attempted to establish the reconcilability of the new witch stereotype and the *Canon Episcopi.* He also refuted the idea that witch's tales could be explained medically, by melancholy. His treatises were published with some modifications in 1490 by the canon lawyer Alvisio Della Croce.

REFERENCES: Jeffrey Burton Russell. *Witchcraft in the Middle Ages.* Ithaca: Cornell University Press, 197; Walter Stephens. *Demon Lovers: Witchcraft, Sex, and the Crisis of Belief.* Chicago and London: University of Chicago Press, 2002.

VOLLMAIR, HANS

The Master of Biberach, Hans Vollmair, served the free imperial city of Biberach in the Holy Roman Empire as executioner and torturer. Carrying out witch persecutions called for special expertise in a torturer beyond the application of pain to extract confessions, and a small number of executioners, of whom Vollmair and Jorg Abriel of Schongau were the most prominent, took the leading role in the late-sixteenth-century south German persecutions. Vollmair was known for expertise in identifying witches and particularly for his adept use of the needle in "witch-pricking," for the detection of **devil's marks** (if the needle, when stuck into the mark, did not draw blood, the suspect was a witch). During the great south German witch-hunts of the period 1586–1591, Vollmair's services were in demand far beyond the small town of Biberach. He participated in the **Obermarchthal witch-hunt.** In Dettingen, at the beginning of the hunts, Vollmair wrung a confession from the horse herder and accused witch Chonrad **Stoeckhlin** by extreme **torture** involving the burning off of his skin. Vollmair then burned Stoeckhlin on January 23, 1587. In 1588, after a severe hailstorm, the poor peasants of the town of Schwabsoien in the bishopric of Augsburg expressed a willingness to sell the communal forest to pay for Vollmair's services. In 1589, accompanied by his stepson and fellow torturer Master Christoph of Biberach, he went to Schwabmunchen, also in the bishopric of Augsburg, to attend a gathering of executioners and their families for a hunt precipitated by the **accusations** of a child. The well-paid Vollmair contracted with the bishop of Augsburg, Marquard vom Berg (bishop, 1576–1591), for a year's service carrying out persecutions. In 1590, he carried out a great persecution in Ellingen, in which at least 72 accused witches were burned.

REFERENCES: Wolfgang Behringer. *Shaman of Oberstdorf: Chonrad Stoeckhlin and the Phantoms of the Night.* Trans.H. C. Erik Midelfort. Charlottesville: University Press of Virginia, 1998; Wolfgang Behringer. *Witchcraft Persecutions in Bavaria: Popular Magic, Religious Zealotry, and Reason of State in Early Modern Europe.* Trans. J. C. Grayson and David Lederer. Cambridge: Cambridge University Press, 1997.

W

WAGSTAFFE, JOHN (1633–1677)

The country gentleman John Wagstaffe's *The Question of Witchcraft Debated* (1669) was one of the most skeptical works published in the late-seventeenth-century English debate on witchcraft. Although it was only about 80 octavo pages, *The Question of Witchcraft Debated* employed a full range of arguments to attack the entire system of belief in witches and witchcraft rather than simply defend particular witches. Wagstaffe addressed standard issues such as the applicability of **Bible** passages denouncing witches to contemporary witches. He firmly aligned himself with classical pagan skeptics of supernatural beliefs such as Marcus Tullius Cicero (106–43 B.C.) and Lucian of Samosata (c. 120–180). He also broadened the traditional English alliance between opposing witch-hunting and anti-Catholicism into a general assault on "priest-craft"—the manipulation of human credulity by power-seeking clerics—Protestants as well as Catholics. Wagstaffe was not antireligious or anti-Christian by his own standards and attacked the powers traditional belief in witchcraft ascribed to witches and the Devil as incompatible with God's benevolence and omnipotence. He expressed sympathy for accused witches and claimed that the state of human knowledge was simply insufficient to assert positively that any event was caused by the Devil's power.

Wagstaffe provoked responses from defenders of witchcraft belief, including **Increase Mather** and Meric **Casaubon.** He responded to his critics in an expanded edition of *The Question of Witchcraft Debated* published in 1671. Wagstaffe's work continued to influence debate after his death. *The Question of Witchcraft Debated* was translated into German in 1711, and *The Impossibility of Witchcraft* (1712), a contribution to the debate on the Jane **Wenham** case, was extensively plagiarized from Wagstaffe.

REFERENCE: Michael Hunter. "The Witchcraft Controversy and the Nature of Free-Thought in Restoration England: John Wagstaffe's *The Question of Witchcraft*

Debated (1669)." In *Science and the Shape of Orthodoxy: Intellectual Change in Late Seventeenth-Century Britain.* 286–307. Woodbridge, England: Boydell Press, 1995.

WALDENSIANS

The Waldensians were a small, underground medieval heretical group founded in the twelfth century by Peter Valdes of Lyon, and surviving by the fifteenth century mostly in remote communities in the Alps. Their religion was based on rejection of what they saw as the wealth and corruption of the Catholic clergy rather than rejection of Catholic doctrine. The Waldensians originally had nothing to do with witchcraft, but in the fifteenth century they became identified with witches to the extent that the French referred to witchcraft generally as Vauderie, or Waldensianism. This identification emerged from the slanders used by the Inquisition and other defenders of Catholic orthodoxy against both witches and heretics. To many medieval Catholic Christians, opposition to the Church was identified with opposition to God, and it was natural to think that whatever their outward respectability, the Waldensians consciously served the devils whose cause they were promoting. From early in the centuries-long Catholic campaign against the Waldensians, they had been charged with secret nocturnal orgies and the worship of devils, charges reinforced by confessions extorted from imprisoned Waldensians under **torture.** In the early fifteenth century, when both inquisitors and secular courts were persecuting witches in the Alps, it was inevitable that those groups identified as holding secret nocturnal and diabolical orgies be called Waldensians, particularly as they existed in the same area as genuine Waldensian communities and were also targets of the Inquisition.

REFERENCE: Norman Cohn. *Europe's Inner Demons: The Demonization of Christians in Medieval Christendom.* Rev. ed. Chicago: University of Chicago Press, 2000.

WALES, WITCH-HUNTING IN

Governed by the same laws as **England,** early modern Wales saw even less witch-hunting. There are 32 recorded cases of **magical** offenses that survive in the records of the four Welsh assize circuits, with 37 people indicted but only 8 found guilty and 5 sentenced to death. The first sentenced to death was also the first indicted for maleficent witchery rather than sorcery, Gwen ferch Ellis, sentenced to hang in 1595. Welsh witch-hunting peaked during the 1650s, when England's commonwealth government aggressively attacked Welsh traditional culture. There were 10 indictments in that decade. The last witchcraft indictment in Wales was in 1698. About 75 percent of the accused witches were women, as were all those who sued others for slander for calling them witches.

Welsh notions of witchcraft seem to have moved closer to those of England during this period. One way this can be traced is the growing popularity of the word "wits," a borrowing from the English "witch." The first surviving appearance of "wits" is in a Welsh-English dictionary printed in 1547. The dictionary identifies witches as women, and growing use of "wits" seems to be linked with a feminization of magic offense. The Welsh term *Rheibiwiyr* (feminine *Rheibes*) was principally used to describe male sorcerers. Welsh witchcraft theory, however, remained unique and only moderately affected by English and Continental demonology. (The only demonology book available in Welsh was the Englishman Robert **Holland's** *Tudor and Gronow*.) **Sabbat** and **satanic pact** do not appear in Welsh cases, and **familiars** only rarely. Welsh witches concentrated on affecting the health of people and livestock through *maleficia*, almost always in the form of a curse. A standard piece of Welsh **countermagic** was to get the original curser to recite a blessing. From the late seventeenth century on, religious dissenters, including Quakers, were frequently believed to be witches. Although witch trials had ended by the eighteenth century, belief in witchcraft and the power of curses continued for centuries after.

REFERENCE: Richard Suggett. "Witchcraft Dynamics in Early Modern Wales." In *Women and Gender in Early Modern Wales*, ed. Michael Roberts and Simone Clarke, 75–103. Cardiff: University of Wales Press, 2000.

WALSH, JOHN

The trial of John Walsh, a **cunning** man, was the subject of the one of the two English witchcraft pamphlets that came out in 1566, the first surviving examples of the genre. Titled *The Examination of John Walsh, before Master Thomas Williams, Commissary to the Reverend Father in God William bishop of Exceter, upon certayne Interrogatories touchyng Wytchcraft and Sorcerye, in the presence of divers gentlemen and others*, the bulk of the manuscript is a transcription of answers that Williams put to Walsh. It is the only English witchcraft pamphlet to recount a church rather than a civil process. The pamphlet also includes a preface, probably by the publisher John Awdeley, putting Walsh's confessions in an anti-Catholic context and recounting scandalous stories of sorcerer-popes. The interrogation offers a look into the world of a cunning man. Walsh claims to have learned the medicine he practiced from "Sir Robert of Dreiton," whom Awdeley claims was a Catholic priest. After first denying he had a familiar, Walsh admitted to receiving one from Sir Robert, which could take the shape of a bird, a dog and a man. He lost the familiar when a local constable had confiscated a **magical** book from him. Walsh describes a number of magical rituals in which he engaged for summoning spirits and white, green and black fairies, from whom he learned who was bewitched. He also described rituals witches used to cause harm but was adamant that he had never used magic for ill, and that anyone who did so lost the power to use it for good. Walsh's final fate is unknown.

REFERENCE: Marion Gibson, ed. *Early Modern Witches: Witchcraft Cases in Contemporary Writing*. London and New York: Routledge, 2000.

WARBOYS WITCH-HUNT

In November 1589, Jane Throckmorton began to suffer from fits. She was the youngest of the five daughters of Robert Throckmorton, a Puritan gentleman of the town of Warboys, and his wife Elizabeth. The fits spread to Throckmorton's other daughters, as well as seven maidservants. There are some indications that the children used the fits to get out of the dull lessons and tedious prayers that were part of the Throckmorton routine and that, by claiming bewitchment, they were able to assume a dominant role in the household, screaming and refusing to conform to their parents' dictates. The children accused an old woman in the neighborhood named Alice Samuel. Robert and Elizabeth do not initially seem to have been eager to believe this, but after **physicians** suggested that the girls' illness was caused by bewitchment and some of their other relatives took the same point of view, a campaign against Samuel, her husband John, and her daughter Agnes was launched. The Throckmortons were a powerful family locally and were able to force Alice and Agnes to live in their house, where they were repeatedly scratched by the children as **countermagic.** A Throckmorton relation, Lady Cromwell, forcibly took a lock of Alice's hair to be burned and died a little over a year later in July 1592, after having strange dreams. Alice confessed to being a witch that Christmas, then retracted her confession, then confessed again. The familars she confessed to having were dun chickens, with humorous names like Pluck and Catch. The three Samuels were tried and convicted of both witchcraft and having killed Lady Cromwell by witchcraft in April 1593. Because by the witchcraft statute of 1563, causing a person's death by witchcraft was a capital offense, they were all hanged. The children immediately ceased their strange and disruptive behavior.

The pamphlet *The Most Strange and Admirable Discoverie of the Three Witches of Warboys, arraigned, convicted and executed at the last Assises at Huntington* (1593) is one of the most detailed accounts of an English witchcraft case, frequently referred to in later literature. Lady Cromwell's surviving husband, Sir Henry Cromwell, who was also lord of the manor, used the Samuels's forfeited assets to endow a sermon to be given in Huntingdon every year against witchcraft. It continued until 1812, although by that time it had metamorphosed into a sermon against belief in witchcraft.

REFERENCES: Marion Gibson. *Reading Witchcraft: Stories of Early English Witches.* London and New York: Routledge, 1999; D. P. Walker. *Unclean Spirits: Possession and Exorcism in France and England in the Late Sixteenth and Early Seventeenth Centuries.* Philadelphia: University of Pennsylvania Press, 1981.

WATER ORDEAL

See Flotation Tests.

WEATHER WITCHING

In the agricultural society of early modern Europe, one of the most devastating **accusations** of *maleficium* that could be made was that of witches' interference with the weather. Accusations of weather witching went back far into the European past, although church authorities had always denied the possibility, preferring that people blame bad weather on their sins rather than the actions of the Devil or witches. Theological opinion was divided on both the Catholic and Protestant sides of the fence. Heinrich **Kramer's** *Malleus Maleficarum* (1486) accepted the possibility of witches altering the weather, as did some Protestant preachers and demonologists. The theory received papal endorsement in the papal decree ***Summis Desiderantes Affectibus*** and was endorsed by all the major demonologists who supported witch-hunting.

A witch riding a goat in the sky causes a storm. From the *Compendium Malleficarum* (1626) by Francesco Maria Guazzo, Italian demonologist. © The Art Archive/Dagli Orti (A).

Weather witching differed from other *maleficia* in that it affected whole communities rather than individuals or families. Perhaps for this reason, it was envisioned as something caused by groups of witches rather than individuals. **Sabbats** were often described as including plans for causing disruptive weather to ruin harvests. (Although witches who caused sickness were sometimes credited, or blamed for, using witchcraft to cause healing or recovery, witches were never accused of causing good weather by diabolical means.) Weather witching accusations frequently characterized large-scale witch-hunts, such as the late-sixteenth-century Trier witch-hunt. These accusations frequently came from the common people. European peasants believed themselves capable of distinguishing between ordinary bad weather and bewitched weather. **Magical** bad weather diverged from expected norms: unusually cold winters, late frosts, cold and wet summers, destructive thunderstorms, hailstorms. The coming of strange forces or objects from the sky had a supernatural flavor. The accepted countermagic for thunderstorms in many parts of Europe was the ringing of church bells, which made the ringers particularly vulnerable to lightning. Hailstorms, which could completely devastate one field while leaving the one next to it untouched, were particularly likely to lead to witchcraft accusations.

The areas most marked by accusations of weather witching were **Germany** and central Europe more generally, a densely populated region particularly vulnerable to bad harvests and crop failure. Rhine valley vineyards, like vineyards everywhere, were liable to near-total destruction by hailstorms, increasing in frequency in the late sixteenth century. Cereal crops were also damaged by the cold and wet weather of the "Little Ice Age." The weak governments and decentralized authority common in the Holy Roman Empire also left much scope for witch-hunting initiative by peasant communities devastated by bad weather and poor harvests. During the peaks of German witch-hunting, from

1560 to the end of the century, and in the 1620s and early 1630s, the agricultural economy was particularly hard hit by cold, wet weather. In **England** and the **northern Netherlands,** by contrast, where the population was much better fed, accusations of weather witching were rare. Weather magic also figured infrequently in witch accusations in more temperate Mediterranean regions, such as Spain and **Italy.**

The other area, besides agriculture, in which weather witching was particularly dreaded was the sea. The most famous storms in witchcraft history affected King **James VI** of **Scotland** on his return from **Denmark** in 1590. The search for the diabolical instigators of this storm touched off the **North Berwick** witch-hunt. On a more humble level, fishing communities like those of **Norway** and the **Basque** country were particularly vulnerable to large oceanic storms, which could carry off a considerable portion of the village's male population.

REFERENCES: Wolfgang Behringer. "Weather, Hunger and Fear: Origins of the European Witch-Hunts in Climate, Society and Mentality." Trans. David Lederer. *German History* 13 (1995): 1–27; Robin Briggs. *Witches and Neighbors: The Social and Cultural Context of European Witchcraft.* New York: Penguin, 1996.

WEBSTER, JOHN

The medical man John Webster was a prominent opponent of traditional witchcraft belief and demonology in later seventeenth-century **England.** His text *The Displaying of Supposed Witchcraft* (1677) was a response to the new, scientific demonology associated with Joseph **Glanvill.** Webster drew from the occult traditions of Paracelsianism and Hermeticism to argue that actions attributed to the demonic powers of witches could be explained by natural **magic** and to defend natural magicians from charges of involvement with demons and **Satan.** He also drew from his own medical experiences, recounting tales of how alleged cases of **possession** were ultimately revealed to be caused by sickness or "melancholy" rather than demons. The concept of possession required demonic bodies, which Webster thought material, to occupy the same space as human bodies, an impossibility. Even if strange events had no natural explanation, he claimed, natural explanations could be discovered in the future, drawing on the ideology of scientific progress that he shared with Glanvill and many others in Restoration England. (Webster's book, denied a license for publication by the church authorities, was eventually licensed by the Royal Society, a scientific group of which Glanvill was a member, indicating the complexity of the relationship between **science** and demonology.) Drawing on Reginald **Scot's** *Discoverie of Witchcraft* (1584), Webster also went over the already well-traveled ground for skeptics of denying the comparability of the witches described in the **Bible** with modern demonic witches.

Webster was well acquainted with previous demonological literature in the skeptical tradition, explicitly defending Scot and Johann **Weyer,** with whom his emphasis on psychological causes of allegedly demonic phenomena has much in common, including charges of poor scholarship and even actual witchhood aimed at them. Despite his wide reading and learning, Webster was an isolated figure, both politically and geographically, removed from the centers of English intellectual life in London and the universities. He had served as a surgeon in the parliamentary armies during the English Civil War, and much of his analysis of witchcraft was aimed at the Royalists who had come into power with the return of the king and the Church of England in 1660. Webster's attack on demonology was also an attack on the mainstream of the Church of England, which Webster found insufficiently Protestant. The demonology of Glanvill and Meric **Casaubon,** another of his main targets, he explained, came from Catholic sources, "the Popish Sink and Dunghills."

Webster was not an intellectually radical opponent of all demonology. He endorsed the reality of the **satanic pact,** although he claimed that such contracts were implicit, simply one variety of the bondage all evil people, not just witches, had with the Devil as opposed to the explicit bartering of soul for demonic powers that was the traditional satanic pact. Despite his acceptance of some aspects of witch belief, Webster was a principal target of the posthumous edition of Glanvill's witchcraft book, *Saducismus Triumphatus* (1681), which included a long letter written by Glanvill's friend, the philosopher Henry More, attacking Webster, as well as Glanvill's defense of the biblical evidence for witches. Although Glanvill and More were usually considered to have won the debate, Webster's work continued to have some influence, and it was published in German in 1719.

REFERENCES: Ian Bostridge. *Witchcraft and Its Transformations, c. 1650–c. 1750.* Oxford: Clarendon Press, 1997; James Sharpe. *Instruments of Darkness: Witchcraft in Early Modern England.* Philadelphia: University of Pennsylvania Press, 1996.

WENHAM, JANE

In 1712, Jane Wenham became the last English person convicted of witchcraft. Wenham was a typical accused witch, an old woman living alone whose reputation for witchcraft dated from several years before her trial. Wenham had had two husbands, the first of whom had died under suspicious circumstances and the second of whom had renounced responsibility for her debts. She had previously been charged with putting a spell on a man after he had refused to let her take some of his straw. The case which led to Wenham's conviction began when she was accused of having bewitched a local serving girl, Anne Thorne. Thorne attempted to cure herself by scratching Wenham, following a common English **countermagical** belief that if the victim could draw blood from the witch, he or she would be cured, but Thorne drew no blood. Wenham was arrested and searched for witches marks. She was also tested by being required to recite the Lord's Prayer, which she failed to do. After confessing and implicating several other women, she was held for the assizes at Hertford. While Wenham was in jail, people claimed a number of mysterious cats, some with Wenham's face, appeared, and the charge laid against her in court was "conversing familiarly with the Devil in the shape of a cat." Although convicted on the basis of her confession and **magical** objects, such as cakes of feathers, found in her room, Wenham received a reprieve from the assize judge and was pardoned shortly afterward by the queen at the judge's behest.

Wenham received many curious visitors while being held for trial, and many more attended the trial itself. Her case was much discussed, and became the subject of several pamphlets. Francis Bragge, author of *A Full and Impartial Account of the Discovery of Sorcery and Witchcraft, Practis'd by Jane Wenham* (1712) and two other pamphlets on the case, used it to argue for the existence of witchcraft and against the skepticism and infidelity of the age. He associated this skepticism with the Whig party, one of the two great British political groups contending for leadership. The area of Hertfordshire where Wenham and Bragge lived was one of great tension between the Church of **England** and the Protestant dissenters, of whom Wenham was one. Dissenters were usually allied with the Whigs, and the Whigs championed Wenham's cause. An anonymous Whig rejoinder, *A Full Confutation of Witchcraft* (1712), defended Wenham, arguing that the Tories, champions of the Church of England and rivals of the Whigs, were superstitious for believing in the powers of witches. Wenham's defenders often attacked Thorne, claiming her charges were caused by sexual frustration and hysteria. Wenham, after her pardon, was provided a cottage by a Whig landowner, in which she peacefully lived out her days until she died in 1730. Francis **Hutchinson,** author of the skeptical *An Historical Essay concerning Witchcraft* (1718), visited her there and reported that she proudly recited the Lord's Prayer. The political polarization the case produced was part of the background to the repeal of the Witchcraft Statute of 1604 in 1736, carried out by a Whig government.

REFERENCES: Ian Bostridge. *Witchcraft and Its Transformations, c. 1650–c. 1750.* Oxford: Clarendon Press, 1997; Phyllis J. Guskin. "The Context of Witchcraft: The Case of Jane Wenham (1712)." *Eighteenth-Century Studies* 15 (1981): 48–71.

WEREWOLVES

The belief in human beings that changed into wolves was an old and widespread one in European culture, appearing in many populations and traceable back to ancient Greece and Rome. Werewolves were not always identified with witches. Heinrich **Kramer's** *Malleus Maleficarum* (1486) and most other early writings on witches take little or no notice of them. Sixteenth-century demonologists did sometimes discuss them. All major writers on the subject, with the exception of Jean **Bodin,** agreed that human beings were not actually transformed into wolves, because this would require a combination of an animal body and human soul, beyond the power of anyone but God. Most ascribed "lycanthropy" to delusions caused by demons who could create an illusion so convincing as to fool both the "werewolf" and any onlookers that a human being had actually become a wolf. Another explanation, with ancient roots, was that werewolves suffered from medical conditions such as an excess of the

A woodcut by Hans Weiditz of a witch turned werewolf attacking travelers. From Dr. Johnn Geiler von Kayserberg's *Die Emeis*, Strassburg, 1517. © Dover Pictorial Archive.

melancholic humor. The two kinds of explanation were not necessarily mutually exclusive, because **Satan** could intervene to heighten the melancholic state. Artificial aids could also be used, as the natural magician Giambattista Della Porta (1535–1615) along with many demonologists ascribed the delusions of the werewolf to the use of drugged ointments. Henri **Boguet,** who devoted more space to the subject than other demonologists, partially concurred. Ordinary people seemed to have been more willing to believe in at least partial **transformations** of human to wolf, often triggered by items such as **magic** wolf skins. (The dominant modern form of the werewolf myth, that werewolfism is a condition triggered involuntarily by the full moon, was only rarely found in early modern Europe.)

Wolves were particularly suited for this mythologizing for two reasons. One was the persistence of wolf populations in many parts of Europe, particularly heavily forested and mountainous regions where wolf predation on livestock and, much more rarely, people, could be a serious problem. It was believed that sometimes devils possessed even ordinary wolves for the purpose of wreaking destruction on humans or livestock. The other reason was the Christian metaphor of society as a flock of sheep under the guidance of a shepherd, which made conceptualizing the enemies of society as wolves a logical next step.

There were a series of well-publicized werewolf cases in the late sixteenth and early seventeenth centuries, beginning with Gilles Garnier of **Franche-Comte.** Garnier, a hermit, had confessed to killing and eating several children and was sentenced to be burned alive in 1574. The next spectacular werewolf case occurred in 1589 in the territory of the elector of Cologne, with the capture of Peter Stubbe, who confessed to incest with his daughter and sister and to killing and eating his son along with many others. Stubbe's case, the only werewolf case in the Cologne witch-hunt, was marked by the assimilation of the werewolf to the witch, because he confessed to having received a magic belt from a **satanic pact** that enabled him to turn to a wolf. (The belt was never found.) Stubbe was sentenced to a slow and painful death involving having his flesh torn with red-hot pincers and his arms and legs broken before beheading. His case was widely known. The French case of Jean **Grenier** in 1603 displays some similar features, although he was not executed. Although these spectacular werewolf cases were men, women were also charged as werewolves.

Interest in werewolves varied greatly by region. Heavily wooded Franche-Comte, home of Boguet and Garnier, was full of werewolves, whereas neighboring **Lorraine** saw few. The British Isles, where wolves were eliminated from **England** by the sixteenth century and were increasingly being hunted out of **Scotland** and **Ireland,** had virtually no werewolf cases. Livonia on the Baltic had an unusual mythology of good werewolves, who like the Friulian *benandanti* fought devils and witches to ensure a good harvest. (Another similarity between werewolves and *benandanti* is that many Slavic peoples, among whom werewolf mythology was strong, believed that persons born with a caul would become werewolves.) Interest in werewolves was dying out among the educated population in western Europe in the seventeenth century. After around 1650, werewolf cases and books on lycanthropy are found only in the Holy Roman Empire and eastern Europe. Ordinary people, however, were slower to give up the idea.

REFERENCES: Carlo Ginzburg. *Ecstacies: Deciphering the Witches' Sabbath*. Trans. Raymond Rosenthal. New York: Pantheon Books, 1991; Charlotte F. Otten, ed. *A Lycanthropy Reader: Werewolves in Western Culture*. Syracuse, N.Y.: Syracuse University Press, 1986.

WESTERSTETTEN, JOHANN CHRISTOPH VON

See Eichstätt Witch-Hunt; Ellwangen Witch-Hunt.

WEYER, JOHANN (1515?–1588)

The German **physician** Johann Weyer was the author of the first great systematic demonology opposing witch-hunting, *Of the Tricks of Demons* (1563). As a youth, Weyer had been a student of the magician and defender of witches Heinrich Cornelius **Agrippa,** and then studied medicine at the Universities of Paris and Orleans. Weyer became municipal physician in the town of Arnhem in 1545, where he handled a mass **possession** case in 1548. From Arnhem he moved to the Dusseldorf court of Duke William of Julich-Berg-Cleve in 1550 as ducal physician. As a physician, Weyer was an intellectually conservative follower of the classical and Arab physicians, who despised the medical innovations of Paracelsus and his followers.

Of the Tricks of the Demons, unlike much later anti-witch-hunt materials, was aimed not at the abuses of the witch-hunt but at the fundamental ideas of witch-hunters. Weyer limited the power of demons, claiming that many events that witch-hunters ascribed to demons actually had material causes. The actions of accused witches were not primarily caused by their relations to demons, but by the feebleness and "melancholy" of deluded old women. (Following Europe's dominant medical theory, Weyer explained melancholy by an excess of black bile, one of the four "humors" of the body.) Weyer had as poor an opinion of women, as did many witch-hunters, although in his opinion women's feebleness made them less culpable. Demons use women's melancholy and feebleness to delude them. Weyer particularly associated erotic delusions with witches' propensity for masturbation and lesbianism.

Although Weyer did not go as far as later opponents of the witch-hunt, such as Reginald **Scot** and Balthasar **Bekker,** in denying the possibility of demons affecting the material world at all, he limited the sphere of demonic action. He believed the Devil acted only with God's permission, and in accordance with the limits of his own nature; thus Weyer denied the possibility of the Devil impregnating witches. Witch flight, **transformation** and the **sabbat** were all delusions. Weyer attacked the **torture** of witches and claimed that the appropriate treatment in most witchcraft cases was medical rather than judicial. He was much harsher on learned magicians, who were far more culpable than deluded, old, female witches. The magician consciously turned away from God by practicing a profession he had forbidden and practicing the idolatrous worship of demons. (Weyer somewhat unconvincingly defended his old master Agrippa from charges of being a demonic magician.) Although physically limited, demons were powerful nonetheless—the Devil was extremely crafty, and demon worship common. Weyer referred to contemporary travel literature to claim that the gods of Native Americans were really demons.

Weyer attacked the concept of the **satanic pact** with arguments based on Roman law. **Satan,** he claimed, could not enter into a legally binding agreement because of his lack of trustworthiness. He also invoked a Roman law doctrine claiming that contracts redounding entirely to the benefit of one party, in this case, the Devil, and entirely to the disadvantage of the other, the witch, were not legally binding. He also asserted that the **Bible** shows no evidence of satanic pacts. Humans could never command demons, whether based on pact or not. Witches described in the Bible, Weyer claimed, were poisoners rather than wielders of **magical** or demonic power. Exodus 22.18 actually commanded death to poisoners rather than witches as early modern people understood them.

Weyer was a moderate Lutheran Protestant, although he worked for the Catholic Duke William, of whom he spoke admiringly, with little evidence of friction. Although not specifically directed against Catholics, *Of the Tricks of Demons* denounces ecclesiastical countermagic and exorcism rites involving sacramentals such as holy water. All countermagic was invalid as relying on material things rather than power of faith. *Of the Tricks of Demons* drew on wide reading in ancient and modern literature as well as many of Weyer's own experiences. He was familiar with Heinrich **Kramer's** *Malleus Maleficarum* (1486), a frequent target of his denunciations, as well as previous antiwitch-hunt writers such as the Italian lawyers Gianfrancesco **Ponzinibio** and Andreas Alciatus.

Of the Tricks of Demons was popular and widely circulated, going through six expanded editions between 1563 and 1583 in the original Latin. The first unauthorized French translation appeared in 1567, and the first unauthorized German translation in 1565. Weyer's own somewhat abridged German translation appeared in 1566. Although the book was not translated into English during the early modern period, it entered the English-language demonological tradition through Scot, who borrowed heavily from Weyer in his *Discoverie of Witchcraft* (1584). Weyer was attacked by leading European intellectuals such as the Heidelberg professor Thomas Erastus (1524–1583), with whom Weyer corresponded and to whom he replied in *Book of Witches* (1577) and much more bitterly by Jean **Bodin** in *On the Demonmania of Sorcerers* (1580). Bodin ridiculed Weyer's legal arguments and attacked him, charging Weyer with being a demonic magician. Weyer replied in the 1583 edition of *Of the Tricks of Demons*. Bodin was generally thought to have won the dispute, and the direct influence of Weyer faded in the seventeenth century. Weyer's direct influence on witch-hunting practice is hard to trace. Ironically, witch-hunting expanded greatly in the decades after the publication of *Of the Tricks of Demons*. Increased use of physicians as consultants on the mental state of accused witches in German trials may be due to Weyer's influence.

REFERENCES: Christopher Baxter. "Johann Weyer's *De Praestigiis Daemonum:* Unsystematic Psychopathology." In *The Damned Art: Essays in the Literature of Witchcraft*, ed. Sydney Anglo, 53–75. Boston: Routledge and Kegan Paul, 1977; J. J. Cobben. *Jan Wier, Devils, Witches and Magic*. Trans. Sal A. Prins. Philadelphia: Dorrance, 1976; Gerhild Scholz Williams. *Defining Dominion: The Discourses of Witchcraft and Magic in Early Modern France and Germany*. Ann Arbor, Michigan: University of Michigan Press, 1995; Johann Weyer. *On Witchcraft: An Abridged Translation of Johann Weyer's De Praestigiis Daemonum*. Ed. Benjamin G. Kohl and H. C. Erik Midelfort. Asheville, N.C.: Pegasus Press, 1998.

WIESENSTEIG WITCH-HUNT

Although poorly documented, the witch-hunt in the small southwestern German territory of Wiesensteig was one of the first in the great wave of witch-hunting that swept **Germany** in the second half of the sixteenth century. In 1562, Wiesensteig was a Lutheran territory ruled by Count Ulrich von Helfenstein. After a severe hailstorm on August 3, 1562, von Helfenstein had several women arrested as witches. Under **torture,** they implicated others, including several people from the neighboring city of **Esslingen** who they claimed to have seen at the **sabbat.** Much to the chagrin of von Helfenstein and Esslingen's Lutheran preacher Thomas Naogeorgius, this disclosure was not followed by a witch-hunt in Esslingen. Wiesensteig itself, where von Helfenstein cooperated with the local Lutheran leader Leonhard Culmann, was a different story, of course, and a sensationalistic pamphlet dated 1563 claimed that Wiesensteig had executed by burning no less than 63 witches. Under outside pressure, von

Helfenstein converted to Catholicism in 1567, and nineteenth-century German historians spent much time arguing whether Wiesensteig was Catholic or Protestant at the time of the witch-hunt. Although it seems clear that during this first Wiesensteig witch-hunt the state and church were Lutheran, the habit of witch-hunting survived von Helfenstein's and the territory's return to the Catholic fold. There were subsequent flare-ups in 1583 (about 25 dead), 1605 (14 dead) and 1611 (5 dead).

REFERENCE: H. C. Erik Midelfort. *Witch-Hunting in Southwestern Germany, 1562–1684.* Stanford: Stanford University Press, 1972.

WITCH-BOTTLE

See Countermagic.

WITCH-FINDERS

Witch-finders were persons who claimed particular expertise in the detection of witches, frequently working outside the judicial system. They were characteristic of many witch-hunts. Witch-finders came from a variety of social backgrounds and roles. Some were **cunning folk,** who identified witches for persons suffering from *maleficia*. Others were judicial professionals, torturers and executioners such as Hans **Vollmair** or Jean Minard, the hangman of Rocroi who identified more than two hundred witches by pricking for the **Devil's mark.** In some areas of **France,** teenage boys claimed they could identify witches by looking in their eyes. Some Spanish witch-finders washed the feet of suspects with holy water looking for a mark in the shape of a crow's foot. Clergy, particularly members of the Catholic religious orders, were sometimes witch-finders. Even witches could become witch-finders. In 1597, the Scottish witch Margaret Atkin, after her conviction, was carried around to various Scottish towns where she found witches, by, she claimed, a mark on them that was invisible to everyone else. She was found to be a fraud when a person she had declared to be a witch was led before her the next day, in different clothing, and declared to be innocent.

Witch-finding could be a profitable business. Cunning folk who identified witches for individuals normally charged for their services, and specialized witch-finders were often called in by communities suffering from what they believed to be witchcraft—plagues, spells of bad weather or poor harvests and other large-scale *maleficia*. These communities wanted witches identified and neutralized quickly, without the cumbersome machinery of the early modern judicial process being set in motion. Local nobles sometimes hired witch-finders or were witch-finders themselves. Some witch-finders, like the Scottish witch-prickers, were actually court employees.

Despite the occasional employment of witch-prickers, freelance witch-finders usually met with disapproval from higher judicial authorities. There were several reasons for this. Many of the techniques of witch-finders relied on a concept of evidence far removed from that of early modern lawyers and magistrates. Witch-finders' activities often led to extrajudicial killings, and their very existence suggested that judicial authority was inadequate to protect the community. Some witch-finders were executed; the Parlement of Toulouse executed three active in the burst of witch-hunting in the early 1640s. These witch-finders had not only blackmailed people by accusing of witchcraft those who did not pay them, but, possibly an even greater sin in the Parlement's eyes, they had pretended authority from the Parlement itself. Given the hostility of the higher courts to most witch-finders, the best areas for their operations were those where higher judicial authority was weak or absent, whether physically remote areas or those undergoing civil unrest. The most celebrated witch-finder of all, "witch-finder general" Matthew **Hopkins,** took advantage of the disorder of the English Civil War to cause the death of dozens or hundreds of witches.

REFERENCE: Robin Briggs. *Witches and Neighbors: The Social and Cultural Context of European Witchcraft.* New York: Penguin, 1996.

WITCH'S MARK

The term "witch's mark" is used with two separate meanings in the literature of witchcraft. The first is as a synonym for **Devil's mark.** The second is restricted to witchcraft in **England** and English colonies, which was characterized by the relationship of the witch and her **familiars,** or "imps." The witch's mark is an extra nipple or protuberance through which female witches (and sometimes male witches) nursed their imps on their blood. It was usually located near the vagina or anus, a belief that grew stronger with the progress of the English witch-hunt, and was supposed to be grotesque and deformed in appearance. The witch's mark was part of the whole distorted parody of motherhood played out by female witches and their familiars. The search for the witch's mark was ordinarily carried out by women, **midwives** or matrons whose familiarity with the female body was assumed. Warts, hemorrhoids, deformations of the labia or even insect bites could all be identified as witch's marks, and such identifications were treated as proofs of witchcraft. The witch's mark also differed from the Devil's mark in that it was not usually thought insensitive to pain.

REFERENCE: James Sharpe. *Instruments of Darkness: Witchcraft in Early Modern England.* Philadelphia: University of Pennsylvania Press, 1996.

WOMEN

See Feminist Historiography; Gender.

WÜRZBURG WITCH-HUNTS

The prince-bishopric of Würzburg was a center of witch-hunting in central **Germany.** The first recorded **execution** there was in 1590. The first major witch-hunt in Würzburg territory occurred under the Catholic Reformation

Prince-Bishop Julius Echter von Mespellbrun (1573–1616). Mespellbrun had taken over the Protestant town of Freudenburg in 1612, on the death of the last representative in the direct male line of the counts of Lowenstein-Wertheim. Mespellbrun's takeover of the territory was accompanied by a witch-hunt that claimed more than 50 victims, although the relation between the two phenomena is not clear. The height of witch-hunting activity during the Mespellbrun era in Wurzburg occurred between July 1616 and June 1617, when more than three hundred witches were sent to the stake.

The next major Würzburg witch-hunt, and one of the bloodiest in the entire history of European witch-hunting, occurred under another reforming prince-bishop, Philipp Adolf von Ehrenberg (bishop, 1623–1631), from 1627 to 1630. Survival of records is incomplete, but the traditional figure is around nine hundred executions. This may be high, because the source is a sensationalistic pamphlet published in 1629, but unquestionably the death toll was large. The full panoply of German witch-hunting was unloosed in Würzburg, with a special Witch Commission to oversee the hunt and the unrestricted use of inventive **torture** to force witches to confess and name accomplices. Like many large-scale German hunts, the Würzburg hunt held no respect for human beings of any social level. In 29 recorded witch burnings in the town of Würzburg from 1627 to February 1629, the dead included several members of the nobility, two learned theologians, five canons of the cathedral, and the wives of an ex-chancellor, a burgomaster, and three councillors. In all, at least 43 members of the clergy are known to have been killed. Von Ehrenberg also executed his own young nephew, Ernst von Ehrenberg. Although most of the early victims were women, as the hunt went on, the **gender** and age stereotype of the witch broke down, and in some of the later burnings a majority of the victims were men. Another development in the course of the witch-hunt was the increased involvement of children as both witnesses and witches. At least 41 children were killed. Although the Würzburg bishops were fierce opponents of Protestants as well as witches, there were no correlations, positive or negative, between areas with a strong Protestant presence and areas of particularly active witch-hunting.

The Würzburg witch-hunt had an influence far beyond its boundaries. Influence from Würzburg helped set off the **Mergentheim witch-hunt** of 1628–1631. In northwestern Germany, unrestrained large-scale witch-hunting became known as "Würzburgisch work," and for the next several decades, German supporters of witch-hunting would invoke von Ehrenberg as a role model.

The persecution came to an end around 1630, after an escapee from the Würzburg prison brought a complaint before the Chamber Court of the Holy Roman Empire at Speyer. An order was issued to von Ehrenberg to desist, and the last prisoners were released on bail in September 1631. The occupation of Würzburg by the Swedish army and von Ehrenberg's death in exile in 1631 ensured that large-scale witch-hunting did not revive. In 1642, the friend of Friedrich von **Spee,** Johann Philip von Schonborn (1605–1673), became bishop of Würzburg and opposed witch-hunts there. Small scale witch-hunts did occasionally happen, and witch trials and executions continued to the mid–eighteenth century.

REFERENCES: Wolfgang Behringer. *Witchcraft Persecutions in Bavaria: Popular Magic, Religious Zealotry, and Reason of State in Early Modern Europe*. Trans. J. C. Grayson and David Lederer. Cambridge: Cambridge University Press, 1997; H. C. Erik Midelfort. *Witch-Hunting in Southwestern Germany, 1562–1684*. Stanford: Stanford University Press, 1972; Hans Sebald. *Witch-Children: From Salem Witch-Hunts to Modern Courtrooms*. Amherst, Mass.: Prometheus Books, 1995; Robert S. Walinski-Kiehl. " 'Godly States,' Confessional Conflict and Witch-Hunting in Early Modern Germany." *Mentalities* 5 (1988): 13–25.

Z

ZAUBERERJACKL TRIALS

From 1677 to 1681, the archbishopric of Salzburg in southeastern **Germany,** under Prince-Bishop Max Gandolf von Khuenburg (bishop, 1668–1687) carried out a series of witch trials, known as the Zaubererjackl or "Magic Jack" trials, with their primary targets gangs of beggars. **Magic** Jack was the adolescent Jacob Koller, a beggar leader and son of beggars widely credited by other beggars to possess magical powers, such as the power to become invisible. Persons who refused to give to beggars were threatened with the vengeance of Magic Jack, adding to his legend and also to the desire of the government to catch and dispose of him. Ideas about magical power seem to have been common in beggar culture, judging by the information some volunteered to interrogators. Beggars were particularly vulnerable to persecution, because they had no position in society, and no one with any power would have a reason to protect them. At least 140 alleged witches, mostly adolescent boys, were killed in the persecution. Magic Jack was not caught and became a legendary figure. The Zaubererjackl trials were invoked as a precedent in legal writing on the crime of witchcraft into the eighteenth century. They also set a precedent for many subsequent trials in Salzburg, in areas on the fringes of the Holy Roman Empire such as Styria, the Tyrol and Carinthia; and in **Bavaria** to around 1722. The stereotype of the witch in southeastern Germany shifted from that of a poor old woman to that of a teenage male beggar.

REFERENCES: Wolfgang Behringer. *Witchcraft Persecutions in Bavaria: Popular Magic, Religious Zealotry, and Reason of State in Early Modern Europe.* Trans. J. C. Grayson and David Lederer. Cambridge: Cambridge University Press, 1997; Robin Briggs. *Witches and Neighbors: The Social and Cultural Context of European Witchcraft.* New York: Penguin, 1996.

ZUGURRAMURDI CASES

The auto-de-fé at Logroño on November 7, 1610, saw the burning of six witches, along with the effigies and remains of five more who had died while being held captive by the **Spanish Inquisition.** These witches all came from the area of Zugurramurdi in the **Basque** country of Spain. This was the greatest—and the last—witch-burning in the history of the Spanish Inquisition.

The Zugurramurdi case began as a spillover from the great witch hunt in Basque **France** being carried out by Pierre de **Lancre.** The first witch, Maria de Ximildegui, had lived in France for several years and claimed she had become a witch there. She returned to Zugurramurdi late in 1608 and shortly afterward began talking about her experiences, claiming that while living in Zugurramurdi she had attended **sabbats** along with other village residents. Most of the persons she accused already had bad reputations. The village priest urged the accused witches to make public confessions in the church and beg their neighbors' forgiveness.

What made the Zugurramurdi case an affair for the Inquisition's intervention was the action of the ambitious Premonstratensian Abbot of Urdax Leon de Aranibar, spiritual and secular lord of Zugarramurdi and Urdax. De Aranibar was probably the one who informed the Logroño tribunal of the events, hoping to be appointed a commissioner, or local agent of the Inquisition, in an area where the Inquisition had little day-to-day presence (a wish duly fulfilled during the witch-hunt). Although the Logroño inquisitors lacked experience with witchcraft, not a major concern of the Inquisition, the tribunal quickly responded. Four Zugurramurdi witches, all women, were summoned to Logroño, where they made voluntary and extraordinarily detailed confessions regarding the sabbats, their relationships with the Devil and the clothed toads they had received as **familiars.** Six other witches voluntarily appeared at Logroño, claiming their original confessions had been coerced and false. The Inquisition imprisoned them as well. After many delays, one of the three inquisitors of Logroño, Jose de Alvarado Valle, a priest in his late 50s, left for Zugurramurdi on August 16, 1609, to investigate the matter. Five more witches confessed. Valle, who had become an enthusiastic witch-hunter, arrested 15 more accused witches, 6 women and 9 men, including a monk and a priest, and sent them to Logroño. He also discovered witches in many other villages in the region and was greatly concerned about the possibility of the area being inundated by French witches fleeing persecution.

The trials of the accused witches at Logroño was running into difficulties because of epidemics that killed nearly half of the prisoners held there. Eventually, the Logroño Inquisition requested permission from the Supreme Council of the Inquisition at Madrid to burn eight witches who had survived the epidemics and refused to confess, even under **torture,** along with effigies and the remains of dead witches who had refused to confess. The Supreme Council spared the two priests, but the other six, including the mothers of the two priests, were duly burned in an auto-de-fé that attracted thousands of spectators, including French dignitaries involved in the persecution of witches on the other side of the Pyrenees. Although the auto-de-fé was followed by a massive flare-up of witch **accusations** in the Basque country including mobs invading the houses of suspected witches, torturing and murdering them, there were no more judicial **executions.** This was due to the efforts of the bishop of Pamplona, ex-inquisitor Antonio Venegas de Figueroa (1550–1614), and of the third inquisitor of Logroño, Alonzo de **Salazar Frias.** Salazar's efforts wrought a change in inquisitorial policy toward witches (or a return to the traditional policy), essentially ending their persecution by the Inquisition.

REFERENCES: Gustav Henningsen. *The Witches' Advocate: Basque Witchcraft and the Spanish Inquisition (1609–1614)*. Reno: University of Nevada Press, 1980; William Monter. *Frontiers of Heresy: The Spanish Inquisition from the Basque Lands to Sicily/* Cambridge: Cambridge University Press, 1990.

BIBLIOGRAPHY

Adam, Isabel. *Witch Hunt: The Great Scottish Witchcraft Trials of 1697*. London: Macmillan, 1978.

Andreski, Stanislav. "The Syphilitic Shock." *Encounter* 58 (1982): 7–26.

Ankarloo, Bengt. "Sweden: The Mass Burnings (1668–1676)." In *Early Modern European Witchcraft: Centres and Peripheries*, ed. Bengt Ankarloo and Gustav Henningsen, 285–317. Oxford: Clarendon Press, 1990.

Bailey, Michael. "The Medieval Concept of the Witches' Sabbath." *Exemplaria: A Journal of Theory in Medieval and Renaissance Studies* 8 (1996): 419–439.

Balleine, G. R. "Witch Trials in Jersey." *Societe Jersaise* 13 (1939): 379–398.

Bankoff, Greg. "Devils, Familiars, and Spaniards: Spheres of Power and the Supernatural in the World of Seberina Candelaria and her Village in Early 19th-Century Philippines." *Journal of Social History* 33 (1999): 37–56.

Barber, Laird H. *An Edition of the Late Lancashire Witches by Thomas Heywood and Richard Brome*. New York and London: Garland, 1979.

Barber, Malcolm. *The Trial of the Templars*. Cambridge: Cambridge University Press, 1978.

Barstow, Anne Llewellyn. *Witchcraze: A New History of the European Witch Hunts*. San Francisco: Pandora, 1994.

Baxter, Christopher. "Jean Bodin's *De La Demonomanie des Sorciers*: The Logic of Persecution." In *The Damned Art: Essays in the Literature of Witchcraft*, ed. Sydney Anglo, 76–105. Boston: Routledge and Kegan Paul, 1977.

Baxter, Christopher. "Johann Weyer's *De Praestigiis Daemonum*: Unsystematic Psychopathology." In *The Damned Art: Essays in the Literature of Witchcraft*, ed. Sydney Anglo, 53–75. Boston: Routledge and Kegan Paul, 1977.

Behar, Ruth. "The Visions of a Guachichil Witch in 1599: A Window on the Subjugation of Mexico's Hunter-Gatherers." *Ethnohistory* 34 (1987): 115–138.

Behringer, Wolfgang. *Shaman of Oberstdorf: Chonrad Stoeckhlin and the Phantoms of the Night*. Translated by H. C. Erik Midelfort. Charlottesville: University Press of Virginia, 1998.

———. "Weather, Hunger and Fear: Origins of the European Witch-Hunts in Climate, Society and Mentality." Trans. David Lederer. *German History* 13 (1995): 1–27.

———. *Witchcraft Persecutions in Bavaria: Popular Magic, Religious Zealotry, and Reason of State in Early Modern Europe.* Translated by J. C. Grayson and David Lederer. Cambridge: Cambridge University Press, 1997.

Bethencourt, Francesco. "Portugal: A Scrupulous Inquisition." *Early Modern European Witchcraft: Centres and Peripheries,* ed. Bengt Ankarloo and Gustav Henningsen, 403–422. Oxford: Clarendon Press, 1990.

Bevers, Edward. "Witchcraft Fears and Psychosocial Factors in Disease." *Journal of Interdisciplinary History* 30 (2000): 573–590.

Black, George F. "A Calendar of Cases of Witchcraft in Scotland, 1510–1727." *Bulletin of the New York Public Library* 41 (1937): 811–847, 917–936; 42 (1938): 34–74.

Blécourt, Willem de. "The Making of the Female Witch: Reflections on Witchcraft and Gender in the Early Modern Period." *Gender and History* 12 (2000): 287–309.

Boerner, Peter, and Sidney Johnson, eds. *Faust through Four Centuries: Retrospect and Analysis.* Tübingen: Max Niemeyer Verlag, 1989.

Bogucka, Maria. "Law and Crime in Poland in Early Modern Times." *Acta Poloniae Historica* 71 (1995): 175–195.

Borst, Arno. *Medieval Worlds: Barbarians, Heretics and Artists in the Middle Ages.* Trans. Eric Hansen. Chicago: University of Chicago Press, 1992.

Bostridge, Ian. *Witchcraft and Its Transformations, c. 1650–c. 1750.* Oxford: Clarendon Press, 1997.

Boyer, Paul, and Stephen Nissenbaum. *Salem Possessed: The Social Origins of Witchcraft.* Cambridge and London: Harvard University Press, 1974.

Brauner, Sigrid. *Fearless Wives and Frightened Shrews: The Construction of the Witch in Early Modern Germany.* Amherst: University of Massachusetts Press, 1995.

Breslaw, Elaine G. *Tituba, Reluctant Witch of Salem: Devilish Indians and Puritan Fantasies.* New York and London: New York University Press, 1996.

Briggs, Robin. *Communities of Belief: Cultural and Social Tension in Early Modern France.* Oxford: Clarendon Press, 1989.

———. *Witches and Neighbors: The Social and Cultural Context of European Witchcraft.* New York: Penguin, 1996.

Burke, Peter. "Witchcraft and Magic in Renaissance Italy: Gianfrancesco Pico and His *Strix.*" In *The Damned Art: Essays in the Literature of Witchcraft,* ed. Sydney Anglo, 32–52. Boston: Routledge and Kegan Paul, 1977.

Burr, George Lincoln. *Narratives of the Witchcraft Cases, 1648–1706.* New York: Charles Scribner's Sons, 1914.

Caporael, Linnda R. "Ergotism: The Satan Loosed in Salem." *Science* 92 (1976): 121–126.

Carlson, Laurie Winn. *A Fever in Salem: A New Interpretation of the New England Witch Trials.* Chicago: Ivan R. Dee, 1999.

Caro Baroja, Julio. *The World of the Witches*. Trans. O. N. V. Glendinning. Chicago: University of Chicago Press, 1965.

Caspar, Max. *Kepler*. Trans. and ed. C. Doris Hellman. London and New York: Abelard-Schuman, 1959.

Certeau, Michel de. *The Possession at Loudun*. Trans. Michael B. Smith. Chicago and London: University of Chicago Press, 2000.

Cervantes, Fernando. *The Devil in the New World: The Impact of Diabolism in New Spain*. New Haven and London: Yale University Press, 1994.

Clark, Stuart. "King James's *Daemonologie*: Witchcraft and Kingcraft." In *The Damned Art: Essays in the Literature of Witchcraft*, ed. Sydney Anglo, 156–181. Boston: Routledge and Kegan Paul, 1977.

———. *Thinking with Demons: The Idea of Witchcraft in Early Modern Europe*. Oxford: Clarendon Press, 1997.

———, and P. T. J. Morgan. "Religion and Magic in Elizabethan Wales: Robert Holland's Dialogue on Witchcraft." *Journal of Ecclesiastical History* 27 (1976): 31–46.

Cobben, J. J. *Jan Wier, Devils, Witches and Magic*. Trans. Sal A. Prins. Philadelphia: Dorrance, 1976.

Cohen, Thomas V., and Elizabeth S. Cohen. *Words and Deeds in Renaissance Rome: Trials before the Papal Magistrates*. Toronto: University of Toronto Press, 1993.

Cohn, Norman. *Europe's Inner Demons: The Demonization of Christians in Medieval Christendom*. Rev. ed. Chicago: University of Chicago Press, 2000.

Corrêa de Melo, Maria Cristina. "Witchcraft in Portugal during the Eighteenth Century, Analysed through the Accusations of the Tribunal do Santo Officio de Evora." In *Transactions of the Eighth International Congress on the Enlightenment*, 573–578. Studies in Voltaire and the Eighteenth Century, no. 303. Oxford: Voltaire Foundation, 1992.

Craker, Wendel D. "Spectral Evidence, Non-Spectral Acts of Witchcraft, and Confession at Salem in 1692." *Historical Journal* 40 (1997): 331–358.

Daly, Mary. *Gyn/Ecology: The Metaethics of Radical Feminism*. Boston: Beacon Press, 1978.

Darst, David H. "Witchcraft in Spain: The Testimony of Martin de Castañega's *Treatise on Superstition and Witchcraft* (1529)." *Proceedings of the American Philosophical Society* 123 (1979): 298–322.

Davidson, Jane P. *The Witch in Northern European Art, 1470–1750*. Freren: Luca Verlag, 1987.

Davies, Owen. "Methodism, the Clergy, and the Popular Belief in Witchcraft and Magic." *History* 82 (1997): 252–265.

Davis, Richard Beale. "The Devil in Virginia in the Seventeenth Century." *The Virginia Magazine of History and Biography* 65 (1957): 131–149.

De Graaf, Robert M. *The Book of the Toad: A Natural and Magical History of Toad-Human Relations*. Rochester, Vt.: Park Street Press, 1991.

de Mello e Souza, Laura. "Witchcraft and Magic Practices in Colonial Brazil: 1580–1770." *Acta Ethnographica Hungarica* 37 (1991/1992): 243–256.

Demos, John Putnam. *Entertaining Satan: Witchcraft and the Culture of Early New England.* New York: Oxford University Press, 1982.

Deutscher, Thomas. "The Role of the Episcopal Tribunal of Novara in the Suppression of Heresy and Witchcraft 1563–1615." *Catholic Historical Review* 77 (1991): 403–421.

Dresen-Conders, Lene. "Witches as Devil's Concubines: On the Origin of Fear of Witches and Protection against Witchcraft." In *Saints and She-Devils: Images of Women in the 15th and 16th Centuries,* ed. Lene Dresen-Conders, 59–82. London: Rubicon Press, 1987.

Dundes, Alan, ed. *The Evil Eye: A Folklore Casebook.* New York and London: Garland, 1981.

Edsman, Carl-Martin. "A Manuscript concerning Inquiries into Witchcraft in Swedish Lappland ("Trolldomsrannsakningar i Lappmarken") 1649–1739 by Erik Nordberg." In *Saami Pre-Christian Religion: Studies on the Oldest Traces of Religion among the Saamis,* ed. Louise Backman and Ake Hultkranz, 121–137. Stockholm: Almqvist and Wiksell International, 1985.

Ehrenreich, Barbara, and Deirdre English. *Witches, Midwives and Nurses: A History of Women Healers.* New York: Feminist Press, 1973.

Ellis, R. C. "The Kirkjubold Affair: A Seventeenth-Century Icelandic Witchcraft Case Analyzed." *The Seventeenth Century* 8 (1993): 217–241.

Estes, Leland. "The Medical Origins of the European Witchcraze: A Hypothesis." *Journal of Social History* 17 (1983): 271–284.

Evans, R. J. W. *The Making of the Habsburg Monarchy: An Interpretation.* Oxford: Clarendon Press, 1979.

Evans-Pritchard, E. E. *Witchcraft, Oracles and Magic among the Azande.* Oxford: Clarendon Press, 1937.

Ewen, C. L'Estrange. *Witchcraft and Demonianism: A Concise Account Derived from Sworn Depositions and Confessions Obtained in the Courts of England and Wales.* London: Heath Cranton, 1933.

Fehrenbach, R. J. "A Pre-1592 English Faust Book and the Date of Marlowe's Doctor Faustus." *The Library,* 7th ser., vol. 2 (2001): 327–335.

Fix, Andrew. *Fallen Angels: Balthasar Bekker, Spirit Belief, and Confessionalism in the Seventeenth Century Dutch Republic.* Dordrecht: Kluwer, 1999.

Ford, John, Thomas Dekker and William Rowley. *The Witch of Edmonton,* ed. Peter Corbin and Douglas Sedge. Manchester and New York: Manchester University Press, 1999.

Freeman, Thomas. "Demons, Deviance and Defiance: John Darrell and the Politics of Exorcism in late Elizabethan England." In *Orthodoxy and Conformity in the English Church, c. 1560–1660,* ed. Peter Lake and Michael Questier, 34–63. Woodbridge, England: Boydell Press, 2000.

Freud, Sigmund. *The Complete Letters of Sigmund Freud to Wilhelm Fleiss 1887–1904.* Ed. and trans. Jeffrey Moussaief-Masson. Cambridge and London: Belknap Press of Harvard University Press, 1985.

Freud, Sigmund. "A Seventeenth-Century Demonological Neurosis." In *The Standard Edition of the Complete Psychological Works of Sigmund Freud, Volume 19*, ed. James Strachey, 67–105. London: Hogarth Press, 1961.

Frijhoff, Willem. "Witchcraft and Its Changing Representation in Eastern Gelderland, from the Sixteenth to the Twentieth Centuries." In *Witchcraft in the Netherlands from the Fourteenth to the Twentieth Century*, ed. Marijke Gijswit-Hofstra and Willem Frijhoff. Rotterdam: Universitaire Pers Rotterdam, 167–180. 1991.

Geis, Gilbert, and Ivan Bunn. *A Trial of Witches: A Seventeenth-Century Witchcraft Persecution*. London and New York: Routledge, 1997.

Gentilcore, David. *From Bishop to Witch: The System of the Sacred in Early Modern Terra d'Otranto*. Manchester and New York: Manchester University Press, 1992.

George Lincoln Burr: His Life by Roland Bainton: Selections from his Writings Ed. Lois Oliphant Gibbons. Ithaca and New York: Cornell University Press, 1943.

Gere, Cathy. "William Harvey's Weak Experiment: The Archeology of an Anecdote." *History Workshop Journal* 51 (spring 2001): 19–36.

Gevirtz, Norman. " 'The Devil Hath Laughed at the Physicians': Witchcraft and Medical Practice in Seventeenth-Century New England." *Journal of the History of Medicine* 55 (2000): 5–36.

Geyer-Kordesch, Johanna. "Whose Enlightenment? Medicine, Witchcraft, Melancholia and Pathology." In *Medicine in the Enlightenment*, ed. Roy Porter, 113–127. Atlanta: Rodopi, 1995.

Gibbons, Lois Oliphant. "A Seventeenth Century Humanitarian: Hermann Löher." In *Persecution and Liberty: Essays in Honor of George Lincoln Burr*, 338–359. New York: Century, 1931.

Gibson, Marion. *Reading Witchcraft: Stories of Early English Witches*. London and New York: Routledge, 1999.

———, ed. *Early Modern Witches: Witchcraft Cases in Contemporary Writing*. London and New York: Routledge, 2000.

Gijswit-Hofstra, Marijke, and Willem Frijhoff, eds. *Witchcraft in the Netherlands from the Fourteenth to the Twentieth Century*. Rotterdam: Universitaire Pers Rotterdam, 1991.

Ginzburg, Carlo. *Ecstacies: Deciphering the Witches' Sabbath*. Trans. Raymond Rosenthal. New York: Pantheon Books, 1991.

———. *The Night Battles: Witchcraft & Agrarian Cults in the Sixteenth & Seventeenth Centuries*. Trans. John Tedeschi and Anne Tedeschi. Baltimore: Johns Hopkins University Press, 1983.

Goodare, Julian. "Women and the Witch-Hunt in Scotland." *Social History* 23 (1998): 288–308.

Guazzo, Francesco Maria. *Compendium Maleficarum*. Ed. Montague Summers, trans. E. A. Ashwin. 1929. Reprint, New York: Dover Press, 1988.

Guskin, Phyllis J. "The Context of Witchcraft: The Case of Jane Wenham (1712)." *Eighteenth-Century Studies* 15 (1981): 48–71.

Harley, David. "Historians as Demonologists: The Myth of the Midwife-Witch." *Social History of Medicine* 3 (1990): 1–26.

Harner, Michael J. "The Role of Hallucinogenic Plants in European Witchcraft." In *Hallucinogens and Shamanism*, ed. Michael J. Harner, 125–150. New York: Oxford University Press, 1973.

Harvey, Margaret. "Papal Witchcraft: The Charges Against Benedict XIII." In *Sanctity and Secularity; the Church and the World. Papers read at the eleventh summer meeting and the twelfth winter meeting of the Ecclesiastical History Society*, ed. Derek Baker, 109–116. Oxford: Published for the Ecclesiastical History Society by Blackwell, 1973.

Hastrup, Kirsten. "Iceland: Sorcerors and Paganism." In *Early Modern European Witchcraft: Centres and Peripheries*, ed. Bengt Ankarloo and Gustav Henningsen, 383–401. Oxford: Clarendon Press, 1990.

Heikkinen, Antero, and Timo Kervinen. "Finland: The Male Domination." In *Early Modern European Witchcraft: Centres and Peripheries*, ed. Bengt Ankarloo and Gustav Henningsen, 319–338. Oxford: Clarendon Press, 1990.

Heinemann, Evelyn. *Witches: A Psychoanalytic Exploration of the Killing of Women*. London and New York: Free Association Books, 2000.

Henningsen, Gustav. "The Ladies from Outside: An Archaic Pattern of the Witches' Sabbath." In *Early Modern European Witchcraft: Centres and Peripheries*, ed. Bengt Ankarloo and Gustav Henningsen, 191–215. Oxford: Clarendon Press, 1990.

———. "Witchcraft in Denmark." *Folklore* 93 (1982): 131–137.

———. "Witchcraft Prosecutions after the End of the Era of the Witch Trials: A Contribution to Danish Ethnology." *ARV: Scandinavian Yearbook of Folklore* 43 (1987): 147–165.

———. *The Witches' Advocate: Basque Witchcraft and the Spanish Inquisition (1609–1614)*. Reno: University of Nevada Press, 1980.

Hester, Marianne. *Lewd Women and Wicked Witches: A Study of the Dynamics of Male Domination*. London and New York: Routledge, 1992.

Hickey, Sally. "Fatal Feeds?: Plants, Livestock Losses, and Witchcraft Accusations in Tudor and Stuart Britain." *Folklore* 101 (1990): 131–142.

Hill, Frances, ed. *The Salem Witch Trials Reader*. N.p.: Da Capo Press, 2000.

Hoak, Dale. "Art, Culture and Mentality in Renaissance Society: The Meaning of Hans Baldung Grien's *Bewitched Groom* (1544)." *Renaissance Quarterly* 38 (1985): 489–510.

Holmes, Clive. "Women: Witches and Witnesses." *Past and Present* 140 (1993): 45–78.

Hults, Linda C. "Baldung and the Witches of Freiburg: The Evidence of Images." *Journal of Interdisciplinary History* 18 (1987): 249–276.

———. "Baldung's *Bewitched Groom* Revisited: Artistic Temperament, Fantasy and the 'Dream of Reason.'" *The Sixteenth Century Journal* 15 (1984): 259–279.

Hunter, Michael. "The Witchcraft Controversy and the Nature of Free-Thought in Restoration England: John Wagstaffe's *The Question of Witch-*

craft Debated (1669)." In *Science and the Shape of Orthodoxy: Intellectual Change in Late Seventeenth-Century Britain*, 286–307. Woodbridge, England: Boydell Press, 1995.

Hutchinson, James. "A Sermon on Witchcraft in 1697." Ed. George Nielson. *Scottish Historical Review* 7 (1910): 390–399.

Hutton, Ronald. *The Triumph of the Moon: A History of Modern Pagan Witchcraft*. Oxford: Oxford University Press, 1999.

Jackson, Louise. "Witches, Wives and Mothers: Witchcraft Persecution and Women's Confessions in Seventeenth-Century England." In *The Witchcraft Reader*, ed. Darren Oldridge, 353–366. London and New York: Routledge, 2002.

Jens Christian v. Johansen. "Denmark: The Sociology of Accusations." *Early Modern European Witchcraft: Centres and Peripheries*, ed. Bengt Ankarloo and Gustav Henningsen, 339–365. Oxford: Clarendon Press, 1990.

———. "Witchcraft in Elsinore 1625–1626." *Mentalities* 3 (1985): 1–8.

———. "Witchcraft, Sin and Repentance: The Decline of Danish Witchcraft Trials." *Acta Ethnographica Hungarica* 37 (1991/1992): 413–423.

Jones, William R. "Political Uses of Sorcery in Medieval Europe." *The Historian* 34 (1972): 670–687.

Kahk, Juhan. "Estonia II: The Crusade Against Idolatry." In *Early Modern European Witchcraft: Centres and Peripheries*, ed. Bengt Ankarloo and Gustav Henningsen, 273–284. Oxford: Clarendon Press, 1990.

Karlsen, Carol F. *The Devil in the Shape of a Woman: Witchcraft in Colonial New England*. New York: Norton, 1987.

Kern, Edmund. "Confessional Identity and Magic in the Late Sixteenth Century: Jakob Bithner and Witchcraft in Styria." *The Sixteenth Century Journal* 25 (1994): 323–340.

Kieckhefer, Richard. *European Witch Trials: Their Foundations in Popular and Learned Culture, 1300–1500*. Berkeley: University of California Press, 1976.

———. *Magic in the Middle Ages*. Cambridge: Cambridge University Press, 1989.

Klaits, Joseph. *Servants of Satan: The Age of the Witch Hunts*. Bloomington: Indiana University Press, 1985.

Klaniczay. Gabor. "Hungary: The Accusations and the Universe of Popular Magic." In *Early Modern European Witchcraft: Centres and Peripheries*, ed. Bengt Ankarloo and Gustav Henningsen. Oxford: Clarendon Press, 1990.

Klaniczay, Gabor. *The Uses of Supernatural Power: The Transformation of Popular Religion in Medieval and Early Modern Europe*. Trans. Susan Singerman, ed. Karen Marsolis. Princeton: Princeton University Press, 1990. 219–256.

Kors, Alan Charles, and Edward Peters, eds. *Witchcraft in Europe 400–1700: A Documentary History*. 2d ed. Revised by Edward Peters. Philadelphia: University of Pennsylvania Press, 2001.

Kreiser, B. Robert. "The Devils of Toulon: Demonic Possession and Religious Politics in Eighteenth Century Provence." In *Church, State, and Society under the Bourbon Kings of France*, ed. Richard M. Golden, 173–221. Lawrence, Kans.: Coronado Press, 1982.

Kunze, Michael. *Highroad to the Stake: A Tale of Witchcraft*. Trans. William E. Yuill. Chicago and London: University of Chicago Press, 1987.

Lapoint, Elwyn C. "Irish Immunity to Witch-Hunting, 1534–1711." *Eire/ Ireland* 27 (1992): 76–92.

Larner, Christina. *Enemies of God: The Witch-Hunt in Scotland*. London: Chatto and Windus, 1981.

———. "Two Late Scottish Witchcraft Tracts: *Witch-Craft Proven* and *The Tryal of Witchcraft*." In *The Damned Art: Essays in the Literature of Witchcraft*, ed. Sydney Anglo, 227–245. Boston: Routledge and Kegan Paul, 1977.

———. *Witchcraft and Religion: The Politics of Popular Belief*. Oxford: Basil Blackwell, 1984.

Lea, Henry Charles. *Materials toward a History of Witchcraft*. 3 vols. New York and London: Thomas Yoseloff, 1957.

Lefroy, J. H. *Memorials of the Discovery and Early Settlement of the Bermudas or Somers Islands 1511–1687*. Bermuda: Bermuda Government Library, 1932.

Le Roy Ladurie, Emmanuel. *Jasmin's Witch*. Trans. Brian Pearce. New York: George Braziller, 1987.

Levack, Brian P. "The Great Scottish Witch Hunt of 1661–1662." *Journal of British Studies* 20 (1980): 90–108.

———. *The Witch-Hunt in Early Modern Europe*. London and New York: Longman, 1987.

Macalpine, Ida, and Richard A. Hunter. *Schizophrenia 1677: A Psychiatric Study of an Illustrated Autobiographical Record of Demonic Possession*. London: William Dawson and Sons, 1956.

MacDonald, Michael, ed. *Witchcraft and Hysteria in Elizabethan London: Edward Jorden and the Mary Glover Case*. London and New York: Tavistock/ Routledge, 1991.

Macfarlane, Alan. "A Tudor Anthropologist: George Gifford's *Discourse* and *Dialogue*." In *The Damned Art: Essays in the Literature of Witchcraft*, ed. Sydney Anglo, 219–256. Boston: Routledge and Kegan Paul, 1977.

———. *Witchcraft in Tudor and Stuart England: A Regional and Comparative Study*. London: Routledge and Kegan Paul, 1970.

Madar, Maia. "Estonia I: Werewolves and Poisoners." In *Early Modern European Witchcraft: Centres and Peripheries*, ed. Bengt Ankarloo and Gustav Henningsen, 257–272. Oxford, England: Clarendon Press, 1990.

Marshman, Michelle. "Exorcism as Empowerment: A New Idiom." *Journal of Religious History* 23 (1999): 265–281.

Martin, Ruth. *Witchcraft and the Inquisition in Venice, 1550–1650*. Oxford: Blackwell, 1989.

Maxwell-Stuart, P. G. *Satan's Conspiracy: Magic and Witchcraft in Sixteenth-Century Scotland*. East Lothian, Scotland: Tuckwell Press, 2001.

———. *Witchcraft in Europe and the New World, 1400–1800*. Houndsmills, England, and New York: Palgrave, 2001.

McGowan, Margaret M. "Pierre de Lancre's *Tableau de l'Inconstance des Mauvais Anges et Demons*: The Sabbat Sensationalized." In *The Damned Art: Essays in the Literature of Witchcraft*, ed. Sydney Anglo, 182–201. Boston: Routledge and Kegan Paul, 1977.

Meek, Christine. "Men, Women, and Magic: Some Cases from Late Medieval Lucca." In *Women in Renaissance and Early Modern Europe*, ed. Christine Meek, 43–66. Dublin: Four Courts Press, 2000.

Megged, Amos. "Magic, Popular Medicine and Gender in Seventeenth-Century Mexico: The Case of Isabel de Montoya." *Social History* 19 (1994): 189–207.

Middlekauf, Robert. *The Mathers: Three Generations of Puritan Intellectuals, 1596–1728*. New York: Oxford University Press, 1971.

Midelfort, H. C. Erik. "Catholic and Lutheran Reactions to Demon Possession in the Late Seventeenth Century: Two Case Histories." *Daphnis* 15 (1986): 623–648.

———. "Heartland of the Witchcraze." *History Today* 31 (1981): 27–36.

———. *Witch Hunting in Southwestern Germany, 1562–1684*. Stanford: Stanford University Press, 1972.

Mitchell, Stephen. "Nordic Witchcraft in Transition: Impotence, Heresy and Diabolism in 14th-Century Bergen." *Scandia* 63 (1997): 17–33.

Monter, William. *Frontiers of Heresy: The Spanish Inquisition from the Basque Lands to Sicily*. Cambridge: Cambridge University Press, 1990.

———. "Scandinavian Witchcraft in Anglo-American Perspective." In *Early Modern European Witchcraft: Centres and Peripheries*, ed. Bengt Ankarloo and Gustav Henningsen, 425–434. Oxford: Clarendon Press, 1990.

———. "Toads and Eucharists: The Male Witches of Normandy, 1564–1660." *French Historical Studies* 20 (1997): 563–595.

———. *Witchcraft in France and Switzerland: The Borderlands During the Reformation*. Ithaca and London: Cornell University Press, 1976.

Mormando, Franco. *The Preacher's Demons: Bernardino of Siena and the Social Underworld of Early Renaissance Italy*. Chicago and London: University of Chicago Press, 1999.

Mossiker, Frances. *The Affair of the Poisons: Louis XIV, Madame de Montespan, and One of History's Greatest Unsolved Mysteries*. New York: Alfred A. Knopf, 1969.

Muchembled, Robert. *Popular Culture and Elite Culture in France 1400–1750*. Trans. Lydia Cochrane. Baton Rouge and London: Louisiana State University Press, 1985.

———. "The Witches of the Cambresis: The Acculturation of the Rural World in the Sixteenth and Seventeenth Centuries." In *Religion and the People, 800–1700*, ed James Obelkevich, 221–276. Chapel Hill: University of North Carolina Press, 1979.

Murray, Margaret Alice. *The Divine King in England: A Study in Anthropology*. London: Faber and Faber, 1954.

———. *The God of the Witches*. London: Sampson Low, Marston, 1931.

————. *The Witch-Cult in Western Europe: A Study in Anthropology*. Oxford: Clarendon Press, 1921.

Myers, A. R. "The Captivity of a Royal Witch: The Household Accounts of Queen Joan of Navarre, 1419–21." *Bulletin of the John Rylands Library Manchester* 24 (1940): 263–284.

Naess, Hans Eyvind. "Norway: The Criminological Context." In *Early Modern European Witchcraft: Centres and Peripheries*, ed. Bengt Ankarloo and Gustav Henningsen, 367–382. Oxford: Clarendon Press, 1990.

Naphy, William G. *Plagues, Poisons and Potions: Plague-Spreading Conspiracies in the Western Alps c. 1530–1640*. Manchester and New York: Manchester University Press, 2002.

Nauert, Charles G., Jr. *Agrippa and the Crisis of Renaissance Thought*. Urbana: University of Illinois Press, 1965.

Neill, W. N. "The Professional Pricker and His Test for Witchcraft." *Scottish Historical Review* 19 (1922): 205–213.

Ni Dhuibhne, Eilis. " 'The Old Woman as Hare': Structure and Meaning in Irish Legend." *Folklore* 104 (1993): 77–85.

Nildin-Wall, Boldil, and Jan Wall, "The Witch as Hare or the Witch's Hare: Popular Legends and Beliefs in Nordic Tradition." *Folklore* 104 (1993): 67–76.

Normand, Lawrence, and Gareth Roberts, eds. *Witchcraft in Early Modern Scotland: James VI's Demonology and the North Berwick Witches*. Exeter, England: University of Exeter Press, 2000.

Notestein, Wallace. *A History of Witchcraft in England from 1558 to 1718*. Washington, D.C.: American Historical Association, 1911.

Oates, Caroline. "The Trial of a Teenage Werewolf, Bordeaux, 1603." *Criminal Justice History* 9 (1988): 1–29.

Oberman, Heiko Augustinius. *Masters of the Reformation: The Emergence of a New Intellectual Climate in Europe*. Trans. Dennis Martin. Cambridge: Cambridge University Press, 1981.

Oldridge, Darren, ed. *The Witchcraft Reader*. London and New York: Routledge, 2002.

O'Neil, Mary. "Magical Healing, Love Magic and the Inquisition in Late Sixteenth-Century Modena." In *Inquisition and Society in Early Modern Europe*, ed. Stephen Haliczer, 88–114. London: Croom Helm, 1987.

Otten, Charlotte F., ed. *A Lycanthropy Reader: Werewolves in Western Culture*. Syracuse, N.Y.: Syracuse University Press, 1986.

Palmer, Philip Mason, and Robert Pattison More. *The Sources of the Faust Tradition: From Simon Magus to Lessing*. 1936. Reprint, New York: Haskell House, 1965.

Parke, Francis Neale. "Witchcraft in Maryland." *Maryland Historical Magazine* 31 (1936): 271–298.

Pearl, Jonathan L. *The Crime of Crimes: Demonology and Politics in France, 1560–1620*. Waterloo, Ontario: Wilfrid Laurier University Press, 1999.

———. "Witchcraft in New France in the Seventeenth Century: The Social Aspect." *Historical Reflections* 4 (1977): 191–205.

Peel, Edgar, and Pat Southern. *The Trials of the Lancashire Witches: A Study of Seventeenth-Century Witchcraft.* New York: Taplinger, 1969.

Peters, Edward. *The Magician, the Witch and the Law.* Philadelphia: University of Pennsylvania Press, 1978.

Pihlajamak, Heikki. " 'Swimming the Witch, Pricking for the Devil's Mark': Ordeals in the Early Modern Witchcraft Trials." *Journal of Legal History* 21 (2000): 35–58.

Purkiss, Diane. "Desire and Its Deformities: Fantasies of Witchcraft in the English Civil War." *The Journal of Medieval and Early Modern Studies* (1997): 103–132.

———. *The Witch in History: Early Modern and Twentieth-Century Representations.* London and New York: Routledge, 1996.

Rapley, Robert. *A Case of Witchcraft: The Trial of Urbain Grandier.* Montreal and Kingston: McGill-Queens University Press, 1998.

Remy, Nicolas. *Demonolatry.* Trans. E. A. Ashwin, and ed. with an Introduction and notes by Montague Summers. London: John Rodker, 1930.

Richardson, Joanna. "Madame de Montespan and the Affair of the Poisons." *History Today* 23 (1973): 588–592.

del Rio, Martin. *Investigations into Magic.* Ed. and trans. P. G. Maxwell-Stuart. Manchester, England: Manchester University Press, 2000.

Robbins, Kevin C. "Magical Emasculation, Popular Anticlericalism, and the Limits of the Reformation in Western France circa 1590." *Journal of Social History* 31 (1997): 61–83.

Robbins, Rossell Hope. *The Encyclopedia of Witchcraft and Demonology.* New York: Crown, 1959.

Roper, Lyndal. " 'Evil Imaginings and Fantasies': Child Witches and the End of the Witch Craze." *Past and Present* 167 (May 2000): 107–139.

———. *Oedipus and the Devil: Witchcraft, Sexuality and Religion in Early Modern Europe.* New York: Routledge, 1994.

Rosenthal, Bernard. *Salem Story: Reading the Witch Trials of 1692.* Cambridge: Cambridge University Press, 1993.

Ross, Eric B. "Syphilis, Misogyny and Witchcraft in 16th-Century Europe." *Current Anthropology* 36 (1995): 333–337.

Ruggiero, Guido. *Binding Passions: Tales of Magic, Marriage and Power at the End of the Renaissance.* New York and Oxford: Oxford University Press, 1993.

Rumsey, Peter Lockwood. *Acts of God and the People, 1620–1730.* Ann Arbor, Michigan: UMI Research Press, 1986.

Russell, Jeffrey Burton. *Mephistopheles: The Devil in the Modern World.* Ithaca and London: Cornell University Press, 1986.

———. *Witchcraft in the Middle Ages.* Ithaca: Cornell University Press, 1972.

Sanders, Andrew. *A Deed without a Name: The Witch in Society and History.* Oxford and Washington, D.C.: Berg, 1995.

Scarre, Geoffrey. *Witchcraft and Magic in Sixteenth- and Seventeenth-Century Europe*. London: Macmillan Education, 1987.

Schutte, Anne Jacobson. *Aspiring Saints: Pretense of Holiness, Inquisition, and Gender in the Republic of Venice, 1618–1750*. Baltimore and London: Johns Hopkins University Press, 2001.

———. " 'Saints' and 'Witches' in Early Modern Italy: Stepsisters or Strangers." In *Time, Space, and Women's Lives in Early Modern Europe*, ed. Anne Jacobson Schutte, Thomas Kuehn and Silvana Seidel Menchi, 153–164. Vol. 53 of *Sixteenth Century Essays and Studies*. Kirksville, Mo.: Truman State University Press, 2001.

Scully, Sally. "Marriage or a Career: Witchcraft as an Alternative in Seventeenth-Century Venice." *Journal of Social History* 28 (1995): 857–876.

Sebald, Hans. *Witch-Children: From Salem Witch-Hunts to Modern Courtrooms*. Amherst, Mass.: Prometheus Books, 1995.

Seward, Desmond. *Richard III: England's Black Legend*. Rev. ed. London: Penguin Books, 1997.

Seymour, St. John D. *Irish Witchcraft and Demonology*. Dublin: Hodges, Figgis, 1913.

Sharpe, James. *The Bewitching of Anne Gunter: A Horrible and True Story of Deception, Witchcraft, Murder and the King of England*. New York: Routledge, 2000.

———. *Instruments of Darkness: Witchcraft in Early Modern England*. Philadelphia: University of Pennsylvania Press, 1996.

Silverblatt, Irene. *Moon, Sun, and Witches: Gender Ideologies and Class in Inca and Colonial Peru*. Princeton: Princeton University Press, 1987.

Simmons, Marc. *Witchcraft in the Southwest: Spanish and Indian Supernaturalism on the Rio Grande*. Flagstaff, Ariz.: Northland Press, 1974.

Simoni, Anna E. C. "Balthasar Bekker and the Beckington Witch." *Quaerendo* 9 (1979): 135–142.

Simpson, Jacqueline. "Margaret Murray: Who Believed Her, and Why?" *Folklore* 105 (1994): 89–96.

Sinclair, George. *Satan's Invisible World Discovered (1685)*. A facsimile reproduction with an Introduction by Clement O. Parsons. Gainesville, Fla.: Scholars' Facsimiles & Reprints, 1969.

Sinistrari, Lodovico Maria. *Demoniality*. Trans. into English from the Latin with Introduction and notes by Montague Summers. London: The Fortune Press, n.d.

Sluhovsky, Moshe. "A Divine Apparition or Demonic Possession?" *The Sixteenth Century Journal* 27 (1996): 1039–1055.

Soman, Alfred. "Decriminalizing Witchcraft: Does the French Experience Provide a European model?" *Criminal Justice History* 10 (1989): 1–22.

———. "The Parlement of Paris and the Great Witch Hunt (1565–1640)." *The Sixteenth Century Journal* 9 (1978): 31–44.

Sorlin, Per. *Wicked Arts: Witchcraft and Magic Trials in Southern Sweden, 1635–1734*. Leiden, The Netherlands: Brill, 1999.

Spanos, Nicholas P., and Jack Gottlieb. "Ergotism and the Salem Village Witch Trials." *Science* 194 (1976): 1390–1394.

Stallybrass, Peter. "*Macbeth* and Witchcraft." In *Focus on Macbeth*, ed. John Russell Brown, 189–209. London: Routledge and Kegan Paul, 1982.

Stephens, Walter. *Demon Lovers: Witchcraft, Sex, and the Crisis of Belief.* Chicago and London: University of Chicago Press, 2002.

Stronks, J. G. "The Significance of Balthasar Bekker's *The Enchanted World.*" In *Witchcraft in the Netherlands from the Fourteenth to the Twentieth Century*, ed. Marijke Gijswit-Hofstra and Willem Frijhoff, 149–156. Rotterdam: Universitaire Pers Rotterdam, 1991.

Suggett, Richard. "Witchcraft Dynamics in Early Modern Wales." In *Women and Gender in Early Modern Wales*, ed. Michael Roberts and Simone Clarke, 75–103. Cardiff: University of Wales Press, 2000.

Sullivan, Margaret A. "The Witches of Durer and Hans Baldung Grien." *Renaissance Quarterly* 53 (2000): 332–401.

Tausiet, María. "Witchcraft as Metaphor: Infanticide and Its Translations in Aragon in the Sixteenth and Seventeenth Centuries." In *Languages of Witchcraft: Narrative, Ideology and Meaning in Early Modern Culture*, ed. Stuart Clark, 179–195. New York: St. Martin's Press, 2001.

Tedeschi, John. "Inquisitorial Law and the Witch." In *Early Modern European Witchcraft: Centres and Peripheries*, ed. Bengt Ankarloo and Gustav Henningsen, 83–118. Oxford: Clarendon Press, 1990.

Thomas, Keith. *Religion and the Decline of Magic.* New York: Charles Scribner's Sons, 1971.

Thompson, Janet A. *Wives, Widows, Witches and Bitches: Women in Seventeenth-Century Devon.* New York: Peter Lang, 1993.

Tourney, Garfield. "The Physician and Witchcraft in Restoration England." *Medical History* 16 (1972): 143–154.

Valetta, Frederick. *Witchcraft, Magic and Superstition in England, 1640–1670.* Aldershot, England: Ashgate, 2000.

Vickers, K. H. *Humphrey Duke of Gloucester: A Biography.* London: A. Constable, 1907.

Vukanovic, T. P. "Witchcraft in the Central Balkans I: Characteristics of Witches." *Folklore* 100 (1989): 1–24.

Walinski-Kiehl, Robert S. "The Devil's Children: Child Witch-Trials in Early Modern Germany." *Continuity and Change* 11 (1996): 171–189.

Walinski-Kiehl, Robert S. " 'Godly States,' Confessional Conflict and Witch-Hunting in Early Modern Germany." *Mentalities* 5 (1988): 13–25.

Walker, Anita M., and Edmund H. Dickermann. " 'A Woman under the Influence': A Case of Alleged Possession in Sixteenth-Century France." *The Sixteenth Century Journal* 22 (1991): 534–544.

Walker, Anita M., and Edmund H. Dickermann. "A Notorious Woman: Possession, Witchcraft and Sexuality in Seventeenth-Century Provence." *Historical Reflections/Reflexions Historiques* 27 (2001): 1–26.

Walker, D. P., *Spiritual and Demonic Magic from Ficino to Campanella*. London: Warburg Institute, University of London, 1958.

Walker, D. P. *Unclean Spirits: Possession and Exorcism in France and England in the Late Sixteenth and Early Seventeenth Centuries*. Philadelphia: University of Pennsylvania Press, 1981.

Walsham, Alexandra. " 'Frantick Hacket': Prophecy, Sorcery, Insanity and the Elizabethan Puritan Movement." *Historical Journal* 40 (1998): 27–66.

Weisman, Richard. *Witchcraft, Magic and Religion in 17th-Century Massachusetts*. Amherst: University of Massachusetts Press, 1984.

Wells, Charlotte. "Leeches on the Body Politic: Xenophobia and Witchcraft in Early Modern French Political Thought." *French Historical Studies* 22 (1999): 351–377.

West, Robert H. *Reginald Scot and Renaissance Writings on Witchcraft*. Boston: Twayne, 1984.

Wiesner-Hanks, Merry E. *Christianity and Sexuality in the Early Modern World: Regulating Desire, Reforming Practice*. London and New York: Routledge, 2000.

Weyer, Johann. *On Witchcraft: An Abridged Translation of Johann Weyer's De Praestigiis Daemonum*, ed. Benjamin G. Kohl and H. C. Erik Midelfort. Asheville, N.C.: Pegasus Press, 1998.

Wilby, Emma. "The Witch's Familiar and the Fairy in Early Modern England and Scotland." *Folklore* 111 (2000): 283–305.

Williams, Bernadette. " 'She was usually placed with the great men and leaders of the land in the public assemblies'—Alice Kyteler: A woman of considerable power." In *Women in Renaissance and Early Modern Europe*, ed. Christine Meek, 67–83. Dublin: Four Courts Press, 2000.

Williams, Gerhild Scholz. *Defining Dominion: The Discourses of Witchcraft and Magic in Early Modern France and Germany*. Ann Arbor: University of Michigan Press, 1995.

Willis, Deborah. *Malevolent Nurture: Witch-Hunting and Maternal Power in Early Modern England*. Ithaca: Cornell University Press, 1995.

Wills, Garry. *Witches and Jesuits: Shakespeare's Macbeth*. New York and Oxford: New York Public Library and Oxford University Press, 1995.

Wilson, Eric. "Institoris at Innsbruck: Heinrich Institoris, the *Summis Desiderantes*, and the Brixen Witch-Trial of 1485." In *Popular Religion in Germany and Central Europe, 1400–1800*, ed. Bob Scribner and Trevor Johnson, 87–100. New York: St. Martin's Press, 1996.

Winship, Michael P. *Seers of God: Puritan Providentialism in the Restoration and the Early Enlightenment*. Baltimore: Johns Hopkins University Press, 1996.

Wooton, David. "Reginald Scot/Abraham Fleming/The Family of Love." In *Languages of Witchcraft: Narrative, Ideology and Meaning in Early Modern Culture*, ed. Stuart Clark, 119–138. New York: St. Martin's Press, 2001.

Wormald, Jenny. "The Witches, the Devil and the King." In *Freedom and Authority, Scotland c. 1050–c. 1650: Historical and Historiographical Essays presented to Grant G. Simpson,* ed. Terry Brotherstone and David Ditch-burne, 165–180. East Lothian, Scotland: Tuckwell Press, 2000.

Young, Alan R. "Elizabeth Lowys: Witch and Social Victim." *History Today* 22 (1972): 251–261.

Zguta, Russell. "The Ordeal by Water (Swimming of Witches) in the East Slavic World." *Slavic Review* 36 (1977): 220–230.

———. "Witchcraft Trials in Seventeenth-Century Russia." *American Historical Review* 82 (1977): 1187–1207.

Zika, Charles. "Durer's Witch, Riding Women and Moral Order." In *Durer and His Culture,* ed. Dagmar Eichberger and Charles Zika, 118–140. Cambridge: Cambridge University Press, 1998.

Zilboorg, Gregory. *The Medical Man and the Witch during the Renaissance.* Baltimore: Johns Hopkins Press, 1935.

USEFUL WEB SITES FOR THE STUDY OF THE WITCH-HUNT

Famous American Trials: Salem Witch Trials 1692; Douglas Lindner, University of Missouri Kansas City: www.law.umkc.edu/faculty/projects/ftrials/salem/salem.htm

Salem Witch Trials: Documentary Archive and Transcription Project; University of Virginia: etext.lib.virginia.edu/salem/witchcraft/home.html

Survey of Scottish Witchcraft, Department of Scottish History, University of Edinburgh: www.arts.ed.ac.uk/witches

The Trial of the Bideford Witches, Frank J. Gent: www.eclipse.co.uk/exeshul/bidefordwitches/

The Trial of the Lowestoft Witches, Ivan Bunn: www.lowestoft.net/ibunn

Witchcraft, Magic, and Witch Trials in Finland, Timo Kervinen and Marko Nenonen: www.chronicon.com/noita/index.en.html

INDEX

About the Author

WILLIAM E. BURNS has taught at the University of Pennsylvania, the University of Maryland, and Mary Washington College. His earlier books include *The Scientific Revolution: A World History Companion* (2001) and *An Age of Wonders: Prodigies in Later Stuart Politics and Culture* (2002).